DANI[illegible]
MAN

by

TERRY M. DUNN

Published by Daneburyverse Books
Printed by Book Printing UK
Remus House, Coltsfoot Drive, Peterborough, PE2 9BF
ISBN: 978-1-9162657-0-7

To Andy, my ever-helpful military advisor. RIP old friend. To Jamie, artistic advisor and an honest critic. A good friend.

And especially to my long-suffering wife Sandy, who silently endured the many field trips, complaints, baffling explanations of half thought out ideas and the long hours of neglect while I sat hunched over the word processor.

1988

1

The high rumble of a straining engine slowly invaded the peacefulness of Salisbury Plain. For a while, in the still afternoon air, it was difficult to determine the direction the sound was coming from. Then, from over a rise, came a single military truck. The four ton, canvass backed wagon revved it's way to the crest of a brow before coming to a halt, air brakes sighing in relief. No sooner had the truck halted when the men in the cab vaulted out, their heavy boots thudding hard onto the packed earth.

The driver went smartly to the rear of the truck and deftly unlatched the tailboard. The other man, who had also emerged from the cab of the wagon, was a Sergeant. He waited impatiently as the tailboard was swung down and the arms of people inside flipped the rear of the canvas up.

"Come on, come on. Front and centre, you lazy bastards!" shouted the Sergeant from beside the truck. He was tall and slim, but imposing enough never the less. His beret was set at the regulation angle and the creases in his lightweights were razor sharp. The white stripes on his sleeves stood out in stark relief against his green woolly-pully. On his left breast, in exactly the right place, was sewn his name flash. Carter.

In immediate response to Sergeant Carters bellow, men began to spill from the wagon and form up in lines beside it. Unlike him, they were dressed in camouflage jacket and trousers, wore fully packed battle order webbing and clutched black, deadly looking self-loading rifles. They dashed to the side of the truck to form up in lines before the sergeant.

The wagon held a full platoon of twenty four men who all knew what the last man to fall in would be on the receiving end of a rollocking. One man jumped energetically from the rear of the wagon, but landed awkwardly and crashed to the ground. Ignoring the flash of pain as the barrel of his rifle struck his cheek, he turned the fall into a clumsy forward roll, swiftly regaining his footing before falling in at the end of a line. Last man or not, Sergeant Carter was not passing up this golden opportunity to have a go at his favourite whipping boy.

He marched purposefully across and glared into the unfortunate soldiers face while his victim stared fixedly out into space, bracing himself for the tirade of abuse coming his way.

Sergeant Carter's blast almost knocked the man off his feet, but he knew better than to react. Just to sway would invoke even more abuse and probably some dirty and disgusting job for him to do when the regiment returned to barracks at the end of the exercise.

"Parrish, you big idle streak of piss, what the fuck are you playing at? Trying to impress your friends with gymnastics are we? Or maybe you are just a useless spastic who can't even do a simple thing like getting out of the back of a four tonner without fucking up! Pull your bloody finger out man, what's up with you! Idle, that's what you are Parrish, bone fucking idle. You are a waste of space Parrish and useless with it. Your contribution to life on this planet is precisely fuck all! What you will achieve in your miserable life could be written on a stamp and still leave room for the queen's head.

Well you'd better get your act together matey, or I'll have you cleaning out the shit houses in the barracks until you reach retirement age! You might be a lazy, idle fucker in your free time but if I catch you slacking I'll...."

Private Parrish was saved any further abuse by the arrival over the brow of a Landrover.

"Men...atten..SHUN!" Shouted Sergeant Carter as the vehicle pulled to a stop, its brakes emitting a high pitched squeal. All the men snapped simultaneously to attention. A Captain climbed from the Landrover and approached the sergeant.

"The men are all ready sir." Reported Sergeant Carter, giving the Captain a crisp salute. The officers return salute in comparison was appallingly sloppy.

"Thank you Sergeant." he said. "OK men, now listen up. The main purpose of Operation Backfire is to test the readiness and abilities of Her Majesties Ground Forces when small, scattered groups of enemy have parachuted in under cover of darkness, tasked with destroying vital installations and generally causing havoc.

We men of the 2nd Battalion the Light Infantry have been designated as one small part of the enemy force. We are to move to our start positions and be ready to move at 2300 hours tonight. Each section is to set off independently to attack their targets, as given to your section commanders at the 0 group meeting earlier today.

You are to cause destruction and mayhem, while avoiding capture for as long as possible. It goes without saying that the CO expects the regiment to give a good account of itself during this exercise. I personally expect nothing less from you. If you make yourselves look good you make me look good. Make me look good and there's a crate of beer for every man here. Fair enough?" There were murmurs of approval from the soldiers before him.

"Right then. Sergeant, make sure they check their equipment. We move out in five minutes."

"Sah!" The Captain again returned the salute then returned to his waiting vehicle.

Sergeant Carter turned to the men. "Right you 'orrible lot. You heard the man, Check your kit, have a last smoke or a wet but we move out in five minutes. Fall OUT!"

As one, they turned to the right and snapped to attention, before breaking away into small groups. Sergeant Carter went to confer with the junior NCOs.

Three men stood together behind the truck, out of the sergeant's sight. The middle of the three was Private Parrish.

According to the quartermaster sergeant major, Parrish was the perfect soldier to kit out. He had the ideal soldiers build. All MOD equipment was designed around a standard size. His size. Six feet tall with a fit, athletic build but not too bulky, Parrish was one of those fortunate people for whom clothes fitted well straight off the peg. It was next to no effort for him to look neat, tidy and smart. Perhaps that was one reason why Sergeant Carter disliked him.

Parrish bit greedily into a Mars bar.

The soldier to his left spoke. "Fuck me Shaun, old 'mad dog' Carter's certainly got it in for you. What did you do, give his missus one?" He laughed.

"No." countered the soldier to Parrish's right. "He just *looks* like his wife. That's enough to piss anybody off."

"He looks nothing like Carters missus." the first soldier disagreed.

"Yeah" agreed Parrish, "I haven't got a beard or a flat chest." They laughed together. Parrish washed down his chocolaty mouthful with a swig from his water bottle. He smacked his lips, which prompted the soldier on his left, private Dunn, to speak.

"I'm looking forward to that crate of beer that I'm going to make the Captain fork out for."

"He's winding you up 'Clive'." said Parrish, using the soldiers nickname with emphasis, "Did you notice all the 'we' this and 'we' that, then he jumps straight back in his Landrover and fucks off! We do all the hard graft and he looks good. I'll bet he even looses the cost of the beer in the mess bills."

"You've just got the hump 'cos Carter is giving you a hard time." It was the soldier to Parrish's right, 'Bunny' Rabbett. "I'm bagging my beer and no mistake."

"Look on the bright side." said Dunn. "Carter will be in the command post with the other senior NCOs and officers. No hassle for the next thirty six hours."

"Yeah." agreed Parrish. "Fuck Carter, let's play soldiers and get pissed on the Captains beer afterwards."

"You'll do for me, cock." said Dunn.

"Knockout!" said Rabbett, giving the thumbs up.

The smiles were wiped from their faces by Sergeant Carter's ear shattering roar.

"Right then you dozy lot! Form up to your section leaders and be ready to move out." As the men gathered around their corporals he added, "And you *will* look good or I will have the whole lot of you sweeping up the parade square with the hairs on your bollocks!"

"Charming." muttered Parrish under his breath.

"MOVE OUT!" barked Sergeant Carter, making several soldiers wince at the power of his voice.

The platoon moved out.

Fourteen miles to the west of the Light Infantry platoons position, another small group of men were moving. They were emerging slowly from one of the deliberately bland and unassuming buildings that made up the bulk of the Porton Down research centre. Security was tight as the small cluster of bodies escorted a slow moving electric tractor on its journey towards the waiting helicopter. A small bogie truck was hitched to the rear of the tractor. It carried a metal box, to all intents and purposes the same as a photographer's equipment box only larger, a three feet square sealed container.

Two civilians escorted the box, along with an Army Colonel and a Lieutenant. Around the perimeter of the heli-pad, armed soldiers stood at regular intervals, facing outwards.

"Do you really think this thing will work?" asked the Colonel to the suited man beside him. The man laughed.

"Colonel Reed, that's not the sort of question you should ask a scientist who has spent a lot of years working on something that's about to be put to the test. Yes, I do think it will work."

"Professor Barstow," it was the Lieutenant. "You are absolutely sure we will be safe travelling with it," he nodded towards the box "Bearing in mind that it *is* radioactive."

The scientist laughed again. "You'll be all right Marston. That's why Reeves here" he nodded at his ever present assistant," and myself are travelling with you in the helicopter. To put your military minds at rest. Your masters in Whitehall had the same misguided worries, hence the chopper. They deemed it much too dangerous to travel by road. Safer and more secure to fly."

Like all true scientists, James Bartholomew Barstow had no real concept of the deviousness of his race. He was immersed in the problematical world of inventive nuclear science. The military however understood only too well the needs of the super powers of the world to keep abreast of the latest developments in technological weapons and counter-weapons. This knowledge included knowing the lengths that another country would go to, to obtain the latest technology to keep the balance of arms for so called world peace.

Professor Barstow's yet to be tested invention was not directly a weapon. That was the thought that had sustained him during its development, whilst allowing himself to accept the funding and facilities of the Ministry of Defence.

The MOD on the other hand, were very quick indeed to realize the massive military potential of professor Barstow's 'tool' as they described it.

When he and his brainchild had first been brought to the attention of the procurement review board there was much scepticism, even outright ridicule.

The proposal of some 'Dr Who like, time machine' was almost laughed off out of hand. That was until the professor was summoned before a specially convened study group and allowed to put forward his idea, proposals and projections of the applications of his device. If it worked.

The board immediately realised that if the device *could* be made to work, the battlefield applications alone would completely change modern warfare as it was known today, never mind the myriad of other uses it could be put to.

Professor Barstow's device was actually in essence a time machine, although he himself preferred the phrase, 'Temporal Displacement Device'.

Besides, 'time machine' was much too short a phrase to encompass the years of work and the many soul destroying setbacks he had put behind him to reach this test point stage for his life's work.

The machine that sat inside the padded steel box was actually a small, atomic powered, spherical particle accelerator.

A brief pulse of power of very high magnitude sent charged particles circulating around the inside of the two and a half foot diameter accelerator, where they increased in just as few milliseconds to light speed plus. The same power pulse activated separate electrical circuits that energized and operated a circular field around the sphere. The field being ten feet in diameter for this small experimental version. Any molecules (objects and people consisting of molecules) inside the field were also accelerated to light speed plus.

According to Einstein's theories, as objects approach the speed of light, time slows down and, at the speed of light, time stands still. Under laboratory conditions, Professor Barstow had reached light speed with his accelerator, then calculated how much extra power was needed to push beyond that mark. Thus in theory creating a machine that would go backwards in time.

The power needed for this incredible acceleration would require a small, controlled nuclear explosion. A minute amount of plutonium therefore formed the core of his device. Combined with the other components, the controlled massive release of nuclear energy would be directed into driving the accelerator contained within the metal sphere.

The circuits that created the field outside the sphere were built from the latest superconductors and required very little of the power from the plutonium. The reactor part of the sphere, not much larger than a softball in actual size, was shielded in the virtually impossible event of a runaway reaction. Either way, the half life of the plutonium variant used, was one hundred and fifty years. Not long at all by nuclear standards. It meant that the radiation would waste away to become just background radiation in a mere five and a half thousand years. If the worst happened, the whole apparatus could be encased in lead and concrete and forgotten about.

But all this was mere scare mongering speculation. By far the most likely point of failure, if any, as far as Professor Barstow was concerned was the actuating mechanism and the ten digit time clock that was built into the side of the sphere. The whole system was about the size of a thick postcard and was powered by the tiniest pulse of energy drawn from the total reaction output. The activating mechanism was still very temperamental and often refused to operate, one of the small bugs still to be ironed out, but not in itself a real problem. The ten digit electronic clock was simply used because that was what was at hand when the machine was built. At this moment it read zero, with a minus sign at the left hand side of the display. When the test was carried out the clock would read in minus time, telling the observers how far back it had travelled. The clock, by dint of its ten digits, could actually read backwards from one second to nine thousand nine hundred and ninety nine years but the intention of the test was to send the device back thirty minutes.

Professor Barstow was by now well into the realms of theoretical temporal physics but he believed that thirty minutes would be as much as the machine could manage. Power output being the restricting factor. He reasoned that in order to keep the molecules at light speed plus would need the continued output of a nuclear reaction. His device would release all its power in a single pulse.

Unknowingly, Professor Barstow had made an error in his calculations and predictions. He had not correctly deduced or allowed for the slingshot effects of inertia and centrifugal force on super-speed molecules. Being at the very forefront of this unknown field and in effect feeling his way blindly with every step, he could not know that the hyper velocity molecules would continue at their peak velocity, once that had been reached. Requiring only a small amount of constant power to retain that velocity, they would only decelerate when the power was almost completely exhausted. Professor

Barstow could not know this, would not and never would know this, without resorting to actual testing.

And so it was that soldiers were loading his Temporal Displacement Device gingerly aboard the Army Air Corps Lynx helicopter that squatted, still and patient, on the Porton Down heli-pad.

The yellow and black radiation warning roundels that adorned the exterior of the steel box were the cause of Lieutenant Marston's apprehension. It was indeed also the reason why, never mind the secrecy of the whole project, the army high command had insisted on its transportation by air rather than road. The logged flight plan dictated that the helicopter fly due west from Porton Down, out over Salisbury Plain, and then swing south. Just to the west of the small market town of Ringwood, near the south coast and on the edge of the New Forest, was the DRA weapons testing centre. That was the aircrafts destination. The whole flight would use the cover of the large scale military exercise being run on 'the plain' as it was known throughout the MOD. Nobody would notice one extra helicopter flight during Operation Backfire and therefore hopefully throw off any unwanted interest from a 'third party'.

Professor Barstow, his quietly efficient assistant Reeves, Colonel Reed and Lieutenant Marston climbed into the helicopter after the metal box had been securely strapped to the floor of the cargo bay. They sat down on the hard metal seats, the soldiers fore of it, the scientists aft.

Lieutenant Marston leant back, trying to get as far away from the offending item as possible. Professor Barstow smiled. "You can still stay behind if you want to." He said.

"No." said the Lieutenant decisively. "I have my orders and mine is not to reason why, mine is but to do..." He stopped when he realised how the quotation ended.

"Or die?" finished the professor. He laughed and slapped the top of the box with his palm. "This thing is safer than flying in this helicopter and surely you know that statistically, flying is still the safest form of travel?" He gave the Lieutenant his most charming grin. The soldier was still unconvinced.

Colonel Reed shook his head then turned and tapped the pilot on the shoulder. The pilot's helmeted head nodded in return and a few seconds later the primary electric motor began its high pitched whine, starting the rotor blades slowly turning. Everyone in the cargo bay checked their seat straps and waited for the helicopter to take off.

2

At a pre-determined grid reference, three miles from their drop off point, the platoon of the Second Battalion the Light Infantry split into its three separate sections. From this point the sections were to operate independently. They had all been allocated targets to attack. The corporals in charge of each section had conferred before the group had set off. They wondered if the targets had been told that they were going to be attacked.

A section operating independently of any higher command was unusual during peacetime or in large scale exercises. The junior NCOs knew that it was a major test for them, more so than the foot sloggers under their control. They wanted to do well and so, in true British squaddie fashion, the whole platoon settled down for a brew while the NCOs cemented their plans before going their separate ways.

The three Corporals had agreed to operate the tried and trusted military planning system. Simplicity. The objective of their plan was to get themselves and their men noticed by the men at the top. The plan to reach that objective was thus:

The three sections would all be in position, ready to attack their individual targets, by 01.15 hours. There they would wait and watch, unobserved, until 02.00. Although the sections would be in different areas of the plain, they would mount a simultaneous attack on their objectives. This would get the top brasses attention. If all the objectives could be taken, each individual leader would of course make his own decision on this, but if they could all be taken it would be a real triumph. Not just for the NCOs, it would reflect well on sergeant Carter, the captain, the CO and ultimately, the whole regiment. It was a bold plan, but if they pulled it off they would be the talk of the battalion.

Hot drinks consumed, the NCOs all shook hands, then lead their squads off in different directions. B squad, including Parrish, Rabbett and Dunn, headed west.

The afternoon sun was very bright, a hot yellow orb, sinking down towards the horizon.

Private Dunn raised his hand in front if his face and squinted through parted fingers at the heavily wooded copse ahead of them. The sun hung in the sky above it and the bank of high trees cast a long shadow on the bare earth. The squad moved towards it.

"Christ, that's bright." Dunn said. "I'll be glad to get in the shade. I can't see a bloody thing."

"You were obviously never a boy scout." said Parrish.

The others turned to look at him. From an inside pocket he had produced and was wearing an impenetrable, black lensed pair of 'blues brothers' sunglasses. He looked quite ridiculous and yet somehow rather dashing in his dark shades and combat clothes. The other soldiers laughed. Parrish casually adjusted the sunglasses.

"Be prepared." he grinned.

"How can you find room to carry *stupid* kit like that?" asked Rabbett incredulously.

"Because, I've got a *stupid* man like you carrying the big bits of kit." Replied Parrish dryly.

When wearing 'battle order' and staying in the field overnight, it was standard procedure to pair off men. They would split their bedding and shelter, swapping loads the next day. Private Rabbett carried his and Parrish's standard issue sleeping bags in a bulky pack on his back, while Parrish had the two ponchos, used to make temporary tents, rolled up tightly and slung on his webbing beneath the kidney pouches. A much more compact, if not much lighter load.

"Bollocks to you." said Rabbett. "Besides, tomorrow you'll be carrying the sleeping bags and that'll be after a night without sleep *and* a section attack. That ought to slow you down a bit, smart arse."

"Of course it will." agreed Parrish to everyone's surprise.

"It will?" asked Rabbett, leaving him wide open to a sarcastic reply.

"Yes." interrupted Private Dunn before Parrish could deliver his scathing answer. He snapped to attention, doing a perfect imitation of Sergeant Carter. "And I'll tell you why matey. Because you're idle Parrish, bone fucking IDLE!" Even the voice and shout was a perfect copy.

The whole section roared with laughter, the sound carrying in the clear air and causing some consternation among the big black birds that had their rookery in the tree tops of the copse.

The Lynx smoothly gathered speed as it skirted the south western corner of Boscombe Down aerodrome. Gently caressing its controls, the pilot looked and felt as at home in his seat as the aircraft did in the airfield environment. They were made for each other.

He deftly flew his aircraft north west, threading his way at an altitude of two thousand feet between the small towns of Great Durnford and Amesbury, totally unaware of the importance of the cargo he carried. Men or machinery, payload was payload to him. He just loved to fly.

Inside the see through map pocket on the right thigh of his flying suit were the directions for this flight. The looping route added a lot of distance to what would normally have been a very short trip. The pilot shook his helmeted head. Why he couldn't fly straight there he didn't know. Still, orders are orders.

The flight plan in his pocket gave reference figures and fresh headings from each turning point but he knew 'the plain' like the back of his hand and had no need to refer to the notations.

The first turn, to head due west along reference line 42, was at grid: 422122. He grinned. Anyone who had ever flown over 'the plain', from the most seasoned Tornado pilot to the greenest trainee in a Chipmunk, knew that at grid: 422122 stood the greatest landmark in the entire country. Stonehenge.

Once there he would veer west along grid line 42, dropping down to five hundred feet as he technically became part of Operation Backfire. On sighting the army camp at Knook, he was to turn due south. Cross the high wooded ridge of Cranbourne Chase, then skirt around the village of Sixpenny Handley and head south east. He estimated touching down at the DRA testing centre, after completing the eighty kilometre jaunt, in about twenty minutes.

In the time it took for the pilot to think these thoughts, Stonehenge rose into view, a few kilometres ahead. He and his co-pilot/observer exchanged knowing smiles. The passengers didn't know. Nor would they understand, even if they had witnessed it. It was a flyers thing.

Easing the stick gently forwards and letting off slightly on the cyclic, he started to descend. Coming in at exactly five hundred feet, he banked the machine around the great monument for the benefit of his passengers, letting them have a good view of the ancient stones, then headed away, directly into the setting sun.

The soldiers moved gratefully into the cool shade of the copse and began to make their way through the trees. The sun was still very warm, even this late in the day. The men worked their way through the copse, stomping heavy footed over the dead wood and fallen foliage. The sounds agitated the already unsettled crows, high up in the leafy canopy.

"I hate crows." came one soldier's voice from where he stood among the tree trunks. "Horrible things. You should see 'em pick the meat off dead sheep on my old man's farm. I hate crows."

"Ask the Corp real nice and he might let you put a few rounds into the nests. Anyway, what's the point in farming dead sheep?" The jokey voice was easily recognizable as Private Dunn's.

The sound of sniggers drifted through the copse.

"Knock it off and keep quiet." called the Corporal from the front.

"Nice thought though." said the first soldier, ignoring the Corporal and Private Dunn. He raised his rifle to his shoulder, squinted along the sight and said quietly to himself, "Blam! blam! blam!"

Private Dunn chuckled at the sight.

The squad walked clear of the copse, then stopped while the Corporal checked his bearing. They were visible to the crows now and the birds cawed loudly down at the intruders.

"Piss off!" shouted the first soldier. A couple of the others laughed. Just then the sound of a helicopter, travelling low and fast, came throbbing to their ears. That was the final straw for the crows and like a black cloud they began to lift noisily off into the sky.

"Look at 'em," said Private Rabbett. "Living here on 'the plain' you'd think they'd be used to the sounds of the army on the move. Silly sods."

The crows wheeled en mass above the trees, finding a thermal above the greenery and suddenly soaring skyward on the pillar of hot air.

The Lynx came skimming up the shallow valley, on a direct line to the small copse, the low, bright sunlight glinting on the windscreen. The pilot glanced down at his instrument panel to check his position, knowing that a few kilometres farther on would be Knook camp.

At that same moment his co-pilot swore loudly. The pilot looked up to see a flock of black birds rising rapidly in front of the speeding helicopter. Calmly he began side slipping to port. The birds were climbing too quickly and the Lynx was flying too fast to avoid the curse of the modern aviator. Bird strike.

The pilot was not overly concerned. It was highly improbable that a bird would manage to find its way into an air intake and, if he could nose the helicopter slightly downwards, the spinning blades would take care of any unfortunate bird that flew within their span. Some poor sod on the ground crew staff would have to wipe off the mess though. He deftly dipped the nose of his aircraft, but the Lynx's approach speed was some two hundred and forty kilometres per hour and the aircraft was among the birds before he could complete the manoeuvre.

Shattered plexiglas exploded around the control cabin as a bird cannoned through the windscreen.

"Shit!" cursed the pilot, squinting his eyes against the flying debris but keeping both hands on the controls. The bird had blasted through the port side windscreen and its remains hit the co-pilot full in the face. The pilot didn't know whether his partner was dead or not but the unfortunate man, his face a mass of blood and exposed bone, slumped forward onto the control column.

Pulling back as hard as he could on the stick pinned by his companion's weight, the pilot barely managed to flatten out the pitch of the aircraft. With less than five hundred feet between him and the ground he knew there was no chance of recovery.

Still struggling with the controls he spoke urgently yet calmly into his mouthpiece, oblivious to the panic behind him in the cargo bay.

"Mayday, mayday..." was all he managed to transmit before the helicopter went in. Hard.

The soldiers just stood, dumbstruck, as they witnessed the bird strike.

For a brief second the helicopter seemed to stagger in the air before heading earthwards. It overshot the copse and the soldier's positions just beyond it, coming down in a shallow dive. For a moment the aircraft levelled out and more than one of the soldiers thought, and hoped, that the craft would pull up. It was not to be.

Maybe six hundred yards from the horrified infantrymen, the stricken helicopter belly flopped into the ground. Its back broke with the impact and it ploughed on a short distance, exploding clods of earth in all directions. The tail rotor arm sheared off and flew apart in a shower of metal fragments. The wildly revving main engine immediately tried to screw itself and the helicopter body into the ground, twisting the buckled body violently to one side before the main rotor blades smashed into the ground. They splintered into long jagged pieces that whirred away into the air. With a screaming shudder the motor seized solid and the whole juddering, disintegrating wreck screeched and ground into silence. Jagged pieces of metal and plastic came fluttering down out of the blue sky and clattered or flopped to the ground.

For a long moment there was a deathly hush. Thin wisps of steam rose steadily from the remains of the engine as dust billowed out and away from the crash site.

A calm, firm voice brought the soldiers to their senses. The radio man Sparks, speaking with surprising control into the mouthpiece of the Clansman PCR 350 he carried, was calling for immediate assistance. The Corporal drew a hasty cross on his map by way of a grid reference then handed it to Sparks before bursting into a run. The others followed suit, racing desperately towards the smashed aircraft.

3

The battered remains of the helicopter sat quiet and still in the centre of a roughly circular area of scattered wreckage.

As the running soldiers reached the edge of this circle, some twenty or so yards from the actual aircraft, they came across a body hurled clear of the wreck. They didn't know who it was, but it was Reeves.

Several of the men pulled up short, having never been this close to death before. The Corporal and Parrish knelt down to check. Their initial reaction was one of horror and then surprise. The body was that of a civilian, dressed in a now ragged and bloodstained suit. He was definitely dead.

All his limbs had been broken in several places. They lay at grotesque and impossible angles. Blood streamed from his mouth, nose and ears. His eyes were unfocused but wide and staring. One man hurriedly turned away and vomited violently.

Parrish, furious at himself for feeling so futile in not being able to do anything for the dead man, snapped angrily.

"Get a grip man! There could be worse inside the chopper."

The outburst sobered the men even more. Parrish unclipped one of the ponchos from his webbing and, with the help of the Corporal, unrolled it and covered the corpse. The rest of the men waited until the pair had finished their grim task then, as a group, they advanced slowly towards the wreck.

Picking their way through the debris, they reached the main body of the helicopter. Before anyone could check inside, a muttered curse came from the smashed cockpit.

The Corporal detailed four men to check inside the cargo bay. The rest followed him around to the front of the craft. As two of the soldiers peered hesitantly in through the broken and bloodstained windscreen, afraid at what they might see, Parrish pulled open the pilots door, the Corporal doing the same on the co-pilots side. The helicopter fuselage was so badly bent out of shape that considerable force was needed to free them.

The pilot was sitting bolt upright in his seat, still conscious. He turned his head slowly and looked Parrish in the eye.

"Bugger!" he said with real feeling. "D'you know, for a second there I thought I could save it. Shit, the CO's going to have my arse for stuffing this chopper."

"I wouldn't worry about it." said Parrish in what he hoped was an unconcerned voice. "Besides, it's probably insured. Don't know what you were doing up there anyway. Flying is for the birds."

"That's a good one." said the pilot who was obviously in deep shock. "Birds."

With that he reached slowly down to pick up a black crow feather that was in his lap. Parrish's eyes followed the arm movement down then saw the pilot's legs. The helicopter has impacted so hard that the floor of the aircraft had buckled upward. In doing so the rudder pedals had pounded into the pilot's feet and the massive shock had shattered both his femurs. Some pieces of bone had perforated the skin and dark red blood was seeping into the cloth of his flying suit. When the pilot saw this he swore again.

The Corporal gently righted the slumped co-pilot.

"How is he?" asked Parrish.

One of the soldiers looking through the front of the aircraft grimaced at the sight of the co-pilots smashed face, barely recognizable as human. Unable to stop the natural action of looking into a person's eyes, the soldier swallowed at the grisly spectre of empty eye sockets. His words just came blurting out.

"If he lives he's gonna need a white stick and a dog."

Strangely, the callousness seemed to go unnoticed. The Corporal checked the co-pilots neck for a pulse. There was a long pause.

"He won't need any white stick." he said quietly.

"Shit!" said the pilot again. Seeming not to notice his own pain, he became deeply distressed on hearing of the death of his partner. He started to cry.

"Steady mate, steady." said Parrish calmly and rested a hand on the man's arm. "We'll have you out of here in a jiffy and away to hospital in no time. Chin up."

The pilot managed a weak smile that immediately died on his face as the Corporal gently let the body slump forward till it came to rest against the top of the instrument panel. He gave it a gentle pat on the shoulder then turned his attention to the two soldiers still watching, unmoving, from in front of the aircraft.

"Right you two," he said forcibly, making them jump. "Get the pilot out *carefully* and make him as comfortable as possible."

All the men had attended first aid courses and didn't need to be told what to do with a casualty. Parrish stepped aside to allow them to get to work. He got the distinct impression that the two squaddies were glad to be told what to do then left to get on with it. He knew the injured pilot would get the best attention they could offer.

"C'mon Parrish. Let's see what's inside this mess."

He nodded and the pair moved along the sides of the fuselage. Both the sliding doors had tom away and were nowhere to be seen. They peered into the cargo bay.

The other four soldiers were already at work. The third dead body was that of Lieutenant Marston. His chest had been crushed by the steel box that had torn free of its securing straps with the force of the impact, before slamming across the cargo bay and crushing him up against the forward bulkhead. The rescuers didn't actually know what had killed him, the open and empty steel box was lying twisted and buckled on the ground just behind Parrish, who was still peering in through the starboard opening.

Dunn and Rabbett were in the process of using their field dressings to tie together the legs of the civilian who was lying prostrate on the floor of the bay. Dunn had checked the man over and quickly come to the conclusion that his pelvis was broken. The injured man was semi-conscious but had answered coherently when asked his name.

"This is James Barstow." Dunn informed the corporal who was also peering in. "Pelvis busted I reckon. Could be internal injuries as well. We'll need something flat to move him on."

At that moment the third soldier returned from his brief forage through the wreckage, dragging behind him one of the missing doors. It was a bit buckled but it would do.

"Good man!" said the Corporal then helped him slide it into the bay alongside professor Barstow.

Parrish leaned in and grasped the man's feet while Rabbett supported his hips and Dunn grasped the man's shoulders.

"All right Jimbo." Dunn said, his face close to Barstow's so that the man might see him clearly. "This might smart a bit but it's got to be done. OK?"

Professor Barstow nodded, teeth gritted in anticipation.

"Right. One, two, three, LIFT!"

The injured man screamed in agony when they lifted him onto his makeshift stretcher, the dreadful sound dying away to sobs, his breath coming in short heaving pants.

"Did that hurt?" asked Dunn in a surprised voice. Barstow allowed the smallest of smiles to escape through his agonized features. "Told you so didn't I. Never mind, we'll have you away to hospital PDQ." Barstow's eyebrows went up in a hopeful gesture. "Trust me," continued Dunn feigning offence. "It hurt when I said it would didn't it? Would I lie to you?" He glanced up at Parrish who smiled a wink in return. Professor Barstow caught the gesture and looked at Parrish, who said,

"You're all right Jimbo.'Clive' is as good as his word."

The thought that filled Barstow's mind was that the only person who had ever called him 'Jimbo' was his mother and that had been when he was a small boy. He drew as much comfort from that thought as he did from the concern of his rescuers.

The fourth soldier, the radio operator, was attending to Colonel Reed. On seeing the man's rank the Corporal jumped up into the wreck and went to help.

"He's out cold but OK I think." said Sparks. "Both his arms are busted. They must have thrashed about in the crash. That cut on his head looks a lot worse than it really is. Head wounds always bleed like a bastard."

The Corporal nodded as he recalled the MOs words that Sparks had just repeated word for word. He used his own field dressing to help secure the colonels arms across his body.

Colonel Reed was still in his seat and the two men unfastened the straps then lifted him up in a fireman's chair, arms linked under his thighs and behind his back. After struggling out of the cargo bay they carried him off about twenty yards and laid him carefully down beside the pilot, who was still being attended to by his own first aid team.

"Watch him." said the Corporal, before he went back to take the fourth corner of professor Barstow's makeshift stretcher. The two soldier's eyes widened at the sight of crowns on the epaulettes of their new patient.

Back in the helicopter the four men gingerly manoeuvred

Professor Barstow to the edge of the cargo bay which was rather inconveniently at knee level to the ground. The two lead men had to take the injured mans weight in a stooping stance until the other pair jumped down and took their corners. Barstow's head also had to be supported as his body was longer than the door he lay on. By the time the stretcher bearers had picked their way through the strewn wreckage and set the professor down with the other injured parties, the sun had crept a lot nearer to the horizon.

The wrecked helicopter threw a long shadow which made the crash site look even more grim.

The soldiers crouched by their charges, able to do little more than keep them as warm and comfortable as they could. The pilot was bearing his pain silently, Colonel Reed was still unconscious and professor Barstow was lying as still as possible, struggling for full consciousness. The three corpses lay in a short row off to one side, wrapped in ponchos. No one looked at them.

"How long before the cavalry arrives, Sparks?" asked the Corporal. The radio operator checked his watch. Amazingly, it had been less than half an hour since the whole nightmarish event had begun.

"I had to call another unit and they put my message through on their bigger radio." He shrugged his shoulders to indicate the radio on his back. "Only got a five kilometre range these. Shouldn't be long now though."

The Corporal just nodded.

At that moment professor Barstow became fully conscious. He tried to sit up and cried out in pain before being eased back down by Parrish.

"Lie still you silly sod. The less you move the better. Be quiet and wait, the medics will be here pretty soon."

"But, my work."

"What?" asked Parrish thinking the man was delirious.

"In the helicopter." insisted professor Barstow. "The machine I've been working on for over ten years. Please, I must have it."

"Fuck off. Anyway, it's probably been smashed to bits."

Barstow had enough sense not to say that it was radioactive and also enough to know that the core should easily withstand any impact that a human being could survive. Either way, it was still his life's work *and* a piece of top secret military hardware.

"Please. I must have it." he begged.

"Look..." began Parrish.

"Jesus, Parrish." interrupted the Corporal, "It won't do him any harm and you haven't got anything else to do. Go and get his bloody machine."

"Yes." Rabbett was not missing a chance for a dig. "The civvie wants his machine. Go and get it, it might make him feel better. Hop to it!"

"'Bunny' Rabbett says hop to it!" said Parrish making the other soldiers smile, "All right, I'll go, but only because I can't stand the diabolical jokes!"

"Please." groaned professor Barstow.

"OK, OK. What exactly does it look like?"

Barstow formed a sphere in the air with his hands. "A round metal ball about so big." His hands were about two and a half feet apart. "Control panel on the side. It's quite heavy."

Parrish heaved himself to his feet. "Here 'Bunny', catch!" He tossed his rifle at the grinning soldier who caught it deftly, the weapon making that unmistakable metallic clatter as it slapped into his outstretched hands.

Parrish spread his arms wide before the gathering of men, looking vaguely like the statue of Christ the Redeemer overlooking Rio de Janeiro.

"The poor bugger's lying there badly injured, needs hospital treatment, there's two more hurt, *three* dead and he wants to play with his heavy metal football!" He shook his head sadly.

"Go on!" chorused the other soldiers, always happy to watch someone else do a chore while they rested.

"I'm going, I'm going." Parrish waved away the gloats and trudged back through the scattered pieces of wreckage to the battered fuselage.

He climbed inside and looked around in the gathering gloom. It was there all right, jammed up where the cargo space narrowed, in the rear of the aircraft. It was quite unremarkable looking and Parrish was not impressed. The steel ball was wedged tight and refused to budge. The soldier impatiently gave it a good solid kick and it jerked free. Almost inaudibly, it started to hum.

Rolling it towards the centre of the bay, the display section came to the top. There was a large dent here, just alongside the panel and very close to the digital readout. All the digits still read zero, the illuminated numbers glowing dully in the half light. Parrish cocked his ear to the muted hum and eyed the row of noughts.

"Don't know how he tunes it in, but he lost that radio station." said Parrish half jokingly, noticing the total lack of manual controls anywhere on the sphere.

It *was* heavy he realized, when he tried to lift it. The steel ball seemed to him to be about as heavy and unmanageable as a half hundred weight bag of spuds but there was no way he was going to give the others the satisfaction of seeing him roll it all the way back to Jimbo.

He grunted as he heaved it up into his arms, gratefully taking some of the weight on the front pouches of his webbing, then made his way to the door.

"Is this it?" he called.

All the faces turned his way and even at that distance he could see Professor Barstow's head nodding eagerly.

Private Dunn called back. "Jimbo says yes and to be extremely careful with it. It's very valuable."

"Oh really!" said Parrish feeling rather silly stood in the doorway, leaning back against the weight of the sphere.

"Come on!" waved the Corporal, beginning to lose patience with all the larking about when there were injured people to be taken care of.

"Keep your hair on." replied Parrish. "What's the rush? I've got plenty of time." He shrugged his shoulders, settled the weight onto his chest and jumped down from the cargo bay.

He never saw the confused looks of baffled surprise, amazement and fear on the faces of the other men. He never saw anything.

As he thudded to the ground there was a muffled click from deep inside the sphere. For one timeless second he was encased in a faint electric blue aura. Then there was a brief but very bright, white light, like an electronic camera flash. It momentarily dazzled the watching men, who looked hurriedly away.

When they looked back, Private Shaun Parrish, 2nd Battalion the Light Infantry, just wasn't there anymore!

3,512 BC

4

The unusually warm summer sun beat steadily down on the unconscious form of Shaun Parrish. He lay on his back, slightly arched because of his webbing beneath him. The reviving rays of light slowly brought him back to his senses. He lay motionless for a few moments longer, eyes squinting up at the almost azure blue sky and adjusting to the brightness.

In a sudden rush of thoughts, he remembered the helicopter crash, the dead and injured and the heavy steel ball. He snapped up into a sitting position and almost fell immediately back down again. His head pounded and a wave of nausea swept over him as his semi-circulars swam, before settling back on an even keel.

"Whoa!" he said aloud, holding his aching head. "Shit! I must have fallen over and cracked my head on something."

It took a few moments, sitting with eyes screwed tightly shut, before the pounding in his head subsided and he again dared to open them. Better. He took a look around. A couple of yards away rested the steel ball. It had obviously rolled away when he had dropped it. Jimbo wouldn't be too pleased about that.

Parrish climbed labouriously to his feet and did a slow three hundred and sixty degree turn. He looked but it was difficult to grasp what he saw and, more to the point, what he didn't see.

There was no sign of the helicopter crash. Nothing. No wreck, not a single broken piece of metal or plastic and no tell tale marks or gouges in the earth. He looked to where the other members of B section should have been sitting, waiting and watching him. No one.

He didn't like it. He didn't like it at all. The only thing that should be there and actually was, the steel ball, sat still as a stone and he walked unsteadily over to it, then around it. At the rear of the sphere was the display panel. It glowed dully, only visible because it was in shadow. Parrish knelt slowly down and read the display.

- 5,500 YRS

Parrish frowned.

"Minus five thousand five hundred Y-R-S?" he read aloud. "Y-R-S? Years? OK, minus five and a half thousand years what? Doesn't make sense." In a state of confusion, he read the panel again. As he watched, the display blinked out, back on again then faded slowly away until the readout was blank. After waiting to see if anything else would happen, which didn't, Parrish stood up and gave the sphere another good kick. It achieved nothing.

He took a longer look around, his head clearer now. It was still Salisbury Plain. 'The plain' always looked the same. Except that it didn't. Not quite. He couldn't put his finger on exactly what was different but it wasn't quite as he remembered it from before.

The copse that B squad had passed through was no longer there, along with the vanished crashed site. It was warmer too. He squinted up at the sun, high up in the blue sky. The sky itself seemed bluer than he could ever remember and the air was clean and sweet. It hit him then that the sun was *high* in the sky, while it had been setting when he had jumped from the cargo bay. He checked his watch. It had stopped and no amount of shaking or tapping could re-start it.

"I don't know what's happening, but I don't like it."

He sat down on the steel ball and thought some more. Nothing made sense in his head. He ran through the sequence of events leading up to his present predicament. Mentally ticking them off, they ran in a logical sequence until the last step. See chopper crash, help injured, get ball, jump from fuselage then somehow end up here. It sounded so stupid and unexplainable that he got angry. Banging his fist on the hard metal beneath him, he leapt to his feet and shouted at the top of his voice.

"What the fuck is going on?!"

The silence that followed the wild outburst did absolutely nothing to boost his flagging spirits.

Pulling his black plastic water bottle from its pouch on his right hip, he took a sip and tried to formulate some sort of plan of action.

OK, he thought, calming himself. The section was moving in a west to east direction across the south of 'the plain'. Now, assuming I'm still in the same area, just to the south of my position maybe six or seven clicks away is the Wylye Valley, the river Wylye and the A36. I'll get to the road, hitch a lift to the nearest phone box and make a few calls. That'll sort out this mess. It must be some kind of training test or something. I'm not sure what but I don't like it one little bit.

Replacing the water bottle, he took a deep breath then, turning to face roughly south in relation to the present position of the sun, he set off, pausing only to give the steel ball one last kick.

Parrish was, if nothing else, resilient. He ambled along at an easy pace, looking all about for any land marks that might help him pinpoint his position.

Not that there are many land marks at all on Salisbury Plain. He began to recover more as he walked, regaining his composure and sense of humour. He took deep breaths of the clean, reviving air and was grateful for the warm sunlight. He opened the front of his combat jacket to cool himself a bit and chewed on a few of the Rollo's that were part of the snacks and sweets section of his twenty four hour rations.

Actually, he thought, it's not that bad a situation to be in. He decided that if it was some sort or army initiative test, he could use his initiative and make the most of it. There was bound to be a handy pub somewhere along the A36 and all pubs have phones. Walking across 'the plain' in the sunshine was thirsty work and a well prepared soldier always carries a few pound coins and fifty pence pieces for just such a chance encounter with a public house. After all, there was no rush and they wouldn't know where he was until he called in.

He really knew, inside himself, that 'some sort of initiative test' was a poor and unsatisfactory explanation for his situation. Still, he didn't intend to let the strange state of affairs get him down or come between him and a pint. There had to be some simple explanation and he had no doubt that all would be made clear to him when he returned to barracks. When he returned though was up to him.

He smiled, thinking about what the rest of the lads might say. No doubt 'Clive' would take the piss but that was OK, let him. Enjoy today because tomorrow you may get shit on from a great height. Probably by sergeant Carter. Dismissing the idea of Carter in favour of Dunn's good humoured leg pulls, he smiled again and started to whistle one of the regimental marches he secretly enjoyed but wouldn't dare admit to his mates. As he walked on southwards there was a definite spring in his step.

The afternoon wore on and Parrish made constant if unhurried progress southwards. As he unaccountably watched the sun make its steady way towards the horizon for a second time in the same day, the river became visible in the distance. In the bottom of its valley some two kilometres distant, the western sunlight glinted and twinkled on its constant, flowing surface. A welcome sight indeed.

Parrish grinned in anticipation of a pie and a pint before making any calls to his superiors. He picked up his pace and started down the gently sloping valley side.

He stopped.

Something was not right with the panoramic view he now held, up and down the valley and across to the other side. It required a long, pensive moment for the reason for his worry to become clear. When he finally made that first connection, others emerged too.

The penny first dropped when Parrish realised that he could hear no traffic noise. None at all. Just twittering birds and the light sounds of windblown trees. No road noises meant no road. He looked hard but there was no sign of it. His eyes scoured all of the valley that could be seen. As he did so, realization dawned as to why 'the plain' didn't quite look the same. There were no fences.

In fact, as he stood stock still, looking up and down the river valley he was suddenly frighteningly aware that there were no signs at all of *any* human habitation.

If a person stands anywhere in the British Isles there is usually some sign of man making or having made past changes to his environment. Even in the remotest parts of the country.

Yet here was Parrish, standing in busiest south Wiltshire, and there was not one single thing or sign to say that people had ever been there. No roads, no fences, tracks, houses, tractor lines, telegraph poles or smoke. Nothing!

For the first time real fear gripped Parrish by the throat. He trembled even in the warm sunshine. His eyes darted desperately but try as he might, he could see no signs of human habitation. Because there were none.

He started to run down the slope that led ultimately to the river.

Stumbling and staggering as he ran, his head flicked, constantly searching left and right, but to no avail. When he reached the riverbank he flopped to the ground, breath ragged and nerves taut. Parrish had crossed the meadow just short of the river where the A36 *should* have been, and collapsed at the river's edge.

"HELLO?" he called out in desperation but was only rewarded with silence.

"What's happening to me? Am I going mad?" he asked himself softly. Then he just sat, hugging his knees tightly to his chest, and started to cry.

Never had a man been so alone.

It took a long time for Parrish to pull himself back together. The desperate loneliness and fear of not knowing what had happened crushed him utterly.

He didn't know it at the time, but on that river bank in the middle of that lonely landscape, he had reached the greatest juncture of his life. Whatever decision he made now would affect the rest of his entire life.

So completely desolate did he feel that even suicide crossed his mind. The very realization that Parrish was actually seriously considering taking his own life jarred him roughly and unpleasantly back to reality. He couldn't believe that he could have sunk so low as to even consider such a thing. Parrish wasn't in the remotest way religious but still he knew that suicide was the basest, most fundamental wrong.

He stopped crying and struggled hard to come to his senses. Unbuckling his webbing and letting it drop to the ground, he staggered to the river's edge, fell to the ground and plunged his face into the water.

It was cold and reviving. He held his head under the surface until his lungs were bursting, as much for proof that he was master of his own life as for its refreshing properties, then emerged, gasping.

Retrieving his webbing and drying his face on a sleeve, almost on auto pilot he started unpacking the right side kidney pouch. The British Empire had been built on what he was after. Through the years it had been the symbol of Great Britain. When a person was distraught, desperate or sad it was the one universal stabilizing thing. It managed to produce a small but morale boosting smile from Parrish.

He made himself a cup of tea.

The white, crystalline hexamine blocks crackled and popped,

pushing up their bright orange flames against the underside of his mess tin. As the water came to the boil Parrish's thinking became clearer. Slurping gratefully and noisily at the pint of steaming hot, sweet tea, he sat back, gathered his thoughts and tried to look rationally at the situation.

He couldn't come up with a good, reasonable explanation as to why he should be the only person around. Or even how it had happened. At the time he did not know or conclude that the steel ball he had held in his arms was actually a rudimentary, prototype time machine. Even young schoolboys knew that time machines were the stuff of pulp science fiction stories, so he never considered that possibility. His attention focused more on his personal predicament.

The tea had a settling, calming effect. It took a while to drink and he used that time to assess the situation. The sun was warm and the river was fresh, cool and clear. He was in no immediate danger. Technically he wasn't lost either. The simple solution to that problem was to follow the river. The question was, did he go up stream to where he knew there should be several small towns, each with a military camp. Or did he accept the situation as he saw it for himself, with no roads, houses or people, and head down stream. What lay in that direction? Would he follow the river right through Salisbury, if it was there, join with the Avon and eventually end up at the sea?

It was the greatest and most difficult of decisions. He pondered seriously the pros and cons until he had finished the hot, restoring drink. Then he packed away his equipment, put on his webbing and stood silent and still beside the flowing water.

With an almost super human effort that went against everything he had ever known, learned or been taught, he reluctantly turned his back on twentieth century life and set off downstream. At first he felt dejected and sorry, suffering an attack of self pity, but he daren't let himself falter. To stop now would destroy him. He pushed on. The feelings didn't pass but he suppressed them, turning them to resignation at his decision. A great bridge in his life had been crossed, with no way back. His footfalls became more purposeful and he became more determined, lifting his head and his spirits.

He was now the master of his destiny. He felt strangely strong. Where he was actually going he wasn't sure. What he would find he didn't know. But he was now open to whatever life had to offer.

An independent and monumental decision had been made, Parrish realised. It shocked him yet at the same time stirred his blood. He was now truly his own man.

5

Keeping the river to the right of him, Parrish made his way easterly along the valley floor. The virgin ground was mostly meadow and the grasses and wild flowers knitted a knee high green carpet, interwoven with splashes of blooming colour. After the first great depression, then the soaring euphoria, he suffered several mood swings. What's going to happen to me? - I can handle it – look out world, here I come!

The mind can only ride that type of emotional roller-coaster for a limited time before the senses become dulled and numb. By a purely instinctive process which Parrish's conscious mind had very little say in at the end, an air of resigned determination settled upon his shoulders. Darwin's natural selection theory, personal mental attitude or British stiff upper lip, who knows? Either way, Parrish's' mind settled and, once he had opened himself to the idea of carrying on as best he could, come what may, it was undoubtedly the best solution to his mental anguish.

It greatly strengthened his resolve. He needed it. All the rest of the afternoon, as he waded his way through the greenery, all he received was more and more conformation of his aloneness. There was nothing to even hint towards habitation by anyone. By force of habit he found himself looking for tracks or footpaths to make his passage easier. There were none.

The sun was now very low in the sky. Parrish hoped that it really would set this time. In his estimation he had walked a good half dozen clicks, when he came to a pronounced bend in the river. With the water on his right and the sun at his back, he knew he faced east. The river turned south towards where Salisbury should be. Looking straight ahead to the higher ground, he could see it was partially wooded. With the sun almost down, midges and mosquitoes were now out on the air and he was glad of his insect repellent.

He decided to climb to the high ground and camp in the woods, away from the insects but still handy for water. He did of course intend to use puritabs on it when he refilled his bottle the next day. The walk to the top of the brow took him another half hour and he barely had time to set up his poncho as a basha and gather a few armfuls of bracken as bedding, before the night closed in.

Parrish left his temporary base and moved along the ridge to the edge of the wood, perhaps half a click. He did and always would think in kilometres. He was after all a product of the metric age and besides, it had been drummed into him in the army. Clearing the woods he found he had a splendid, scenic twilight view back along the river valley he had walked and also across the valley on the other side of the ridge he now occupied.

He waited patiently until it was completely dark. It was the blackest yet clearest night he had ever witnessed. The night sky was absolutely awash with beautiful, twinkling stars. It was actually difficult to see any dark sky between the bright pinpricks of light. He had never guessed that there were so many stars in the heavens.

The land was an undulating carpet of black velvet. As far as the eye could see in every direction was an all enveloping blackness. There was not a single light to be seen anywhere.

"You really are alone, matey." he said in a quietly awed voice.

Unaccountably, the feeling that washed over him was not one of fear but of sadness. What in heaven's name had happened to all the people? Why hadn't whatever happened to them, happened to him? He gazed quietly into the darkness for a long while, then returned to his basha.

Heating two small ration tins in boiling water, he cooked the bacon burgers and beans in tomato sauce inside them. Half of the boiled water was used to make up some instant mashed potato and the rest went into another cup of tea. Parrish ate and drank in silence, packing away his kit when he had finished and burying all the empty wrappers and tins. Then he settled back to sleep. He lay on his back under his suspended poncho, looking out and up through the leafy trees at the few stars he could see. A light breeze rustled the green canopy. With the warm evening, the soothing sounds and his physical and mental fatigue, he soon found his eyelids growing unstoppably heavy. As he drifted off to sleep he imagined he heard far off animal noises, calling into the night, but dismissed them as a dream.

He was in the cargo bay of a helicopter. It was flying but the altimeter said minus five and a half thousand years. Suddenly the pilot seemed to lose control. It dived. He struggled to reach the controls but couldn't, trapped in a tight corner by a heavy steel ball. His desperately clawing hands managed to open the door to the flight deck. Everyone was gone. The helicopter plunged earthwards. On the ground he could see B squad waiting, watching and laughing. Kick the steel ball as hard as he could, it wouldn't move. Trapped, powerless and screaming for help, he knew there was no one, anywhere, to save him. The ground rushed up. Impact was imminent! He awoke with a violent jerk. Rigidly upright, he was breathing hard and in a cold sweat.

The sun was again smiling down from just above the horizon and chirpy birds were singing the last bars of the dawn chorus. Parrish rubbed his hands roughly across his face and waited till his heart had stopped pounding. Shaking his head, he ran his fingers through his short hair then sorted out some breakfast. He didn't want to waste any hexamine blocks heating water just for a cuppa and a shave, so he restricted himself to a packet of biscuits AB brown. Sparing a small amount to splash on his face and clean his teeth, he used the last of the water on a powdered orange drink, then packed away and rolled up his poncho while sucking on a couple of boiled sweets.

Making sure he had left nothing behind, he strode again out to his vantage point at the edge of the copse. In the daylight it was now possible to see into the valley beyond his ridge. There was another river at its bottom which he knew was the famous river Avon. It ran, from its source in the north of the county, almost directly south all the way to the sea. Parrish could as easily follow the Avon as the Wylye and he disliked backtracking, to him it smacked of failure. It was a purely personal choice and so he set off, still actually travelling in an easterly direction, down the gentle slope of the Avon river valley.

He guessed with unerring accuracy the distance to the river as one and a half kilometres. Just a short, bracing stretch of the legs before being able to refill his water bottle. It didn't take too long and, when he had reached the water's edge, he checked his watch to see exactly how long, again out of habit. The thing hadn't worked yesterday and it still wasn't working. He unstrapped it from his wrist.

"Worse than useless, it's a bloody nuisance." he said and hurled it aggressively into the river where it disappeared with a plop.

After Parrish had refilled his water bottle he popped a puritab into the clear liquid, screwed the top closed and secured the container in its pouch.

Before he turned to head south he looked casually up the valley to the north. It was again meadowland either side of the flow, but something caught his now much more observant eye. There appeared to be, a little way up on the other side of the river, a faint line in the long grass. It snaked up the valley slope in an almost straight line and disappeared over the far brow. He investigated.

As he drew near he saw that it was not much more than a slight flattening of the meadow grass but it certainly looked similar to the path he had made while moving through the Wylye valley meadows yesterday.

Having no worries that anyone might be around to catch him with his pants around his ankles, he stripped naked from the waist down and, holding his trousers and boots above his head, gingerly waded across the river. It was pleasantly cool and at its deepest it flowed around the tops of his thighs. He felt quite refreshed as he re dressed on the other bank.

On inspection, the grass had certainly been trodden down by something. Or someone. Parrish hunted back and forth along the river's edge for a few minutes looking for any tell tale signs, perhaps even a bare footed imprint. Finding nothing, he was for a moment disappointed, then chuckled.

"Who do you think you are?" he asked himself. "Robinson Crusoe?"

Obviously the path demanded further investigation. It was most unlikely that a person had made the faint trail, more probably a deer or something come to the water to drink. On the other hand it was the only thing he had seen that offered even the slightest hope of another person or persons being in the area. Besides, did he have anything better to do?

The line of flattened grass led him up over the brow and onto the rolling slopes beyond. It was densely wooded in places and open in others. It occurred to him that apart from the missing patchwork of crop fields and a lot more trees, the landscape was the same. Things didn't look so different.

The faint track faded away over open ground but was easily picked up again where there was any extensive ground cover. Whatever it was that had passed this way he mused, it knew where it was going, virtually in a straight line to the east.

Another hours walking found him being led by the track to an area of open ground, devoid of any vegetation. There were many holes in the ground here, possibly twenty or thirty. Some were a foot deep, others as much as six or eight. All around the holes, scattered at random on the dry earth were chips and chunks of dark, glistening flint.

Parrish would never know, but it was a touch of irony that the ground he stood on was not too far south of where, in another fifty five centuries, Boscome Down aerodrome would be built. More so, he was less than a kilometre from the spot where, in five and a half thousand years time, a helicopter would take off and begin the events leading up to where, and when, he now found himself.

He walked around, kicking at the odd flint nodule, not quite sure what he was looking at. Just strange holes in the ground with the debris from them scattered all around. Before he could ponder more on the subject he spotted the track again. Still leading east but this time much more pronounced. The grass was just about worn away and patches of earth were clearly visible.

He had gone not ten paces along the track when he stopped suddenly. In a patch of soft soil, just in front of his booted feet, was a footprint! Not some bullshit Robinson Crusoe imaginings, but a real footprint. Parrish knelt to examine it, barely able to contain his joy and excitement. On closer inspection he saw it was small. Too small to be a man's. OK then a kid but it was definitely human.

He hunted about but found no more prints, even after looking again around the strange holes. In one of them he saw a piece of bone and jumped in to pick it up. At the base of the hole walls were gouge marks. Parrish knelt and dug into the earth with the piece of bone. It made the same marks.

Climbing back out, he returned to the footprint, still clutching the bone fragment. It was another puzzle. Some kids, or at least one, had been digging out, even mining, flint. What for he didn't know. Perhaps the answer lay at the end of the path. Tossing the bone to one side he set off with deliberate strides along the much more prominent and definitely foot trodden path.

There was no point in exhausting himself unnecessarily. He

slowed his pace and concentrated on studying the surrounding countryside. The trees were more prolific than he recalled, being very dense woodland in places. They were in fact taller and of bigger girth than twentieth century trees, but Parrish was not to know this. Indeed, who at all takes notice of the height of trees.

The sun moved towards its zenith and Parrish was already taking regular sips of water. It was almost uncomfortably warm, and not yet high summer.

On deciding to stop for lunch, Parrish checked his supplies. It was easily possible to string out the contents of a twenty four hour ration pack over two days and, at a pinch, even three. Soon though he would have to start relying on the skills taught to him during his survival training. Like every other foot soldier, Parrish had attended extensive 'survival in the field' courses and carried the survival equipment issued by the MOD. Included in this kit was their excellent knife, secure in its leather sheath squeezed in between his water bottle pouch and right side ammo pouch. A firm recommendation by the survival instructors was the tobacco tin full of essential pieces of kit sold by a Penrith company called, appropriately enough, Survival Aids Limited. Every good soldier should have one, they said, and Parrish was proud of the fact that he was a good soldier.

The training that all soldiers undergo is concise and emphatic. It all comes down to three things. Shelter, food and water. Parrish was quite capable of building a sturdy temporary or even more permanent shelter if necessary. Streams and rivers abounded in what he still recognised as the Salisbury Plain area. For food he could catch fish or small animals. He knew about traps and deadfalls and the Survival Aids kit included fishhooks and snares. It also included a flint and steel for starting fires. He could use it once his Zippo had expired but there was an ample supply of flint just lying about on the ground.

He sat in the shade of a positively huge, sprawling oak tree and ate the second pack of AB biscuits, spreading ham paste on them. Reclining against the gnarled, mottled trunk he lay still, just soaking up the peaceful ambiance of the calm air, warm sunshine and magnificently unspoiled scenery. The restful, pleasant feeling didn't last. Constricting thoughts of helicopter crashes, dead men and vanished people, all still unexplainable, soured the midday repose. He rose resignedly to his feet, pulled on his webbing and set off again, picking occasionally at the mixed fruit and nuts from the small plastic packet they came supplied in.

Still, thought Parrish as he walked, look on the bright side. If you have to be alone, you could be in a lot worse places. After all, the scenery is breathtaking. As if to make his point he opened his arms wide and did a slow three hundred and sixty degree turn, scanning the horizon as he did so. When he returned to his start point, facing along the track, ahead of him was a large steep banked knoll about three kilometres distant. Almost a hill, it was more prominent than the rest of the undulating ridges and vales he could see. The sight stopped him dead in his tracks, and not because it was impressive, dominating the surrounding landscape.

It was because of the fine column of wood smoke that spiralled up from the top of it into the still summer air.

6

The first thing he noticed as he drew nearer to the flat topped hill was the close cropped grass underfoot and the occasional pile of sheep droppings. The unmistakable signs of organized farming made Parrish smile. Things were looking up. Indeed, looking up at the top of the knoll, he could vaguely see some sort of low construction work. It took some effort to stop himself from breaking into a run but with a good kilometre still between him and the hill he kept to his disciplined pace. A thousand questions whirled around inside his head and he used the time to order them. It wouldn't look very good if he arrived a breathless, gibbering idiot.

Parrish closed steadily. The closer he got the more puzzled he became. The smoke that he had first seen was actually produced by more than one fire. Several separate columns rose from the top of the hill and combined higher up in the sky. That was why it had been visible from such a distance. Although there was obviously more than one fire source, he could still see no buildings on the top of the plateau.

At five hundred meters he could plainly see a long, low wall along the top. It didn't extend right across the top of the knoll. Parrish walked, in a state of complete bemusement, right up to the base of the knoll. From his low viewpoint he couldn't see the wall and so climbed steadily till he reached the brow.

The mysterious wall was actually a three meter high fence or barrier, perhaps thirty or so meters back from the lip of the hill, made entirely of telegraph pole sized tree trunks. They formed an impenetrable wall that curved away on both sides. If it continued the same curve, Parrish reasoned, then the wall enclosed a large circular compound. He would have liked to inspect it closer but could not, because of the deep, steep sided ditch that had been dug between where he stood at the lip of the hill and the wooden wall. It too went off to both sides in a curve, keeping a constant distance from the base of the wall.

As a soldier Parrish instantly recognized crude but effective defences. The bottom of the ditch was meticulously tidy and deep, five or six meters below the surface.

Unable to reach the wall, Parrish started to walk anti-clockwise along the edge of the defence ditch. It was only when he started walking that he became aware of the people watching him. The tops of their heads were barely visible behind the top of the wall, but they moved when he did.

"Hello! Hello there." He smiled joyfully and waved his arms. "How do you get into that thing? Around this way?" He pointed. There was no reply.

"Hey, can you hear me? What kind of a camp is this?" Still no answer. Shit, he thought, I hope they're not new age travellers or hippies. They hate authority and I look more than just a bit establishment in my soldier suit.

"I'm lost, where is this?" Still he received no acknowledgement or answer from the hidden watchers. Parrish began to get annoyed. He had been through a stressful, worrying time and was in no mood to play silly buggers.

"Stop fucking about!" he yelled. "Answer me!"

He was answered with more silence.

Fuck it, he said to himself and set off angrily around the edge of the ditch. He'd find his own way in and then he'd get some answers. And they'd better watch it. The first man to give him any lip would get a smack. He didn't need this sort of aggro.

There were more surprises when he reached the other side, the south eastern aspect of the walls, for there was the entrance. But it was no ordinary entrance. The two ends of the ditched almost met here. One finished directly in front of the entrance way to the circular compound. The other end swerved outward and overlapped that of the first. The effect was that the only path into the fort, for that was now what Parrish recognized it as, formed a sweeping 'S'. To enter the fort it would be necessary to negotiate the ditch ends, in full view of the watchers behind the wall, fully exposed to fire. Even Parrish had to admit that it was a simple but very effective protection system.

All this was academic though. Even if Parrish walked the exposed path he would still be unable to enter the fort. A wide two piece gate made of the same posts as the wall was closed across what he assumed to be the only entrance.

"C'mon," he yelled, half furious and half desperate. "Don't fuck about. Let me in!"

Still the barely visible heads watched in silence. Try as he might, Parrish could not get the fort people to open up. No amount of cajoling, pleading or threatening produced even the slightest reaction. After twenty minutes of shouting a one sided conversation he gave up, turned his back on the fort and walked down the more gently sloping approach road to level ground.

He spent some time exploring the outbuildings that squatted under the shadow of the fort, just off to the left of the track way that ended at the foot of the slope. The buildings were in the corner of a fenced area which was itself segmented off into small corrals. The fences were very rudimentary, made of thin tree trunks, similar he thought to the corrals seen in old western movies. The buildings themselves were crude too. Mud walls and thatched roofs. Simple barns for keeping animals in during bad weather. Sheep, judging from the old, dried droppings that littered their earth floors.

He stepped back out into the sunlight, feeling the eyes of the watchers still on him. Ignoring them and drawing a tingle of pleasure from it, he gazed out across the valley he could not see when he had approached from the other side of the hill. This is more like it, he thought.

The immediate valley had been cleared of forest and was a series of small patchwork fields. They were not what Parrish considered proper fields but more in the way of allotments. After a few moments scrutiny he became aware that each set of allotments of maybe eight to twelve small squares was separate from the other sets. The gaps between each allotment were left to grass and the whole effect was like that of a flat, two dimensional maze.

Beyond the chequered earthworks was open grassland that sloped gently up to a thick wood on the near horizon. On the grassland grazed a quite substantial heard of sheep. Maybe two to two hundred and fifty animals. Well, at least he knew where the droppings came from. The overall effect of the grazing sheep, well tilled allotments and the silent watchers, even if they had chosen to ignore him, gave Parrish a feeling of security. He knew that he wasn't alone anymore and felt a great sense of relief. It also tempered his anger and he gave the people in the fort a more measured look. A smile creased his features. He could play them at their own game.

Moving back to the outbuildings, he selected one that gave him a good, unobstructed view of the hill fort. After removing his webbing he sat down with his back against the wattle and daub. He watched and waited in the sunlight. Whenever you're ready, he thought. You're in there and I'm out here, but also out here are your food and animals. You want 'em back? Come and talk to me.

The afternoon drew on towards its close. Parrish continued watching the entrance to the fort from his now shady position. They weren't always visible but he knew there was a constant surveillance on him from the watchers behind the wall.

Parrish had developed his own waiting technique over the eight years he had served in Her Majesties Forces. The whole basis of the military system seemed built on the 'hurry up and wait' premise. Apart from the constant waiting for kit, be it requested or supplied, there was waiting for orders, for information, or simply waiting in lines for anything from food to remembrance parades.

On the numerous and varied exercises that the army continuously ran, from battalion right down to platoon or section strength, the main requirement was patience. As one of the basic building blocks of the British Army, namely the humble foot soldier, it was Parrish's dubious pleasure to be exercised and trained almost constantly. Night exercises, day exercises, weekend, week or fortnight long exercises. You name it, he had done it. During those exercises it was always wait. Move to your position and wait, check your equipment and stand by, position your observation post on that hill and watch.

Waiting and watching was one skill that Parrish had particularly worked on. The secret was, during an extended period of inactivity, not to let your mind run riot. To try and switch off the imagination but stay watchful. Be alert but be still. He found that the main enemies of quiet watchfulness were panic or uncertainty and discomfort. The panic and uncertainty usually went hand in hand when confusion reared its ugly head and discomfort, more often than not, meant cramped conditions or bad weather. Sometimes both.

Parrish sat, warm and comfortable, in the evening shade, facing a settlement where he knew there were people. Thus the main problem that had worried him since the disappearance of the helicopter crash and everything around it, was solved. Discovering the people at the fort had lifted a great weight from his shoulders. He rested easy.

Rested and watched.

The day drew to a close. Before it got too dark to see, Parrish made himself a mug of hot black coffee using one of the instant granules sachets from the drinks pack. The caffeine would help him through the night.

It amused him that there was a thinly disguised flurry of interest when he brewed up. Anyone would think they had never seen a hexi stove, mess tins or zippo lighter. He packed the cooking equipment away into his webbing and put it back on. He didn't want to lose it in the dark and, if the coming night was anything like last night, it would be blacker than the inside of a pocket.

Parrish sipped his steaming hot coffee in the gathering darkness, grudgingly admitting that the fort dwellers knew a bit about night time observation. They had no lights near them, although there were fires burning far beyond the fort wall. It is always better observing from the darkness out into the night, rather than have your night vision ruined by nearby or back lighting.

Finishing the drink in total darkness, Parrish put away the fifty eight pattern mug by feel and continued his relaxed watch. He would not move but he wouldn't sleep either. Hopefully they would think he had gone to sleep and come out to investigate him. Between three and four in the morning, he guessed. When they finally got too inquisitive he would jump on the bastards and sort them out. He waited.

There had been a time, during one of his tours of Northern Ireland, when he had been paid a compliment on his waiting by a second Lieutenant who commanded a vehicle checkpoint just outside Londonderry.

It had rained for two days solid. Parrish had been detailed to cover the checkpoint soldiers who stopped and searched the vehicles, by standing off to one side of the road alongside a tall hedgerow. He wore his camouflage pattern waterproofs and held with almost casual readiness his loaded and cocked rifle. He had been standing motionless in the steady rain for over three hours. Merging in with the mottled foliage of the hedgerow, you had to look twice to make sure he was still there.

Inside the sandbagged observation post, the lieutenant had decided that Parrish had fallen asleep on his feet and went angrily out into the rain to give him a rocket and wake him up. The officer, approaching from behind, got barely within twenty feet him of him, when Parrish whirled at high speed, dropping to one knee.

"Halt or I fire!" He commanded.

The surprised and rattled officer found himself looking straight into the barrel of a loaded gun. Parrish immediately put up his weapon.

"Sorry sir, but you shouldn't sneak up on a man like that."

"Fuck me Parrish, you nearly scared the shit out of me."

"Sorry sir." he repeated, not really caring either way.

"That's OK soldier. I thought you were kipping." Parrish just shook his head and smiled at the insult, like they were trained to in Northern Ireland. The officer wasn't going to apologize for the insult but a good commander knew the value of a complimentary pat on the back.

"Good work Parrish. Nice to see that someone is switched on. Jesus, I swear that you could out wait a stone."

Parrish nodded in acceptance. The conversation seemed to be at an end. The two men stood facing each other in the rain for a few seconds, then the officer turned and hurried back to his warm and dry ops post. Parrish returned to his ever watchful position beside the hedge. In the rain.

Now, in the blackness of the unlit countryside, he still sat back against the mud wall. The night sky was clear but there was no moon. Time crept by on tiptoe. Parrish could see occasional movement from the ramparts of the fort. He didn't give them the satisfaction of seeing any movement from him. And still the night dragged on. It was a long stag, even for Parrish. He was tired but determined not to sleep.

Finally, away to the east, the merest glimmer of light on the horizon announced the false dawn. He was most surprised that no one had emerged from the fort. Perhaps he had misjudged them.

He let out a silent yawn and was deliberating finally moving his limbs to enjoy a good stretch when he heard the noise. It was faint but unmistakable. His ears strained against the silence. Then he heard a definite footfall, just beyond his vision, around the corner of the mud wall to his left.

He had been awake well over twenty hours by now and the fatigue had made him slower than usual. Leaping to his feet he turned to face the man who stepped out into the half light. Parrish had time to register the fact that he looked kind of short, before he heard a second noise behind him. He spun, just in time to see the club or mace that blurred towards him out of the darkness. Trying to roll with the blow, he only partially succeeded. The blunt edged weapon struck him just below and behind the right ear. Multicoloured lights exploded in his vision and he went down, unconscious before he hit the dirt.

7

Parrish awoke to find himself in virtual darkness. He groaned and lifted slowly into a sitting position. Massaging the base of his skull he risked a squint through slitted eyes. Dark.

It seemed unbelievable that it could still be night and he wished this crazy world would get its clock sorted out. He seemed to recall that dawn was breaking when... It all came back to him in a rush. Some bastard had blind-sided him and damn near cracked his skull. His fingers tenderly probed at the squishy, swollen lump behind his ear. They came away sticky with semi-congealed blood. The pounding inside his head was, never the less, bearable and opening his eyes fully, he looked around him.

It wasn't dark, just very subdued. He was sitting on a bed of straw inside a small circular mud hut, similar in construction to the rough barn he had spent all the previous night leaning against. The conical roof was thatched. There was the occasional chink of light breaking through it here and there. The wattle and daub walls were low, only about a meter high. As his eyes adjusted to the half light he saw that the hut was no more than four meters across. He was seated towards the rear and directly opposite him was a doorway, covered by a coarse woollen blanket. Sunlight was trying to get in around the edges of that too. Taking advantage of the shadowy conditions he allowed himself a few minutes for his thumping head to settle. He discovered his back ached too. He had been lying unconscious on top of his bulky webbing at an unnatural angle. He removed the load system and placed it on the straw beside him, then massaged his back and let out a long groan of relief.

Hardly had the sound left his lips when the blanket over the door was thrown aside and a gaggle of men burst in. They gathered before him. Parrish squinted for a second against the sudden brightness from the doorway, waiting a few seconds while his eyes adjusted. Still sitting, he looked up at the group. Not that far up though. They were all small men. He figured the tallest of them to be only five foot three or four.

Parrish had always used metric measurements for distance,

heights and depth, it was the army way. But the MOD still used feet and inches for personal measurements and imperial tons for weight and thus, so did he.

The tallest of the men stood directly in front of Parrish which he took to mean that he was the leader. He never spoke but glared down at him. Another short man came in carrying a blazing torch. This man came around from behind the group and stood to one side, slightly back but midway between the sitting Parrish and the standing man.

Everything was suddenly thrown into sharp relief and Parrish was shocked. He had been clinging to the idea that the short people were tallish kids or teenagers. The man who stood before him looked thirty five to forty. In fact, the eldest man of the entire group was only twenty six summers old. But that wasn't all.

Every man jack of them was dressed in buckskins, rough leather boots and coarse woollen capes. All the stitching that he could see, on their clothes or boots, was rough too, with big thick cords of leather or spun wool. They all sported beards and long wild hair, had hard eyes and a variety of basic line or dot tattoos on their faces and bare arms, blue or black in colour.

Parrish couldn't figure it. They all looked a lot like a movie producer's idea of cave men. Even the hut fitted the picture. Was it some sort of film set? He dismissed the notion as stupid but still couldn't explain the situation he found himself in. He offered a smile.

"Hello there, what's happening then?"

The lead man frowned for a moment, then spat a long load of gibberish at him. Parrish was taken aback and listened to the tirade in shocked silence. Two things immediately struck him. One was that the mumbo-jumbo sounded vaguely similar to the totally baffling Gaelic that his Irish grandfather had tried to teach him as a boy. The other was that the accent of the gibberish was reminiscent of Sergeant Carter in full flow.

"Huh?" was all he could say when the man had finished. Combined with the events of the last two day, Parrish wouldn't have argued if he'd been told he'd gone completely mad.

The lead man attacked him verbally again, this time even more aggressively. Parrish knew a slagging down when he heard one, no matter what the language. He didn't like it and he didn't have to take it.

Pointing a finger he said, "Now that's enough, watch your lip. Shut it or I'll shut it for you."

The small man was taken aback when Parrish stabbed his finger towards him, but returned the threat by producing a dagger from somewhere behind his back and thrusting it threateningly into Parrish's face.

Parrish wasn't the least bit frightened of intimidated. He simply examined the offending item. It was almost a mistake to describe it as a dagger. The man gripped an eight inch stick with a flat, three inch diamond shaped piece of flint lashed to the end of it.

To the small mans utter amazement, Parrish actually laughed out loud.

"Fuck me. Where did you get that? It looks straight out of the Stone Age."

And that was when he knew.

It hit him like a sledgehammer. His face froze. The small man mistakenly took Parrish's expression to be the one he had originally expected. He grinned with small, square ended teeth. Parrish never noticed. He was wrestling with the turmoil inside his mind.

The *Stone Age*!

No fences, houses or fields. Small people. Ditched and walled hill forts. Flint tools and mines. It all fitted.

But it couldn't be. How? In his heart he knew how, although he found it almost too hard to believe. It was the helicopter crash, Jimbo and that blasted steel ball! He hadn't the faintest idea how the ball had done it but he now knew the significance of minus five thousand five hundred years. It didn't take a mathematical genius to figure out where that would put a man back in time from nineteen eighty eight.

Three and a half thousand years before the birth of Christ!

It was incredible. Too incredible to be true. Parrish refused to believe it and shook his head. It couldn't be.

Totally disregarding the potential threat to his life, and to the small man's utter surprise, Parrish slapped the stone dagger absently aside. He rose swiftly to his feet, pushed through the astounded and rapidly recoiling group and, after stooping through the low door, staggered out into the sunlight.

He wasn't in the centre of the camp but it was possible to see most of it from where he stood. Similarly, most of the camps inhabitants could see him. The entire place came to a halt as everyone stared at the strangely dressed giant who stood in their midst. Parrish looked around, jaw slack and eyes wide.

It really was a Stone Age encampment.

There were a number of circular wattle and daub huts with tall, thatched roofs. They varied in size but even the smallest was a good ten meters across the base. These buildings, and Parrish used the word 'buildings' loosely, were well spaced within the walled compound. The timber wall wasn't nearly so high when viewed from the inside because of the earth walkway that was banked up against it. The compound itself seemed much too large for the number of huts inside it. There was a lot of empty, grass covered space.

All this though was lost on Parrish as he stood, astounded at his situation. It was the people he was shocked by. Shocked and shattered. He felt devastated. His earlier discovery of people in the empty landscape had been his one firm hand hold on sanity when he had been alone. Now, just when he thought he had found salvation, someone had stamped on his fingers. To him, the inhabitants of the fort were only just people. A cruel thing to say but that was his immediate feeling as he looked about. The objects of his observation were themselves staring at him, staring at them. Several others emerged from huts to look at him as well.

They were all short. Like the men he'd seen inside the hut, all the adult males were between five and five feet four. The women were even shorter. Ones that he could see ranged from an almost midget like four and a half foot up to just under five feet. An incidental observation was that even from his brief glances he could see that the women were grossly subservient to the men. They cowered whenever a man passed, or walked with head bowed, several paces behind.

In the all revealing daylight he also realised that everyone looked old before their time. It was a difficult feeling to explain. They looked somehow young and yet worn out. He got only a fleeting glance of some raggedy, half wild children. They had run and hid when he burst from the hut.

Every single soul except him wore rough buckskin jerkins, jackets, skirts or loincloths and woollen capes. There were semi-prepared skins tensioned over drying frames and exposed to the sun, outside most of the huts. Propped up near the entrances to the huts were unstrung bows, flint headed spears and small quivers of short, feather fletched arrows. He knew without having to check that they would have flint heads fitted to them.

It was almost too much for him to handle at that moment. A Neolithic nightmare. He stood still, arms limp at his sides. All the will to fight seemed to just drain out of him. He felt totally crushed. A feeling swamped over him that he hadn't experienced since boyhood. He wanted to cry. Never had he felt such bottomless, heartbreaking despair.

Another tirade of gibberish abuse from behind made him turn around. The group of men who had been with him inside, were standing a few feet away. The lead man looked into Parrish's eyes and knew the big man was near to breaking point. He started forward, raising his stone dagger.

Indeed, Parrish was at the end of his tether. He was ready to give it all up when a movement at the back of the group caught his eye. One of the small men was sloping off, hopefully unnoticed, with Parrish's webbing.

That jumble of olive drab pouches was the one and only thing that still connected Parrish with the twentieth century. He needed that webbing like a drowning man needs a lifejacket.

Again, with total disregard for his personal safety, he pushed aside the leader's daggered threat and caught up with the man with his webbing. He was oblivious to the fact that the whole camp watched in stony silence. Parrish grabbed a trailing end of his webbing while the Neolithic man held on to another. A brief tug of war ensued. It didn't last long. Parrish out powered his opponent by almost a foot in height and over four stone in weight. Snatching the equipment away, Parrish held it tightly against his chest and glared down at the would be thief.

The smaller man was obviously furious. He too produced a flint dagger and threatened Parrish with it. The soldier just stared down at him. This inaction infuriated the man even further. He shouted a stream of unintelligible words while all the time waving his arms energetically in the air. When he finally finished he rammed the dagger up under Parrish's chin, the surprisingly sharp point just pricking his Adams apple. Still the soldier just stared down. There was a long, long moment of tense silence. Not a sound from anyone.

Then, the small man slowly withdrew his dagger and looked Parrish in the eye. He spoke more gibberish, this time slow and deliberate, then spat emphatically into the soldiers face before turning his back and walking away. Parrish needed no translation to recognize contempt. He turned to look at the other men who still stood behind him. They too slowly turned their backs and walked away. Parrish scanned the camp. The entire population turned their backs, and went about their business, paying him no more attention. He was ridiculed and ignored. An outcast. They would not waste time even looking at him.

Even though Parrish could not understand a single word they spoke or grasp anything about the society they lived in, their habits, religion or rituals, it was still the most painful and cutting insult he had ever received. To be totally shunned in a world where he had no roots, no friends and no place was completely devastating.

He just stood for several minutes in stunned silence. Even people who passed near him during that time did not acknowledge his presence. He might as well have been a pillar of stone.

Perhaps a normal person would have crumbled completely then. Parrish almost did but he had been through a similar feeling of loneliness two days earlier on the bank of the river Wylye. It didn't make the unhappy event any easier to bear but at least he knew from bitter experience that whatever happened, life did go on. Almost instinctively he fell back on his army training. That told him that the first objective in any survival situation was to establish a base.

Parrish wandered off. Nobody paid him the slightest attention. Almost in a complete daze he found the most secluded part of the circular encampment. On the higher part of the enclosure, the north western aspect, there were no buildings or people. The reason was because it was the most exposed part of the camp and took the brunt of the cold winter winds.

At that moment in time Parrish neither knew nor cared. He sank to the ground and sat, cross legged, still clutching his webbing to him.

It was the second time in three days that he actually contemplated suicide.

8

It took a while for Parrish to get his head together for a second time.

All the rest of the day he sat on his rise at the rear of the encampment. Again he experienced the deep, deep trough of despair before it was even possible to begin the painful climb back up to an emotionally even keel.

At least he now knew where he was, or rather, when! True, he was already semi-prepared for a more lonely life by his two day wanderings through an empty landscape but what really shook him, what he had the utmost difficulty coming to terms with, was the loss of everything and everyone he knew.

The twentieth century was gone from him forever. It was heartbreaking to realize that his parents, friends and even his enemies were just simply no longer there. Not even born yet. Not for another fifty five centuries! Just the concept alone was difficult to grasp.

A strange thing. After Parrish had left school, he had enlisted in the Light Infantry and drifted away from any close ties he had with his parents. He was an only child and had developed a strong sense of independence early in life. That didn't make their loss any easier to bear. He suddenly felt dreadfully homesick for the first time in years.

The most terrible thing of all was that he knew he could never make the return trip. To quote the eloquent phraseology of Sergeant Carter, what he knew about time travel he could write on a postage stamp, if stamps had been around where he now was! Nearer to his own level of understanding, the steel ball was now two days walk away and even if he went back and retrieved it, he still wouldn't know what to do with it. He had no way of knowing how to start it, stop it or aim it.

Parrish of course could not know that the machine was now nothing more than so much scrap, being as it were a one shot, throw away prototype.

When Parrish finally did manage to get past the thoughts that he had lost everything he had been born or grown up with, he then had to struggle with the problems that plagued his immediate position. And his future, if any.

He was totally alone.

There was no one or anything that he could call on for assistance. He couldn't even speak the Gaelic/Celtic type gibberish lingo that these Stone Age people used. It frightened him more than he realised, that not a soul in the whole country, or on the entire planet for that matter, spoke a single word of English.

He didn't notice it on a conscious level, but Parrish's mind was beginning to come to terms with his predicament because, as soon as he considered the idea of planetary thinking, he corrected himself.

Don't waste time thinking about global problems Parrish. From now on your world is the same size as these cave men. If the edge of Salisbury Plain is two days walk away, and that's now your only mode of transport, then it's doubtful you will ever travel more than fifty or sixty kilometres from here during the rest of your life.

It was another jolting shock to his system, but Parrish was beginning to learn how to ride these mental knocks. Like a surfer. His numbed senses let them wash over him or else he just slid along with them.

It finally came down to a limited number of choices. He could leave this encampment and try to make a go of it alone. Or stay here as an outcast, ignored by one and all, and try to fit in somehow with this crude, barbaric society, or just say sod it and hang himself up in the nearest tree. His army training once more came to the fore and told him that there was no rush to make any decision. Take some time to consider the options. Wait.

And so he sat on his little patch of high ground, with the north western section of the wall at his back and the whole of the encampment spread out before him. To keep his mind busy and in order to push away the swamping fears that tried to crowd him, he watched the camp. Observed it. Tried to understand the systems and organization of it. Standard procedure for a forward observation post. Watch and learn. Positions and patterns.

The day continued to run its course. Parrish just sat and watched, indifferent to the warm sunshine or his grumbling stomach. The camp was like nothing he'd ever seen before and he had to admit that he found it totally fascinating. It seemed somehow almost a privilege to be a fly on the wall here. A right there on the spot observer of Neolithic life.

He had never been really deeply interested archaeology or pre-history, but, he and everyone he knew, correction, had known, was curious about stone age life. Remember how popular all those cave man and dinosaur movies were? One Million Years BC and all that?

Just from a few hours casual observation Parrish realised that the ancient life depicted in those films was total crap. No poncing around in little fur loincloths and carrying big, rounded clubs to bop women on the head with then drag away by the hair. Life here was tough. For a start, the people here looked barely well fed and this was summer time. What it was like in the winter he dreaded to think.

He watched the people closely. They were smaller than him all right, but apart from that, the same. No steeply sloping foreheads or pronounced, ape like lower jaws. They all looked athletically wiry, like modern day marathon runners. He never saw a single fat or even slightly obese person.

No one had as yet invented the chair. They all just squatted on their haunches whenever they parked anywhere.

There was a steady dribble of people passing in and out of the fort entrance. It was interesting to note that the people moved about in small groups which corresponded to individual huts. Parrish decided these groups were family units. As the day wore on it became obvious that each hut held one family and that each family kept more or less to itself.

These family units seem to consist of two or three men and five or six women, plus however many kids were there. Thus, each hut seemed to hold at least two generations of a family, and each man had more than one wife.

From his elevated position it was possible to see beyond the south facing aspect of the encampment, the wall, and right out over the cleared valley. It soon became clear, by keeping tabs on selected family groups, that each family had its own individual allotment. Also, that no one family helped any other family as far as the basic farming was concerned. It seemed you either stood or fell on your own endeavours. Parrish shrugged. It was a selfish, wasteful and potentially dangerous system but he wasn't surprise to find that even this early in man’s development, the 'look after number one' rule was already evident.

It didn't surprise him either that the women were the work horses of the community. Household chores, from gathering water, firewood and rounding up children, right through to clothing manufacture. You name it, they did it. He did though find it somehow annoying and insulting how the women cowered and bowed whenever a man passed near them.

The children, and it was difficult to tell their ages because of the height difference and their grubby, wild appearance, ran around totally out of control. They still had little concept of the family unit and moved at will among the huts, taking care not to get too close to an adult male. The men were quick to deliver a cuff to the side of the head, seemingly just for the hell of it.

From his lone vantage point Parrish could see all the huts in the encampment. There were an even dozen, plus one extra large one smack in the centre of the camp. The others surrounded it in a well spaced, roughly circular pattern. Here Parrish had to make several assumptions but, using what he could see as a guideline, he wasn't too far wide of the mark.

He guessed that the giant hut was some sort of gathering place for the whole camp. He didn't like to use the word tribe. It made them sound like they were the only ones of their kind. He fervently hoped there might be more people elsewhere.

Assuming two men and five women to a hut, there were roughly a hundred adults in the camp, plus the children who were impossible to count, moving about the camp like fleas on a dog. Maybe fifteen to twenty youngsters then.

With a hundred and twenty odd mouths to feed, even split into family units, Parrish knew without a doubt that the small allotments of rough wheat and root vegetables was nowhere near enough to feed them all. He figured most of their food was hunted and the farmed goods just supplemented their diet. That brought up the subject of the sheep. Parrish watched and considered for a long while before coming to his conclusion.

The sheep belonged to everyone. With over two sheep to every person, plus lambs, the flock provided wool, meat and implements made from their bones, for the whole camp.

At that point Parrish finally had the whole camp system sussed.

The families lived separately in their individual groups, tending their own allotments, getting their own water, firewood et cetera, and stuff everybody else. They did however band together for the mass benefit of the large sheep flock. It was also more than likely that the men hunted together in perhaps one or two large groups. That a large hunting party would be more successful than any individual efforts was good sense, bringing in larger quantities of meat.

The whole camp was also enclosed in the defensive wall and ditch system that he had come up against a day earlier. Communal protection yes, but from what or who? Parrish doubted that there were more than a few thousand people in the whole of Britain judging by the poor standard of living he saw before him.

He continued to watch.

Each main hut had one or more small huts of the same design nearby. They seemed to be storage areas for the most part. It was in one of these that Parrish had found himself when he recovered from his daybreak attack. He grimaced and tenderly touched the sensitive spot behind his ear.

Some things however didn't quite fit with this rough and ready camp life. He could see why this hilltop had been chosen for a village site, it commanded unobstructed views all round and ease of protection once the defences were built, but it had no source of water. At least not inside the camp. The women made regular trips outside, off to the north, where the dense woods were only half a kilometre away. There was obviously a small river or stream inside it because they returned with skin bags full of water. Some women made five or six trips in the one day.

Another odd thing were the inhabitants of some of the small peripheral huts. Admittedly there were only two or three individuals but it did seem strange. One of these was an old lady whose hut was the one closest to him, behind the nearest main hut and almost not part of the village at all. Her little hovel was in a dilapidated condition with tufts missing from the thatch and holes in the mud walls. He watched her scratching about for a few scraps of food, occasionally being teased by the children. He wondered if she too was an outcast.

The only reasonable explanation Parrish could come up with was that somehow she had lost, been separated or expelled from her family unit and made to fend for herself. Whatever had happened, it must have been earlier in this year. From what he could see of her lifestyle, Parrish couldn't see her making it through even a mild winter.

It was very near the end of the day before a small smile finally came to his lips and wrinkled his normally, well at least until two days ago, happy and joking features.

What brought about this small amount of cheer was the discovery that, however primitive these stone age people, they were still human. Although he had been cast out and the whole camp had decided not even to acknowledge him, they were still curious and kept sneaking glances in his direction.

The raggedy children were even more bold. A couple of them, and he couldn't tell if they were boys or girls, crept from behind the nearest hut and stared openly at him until a woman appeared and cuffed them away. Even then, she herself looked his way for a few seconds before going on about her business.

Parrish enjoyed his small smile and decided then that he would at least cross off stringing himself up from his list.

He set up his hexi stove and mess tins and cooked himself an evening meal of tinned curried chicken and boiled rice. He kept the empty tin now that he knew there was no metal about, anywhere. He wished that he hadn't buried the last one.

All the time he cooked and ate, the camp people could barely contain their curiosity. How did the tall stranger make fire so quickly and what were his strange shiny pots made of?

Parrish could feel their bursting inquisitiveness, which made him smile all the more. Things were definitely picking up. He didn't feel quite so desperate now. He finally packed his kit away, thinking the day was ending quite a bit brighter than it started. Not so.

As the daylight began to fade, the sky began to cloud over. Before it was fully dark it had started to rain and Parrish spent a miserable night hunched beneath his poncho. It rained hard. He now knew why their huts were so sturdily built and with such thick thatch.

Parrish somehow managed to stay mostly dry under his body hugging shelter but he felt damp and cold. The rain drummed down on him on and off for most of the night. His second successive night without much sleep.

The morning broke dull and overcast but with the promise of an improvement. The rain was now more off than on but didn't stop completely until mid morning. Parrish had no choice but to sit and wait it out.

When it finally did stop he was determined not to get caught out again and set about planning to building himself a more sturdy, all be it still temporary shelter. Taking a leaf from the cave men's book he settled on a type of lean-to with a low back and solid sides. The easiest and quickest way to accomplish this would be to make the same type of walls as utilized by the huts below him. Interweave thin boughs together into squares or rectangles, similar to wattle fence panels. Easily said. The problem was collecting the material. There was plenty of it about but it was all *outside* the encampment. He didn't envisage any trouble leaving but the big question was, would they allow him back in?

Parrish had no choice really. He knew he would be in a very sorry state if he spent another night in the open without sleep, and to sleep he needed a shelter.

After strapping on his equipment he walked slowly around the edge of the village, under the shadow of the wall, until he was near the main gate. No one paid him any attention. He tagged on to the rear of a group of people on their way out. Parrish bowed his head and slouched to try and make himself less conspicuous, but being so much taller and dressed in camouflage jacket and trousers, he knew he stood out like a bacon butty at a bar mitzvah!

Still no one appeared to notice him. It seemed even the smallest of the children never considered him a threat.

Once outside, Parrish waited in the shelter of the barns until another group appeared, on their way into the fort. He again tagged on behind and, sure enough although he himself was surprised, he was allowed to enter, seemingly unnoticed. He did this twice more. He imagined the camp inhabitants thought him crazy, which wasn't far from the truth. Anyway, it appeared he could pass in and out of the fort with impunity.

Finally satisfied, he set off on his plan of action. He went north into the woods and found the camps water source by following the well worn path. The water was not so much a river as more of a large stream. Gravel bottomed, it varied in width along the stretch he could see from four or five meters at its widest to fast flowing bottlenecks with less than two meters between banks. He walked up and down the bank for a while, ignoring the curious and puzzled glances from the women who filled their water bags. No men here.

Here and there, close to the bank he could see submerged, conical shaped wicker-type baskets. They were crude fish traps to catch some of the many brown trout that swam about in the current. As Parrish filled his water bottle he debated how successful they might be. It looked like these Neolithic people ate fish when they could get it but didn't try too hard to catch them. Perhaps too much effort required for too small a reward?

Parrish turned his back on the women and moved off, upstream. Half a click further on, he found several well worn animal runs along the riverbank. They looked promising; so along these runs he set up three snares, staking their ends well into the ground with long, forked pegs cut from the branches of a nearby tree.

Traps laid, he went off into the woods. There were more than enough young saplings to make his wattle panels and he set too with his MOD survival knife. With a keen edged seven inch blade of quarter inch wide carbon steel it was well designed for chopping and cutting. It made it hardly ever necessary to need more than one good blow to cut through the inch thick stems. In a short time he had a bundle of boughs he was unable to link his arms round. Tying them together with a length of paracord, he grunted the bundle onto his back and carried it back to camp.

Ignoring the sly glances as he entered the encampment, he again followed the inside of the wall around to the back of the camp and returned to his original spot. He marked out where the shelter was to be erected, cleared the oblong patch of ground of any stones or other rubbish and bent to his task.

It is always the case. The bundle he had collected was nowhere near enough raw material and in all Parrish had to make three trips to complete his shelter.

It was late afternoon by the time he had finished and stepped back to admire his work. It would do, he decided. At least one small, morale boosting victory today. What he had built was in effect an eight by four wicker shed with one open side which faced south east. The corner stakes were driven well into the ground and the side and roof panels securely lashed to them. The next day Parrish would coat the walls in mud like the Neolithic huts and turf the roof, but for tonight he would waterproof it by covering the top with his poncho.

Three feet in front of the open side of his wicker 'hut' he drove two short and sturdy stakes into the ground and wedged short lengths of trunk against them, making a low wall about two and a half feet high. This wall had a number of uses, not least as a wind break if the wind did swing round, but its primary use was as a heat reflector for the fire that he intended to build in front of it. That would be his last job of the day before he settled down to eat the last of his ration pack. Tomorrow he would have to concentrate on finding and gathering food.

Parrish returned to the woods for the final time and spent half an hour collecting as big a supply of firewood as he could carry to add to the pile of off cuts from the wattle boughs.

The evening drew steadily on, with only a few hours of daylight left. Almost as an afterthought he checked his traps. It is said that you make your own luck but seems a lot more likely that common sense prevails. Either way, Parrish was pleasantly surprised to see that one of his snares held a catch. He nodded to himself. Another small victory.

The unfortunate animal was a medium sized otter. It squirmed desperately against the ever tightening noose. Parrish wasted no time, pinning it down with a heavy boot on the back then despatching it cleanly with one blow from the hilt of his knife. He hung the animal head down from a tree a little way off in the woods, cut its throat to let it bleed and went to check the rest of his traps. They were empty and he left them in place. Next he dug up some worms and used them to bait hooks which he suspended in mid stream from long fishing poles, freshly cut and pegged securely down on the bank. Then he returned to his first catch.

Parrish was happy enough to get the otter but a little surprised. He thought that if he caught anything, it would most likely be a rabbit. He was not to know that there would not be any rabbits around for a long time yet, the creatures not being originally indigenous to Great Britain but introduced to these shores by the Romans.

Tying the otter to his belt and heaving the collected timber onto his back, he made his way back to the encampment. The Neolithic people found it even more difficult not to stare at him with both his firewood *and* his catch. Again Parrish ignored them as he staggered up to his campsite. Fuck 'em, he thought, I can look after myself. I don't need your help, even if you offered any. Which they didn't.

He swiftly gutted and skinned the otter with his pocket knife, hanging the pelt on the side of his hut, then concentrated on getting a fire going. Task accomplished, he then cut strips of meat from the back and shoulders of the carcass, diced it up and added it to some water to make a basic stew. He threw in the tiny kidneys and heart too. The larger haunches of meat from the animal's hind quarters he intended to cut into thin strips and dry in tomorrow's sun to make jerky.

With that same sun beginning to sink below the horizon, his stew came to the boil. He let it simmer on for twenty minutes. It actually didn't smell too bad and Parrish allowed another smile to play on his face. At least he wouldn't have to east more army rations.

Thus the day ended well. Parrish ate his surprisingly good stew before settling down on the hard ground inside his basic house. The fire was warm on his face and his belly was full. He had shelter, fire and food, well at least for now. Who knew what tomorrow might bring?

He slept well.

9

Parrish slept on past the sunrise and was finally woken by ominous, shuffling sounds. Someone was moving about outside his hut. Instantly awake and alert, he rose silently to his feet and crept out to find a kid, closely inspecting the now slightly odourous otter pelt. He grabbed the unsuspecting, dirt streaked child roughly by the shoulder making him visibly jump with surprise. He was about the same size as a modern nine year old but Parrish guessed him to be about twelve.

The nipper struggled for a moment in the inescapable grip before remembering who it was that held him. He stopped writhing and stared the tall man boldly in the eye. Parrish's hard stare was nothing like the timid, frightened gaze of a few days earlier. The boy's defiant glare died on his face and changed to fear. He cowered, shielding his face with his arms.

Parrish hauled the reluctant youth up to the side of the wicker hut and snatched the otter pelt down with his free hand, ramming it up close under the nipper's nose.

"Is this what you were after?" he said in an aggressive growl, "Is it?" He shook the boy who just whimpered, keeping his arms up.

"Well here," Parrish slapped the smelly skin against the boy's puny chest. "Take it!"

Surprise mixed with the fear on the boys face.

"Take it." he repeated, less aggressively.

The boy took the skin in both hands, eyes never leaving the big man's face. Parrish held his gaze for a long moment, then released his grip. The nipper seemed frozen to the spot for a moment, then tore away and off down the slope at breakneck speed. Parrish's laughter followed him all the way.

A good start to the day.

He went back into his hut and had a 'squaddie' wash, just splashing a palm full of water onto his face, before starting on the tasks he had set himself for the day.

With some thin twigs he made himself an open weave, wicker square which he suspended from the front of his hut on long green sticks. It hung in this suspended position high above his camp fire. He had deliberately made it a very open weave so it could be used as both a platform to dry his meat strips and also to smoke things on.

Smoking and drying were the only ways he could remember to preserve food and make it last longer. It was very important for him to build up a reserve so he could spend more time on other equally as important tasks, rather than all his time collecting things to eat. Parrish needed the practice too. He had not forgotten that it would inevitably be winter. Not a cheering thought. He cut the meat off the otter carcass and sliced it into long thin strips. The drying rack was high enough above the fire to offer uninterrupted sun all day. After stirring up the previous nights ashes and re-starting the fire, he kept it smouldering, occasionally adding a few green leaves to produce enough smoke to keep any flies at bay. He left the meat to dry and got on with the next task.

Behind his hut he cut turfs from the ground, trimmed then laid them carefully on his roof, ensuring a good fit. It would keep the rain off, especially if the grass lived on and knitted the turfs together. The now bare patch of ground behind the hut presented itself as a perfect mud hole. Parrish's' only problem was the lack of water to make his mud. He could really use one of those skin bags. Fortune smiled on him then.

While standing, contemplating his dilemma, he became aware that he was being watched. He was by now well used to the sly glances he got from the camp people but this was different.

The source of the stare was the old lady who lived in the small, battered hut nearest him. On closer inspection it wasn't actually Parrish she was staring at, but his drying meat. There was hardly enough for him, let alone anyone else. His eyes fell on the now fly specked, stringy remains of the otter. He picked it up by the neck and walked down to the old woman's hut. She immediately darted inside and peered out, terrified, from beyond the doorway. Hanging from around the entrance were several of the skin water bags. Parrish removed one from its peg and held it to his chest, offering out the carcass. The old lady just cowered. Parrish repeated his gestures. Even fearful that she might be struck down the moment she emerged from her hovel, hunger overcame her fear. She reached slowly and timidly out, then snatched the carcass from his grasp. He nodded and smiled, holding her eyes. She stared back. He nodded again. This time she nodded in return but he knew it was asking too much for a smile as well. Parrish gracefully bowed low, he wasn't sure why, it just seemed the right thing to do, then walked away. He hadn't gone five paces before the old lady fell onto the carcass, gnawing noisily at the bones. The sound made Parrish shudder. He didn't look back.

Armed with his 'new' water bag, which held a good few gallons as opposed to his water bottles two pints, he set off towards the stream. Parrish's confidence was back and he decided he'd had enough of cowering like the women of the camp. He didn't fit in with these Stone Age people but he was damned if he was going to be afraid of them. This time, when he set off towards the main gate, he went straight through the centre of the camp. He walked tall and straight in a bold effort to show he wasn't intimidated and perhaps also to dish out a little intimidation of his own. He did have enough sense to give the extra large gathering hut a wide berth. It was obviously very significant in some way and he knew he had to show it respect but he still walked on through like he hadn't a care in the world.

As usual, the men totally ignored him. The women stole glances when they thought nobody was looking. He recognized the boy he'd given the pelt to and threw him a wave. The boy gave a small, hesitant wave in return before vanishing into a hut at high speed.

When Parrish finally made the main gate and exited the camp he found himself holding his breath. It burst from his lungs with an audible whoosh and he wiped his sweating brow with the back of his hand.

Parrish spent the rest of the morning playing mud pies. As well as being essential to his welfare, it was plain good fun. He stripped off to just his trousers and, with glorious goo squishing between his fingers and toes, slapped thick wet mud onto his wattle walls. Not a heavy mud and straw mix like the big huts but enough of a layer to fill in all the holes and make his hut wind proof. By the time he had finished the sun was high in the sky and He was plastered in wet and rapidly drying mud. It demanded a trip to the stream for removal.

"Now I know how a London Brick feels." he said aloud, looking down at his caked torso.

It was at this point that Parrish decided to take a leap of faith. He left the camp, heading for the stream carrying only his boots and wash kit, leaving his precious webbing behind. He wasn't overjoyed at the idea but he knew that sooner or later he would accumulate so much extra equipment and paraphernalia that it would be impossible for him to carry it all around. So, he left his kit back at base, hoping it would still be there when he returned. He didn't know what he'd do if it wasn't, but he felt the time had come to make a gesture, to himself as much as to anyone else, and show that there was at least an element of trust.

Well down stream of the watering place, Parrish jumped into the water, washed himself and his trousers then had a cold water shave. It was another warm day and it took only half an hour for his cammo lightweights to dry, while he sunned himself, buck naked, on the grassy bank.

Before he returned to base he checked his traps and hooks. Nothing. Walking back through the camp dressed only in trousers and boots, he was suddenly very self conscious of the women's more open glances and the men's hostility. By the time he realised what a stupid move it was he had no choice but to carry on. Even by twentieth century standards he was considered a fine figure of a man. In a Neolithic village inhabited by small men and oppressed women he couldn't help but be noticed. The women who dared a glance looked at him the way a child stares in through a sweet shop window.

The men on the other hand saw him as an affront to their masculinity and dominance. He could feel their disapproval and anger.

Parrish hurried back to his hut, pulled on his tee shirt and kept out of the way, staying near his mud splattered home all the rest of the day. At least his equipment was still there, apparently undisturbed.

His jerky was still drying and he had, foolishly he now realised, given away the remains of his first catch. He ate the last of his rations apart from the sweets. It was while he was munching on an odd morsel of pre-packed food that the boy he had grabbed earlier, appeared close to the old ladies hut. Parrish waved the boy to approach. He was ignored. Parrish offered him a Rollo but was still ignored. He bit the sweet in half, made yum-yum noises and faces, put the half Rollo on the ground and retreated. The boy darted up the slope, popped the sweet greedily into his mouth and chewed appreciatively, his eyes never leaving Parrish. The big man nodded. The boy just watched. Parrish nodded again and held another Rollo out on his palm, squatting down on his haunches to show he was waiting, plus getting down to the lads level so as not to intimidate him with his size. After a while the boy plucked up the courage to approach, and reached out for the sweet. Parrishs[1] hand snapped shut over the morsel and the boy froze, wondering what happened next. Parrish smiled at the boy then slowly opened his hand. The boy smiled too, took the sweet and hunched down opposite him but at a respectable distance, popping the sweet into his mouth.

They sat like that for a while, just eyeing each other. Parrish knew what was coming even if the boy didn't. He was going to have to do the corny 'me Tarzan you Jane' act. It was difficult to believe, but he could see no other way of breaking the ice. It seemed so silly that he had to stop himself from laughing at the ridiculousness of the situation. He tapped himself lightly on the chest.

"Parrish." he said. "Parr-ish."

The boy just looked. Parrish repeated himself. Twice more after that and still the boy just watched. Parrish tried again and still got no reaction. He gave up and looked down at his boots.

The boy said, "Parr-ish." with no inflection at all.

Parrish eyed him with a smile and nodded vigorously while pointing at his own chest.

"Par-ish ..... Parrish." The boy's accent was heavy on the 'Parr' and very light in the 'ish' but it was close enough.

Parrish threw the nipper another Rollo before thumping himself on the chest.

"Parrish" he said, then pointed at the boy with a questioning expression on his face. The boy understood what he wanted, it was visible in his eyes. He chewed with obvious pleasure on the Rollo, seeming to consider the question until he had finished extracting every last drop of flavour from the sweet.

"Tomps." he said.

Well that's what it sounded like. The accent was heavy and Parrish had to listen hard. He tried to repeat the word.

"Tomps?" he said. His pronunciation was bad but the boy nodded.

Parrish grinned and the two spent the next few minutes pointing at each other and repeating their names. The boy soon got the hang of Parrish's but the tall man ended up practically calling the boy 'Tomas'.

Tomps didn't seem to mind.

There was a call from somewhere down in the camp and Tomps made to leave. Parrish rose when he did and watched as the boy ran off down the slope. He stopped near the bottom and turned to look at Parrish, calling out his name. Parrish called back and waved. He got a return wave before the boy vanished between the huts.

Parrish stared after the lad and hoped that he would return for another 'chat'. Mind you, he was now down to his last couple of Rollo's.

That night there was the sound of drums in the village. Surrounded by blazing bonfires and torches, the huge centre hut was lit up like a Christmas tree. It seemed that everyone was there. Everyone except him. Parrish watched from his vantage point. Of course he was curious but there was no way he was going down there to find out. Gate crash a party in this rough neighbourhood and you could wind up just a bit dead. The drums and chanting carried on late into the night.

The next morning he watched as a band of twelve to fifteen men and a couple of the older kids left the camp and set off towards the forests on the horizon. They were all armed to the teeth with a selection of bows and arrows, spears, clubs, axes, daggers and slings. No matter that they were all made of flint, bone or stone. They still looked very deadly. Parrish couldn't tell or guess if the band was a hunting or war party. He didn't ponder the question too long. He had a problem of his own.

Food. Or rather, lack of food. He had checked his traps and hooks again. Nothing.

All that morning he systematically searched the local woods and copses for animal tracks or spore. A few signs came to light and he set about making traps like he'd been taught in survival school. Again it was practice, as well as practical, as he made and tried out an assortment of traps. They varied from the famous whippy young tree attached to a hidden noose on the forest floor, to an evil looking deadfall trap with sharpened spikes lashed to a carefully balanced log, poised above a trip wire along an animal trail.

But that didn't solve his immediate problem. His stomach rumbled. The drying jerky was still not ready and anyway, the more it dried the less of it there seemed to be. He would need a lot more of that. Other options had to be considered. The local stream was absolutely teeming with trout but they seemed oblivious to his modern hooks or the Neolithic basket traps. He could catch them if he were allowed to dam up the stream and create a pool but he doubted the idea would go down very well with the local inhabitants.

Just to put something inside his belly, Parrish decided to follow, at a respectable distance, a group of women who were wandering purposefully through the forest. He watched what they were doing while they just watched him out of the corner of their eyes.

The women were collecting berries and herbs. Parrish saw which ones they picked and followed suit, popping as many into his mouth as he put into his mess tin. Some of the plants he recognized, like the wild parsley, thyme and mint, and he couldn't disguise his delight when they came to a large patch of wild strawberries. He also recognized a clump of apple trees they passed through although the fruit was nowhere near ripe. All the locations were memorized.

Pockets stuffed full of herbs and mess tin brimming with berries, he returned to his hut. It was his intention to dry the herbs and hang them inside his hut to be used as *a food* supplement. If he ever managed to catch any food.

Now that most of the men were away from the camp, the women and children were less inhibited. The whole encampment seemed to change character. More relaxed, almost amiable. The women chatted freely amongst themselves while they worked and there was the occasional burst of female laughter. There was still a small nucleus of men about the camp but they kept to themselves, tending the sheep or sharpening, re-shaping or making fresh implements and weapons. Parrish smiled at their apparent busyness. To him they just looked out numbered.

He assessed the few small in roads he had made into village life. Not much but it was a start. He was a hit with the old lady. She would nod when he passed by and point to the picked clean otter skull that had pride of place on the end of a pole outside her hut. Parrish would nod a return.

The boy came back to visit him. He sat opposite Parrish and spoke his name which itself alone was a morale booster. He spent some time with the tall man during the next few days, sharing his tins of berries and the last of the Rollo's, but when the Rollo's ran out, he did too.

Parrish used the time to try and gather a few words of the local lingo. Being taught a foreign language by a foreign twelve year old is not recommended and he didn't get very far. All he got for two days work was half a dozen words. It was a case of point at an object and have Tomps name it. At least that was what he hoped Tomps was doing. There was no way of knowing whether the boy was telling him the correct name or just making some idle comment about what they were pointing at. Some of the words sounded vaguely familiar in a distant sort of way and it was those words that Parrish was pretty sure were right. He got the word for sheep OK, plus his best snippet of information, the name of the encampment.

Parrish was actually quite close in his assessment of the language, calling it a Gaelic/Celtic mish-mash. Perhaps in another millennium or two the language would become more refined, separate tongues, but for now it was a jumble of rudimentary dialects, most of them barely recognizable as the forerunners of complex and eloquent languages. Be that as it may, Parrish did recognize one word that was very significant to him.

In Gaelic the word - DANA or DANE means resolute or determined.

The Celtic word - BRE means hill.

After much gesticulating of arms and pointing at the ground and the camp, Parrish got Tomas to understand that he wanted to know the name of the encampment. Tomas told him the name, DANA-BRE which the lad understood as resolute hill, or more basically, sturdy place.

Parrish was overjoyed at this news. He now knew from the name of the encampment *and* his location in the south coast area. To Parrish, DANA-BRE sounded very similar to the name of a place he knew that corresponded closely to the area he had left a few days ago, or was it five and a half thousand years ago. He knew there was, or would be an Iron Age hill fort on the site with that name. Perhaps the archaeologists had got it wrong in not dating the hill fort back to the Neolithic age. Parrish didn't care. He was here now and he now knew where 'here' was.

Danebury!

10

For another three days Parrish had no success whatsoever with any of his traps. He lived off berries and the few measly strips of jerky that he had dried. The dark, grainy strips were not half as repulsive as they looked, being practically tasteless and as hard as nails. Even so, his stomach thought his throat had been cut.

It was more frustrating than anything else. The permanent feeling of hunger was tolerable, if uncomfortable. He wouldn't completely starve and there was plenty of water so he wouldn't die. It was just that there seemed to be some kind of block to him catching animals for food. Parrish felt, deep down, that once he had made his first intentional catch, things would fall into place. He didn't count the otter, looking on that as pure fluke. The object was to become an aggressive, systematic hunter and have a regular inflow of trapped and deliberately caught food, not relying on blind luck to stock his larder. Break his duck and he knew he would be one step closer to nature and more able to take advantage of the bounties it had to offer.

More and more, his mind turned towards 'food procurement' as he liked to put it. At no time did it occur to him that perhaps he was trying to be too scientific in his approach. After all, nature is a very inexact science at best. All the tracks and spore that could be found on the forest floor proved there were plenty of animals about. He had heard the echoing calls of some sort of wildfowl but had never seen any of the elusive creatures. There were sometimes birds to be seen, high up in the sky, but they were so far out of reach. Parrish was trying to defeat an unseen adversary. The only place where he was actually sure there was food to be caught, and that was because he could see them, was in the stream.

Those brown trout. What he couldn't do with a couple of those! Bake them in his fires hot ashes, grill them above the glowing heat or make a nice fish stew. He could smoke them too so they'd keep for later. He tortured himself with the thoughts. But to do those things, first he had to catch the elusive little bastards.

Then he had a brain wave. He'd cheat!

Grabbing his webbing, which was hanging from pegs inside his hut, he dipped into the right side front ammo pouch.

He had all but forgotten that before he had been hurled back in time, B squad had been tasked to do a section attack, by night, on some undisclosed target. For maximum effect, the soldiers had been issued with plenty of blank rounds, *and* pyrotechnics. Parrish, like most soldiers, always appreciated a big bang or two.

His left side front ammo pouch was stuffed full of 7.62mm blank firing rifle rounds. The right side front however, was only half full of blanks. The rest of the pouch was filled with the long tubular shapes of three mark eight thunderflashes!

So, with a 'mark eight' concealed in his pocket and an evil grin on his face, Parish set off towards the trout filled stream. Once there he tracked along the river bank until he came upon a narrow, fast flowing bottleneck with a wide, slower moving pool just upstream of it. This pool had lots of trout in it.

Stripping off, he stepped into the water and waded up into the centre of the bottleneck, leaning forward against the current.

He had tied a stone to the thunderflash and held it tightly in his hand. Looking upstream into the sunlit pool before him, he grinned at the darting shadows beneath the surface that were unsuspecting trout. There was that delicious moment that only people who have ever used explosives know, when you are about to unleash chaos, destruction and noise and the rest of the word is totally unsuspecting and unprepared. Then, he unwrapped the striker and exposed the fuse. Drawing the striker sharply across the top of the fuse, it immediately started to fizz furiously.

"Grenade!" shouted Parrish gleefully and launched the weighted bomb in a graceful arc that finished with a small bright splash in the centre of the pool. There followed a few seconds silence as it sank into the clear water, while ripples moved unhurriedly outwards from the source of the splash.

With a dull 'whump', the thunderflash detonated. A white plume of water climbed into the sky. Parrish clapped his hands together then punched the air.

"Yes!"

He felt the pressure wave in the water against his legs. The airborne water splashed back into the pool and the water settled back to normal. After a few seconds all trace of the explosion was gone and there was a long silence. Parrish's face fell. Nothing was happening.

Then a single stunned fish rose slowly to the surface. Followed by another. And another. The constant flow carried the limp fishes towards Parrish and as they reached him he tossed them onto the bank. And kept tossing them onto the bank! There were lots of fish and for several minutes Parrish was inundated with the stunned creatures.

By the time he had thrown ashore the last fish there were more than two dozen good sized trout on the bank. Some little fish, dace or similar, were also stunned or killed by the blast but slipped by unnoticed and were carried away by the current.

Parrish climbed onto dry land and despatched the fish before getting dressed. He had honestly only expected to nab two or three and was for a moment at a loss as to what to do with his huge catch.

He cut a long thin pole from a tree and threaded the fish onto it through the gills. Twenty eight fresh brown trout!

With the pole on his shoulder, balanced by an equal amount of trout fore and aft, he walked back to camp, well pleased.

All the inhabitants there were totally astounded, not just that he had made a catch, but also by the sheer size of it.

Parish had far more fish than he could handle and, as much to show off as to demonstrate goodwill, he went slowly round the camp handing out fish, one to each hut. He got no thanks but the gifts were all accepted.

Finally, leaving the camps inhabitants to make of him what they will, he returned to his hut. As a last thought, he stopped off at the old ladies hut en route. She watched him approach without fear and was delighted when he gave her a fish too. She thanked him with a smile and a nod. At least one of them has some manners he thought, and so she should, a whole fish to herself while the others got one per hut was pretty generous. Suddenly Parrish realised that he was beginning to get a bit big headed about the whole thing. After all, he had cheated, hadn't he.

Parrish spent the rest of the day smoking and curing his fish. He rounded the evening off nicely with a fish and herb stew. It was good, like he knew it would be.

He congratulated himself on the success of his fishing trip, looked with satisfaction at the row of fish now stocking his larder, and settled back to enjoy his tasty, basic bouillabaisse.

The following morning an event occurred that pleased Parrish, endeared to him the downtrodden women of the camp and also enlightened him to one of the main Neolithic traits of the camp where he now lived. Barter.

He was walking through the camp, now being more watched than stared at, when he was confronted by a group of the women. A delegation. The looks on their faces told him they were intimidated by him, probably more by his maleness rather than his reputation, but were determined to do what they thought had to be done.

He looked down at the small creatures, opened his arms wide and smiled.

"Ladies?"

The women had no idea what he had said or what the arm gesture meant but they knew the smile. To Parrish it seemed that smiling and nodding were his only means of communication.

A woman stepped forward from the group, carrying one of the woollen capes that everyone in the camp wore, draped over her arm.

"Parrish." she said, indicating that probably the whole encampment knew his name. Good old Tomas.

He nodded and grinned even more.

The woman offered him the cape and his smile turned to a look of bewilderment. Another woman stepped forward as moral support for her compatriot and said a word that Parrish obviously did not understand. He shrugged and the second woman repeated the word, making the sign of a swimming fish with her hand.

Light dawned. He nodded and made the fish sign. So did the woman and repeated the word. Parrish tried the word a few times on his uneducated tongue and so added another word to his still very limited vocabulary.

The first woman said the word 'fish' and slapped her chest, then offered out the cape. Just like his trade of the otter carcass for the old ladies water bag. He knew then that the camp worked a rough bartering system of goods between individuals, maybe even between families too. The cape was being offered in exchange for the fish and it would be an insult not to take it.

Parrish duly accepted the gift, correction, trade and bowed to the ladies. They all thought this was funny and giggled, lightening the rather tense atmosphere.

He tried on the cape. It had a wooden toggle and loop clasp at the neck to secure it. The cloth rested heavily on his shoulders and hung straight down his back. He appreciated that thought had gone into its manufacture because it came to just below his knees, the hem just brushing the tops of his calf muscles. That was the same length as all the capes worn throughout the camp, and the ladies had obviously allowed for his extra height when they had sewn together the woollen squares that the cape was made from.

It was a bit scratchy but one hundred percent pure wool and nice and thick. Wearing it, a man always had with him a blanket, a warm coat and weatherproofing up to a point. With this under his poncho, he realised that he could handle most types of weather if he was away from the shelter of the camp. What a tremendous piece of kit and a marvellous gift! It hardly seemed fair to accept it in exchange for a few measly fish. Parrish was delighted. He swept it through the air, spreading it wide with his arms, then did a twirl to see how it felt, impressed with the way it settled back naturally over his shoulders. Holding onto one edge he did a splendid Sir Walter Raleigh bow in appreciation.

The women giggled again, realizing that he was very pleased with the cape, and pleased to have their work appreciated. Parrish nodded once more as if knowing what they were thinking. The women nodded in return then hurried away in a tight huddle, chattering eagerly among themselves.

After the pleasant fish event, there followed the not so pleasant, but equally important meat event.

The very next morning the hunting party returned. Parrish now knew that they were indeed a hunting party because they carried several large carcasses suspended from poles, just like the cannibals in old black and white movies used, to carry off their prospective lunches. The catch itself was very interesting. It included several deer and a wild pig or boar, but what most impressed Parrish was the huge elk that practically dragged on the ground as it was carried. There weren't many of those about on Salisbury Plain when he was there! He was also quite green with envy at the size of their catch, *and* no cheating with any twentieth century technology either!

The party made their way straight to the centre of the camp and all the other inhabitants immediately gathered round. Parrish went down to watch but stayed at the back of the crowd. It was no effort to see over the top of their heads anyway. The carcasses were gutted and skinned and the skins put to one side for later attention. The same with the edible pieces of offal. All except the hearts.

A strange man suddenly burst from the entrance of the giant centre hut. He wore a brightly coloured cape and an elaborate headdress with long feathers and bright flowers. What a grown man was doing with flowers in his hair Parrish had no idea. Didn't he realize how silly he looked?

The man started chanting and leaping about, moving his hands in writhing, snake like motions over the heads of the men who each held a heart. It seemed reasonable to assume that these were the men who had made the actual kills. The chanting continued for several minutes and the crowd watched sombrely from the sidelines as the feather and flower man made strange signs over the dark red hearts. He stopped abruptly, then shouted what sounded like an oath or brief command, and pointed theatrically at the hearts. As fast as they could, the men holding the hearts ate them, blood plastering their faces, hands and arms. To Parrish it all looked quite revolting.

Strange ceremony over, several men bent to the carcasses and started cutting large hunks of meat off with broad, yet flat stone knives, handing the chunks out to the outstretched hands of the crowd. It looked badly organized but was fairly done. When a person had received a portion, he or she immediately retired from the crowd.

The mob began to thin and Parrish thought he would chance his arm.

The man who was quartering the animal nearest him cut off a large piece of meat and was about to slap it into his palm when, seeing whose palm it was, stopped dead. There was a stony silence as all eyes turned to Parrish and the butcher.

A man in the crowd said something which the butcher seemed to question. A second voice backed up the first and a short conversation ensued. It was all totally incomprehensible to the tall man but he did hear his new word fish more than once. Finally the butcher nodded and slapped the meat into Parrish's' eager hand.

Emulating what the others had done, he turned to leave the group. Suddenly the meat was slapped roughly from his grasp and it flopped to the ground.

Parrish looked up from the fallen meat to see who had knocked it from his hand. He recognized the man. Recognized him not only by the single black slash across the face that was his full complement of eyebrows but also by the angry look in his eyes. It was the man who had tried to steal his webbing that first day.

Averting his own eyes, Parrish knelt to pick up his meat. The Neolithic man attempted to kick him in the face. Parrish saw the attack coming and tried to avoid it by swaying to one side. The kick went hard into his shoulder and toppled him onto his back in the dirt.

Parrish did not find out until much later that his Stone Age assailant had apparently been shamed, dishonoured if you like, by the incident with the webbing. Barter was indeed an important system used within the camp, along with equal shares for all when it concerned hunting or sheep. Theft however, was very heavily frowned upon.

Incidentally, it was the reason why Parrish's old lady had been banished to her distant, dilapidated hut, after she had stolen from other camp members while desperate for food.

On that eventful first day, Parrish had exposed his now determined assailant during an attempted theft, and to exonerate himself the man had immediately challenged Parrish. Not knowing this and also being in a state of shock at the time, Parrish had denied the man satisfaction or redemption of his honour. He also showed himself to be a coward before the whole encampment.

It had never happened before and the camp people were not sure how to react. They shunned Parrish completely and the Neolithic man lost all standing in the community. The effects were slightly lost on the uncomprehending tall man but it was a continuous insult to the Neolithic one. Now was his chosen time for retribution.

The aggressive man stood astride the glistening lump of meat in an open challenge. Parrish rose slowly to his feet, keeping a respectable distance between them, and gave the man a hard stare, holding eye to eye contact. It was another open insult to the smaller man and he would have none of it. He leapt forwards with a cry, hands reaching out for Parrish's throat.

Stepping smartly to his right as the man lunged, Parrish deflected the outstretched arms away with his left hand and punched the man in the side of the rib cage with his right as he passed by. The smaller man grunted with pain, staggering sideways to retain his balance and turned to face Parrish, surprised by the tall mans swiftness.

There was a momentary pause, but now it was Parrish who was determined not to let the matter of honour pass. He made 'come hither' gestures to the small man with his hands.

"Whenever you're ready, 'Eyebrows'. If you like to dish out kicking's you've got to be prepared to take them too. C'mon!"

'Eyebrows' didn't understand a single word but got the general tone of the comment all right. He snatched free the flint dagger that was tucked into the back of his tunic belt. There were murmurs from the crowd. Parrish couldn't tell if they were of approval or disapproval but no one stepped in to stop the fight.

He dropped into a well balanced crouch.

"C'mon." he waved again, speaking in a sly, threatening voice. "I'll teach you to pull a knife on a Light Infantryman, you Piltdown ponce! C'mon!" His insult was freely understood, even if the actual words weren't.

In a fury, Eyebrows lunged, dagger searching for Parrish's heart. The short man had a correspondingly short reach and his attack was well telegraphed. Parrish grasped the man's wrist with both hands as he came in, then ducked under the arm, pirouetting on the balls of his feet as he straightened back up, twisting the arm until it locked up hard against its tortured muscles. Again the small man grunted in pain, having no choice but to bend forwards in the direction of the twist, the dagger dropping from his grasp. As the man's head went down, it met Parrish's boot coming up. The force of the blow snapped the man back up and, when Parrish released his grip, he sprawled on his back on the ground. His nose was smashed and blood streamed down the unconscious man's face. The crowd watched in stunned silence.

Parrish stooped and picked up his meat, then the dagger which lay nearby, and with a 'take that' look at the prostrate man, tucked the weapon in his belt.

The other men looked at Parrish with new eyes. He just slapped the side of meat loudly with his palm and pointed to his chest. He received a chorus of nods.

Two women went to Eyebrows aid and helped the now semi-conscious man to his feet. He staggered away, clutching at his battered face, shunning their assistance.

A call from the butcher brought everyone's attention back to matter of sharing out the meat and after a few moments the whole incident seemed forgotten.

Some of the men now acknowledged Parrish as he passed them by on the way back to his hut, clutching his prize. Parrish nodded back. Apparently he had redeemed himself in their eyes.

He laughed. It seemed he was getting more popular by the day!

11

Parrish was now in the strange and not all together pleasant position of being acknowledged but not really accepted. He likened it to walking through the streets of a foreign city. People could see you were there and would usually acknowledge you, if you did them, but they didn't really care if you were actually there or not.

He did however use his new found freedom of the camp to stroll apparently aimlessly about, while gathering any snippets of information that might help him understand more about his new 'theatre of operations'. He called it that because it definitely did not feel like home!

It was soon apparent that not every family hut was identical. They were in terms of their construction, with wattle and daub walls about four or five feet high and having thatched conical roofs. The roof pitches were all the same, at about forty five to fifty degrees. It had probably evolved as the best angle to repel the elements. All the living quarters huts were approximately the same diameter, no matter how large or small the family that lived inside it. About ten meters across at the base being the norm.

This of course did not include the great roundhouse in the centre if the camp, it being of the same construction but much bigger, perhaps thirty meters plus across. Parrish still gave it a wide berth. All the Neolithic people seemed to have a certain reverence for the building, it was noticeable by their change in attitude whenever they passed close by it.

There was one other hut that was different.

This hut had a sort of long porch built onto its entrance way. Almost a short tunnel, it too had a thatched roof. The two thick wooden pillars that stood, one either side of this entrance porch, were adorned with various animal skulls. On closer examination, Parrish could see ornate carvings on the posts, strange symbols and signs. There were also markings on the skulls. Cross hatches, off- set squares or spirals. They were painted on with the same blue/black ink that the tattoos on men of the camp appeared to be drawn with.

This was the Chieftains hut.

The camp inhabitants elected a new Chieftain whenever the vacancy arose. The vacancy arose on the death of the Chieftain.

It was he who had the final say on settling any domestic disputes or inter-family quarrels that could not be settled amongst the warring factions and disrupted the smooth running of the camp. It also fell to the Chieftain to ensure that the camp defences were up to scratch. He would delegate out any work to be done to either the ditch or wall, ensuring that no one families workload was so great as to upset its own domestic affairs and put the people at risk if their winter reparations were too adversely affected. Of course, if a bad or vindictive Chieftain was elected, he could virtually exterminate a family he didn't like by keeping them so busy during the summer that they could not prepare sufficiently for the cold season.

Ironically, Chieftains were not elected by dint of their sensibility, skill in defence planning, sense of fair play or even general feeling of responsibility towards the camp and a wish to promote the continuing forward perpetuation of the whole fort and community under his control.

The Chieftain was almost always chosen because of his hunting prowess. He who led the most successful hunting parties over the seasons gained in stature and reputation.

On the not so rare occasions when the crop failed or the flocks were somehow decimated, making village food supplies scarce, the Chieftain would lead a raiding party against another village. It was a harsh reality, but if things became so desperate, it was then a case of steal from another village, risking violent death, or die slowly in the cold harsh winter. It was a double irony that a village would have to resort to the action they abhorred most to improve their chances of survival. Theft.

He who was the strongest and bravest during raids, or brought home the most fruitful bounty during hunts, had pole position for the post of Chieftain if the current Chieftain looked likely to die.

To a people who until a century or so before had relied entirely on hunting as their means of gathering food, the system for choosing Chieftains seemed wise and worked well enough. But times were changing and now very rudimentary farming techniques were coming into use. The new farming/hunting lifestyle was *a vast* improvement on their former living pattern, offering on the whole a more regular supply of food. The people were still at the mercy of the actions of the earth, forests and animals around them, but to a much lesser extent than when relying solely on catching animals which not only did not want to be killed, but also roved freely over the landscape and were sometimes difficult or even impossible to find.

Neolithic lifestyles were on the change, but the people themselves were still very set in their ways. It seems people always will be. The rituals that had been used for many hundreds of centuries were deeply ingrained and it would take much to change them.

And so, encampments across the land still selected their Chieftains using the tried and tested 'best man' system. Usually it seemed to work well enough but a village could do itself great harm or even sign its own death warrant if it chose a stupid, vindictive or very selfish Chieftain. Especially if the arrival of a bad Chieftain coincided with the arrival of a run of bad seasons.

Being Chieftain was naturally a position of honour and as such was rewarded with the best that the camp could offer. The best skins, choicest cut from the meat and first offer on the best women, most likely to bear sons. It was also a position of great power and could be used for personal gain. For instance, The Chieftain could instruct people to make repairs to his hut, irrespective of the fact that the people he instructed may have urgent repairs to do on their own homes. This could, and did happen, after the camp had been ravaged by a particularly severe storm, and was a gross misuse of power by the Chieftain.

The villagers had no recourse though. They had elected him and his say was final.

The only man who did not come directly under his control was the holy/medicine man.

His however, was a completely different lifestyle to anyone else in the village. He was, to all intents and purposes, 'kept' by the villagers as their connection, so they believed, to the earth and thus guaranteeing a good rapport with Mother Nature and continued good fortune with their hunting and farming. Even the Chieftain listened when he spoke. Ultimately another position of usable or abusable power.

Parrish found during his wanderings that almost all the huts had at least one storage hut behind it, some several more. They were living quarters huts in miniature. Peeking discreetly inside a few, he could see that they were used exclusively for storage and held a plethora of diverse and sometimes baffling items. These ranged from rudimentary tilling tools like hoes and picks made from antlers and shoulder blade shovels, to big mounds of moist clay. There were some things that he could only guess as to what their uses were, but the clay tied in nicely with the stone and clay built kilns that squatted close to the ground here and there, always a safe distance from the potential fire hazards of the thatched buildings.

He hadn't seen much at all in the way of pottery but it was obviously fired in these kilns and used somewhere, most probably inside the huts. There was no doubt in his mind that the wares these people made would be rough hewn and crude, but it would sure be nice if he could use some more suitable crockery than his battered mess tins. Perhaps he could trade for some at a later date?

Another curious find were the small pits. They were dotted at regular intervals around the interior of the encampment, just back from the foot of the parapet walkway that permitted the people to see over the wall. There were quite a few of them and they were all empty. Parrish lay on his belly and peered into them to try and discover what they were used for. The scattering of seeds in the bottom told him the answer. Storage pits for grain.

The pits were narrow necked but wide based and with flat bottoms. They varied in depth from three to six feet. How the Neolithic people had discovered that grain stored in this way would keep, sometimes for up to a year, was an undisclosed mystery.

The way it worked was both clever and yet simple. Once the filled pit was hermetically sealed, the grain in contact with the damp pit sides started to germinate. Fungus would then act upon it. The resulting fungi would use up the oxygen in the pit and it would be replaced with carbon dioxide which quickly ended the biological process. So long as the pit remained sealed and the grain dry, it would be preserved. Up to six to nine months was not uncommon.

The reason they were now empty was that all the grain had been used up. Even the ruined, fungus covered grain around the edges was not wasted. It was still suitable as animal fodder. Soon it would be autumn and when the coarse spelt wheat and six row barley had been harvested, the pits would be re-filled and so help to tide the inhabitants over during the cold season.

So it seemed the people also shared equally their grain crop. Parrish moved on with yet another useful insight into camp life.

He spied a man sitting cross-legged before the entrance to a storage hut and walked over, sitting down on the ground opposite him. Looking in through the doorway behind him, he could see the hut was brimming with variously shaped, knobbly white and black flint nodules. The Neolithic man had a towel sized irregular rectangle of hide across his lap, a flap of the same hide in his hand and, laid out neatly beside him, a selection of different stone hammers. Some were long and club ended, like pestles without their mortars, others were completely round, varying in size from a pebble to a clenched fist. Others again were tapered at one end, looking much like big teardrops carved in stone. All were smooth and highly polished.

Parrish watched, totally enthralled at the smaller mans skill and dexterity. He selected, with great deliberation, a seemingly innocuous nodule from one of the many piles inside the hut, then made himself comfortable once more on the ground. After inspecting the flint to determine the fissure lines, he struck it one single, crisp blow with his biggest hammer and it seemed to fall into perfect, smooth sided shards.

After laying the pieces out on the ground before him, he selected a suitable piece and started to chip and flake away at it. Before Parrish's astounded eyes the lump of flint became an exquisite axe head, skin scraper, dagger point or arrowhead.

The arrowheads fell into two distinct types. The first were diamond shaped, perfect miniatures of dagger heads, including the one he now wore tucked into his belt. The second type were barbed broadheads, wonderful to look at but obviously capable of inflicting terrible wounds and being difficult to remove.

Parrish had watched closely the return of the hunting party and noted that their arrow and spear heads all had diamond shaped tips. A shape ideally suited for deep penetration to reach the vital organs while still causing minimum meat damage. The broadheads on the other hand seemed specifically designed to be used on only one thing. People.

It was at least a small comfort that the skilled flint knapper made many diamond heads and very few of the other type.

After a while of working silently under Parrish's all seeing gaze, the knapper selected a medium sized flint shard from among his pieces, put it into a loose fold of hide and handed it to Parrish. Was there a small twinkle in the man's eye? The tall man held it in his open palm, looked for a thoughtful moment at the choice of stone hammers then selected a medium sized one, looking to the knapper for approval. He nodded. Parrish pointed to a corner of his piece of flint and the knapper nodded again. Copying what he had just been watching, Parrish struck the corner of the piece of stone smartly with the hammer. The lump of flint smashed into a myriad of shiny black, jagged fragments. Parrish looked up, dismayed.

The knapper slapped his thighs and roared with laughter. The tall man was surprised for a moment, then started laughing too, enjoying the knapper enjoying his joke at Parrish's expense.

He bowed his head, acknowledging the knapper's superior skill, and humbly handed back the hammer and the folded piece of hide, now filled with broken flint splinters. The knapper accepted the compliment and his tools, nodded in gratification, and returned to his work, still chuckling to himself.

Parrish patted the man on the shoulder, rose to his feet and walked away. Yes, he *had* enjoyed the joke even if it was on him, and yes, it had felt good. Better make the most of it, he thought. Laughs seemed few and far between in Danebury.

12.

Success!

Parrish finally started catching game in his traps. And as suspected, once he had deliberately trapped, a sort of pattern started to emerge. As he gained more and more knowledge of the different creatures that were available to him, his success rate grew.

He started to understand the habits and cycles of the creatures of the field and forest. Where he caught certain types of animals and when. If they were nocturnal, lived near water, burrowed underground or inhabited the trees. All these things he learned from the position of his traps, the creatures caught in them and when they were caught.

It finally sank in that if a person knew where and when to trap, there was food in abundance, well at least on an individual level.

The animal population of the Neolithic Hampshire basin overwhelmingly outnumbered the small cluster of people who they shared it with.

Parrish now had a large supply of dried and smoked meats and fish in his personal larder. He was quite proud of his accomplishments in his new field of endeavour.

Even so, day to day life was still a struggle on many other levels. The bare necessities of life he now had fully covered. Shelter, food, fire and water were his to control. These things however were just the basic building blocks of existence and sustenance.

Parrish still had no companionship and no goal in life to aim at. Now that he actually had free time, it weighed heavily on him. He would spend long spells brooding quietly, or just watching the camp solemnly from his little patch of higher ground. Memories from his past, Danebury's far distant future, would fill his mind and cloud it, making him morose, lonely and homesick. It was something he knew there was no cure for.

Over a month had passed since his arrival into the past and he was now fairly well accepted as a face among the crowd at Danebury. But that was it. He still stood alone as the tall man in camouflage fatigues. In an attempt to blend in, for it was his wish to try and fit in with the Neolithic people as much as he could, he had stopped shaving and was working on a beard. He would keep the face fuzz short because it did so annoy him, but he was very self conscious of being the only adult male with no face hair.

His clothes were another sore point. He kept them reasonably clean and they were by design very hard wearing, but nothing like the buckskins worn by everyone but him. He had attempted to make clothes from his collection of skins but basic dressmaking or even simple sewing techniques were totally alien to him. A pair of rather ineffective badger skin gaiters were his only success. Even a reasonably well fitting hat, something Parrish considered simplicity itself, was beyond his pathetic sewing skills.

Unaware and totally unconcerned about Parrish's morose moods and deep sadness, the people of the camp went on about their collective and individual business. He was still free to move about the camp at will, but it no longer cheered him to do so. He was in the village and yet, not *in* the village.

He tried to use his time constructively, attempting to gather any more words to add to the motley collection of the dozen or so that he had learnt to date. The trouble was that with no second person to teach him the language, he was getting nowhere fast!

It became one of his daily exercises to try and assess the feeling of the camp. The mood of the people. Perhaps that was why he was so quick to notice the sudden change. A tightness and heightening of tension with an undercurrent of worry, almost fear, suddenly changed the whole tone of the people, shattering the usual ambiance of the camp. Parrish immediately retreated to his hut and began to observe the encampment with renewed, hawk like interest.

He watched men in groups of three go out on night watches for the next couple of nights. They moved out at dusk and watched over the now very large flock. Most of the lambs had survived the spring and were growing fat on the lush green grass the flourished under the hot summer sun. The men returned, tired, the following morning to make way for the day watch. Parrish smiled at their inability to organize any kind of rota system for these night stags.

Before the groups of men set out and after they returned, there would be heated discussions. Sometimes these animated exchanges would have to be brought to an abrupt halt by the intervention and sharp words of the man in charge. It was always the same man.

Parrish would amble down into the camp when he could see these meetings about to take place. They were hardly planning sessions, reminding him more of playground groups arguing over who was picking who for some childish game. He couldn't understand what was being said except for the word sheep. It all added up to the fact that the people were worried, it affected the sheep in some way, and whatever it was, they didn't know what to do about it.

Parrish couldn't say why he did it, even if anyone would have been able to understand him, but that fourth evening during the arguing session, he volunteered. It went against everything he knew, his army training and plain common sense, but he volunteered.

It was doubly amazing because it wasn't an easy thing to do, with only sign language, nods and smiles to work with.

The three men who had been tasked that evening were about to make their way towards the main gate when Parrish tapped one on the shoulder. He pointed to the man and made what he considered to be a universal 'stay' gesture with his palm, then tapped his own chest and pointed out towards the flock, grazing at the forests edge on the near horizon. He had to repeat himself several times and a small crowd had gathered to watch.

The small man understood all right. He was waiting for the arrival of the Chieftain, who had immediately been sent for. The head man was still as yet unknown to Parrish. The sheep flock was of vital importance to the welfare of the whole village and to put it under any sort of risk, even concerning just one man, was not a decision to be taken by a lowly villager.

Parrish was still repeating his signs when the Chieftain appeared at the edge of the crowd. He seemed to consider the question for a few moments then nodded almost imperceptibly to the villager who was the centre of Parrish's attention.

The small man finally nodded to his tall volunteer and gestured to the open gate. Parrish nodded back and set off towards the distant flock. He had only gone a few paces when he himself was tapped on the shoulder and turned to see the man whose stag he had just taken. The small man offered out his bow and a bark made quiver holding several arrows. Parrish took the weapon and inspected it with a military eye. It was short. Four and a half feet long in its unstrung state. The arrows were straight, sharp and well fletched but not much longer than two foot gardening sticks.

A kids toy, thought Parrish. He made to return it to its owner but when he looked up the man was nowhere in sight, lost among the dispersing crowd. He shrugged, held the little weapon loosely at his side and fell in behind the other men. The one tall and two short men walked slowly away towards the forests edge in the gathering dusk.

One of the other men pointed to the base of a large tree on the edge of the forest and gestured to him, using the same 'wait' sign. Parrish sat. The area between him and the sheep was open, the dense woodland at his back. The two Neolithic men moved away and took up their own positions in small, purpose made hides in the fields, either side of the flock and nearer to the fort. Parrish knew he had gotten the shit detail. That was OK by him though, it wasn't the first time.

He memorized what he could of the area before the light finally went. As soon as it was fully dark he moved, silent and unseen, to a better position about fifty meters to his right and climbed up into a tree, settling down on a broad branch about six feet above the ground. Parrish had no idea what he was supposed to be watching for but he had no intention of being caught off guard in the ground. He smiled at the little bow resting across his lap, jammed one end against the tree trunk and easily bent it into an arc, hooking the eyed end of the bow string into its notch. The weapon was even shorter when strung. He made himself as comfortable as possible and settled down, gradually working into his waiting technique.

Occasionally he could hear the other lookouts shuffling, grunting or fidgeting in their little bunkers, away out in the darkness. He grinned. They thought it was clever, giving him the duff detail, but it was they who were having an uncomfortable night of it.

Finally, the night was silent and Parrish knew without having to check that the two men had both fallen asleep.

A last quarter moon crept slowly up into the patchy night sky and offered the land the feeble benefit of what little light it could throw down. The countryside was washed by the faint blue glow, making any shadows black as ink. The sheep were silhouetted dully against the soft red glow from fires burning within the encampment. Parrish looked on the bright side. At least it wasn't cold.

The night wore on.

Parrish sat quiet and still in his tree. He smiled at the parallel. When he had first realized that he had done what was thought to be impossible and travelled back in time, he almost went mad. Had almost been 'out of his tree' as 'Clive' would have put it. Pictures of the wisecracking squaddie popped into his head, along with other people he knew he would almost certainly never see again. Even 'mad dog' Carters miserable mug. He wondered what *he* would make of him vanishing without a trace while on exercise. As senior NCO, Carter was ultimately responsible for the men.

On a purely personal level, Parrish hoped his baffling disappearance had dropped good old 'mad dog' into the brown smelly stuff from a great height! He considered whether or not there was any possibility of him returning to the modern age. Would Jimbo be able to make another machine, then have the army send someone to come and get him? How long did he say it had taken him to build the damn machine, ten years? If it had cost millions, would the powers that be justify the expense of getting him back? More to the point, did they even have the slightest idea where or when he actually was? Parrish knew that he could go on and on and really drive himself nuts.

He wasn't sure how long he'd been pondering these and other questions, but he was jarred back to his present reality by the soft sounds of movement in the forest undergrowth behind him. The overlapping sounds told him that there was more than one of whoever or whatever they were. He decided to allow the mysterious night patrol to pass him by, then alert the other sentries and leave it to them. He looked forward to sneaking up on the sleeping men unseen, scaring the crap out of them when he woke them up.

Well up out of harm's way on his fat branch, his eyes and ears reached out into the darkness for sound or movement.

So silent, as they moved across the ground, that they impressed him with their stealth, two dogs appeared quite close to the base of his tree. They were silvery grey looking in the faint moonlight. A third dog appeared just off to his left and the three stood, sniffing the night air. Even in the poor light and at a distance, Parrish could see the sheep getting restless, immediately unsettled by the appearance of these wild canines.

Dogs? Thought Parrish. All this fuss over a few poxy dogs? Christ,

I'd *give* them a sheep each and send them on their way. Sod it. Let's see how this thing works.

He knocked an arrow into the bowstring then pulled back against the tension as far as the short arrow would allow. He still could not believe that the little weapon was anything more that a toy. The arrows should have had round, red suckers on the ends.

Holding the bow in tension correctly, with three fingers on the string, but with both arms bent because of the short pull, he felt like some huge Cupid. Or Eros on his plinth, dressed in cammo. Boy, was he glad his mates couldn't see him now!

Aiming along his arm at the dog on his left, about fifteen meters away, he let fly. To his surprise the arrow flew straight and true, plunging deep into the dogs shoulder with an audible thud. With just a strangle cough coming from its throat, the animal dropped to the ground, dead. The other two beasts hadn't even noticed, their attention still focused on the nervous sheep. Parrish's first reaction was amazement at the success of his impromptu archery display, but that soon turned to delight. This was turning out to be fun.

He knocked a second arrow and launched it into the back of the nearest of the remaining pair, only a few yards away below his position. Again he was impressed by the penetration of the little flint headed missile as the second dog too was killed outright. This slaying alerted the last dog. It immediately got very skittish, sniffing the air rapidly and running back and forth between the two dead animals, not knowing what was going on.

Parrish was having a good time. He slung the quiver around his neck, readied another arrow in the bow and jumped lightly to the ground to have a go at the third animal. It wasn't sure what to make of him and weaved about, dithering at the edge of the forest. Parrish loosed his arrow and it again flew true, revealing the fact that he had within him the makings of a very good bowman. The slender shaft bit deep into the dog's rear quarter. The animal howled in agony and tried to pull out the source of the pain with its teeth. Parrish was in the process of readying a fourth arrow to put the beast out of its misery when the rest of the pack materialized out of the darkness of the forest. There were maybe eight or ten animals. Several emitted low menacing growls.

"Ohhhh, shit!" said Parrish aloud and started to back away from the dogs, out onto the open ground. He shot the arrow hurriedly into the pack but they were so closely grouped that he still scored a hit. The beast didn't die because it too started to howl.

The animals closed in. Parrish hastily loosed another arrow at the dog closest to him. It went straight down the beast's throat and killed it. The animal fell to the ground but Parrish wasn't gloating now. He was close enough to the dead dog to see the grey and black markings on the animal's flanks.

Not dogs. Wolves!

His next arrow was his last and he blew it. Missing the animal he aimed at, it thudded harmlessly into the hard earth.

The wolves attacked. Parrish shattered his bow across the face of the first wolf that leapt at him, successfully fending off the beasts attack, and it went right by him. However, the following animal was right behind the first and took him on his right forearm, teeth biting deep. Parrish yelled in pain, dropped the splintered remains of the bow and pounded the animals face with his free hand. A moment later another wolf bit hard onto his right thigh while a third attacked the same leg, below the knee. They were trying to drag him down in order to finish him off, while he struggled to keep his feet.

Pandemonium reigned. The other wolves circled, looking for an opening, while the three beasts hung on Parrish, shaking themselves violently in an attempt to overbalance and topple him. The only reason he had not already gone down was the smaller size and thus lighter weight of the Neolithic wolves. Fighting for his very life, Parrish snatched the flint dagger from his belt and plunged it with all his might into the body of the beast on his arm. It howled and released its grip, flopping to the ground. He was allowed no time to recover. Another animal leapt, teeth flashing for his throat. The instinctive reaction of protecting his face with his arms deflected the main thrust of the attack and, as an alternative, the beast accepted the next, nearest point of vulnerability. Its fangs slashed into his shoulder. The weight of animals and the pain were too much to bear and he fell to the ground.

The final attack never came. Flickering light pushed back the night. An arrow suddenly materialized through the neck of the animal on top of him. Blood burst from the beasts vicious jaws, splashing onto his face. He threw off the dead weight with an agonized cry and struggled to his feet, stabbing savagely at the wolf still hanging tenaciously onto his thigh, the stone dagger slippery with blood. He kicked free of the wolf on his lower leg. It fell away unresisting, dying from the several arrows embedded it.

Parrish screamed in wild fury and wide eyed fear, dagger clenched in his fist, whirling in search of more attacking beasts. He was confronted by a large group of the camp people. Some were holding aloft brightly blazing torches which illuminated the whole area with a ghostly, dancing light. Others were loosing arrows at the few remaining wolves that were fleeing into the forest.

The people stared at him, a tower of wild fury, dripping blood from multiple wounds and still clutching his blood drenched dagger at the ready.

Through his red mist of pain, all Parrish could see was vague moving outlines and believed he was about to be attacked again. He let out a savage cry which made the crowd recoil instinctively, such was it's vicious ferocity.

Then the tall mans eyes went wide, as the last of his strength ebbed away. His arms dropped limply to his sides. He swayed for a long moment then fell forward, unconscious before he hit the ground.

13

Sunlight was pushing in through the many small gaps in the thatch that Parrish found himself looking up at. He was laying on his back, mind rapidly clearing as he came fully awake.

He remembered. Wolves!

He wasn't dead anyway, well at least not yet. There wasn't much pain either. Maybe things weren't so bad after all. But where was he?

It was the second time he had woken to find himself lying in one of the camps smaller, ancillary huts. Judging by the state of the roof, this hut was in pretty poor condition. A sudden thought jarred him. They had brought him back to camp after he had single handedly saved their damned sheep, then tossed him in some old decrepit hut and left him to die! The bastards!

His intention was to jump up out of bed. He got as far as a half sitting position before crying out in pain and flopping back. The distressed shout alerted someone though, because he had barely recovered his breath when the woollen door cover was thrown back. A bright shaft of sunlight angled in, cutting through the gloom. Parrish looked to see who was coming in. He couldn't help but notice that there were a few holes in the walls of the hut too.

The very small person that entered, it was hardly necessary for the individual to stoop through the opening, held a lamp. Well, a lamp of sorts. It was a rough clay bowl, deep like a breakfast cereal bowl but instead of holding cornflakes it was full of tallow fat. There was a lighted wick floating in it. The flickering yellow flame illuminated the interior of the hut surprisingly well and as the person approached, he could see the features behind the light. It was the face of his neighbour, the old lady.

He didn't understand what was going on but at least he now knew where he was. He would have much preferred to be in his own hut, even if hers was a lot more roomy. At least his didn't look like it might fall down at any minute.

She smiled and placed the lamp in a twine woven hanging basket that hung down on a long cord from the roof of her hut, then knelt down beside his bed. Bed was a loose description. He was lying on a woven straw mat, covered in furs. Parrish wasn't complaining. Compared to his own hard ground and bracken bed it was a vast improvement. He was completely naked but covered by a large, soft hide of some beast that he couldn't identify. He made to rise but the old lady put her palm on his chest and pushed him back down, saying something that he couldn't understand but ended with his name.

There must have been a puzzled look on his face because she shook her head and hands in a 'doesn't matter' gesture and smiled down at him. He knew he was helpless and that made her unafraid. It's easy for the mouse to be brave if the cat has lost his claws. She put a weather beaten hand to his forehead. He wasn't hot. She nodded in satisfaction and then unwrapped a heaped bundle of broad dock leaves that sat near the bedside. Inside the leaves was a mound of what looked like yellowish brown muck. It had a strange foresty sort of odour. Parrish knew it had to be some sort of poultice.

Not standing on ceremony and without a moments warning, the old lady grasped the edge of Parrish's hide blanket and, with one brisk movement, swept it off him. Stunned, Parrish lay motionless, completely exposed and vulnerable in his nudity. She gave a brief, knowing smile and tapped his limp penis with a finger before making the fisherman sign for 'big' with her hands. He flushed and covered his genitals as best he could with his left hand. It was the only arm that seemed to want to move. The old lady laughed briefly at his embarrassment then bent over his white, muscular body.

Parrish watched her work, unresisting. He realised that he wasn't completely naked after all. Wherever he had been savaged, upper and lower right leg, right forearm and across the left side of his neck and shoulder, were green leaf dressings. They were held in place by thin leather cords. Strange, he could hardly feel them. He wondered in a semi-detached way if the reason why was either through nerve damage, or some sort of anaesthetic quality in the strong smelling poultice he knew would be under the leaves.

Parrish forgot about his embarrassment and used his good arm to prop himself up to better see what the old lady was doing with his leg. She deftly undid the cords, which seemed to be secured with a quick release knot of some description, and with surprising gentleness, peeled away the big green leaves. The poultice lifted cleanly off with the leaves and Parrish grimaced at the sight of his leg. From just below the knee to the thinner part of his calf, and along a ten inch section of his mid upper thigh, his leg was slashed wide open. Dark red, almost purple meat glistened inside the wounds. Parrish's first reaction was a hard swallow. Didn't they know how to sew things up around here? Mind you, he knew about debridement and perhaps somehow the Neolithic people did too. The wound looked clean enough and the old lady seemed pleased with it.

"If I start frothing at the mouth, just pick up one of your stone clubs and beat my brains out with it." Parrish tried to relieve his tension and worry with a poor joke. It was totally wasted on the old lady, he knew. She didn't speak English for a start. She looked blankly at him for a moment, making Parrish feel foolish, and returned to her work.

After applying some fresh poultice and re-tying the cords, she set to work on his arm. More of the same. Wicked, slashing bite marks.

By the time the old lady had finished dressing his neck and shoulder wound, all the colour had drained from Parrish's face. She took a marble sized blob of the poultice between her finger and thumb and smeared it onto his face, just below the outside corner of his right eye, on the prominent part of his cheekbone. It was only then that he noticed his face was indeed sore there. Touching the spot tenderly with his fingers he could feel a mottled, lined surface. He didn't recall ever being bitten or struck there during his fracas with the wolves.

The old lady slapped his hand away from the face wound and replaced his blanket, patted him on the shoulder and left abruptly, leaving the door flap open to allow the light and air in. Pale faced and weak from shock, Parrish was grateful. For so called primitive man, these people could sometimes be very thoughtful.

A short time later, although Parrish had no way of telling how long she had been gone, the old lady returned with a another clay bowl, this time full of some sort of hot broth. It didn't taste particularly nice but he was glad of it and scoffed down the lot. The old lady was pleased with that too.

She spoke, pointing at herself and Parrish, then at the interior of the hut, finishing with open hands. Parrish just shrugged with his eyebrows. She nodded. Well, he thought. It looks like I've just agreed to something without having a clue what it is.

The old lady lifted down the tallow lamp and left without another word, flipping down the door blanket behind her. Parrish lay back in the gloom and stared up at the patchy thatch work. Lamp or no lamp, he was as much in the dark as ever!

Without knowing it, through his positive attitude and grim determination to get back on his feet, Parrish saved himself from certain death. The Neolithic times, the harsh way of life and the rugged people who lived it only allowed a short time for wounds to heal. Here, injuries were either minor or fatal! If a person was injured and was to be incapacitated for a long time, they were considered worse than useless to the community. A burden on the already over burdened people who lived short lives of hard toil and also on the steady downhill slope to death anyway. The reward for serious injury was ritual execution, though in the eyes of Neolithic man it was not so much cold blooded murder, more like putting a wounded beast out of its misery.

It was thus fortunate, but unappreciative of the danger, that Parrish was determined to be back to full health as quickly as possible, for his own reasons. To get out of the colander of a hut he lay in as much as to regain mastery over his own life.

The first part of his directive he was not destined to achieve for quite some time. The very next day, the little old lady began to move all his personal effects and equipment out of his wicker shed and into her hut. Parrish shot questions at her constantly but she could not understand him so she ignored him. Accepting defeat, he just watched, finally realizing that what he had unknowingly agreed to the previous day was to move in with the old crone while she took care of him. He wasn't too pleased with the idea but, after reasoning it out, knew that with the gifts of food he had bestowed upon her, she was obligated to return his favours somehow, so perhaps she wasn't looking after him purely out of love. He smiled at his little joke and his expression caused the old lady to throw him a puzzled look.

The second part of his directive, to be up and about, ASAP, started when the old lady dumped a pile of bits on the ground beside him. He recognized the items as the things from the pockets of his combat jacket. Parrish was immediately alarmed and gestured frantically to her, miming putting on a coat. Not an easy task with a bandaged arm and neck. She gave an understanding nod and disappeared through the door, returning almost immediately with his combat jacket and trousers. The jacket was badly torn about the shoulder, collar and arm. The left leg of his lightweights was almost completely shredded. Both garments were encrusted with liberal amounts of blood, both his and the wolves. The old lady rubbed the garments together and Parrish understood that they were to be washed. He nodded and the old lady left him, going about her business while he went carefully through his little pile of kit, checking the contents.

The next morning the old lady appeared with a fresh helping of poultice in one hand and his clothes in the other, clean but still ragged. She put the garments down and started to uncover his wounds. Parrish waited until they were fully exposed then stopped her from applying more of the heady poultice. He inspected the muscle damage. It was all clean and free from infection. Pointing to a beige coloured, rectangular package among his small pile of kit he said with accompanying signs,

"You! Bring that here!" He had seen more than enough of the men's behaviour to know that being assertive with the women was particularly effective in getting results. Sure enough, she nodded and quickly brought him the package. It was one of his two field dressings and the old lady watched with fascination as he broke open the pack and unravelled the huge sterile gauze pad and the long bandage. He guided the woman's hands to the skin either side of the long, open slash on his thigh and pushed the hands towards each other until the edges of the wound butted together. He grunted with the sharp jab of pain but when he removed his hands, hers still held the wound closed. Covering it with the gauze, he wound the long end of the bandage tightly around his thigh and tied it off with a knot. He made swirling finger signs with his finger near the lower wound to indicate that he needed a bandage for that too. No point in using up all his field dressings in one go if something else could be found to do the job. She nodded vigorously and went to the far side of the hut, returning with some long, two inch wide strips of soft leather.

"Excellent." he said out loud. "Thank you... just what the hell is your name anyway?"

The old lady just looked blankly at him and so Parrish did his 'me Tarzan, you Jane' act for the second time.

"Me Parrish." She nodded and he pointed at her. "You?"

"Oona."

Shit, Parrish thought, they really do have those stupid sounding mono syllabic names. Just like in those cheapo caveman 'B' movies. He nodded and grinned at the old woman never the less.

"OK, Oona. Same again on the other wounds."

Together they then bandaged his lower leg and arm in the same way, using a smear of poultice and a covering of leaves to protect the exposed edges of the wounds from the definitely NOT sterile leather strips. His neck and shoulder injuries were not so easy to bandage but not so severe either. He eventually settled on covering the cuts with poultice and leaves and holding it all in place with his tee shirt, worn back to front so there was undamaged cloth over it. Not brilliant but it would do.

Parrish lay back to catch his breath after all the pushing and pulling of his injuries and watched Oona with fascination and barely disguised pleasure. She sat cross-legged on the floor, examining his jacket closely. The small, tight, machine sewn stitches astounded her. She went over every seam she could find in minute detail. Finally she returned to the ragged tears in the shoulder, went again to her side of the hut and returned with a bone needle and some thick thread. The thread was much nearer to twine than cotton and the needle, although beautifully made, was almost three inches long and had an eye you could pass a straw through. Even so, it took her two attempts to thread the needle.

"Oona," called Parrish softly, causing her to look up from her deliberations. "Bring me my webbing."

She didn't understand.

"Webbing." he repeated and pointed at the tangled mess of pouches and straps on the floor beyond the end of his bed. She picked it up and handed it to him. He pointed to it, saying, "Webbing."

"Webbing." repeated Oona not too successfully. Parrish knew it was futile to try and teach all the Neolithic people English, but at the same time realised that he had before him a golden opportunity for someone to teach him their Gaelic/Celtic mumbo-jumbo. Oona! He smiled at her for a long second, then dipped into one of his pouches, emptying it until he found what he knew was in there. His sailor's housewife. He selected a medium sized needle and the small bobbin of green thread. He threaded the needle with a good length, knotted the loose end then offered it to her. She hesitated before taking it gingerly from his fingers, then examined it fully, ending with her inadvertently jabbing her thumb with it. A small red dome of blood mushroomed up from the tiny puncture. She didn't seem to feel the prick but Parrish winced and said 'ouch' for her. At the sound of his voice she looked up at him. Her face said it all. She couldn't have looked more pleased if Parrish had handed her a gold bar.

"Good?" asked Parrish, nodding. Oona nodded back, still grinning from ear to ear. He picked up the bone needle, pointed to it and then the steel one in her hand, and looked questioningly at Oona. She cottoned on, spoke the word and Parrish had the Neolithic word for needle, one more to add to his collection. Satisfied, he pointed to his jacket and made sewing movements. Oona nodded for the umpteenth time and eagerly set to work on the jacket, keen to play with her new toy. He thought that the jacket would be all right, although he held out little hope for the trousers.

For the next couple of days Parrish lay back, recuperating and keeping a close eye on his wounds. The time was by no means wasted though. He questioned Oona constantly, pointing at objects and asking for their names. She soon got the gist of this game and was then even more helpful than ever. And so he slowly started to expand his vocabulary, a process that he continued to do, all the time he lived with Oona. A time that was eventually to expand into many months.

The process was simple enough with simple objects. Objects that he could see and point to. Abstract items however were a completely different kettle of fish. The same with the Gaelic/Celtic grammar, although luckily there wasn't a whole lot of that.

Getting to grips with any abstract words always needed a great deal of gesturing, signs, play acting and above all, patience. Sometimes, no matter what Parrish did, the exercise still ended in failure. How, for instance, does one sign or act out the difference between 'want' and 'need'?

As he learned more and more it became increasingly evident that the grammar was very rudimentary and in some areas the actual vocabulary was very limited. Even years later, when he sometimes wanted to say something in particular, he had to stop, think, and simplify the words, distilling them down to a more basic form.

Some words, like 'idea or 'consider' were almost beyond the Neolithic ability to comprehend at all, even though they used the words concept every day. Parrish also missed words that just weren't in their vocabulary. Simple words that used to give him pleasure.

'Beer' was one word. 'Music' was another. When it came to music, it was beating on log or skin drums or nothing with these people. The first time Parrish had whistled while he worked it astounded everyone. He spent the next several hours giving all and sundry whistling demonstrations and lessons. For the next few weeks, Danebury was filled with constantly twittering idiots before the fad died away. Then they seemed to forget all about it. It served no useful purpose.

Seven days after the wolf attack, Parrish made his first appearance outside the hut. He had gotten Oona to cut him a crutch from the description he gave and a drawing in the dirt floor. OK, the first one she cut was too short, but he blamed himself for not specifying the length. She thought she was in for a beating when she understood that it was wrong, but he just sent her away to get another one. This one was the right length, even if it wasn't very comfortable.

He managed one complete, crutch hopping lap around the hut before going back inside and collapsing with exhaustion, although the fatigue was laced through with satisfaction. He had been seen by the people too and several had nodded with satisfaction and some appreciation. Parrish took it to mean that they were pleased to see him. They were actually pleased that it wouldn't be necessary to kill him after all. There were few enough of them as it was.

Another unappreciated effect of this was that the Neolithic people did now actually care what happened to him, one way or the other. They recognized that he had done solid work in protecting the flock and that it would have been a sad waste to kill him. He had unknowingly ingratiated himself in one more small way to the people of Danebury. Another slight but never the less significant in road towards being accepted by the village, and thus becoming part of it.

Another of Parrish's misconceptions was that the people were nodding approval of his new trousers. Wrong! They couldn't care less what kind of pants he wore. There was no such thing as fashion clothing in 3,500BC. The watchwords here were utility, warmth and hard wearing. Parrish's lightweights were indeed way beyond repair although they were not discarded. It was still possible to chop off the legs and use them as shorts, he thought. To replace them, Oona had made him a pair of leather trousers. His first buckskins.

She found it relatively easy to get the fit right. Parrish was her living mannequin, always at her disposal. She regularly offered the partially made garment up to his legs in impromptu fitting sessions. It annoyed Parrish although he said nothing, and when they were finished, he tried them on with dubious trepidation. He'd needn't have worried. They were soft, comfortable and a surprisingly good fit. There was no fly and they had a leather drawstring fastening instead of a belt but these were minor gripes. Close your eyes, he thought, and they felt like heavy denim jeans. He thanked Oona profusely and she was pleased because, unknown to Parrish, she had worked uncharacteristically hard on a standard item of clothing that would normally be just thrown together. The seams had been sewn with the large bone needle but she had kept the stitching close and tight, doing her best to replicate the machine sewing on his other clothes. The regularity and tightness of it still amazed her, especially on the heavy leather of his combat boots. The mysterious, strange texture of the boots moulded rubber soles left her shaking her head in bewilderment.

The tall man was so pleased that he told Oona, with much signing, pointing and drawing, that all the other skins he had amassed were at her disposal and she could make more clothes for both himself and her. She finally nodded and Parrish was smugly pleased with himself, thinking that Oona would greatly appreciate the gesture. She did not complain but Parrish didn't realize until several days later what he had done. On top of taking care of him, including gathering food, firewood and water, he had heaped upon her even more work. When he understood, he was mortified but could then do nothing. Even if he could have told Oona, retraction would have caused him to lose face and even run the risk of ridicule. It might undo all the work he had put into attempting to gain acceptance into the village.

He severely reprimanded himself and vowed to consider his actions more fully in the future. Parrish knew he now owed Oona, a debt he was fully determined to repay. That was the way of things at Danebury. The thought seemed natural to him and he never questioned it.

Not only was he making inroads into Neolithic life, it was making inroads into him.

14

For a further seven days the tall man made regular trips around the battered hut he now lived in. He fully understood that the trick to swift, full tissue regeneration was gentle, blood circulating exercise without pulling the wounds open. Back in the time he had come from, or was it forward, two weeks was the usual length of time before stitches would be removed. Parrish was determined not to put back the healing process by being too aggressive with the exercises.

Oona however, knew the fate that befell badly injured people and so contrived to keep her new charge visibly busy. She didn't want him put to death, for she had developed quite a liking for her brave but very stupid patient. It was good to be busy for a purpose again, good to be useful. She considered herself very advanced in years, her actual age being thirty six summers, and it was very pleasing to have her mothering instincts come to the surface again. Her new 'boy' was big and brave, of that she had no doubt, but not very bright. For a start, a child only five summers old spoke better than he and the big man had no idea how to live. Building a square house instead of a round one was stupid, as was sleeping on the bare ground. He couldn't even make clothes to keep out the cold. For all his obvious strength he was weak too. Several times when she had done the things that he had asked, badly or wrong, the expected beating had never come. He had simply asked her to do it again. She was never the less, greatly impressed and amazed by some of the things he owned and besides, in her heart she sensed that he was a good man.

She was very grateful for the lack of physical abuse. Although she was pleased and eager to tend to his wounds and take responsibility for his welfare, it was a serious strain on her. Years of hard, relentless toil had taken their toll. She was not as strong as she used to be and deep down inside herself, knew that she was not much longer for this life. Soon the sky spirits would take her and return her to the arms of the Earth Goddess. This she kept from her new charge, along with the ever present threat of death that hung over him while he ran the risk of taking so long to recover.

And so, to be visibly useful, by the fourteenth day of Parrish's apparently long convalescence, he found himself sitting with his back against the hut, a stone axe in his good hand. He hadn't minded in the least when Oona had first tentatively put forward the suggestion to him. It was good, blood pumping exercise without running the risk of too much limb movement. Trapping lengths of log under his right leg, he swung the axe with one handed awkwardness and slowly chopped up the timber Oona brought to be converted into firewood. Occasionally people might pass nearby while bustling about the camp and would nod or just glance in his direction. He tended to ignore them mostly. He also never saw the small smile of satisfaction on Oona's wrinkled face.

A few more days passed and Parrish started to gingerly stretch and bend his leg. The wounds were healing nicely, the edges bright red but not in the least bit puffy. He went carefully but now started to use both arms when doing tasks, be it chopping wood, cleaning out cooking pots, starting fires or whatever else needed to be done that was not too strenuous and near to the hut. It was while chopping more kindling that a shadow fell across his seated form. He looked up, squinting against the bright blue sky, and recognized the dark line of eyebrows across the man's face and the badly broken nose.

Oh shit, he thought. Not now, please not now. Parrish struggled to his feet, keeping hold of the axe, taking most of his weight on his good leg but putting some onto the sore one in the hope of giving the impression that he was OK and not going to be an easy target. He looked down at the man, glad of the immediate height advantage. Eyebrows stared straight back up at him, totally un-fazed by the posturing.

"Parrish." he said and shoved out his hand. Parrish couldn't help it, he flinched. In the man's hand was the flint dagger that had been taken from him when he had been on the receiving end of Parrish's kicking. Eyebrows offered the weapon again.

"Wolves." he said, knowing to keep the exchange simple for this big idiot, and made stabbing gestures with the dagger.

"Oh, right." Parrish realized with relief that the man was simply returning the weapon he must have dropped during the attack. He was glad that the Neolithic man didn't seem to bear a grudge about being beaten in a fight. Dropping the axe, Parrish took the dagger in his good hand. Eyebrows nodded and made to move away.

"Ah... hang on a minute." Parrish didn't know the man's name but he didn't want to leave it at that. The dagger wasn't originally his. He had stolen it from Eyebrows after the fight.

The Neolithic man turned back to face him and the dark eyebrows raised in question. Parrish pointed at himself, Oona then Eyebrows in succession, naming them as he did so.

"Parrish, Oona...?"

"Klud." he said flatly.

"Well, here Klud, this was originally yours after all." said Parrish and offered the dagger back. Apart from his name, the words were unintelligible but the smaller man was not stupid and knew what the big man was attempting. An offer of friendship and honesty. His changing view of this unknown giant was getting steadily better. In fact, he had been impressed with the swift and sure way he had been dealt with that day when the hunting party had returned. He knew to his cost how badly he had misjudged the man. If he had done the same to any other man in the village he would not be alive now and was grateful for that.

Klud fingered his broken nose for a moment then accepted the dagger. Parrish nodded, sensing that the dagger had been accepted as much as a peace offering as simply returning the man's property. Klud held the dagger up between them, then reached behind his back and produced from beneath his cape another dagger, holding it up next to the first. They were practically identical. The small man had obviously replaced the one he had lost. He looked briefly from one to the other then handed the original dagger back to Parrish.

Parrish accepted the gift and Klud laughed. A short, barking sound. Parrish laughed too and the tension was gone, their past conflict forgotten. Klud pointed to Parrish's bandages and the great eyebrows raised again in question. Parrish nodded and the Neolithic man grunted in approval. He clapped Parrish on the arm and turned, setting off into the centre of the village.

Parrish stared after him, a warm glow of achievement filling his chest.

Oona appeared at his side.

"Good." she said.

"Yes." agreed Parrish in Gaelic/Celtic. "Good."

By the time the moon had completed its twenty eight day cycle Parrish had discarded his crutch and was walking, all be it with a pronounced limp, easily about the camp. He returned to his mud and turf covered wicker hut and checked it out. His once extensive food reserve was practically gone and the place was empty, all his kit now inside Oona's hut. At first he was furious that his food had been stolen but before he had taken many paces back down the slope towards a confrontation with Oona he realized that she had been using the food to sustain them both. It was as perfectly reasonable to expect her to do this as it was unreasonable to expect the old lady to go hunting. As he stood on his original patch of high ground and looked down on her battered hut, watching her doddering about beside the outside fire, he finally grasped what a great burden he must be to the old woman. She had taken care of him, done all that he had asked and never complained, bless her. His earlier thoughts of when he had first seen her, how he couldn't see her making it through even a mild winter, suddenly choked him. He had to admit it, he actually liked the old bat.

A sense of determination gripped him. You *will* make it through the winter Oona, he decided, seizing the chance to repay the debt he owed. You've helped me and now I will help you. We'll get through it together.

That day he spent checking and re-setting his traps. They were of course empty, all the baits were long gone and any animals that had been caught had been devoured by other predators and scavengers. He moved slowly, still wary of his recent injuries, and the re-setting took all day. He got a good night’s sleep, made all the better now that he had set himself a task and given himself a direction, and the following morning started on the repairs to Oona's, correction, their hut. He filled in all the holes in the wattle a daub walls and then gave the whole lot a fresh layer of mud just for good measure.

Summer was not yet at its end but Parrish was determined not to waste any time. He had no idea whether the late seasons were wet and mild or cold and wintery. After lashing together a ladder from branches he set to work on the thatch. He had never thatched in his life but removing all the damaged and rotted straw allowed him to see how it had been applied. He cropped the long meadow grasses, stacked it in small stooks, allowed it to dry in the warm sun then set about replacing the thatch, damaged and holed parts first, the rest later.

Oona was pleased with all the repairs and especially grateful when Parrish started bringing in animals that had been trapped. The food supply that she had been using was getting desperately low. She also worried that Parrish was working too hard too soon after his savaging but he pooh-poohed her fears. He had never felt better in his life. Like Oona, he too appreciated how good it felt to be really useful.

In the evenings the pair would sit beside the outside fire in the clean sweet air, and while they worked on skins, firewood, or any other chore that needed doing, Oona coached Parrish on her native language.

His words were still extremely basic but now, more often than not, he could make himself understood if he kept the conversation simple.

Language wasn't the only thing he was learning. He was constantly being introduced to new eye openers. The Neolithic people were nowhere near as stupid as he had first thought. Take meat for instance.

Jerky was jerky and the villagers dried it in the sun just like he did. But hocks and sides of meat were not smoked the same way he had smoked his. They thought bigger. Huge chunks of meat hung on leather cords from the high ceilings inside their conical roofed huts. Parrish didn't know this until Oona had done the same with the first animal he had brought in from a successful trap.

She had skinned it deftly with a sharp flint. Then gutted it, keeping all the offal, some to eat and some to make into gut or sinew for bindings. Then she hoisted the carcass up into the roof space on a leather strap. Parrish was amazed and horrified until Oona laboriously explained to him that if the internal fire was kept alight, as it usually was, then the side of meat would smoke naturally and slowly, making it last even longer, where the smoke gathered in the roof space. He had already noted that none of the other larger family huts had a chimney, the smoke from their fires filtering out through the thatch. He wasn't to know, but keeping the roof space smoky also kept insects and other pests at bay too. Parrish nodded when he finally understood. It was neat, clean, tidy and downright clever.

Parrish continued to work well and Oona complimented his manual labour by taking care of the domestic chores. Between them they had soon established a good buffer against the oncoming ravages of winter with a plentiful supply of food, skins for warmth and lots of firewood. Parrish filled his wicker hut with chopped logs, not intending to use them until regular supplies became scarce.

He got Oona to show him her garden plot among all the other allotments. It was just a wild mass of weeds and grasses, totally beyond salvation for the remainder of this year. He contented himself with the knowledge that leaving it fallow for a year would at least make the ground fertile for the following years planting. He looked at the other plots, admiring the neat, good looking patchwork crops of wheat and barley. It didn't resemble at all what he knew as wheat. For a start, the stems varied greatly in length from not more than a foot above the ground to some that were waist high, his waist that is. The wheat ears were different too, only six or eight seeds a side. If he expected to be permitted to have some wheat seed of his own to plant next year, it was obvious that he would have to help out with the harvest this year. That harvest could only be a few weeks away. He asked Oona this in his simple words and she nodded in confirmation.

"Fair enough." said Parrish in English.

"OK." said Oona, also in English. Parrish smiled. Seems like he wasn't the only one learning new words.

Parrish took a slow stroll out beyond the milling, bleating sheep flock to the edge of the forest and found the area where he had been attacked by the wolf pack. There was no sign of the night time drama that had taken place. Hunting about for any traces, all he could find was the smashed remains of the bow that had been loaned to him and a single, broken arrow shaft. These he gathered up and carried back with him to Danebury.

He had intended to hang the bits on the hut wall as a memento but, as luck would have it, no sooner had he entered the encampment when he almost physically bumped into the very man who had given him the bow. Stuck momentarily as to what to do, Parrish shrugged his shoulders and offered out the broken fragments to the man.

The fellow who faced him was five foot one, bordering on being thick set and had good shoulders beneath his cape. His eyes glittered with some private amusement. He shook his head.

"No matter Parrish. I have made another bow."

To his great pleasure, Parrish heard the words, 'no ... Parrish ... I... made ...bow.' He actually understood!

The small man nodded when he saw from Parrish's expression that he had grasped what he had said. They faced each other for a long second and Parrish decided to try his luck. His words were halting and with a stilted accent but he hoped the Neolithic man would understand.

"Make ... Parrish ... bow?" He finished the short, almost sentence on an upward note and open hands, over emphasizing it as a question.

The small archer was a little surprised by the question, which he fully understood.

Every male in the whole village knew how to make his own weapons. It was one of the essential skills that were taught from a very early age. Admittedly, flint knapping was usually only fully mastered by a few especially gifted individuals who then did well from their skill through barter, but bows, arrows, spear, axe and dagger shafts surely everyone knew how to make? Well, not Parrish it seemed. The giant man from some distant place must have had a deprived upbringing. He was also surprised by the request because, judging by the wolves that had been shot, he seemed to have a definite skill with the bow. Even if Parrish could not make a bow, he certainly knew how to use one.

He would of course make him a bow. At least in gratitude for saving many of the sheep which would be vital in the coming winter, if not only for personal gain. If Parrish wanted the bow when he had made it, he would surely barter for it.

"Yes."

Parrish clapped his hands together with joy. He then put the inside edge of his hand stiffly up alongside his eyebrows like a badly executed salute.

"Bow ... this big. Big bow." he said, asking the small archer to construct a bow taller that the man himself. The small mans eyebrows shot up but he never spoke. He gauged the suggested length swiftly with a practiced eye, thought for a second then nodded in agreement.

Parrish decided to push his luck a little further. After all, what use was a weapon without projectiles.

"Arrow?"

The question confirmed what the small archer thought about Parrish's stupidity and ignorance of even basic but vital functions of normal daily life. The big idiot couldn't even make a simple, straight shaft.

"I will show you how to make them but then you must make your own."

The sentence was still too complex for Parrish's rudimentary Gaelic/Celtic knowledge but he could tell by the accent that it wasn't a negative reply. The archer beckoned him with a wave and set off into the camp, Parrish right behind him.

They came to one of the large family huts and for a moment Parrish thought they might actually enter, but they went on beyond it to one of the small ancillary huts, identical externally to the one he and Oona lived in. From inside it, the small man produced a selection of willow stems. All were fairly straight and cut a good bit longer than needed to make arrows. Parrish noted that they had been sun dried.

Selecting a shaft deliberately for its slight, wandering crookedness, the small archer showed it to Parrish, ideal to demonstrate the art of shaft straightening. The duo made their way back to the main hut and settled on the ground beside the low, but still hot, outside fire there. The tall man watched with intense fascination as the Neolithic archer gently heated the crooked sections before teasing them straight over his knee, sometimes using a long, flat bone with a hole drilled through its face. He threaded the shaft through the hole and gave it lateral twists where the bends were at their worst. An arrow wrench. Eyeing along the shaft several times while twirling it in his fingers, the archer was finally satisfied. He quickly scraped along the length of the shaft with the edge of his flint dagger, skilfully taking off tiny shaves here and there. When he had finished, he showed the now straight shaft to Parrish and allowed him briefly to inspect it. He nodded.

Next the archer put a neat semi-circular nock in one end of the shaft with the abrasive, sawing action of a different flint tool. Then he carefully split the opposite end for about two inches, again using his keen edged dagger, ready for the flint arrowhead to be inserted and secured. But that didn't happen just yet. First the shaft had to be fletched.

The man disappeared briefly into his family hut and returned with some long, wing feathers clutched tightly in his hand. Parrish was impressed. He hadn't managed to catch any birds yet.

In the archers other palm was a small thin sliver of very good quality flint. With it he split several of the big feathers down the centre of the quill, then used it to shave off an inch or so of excess feather fronds at each end of the feather halves. Gauging their length from the nock downwards along the shaft, he inverted the feather halves and bound the scraped ends to the shaft with fine sinew. Parrish watched every operation closely. The three half-feathers lay down along the shaft, the slit quill centres uppermost, at one hundred and twenty degree increments to each other, their lashed ends perhaps six inches from the nock. The archer let Parrish inspect the arrow again then bent the feathers back against their bindings till the quills lay flat against the shaft, the feather fronds standing proud, their free ends at the nock. Parrish nodded as the archer trimmed excess fronds from the top before pulling all three tight and binding them with more sinew, securing them and reinforcing the nock at the same time. Laying the feathers on a flat piece of wood, the archer trimmed them square with his flint then held up the finished article for Parrish to see. A beautifully fletched, three feathered shaft.

While Parrish closely inspected the marvellous piece of workmanship in minute detail, the archer brought out from his hut a small wicker basket and from it he selected a diamond shaped arrow head. Taking back the shaft he deftly slotted the flint into place and secured it firmly with more sinew. He handed the finished arrow back to Parrish with a grin and a 'voila' expression of the hands.

Parrish looked at the arrow with envy. It was obviously much too short for him to use to his full potential, an exact copy of the little ones he had shot the wolves with, but it was truly a thing of beauty in its own right. After some long moments of inspection he handed it reluctantly back.

"Now you know how, you must go and make your own arrows, Parrish."

Parrish didn't understand and gave the skilful man a puzzled look. The small man pointed at Parrish then made imitative binding movements over the new arrow. He understood.

"Thank." he said in his sparse Gaelic/Celtic, patted the man on the shoulder and bowed, then rose gingerly to his feet and immediately set off to start gathering his own arrow making components.

15

Harvest time. The sun didn't climb as high in the sky now but the wheat and barley had already soaked up its bright rays and now reflected it back in a glorious, golden brown.

The evening before the harvesting was due to take place, Oona went with all the other villagers to the great centre hut. Everyone was there. Everyone except Parrish.

She labouriously but sympathetically explained to him that he had no place there yet. There was to be a gathering, to ask for good weather during the harvest. His Gaelic/Celtic vocabulary was not yet big enough for him to understand that what she actually said was that all the people would give thanks. The Earth Goddess had been gracious and given the village a good summer season and a bountiful harvest because they had not offended her during the year. Tonight they would humbly ask for seven days uninterrupted good weather so they could dry, thresh and winnow the harvest.

Parrish had already guessed that it was inside the great hut where they worshipped whatever gods they believed in. So they were going to have another ceremony. Big deal. There had been others since he had arrived in the encampment and he'd gotten by OK so far without attending them.

Looking at it objectively, he reasoned, it seemed that the people of Danebury, and probably all the rest of Neolithic man, were very heavily into ceremonies. Every time a hunting party went out, which averaged about one a month, the night before was spent doing heaven knows what inside the great hut. He could hear the throbbing of drums and occasional chants. Parrish feigned indifference to it all in front of Oona, but he had to admit that it stung him to be left out. He told himself it wasn't out and out jealousy, but he would still have liked to have been there.

It was a cutting reminder that the villagers still saw him as an outsider and he knew what the people really thought of him. It was quite a twist of irony that these Stone Age people actually considered *him* to be a godless heathen! Even so, he would still have liked to have been involved in some small way.

When Oona tentatively gestured that she ought to go, Parrish felt like saying that she shouldn't bother, it was all mumbo-jumbo and a waste of time, but that would have been the green eyed monster talking, so he held his tongue. Hiding his disappointment, he waved her on her way, not registering at all that she was actually asking his permission to go. He still had not come to terms with the notion that women were not wives and people in their own right but just the property of the men that owned them. If he had wanted to be really spiteful he could have refused her permission to attend the ceremony and she would have had to obey, no matter how crucial and necessary she thought the ritual. After she had gone, Parrish went back to the symbolic solitude of his now log filled wicker hut on the high ground, sat with his back against one wall and looked down in the gathering dusk at the illuminated centre hut, with its muffled drum sounds and raised voices. Now completely alone, he could finally admit that he was just plain jealous and wished he was down there too.

Early the following morning the villagers congregated outside the hill fort in front of the patchwork fields of wheat and barley. Parrish was impressed. It was the first time he had seen the whole village acting together for one purpose. Everyone was there.

The elder children had been tasked to take care of the youngsters while the harvesting took place and to stand by ready, whenever called for, with drinking water. Every man who could wield a sickle was ready and waiting. The women stood behind them, ready to tie the fresh cut crops into small stooks and arrange them into the best drying positions. There were large tassels of thin tying cords hanging from straps looped about their waists. Parrish didn't envy them the job. Because the crop stems varied so much in length, he could see that it would be hard, back breaking work. Just cutting the stuff would be hard enough.

Parrish lined up with the other men to collect a sickle from the strange looking flower and feather man who was dispensing them singly from a neatly stacked pile in front of him. The little man gestured in the air with his hands over each tool before the recipient was allowed to take it, all the time uttering odd sounding words in a low voice.

Parrish still found it necessary to suppress a grin whenever he saw the funny looking little man with the totally outrageous hat. With his odd antics and clothes, plus the obvious reverence with which the rest of the villagers treated him, Parrish likened him to a jungle witch doctor. Still, he didn't seem in the least bit aggressive or threatening so perhaps the label was a little unkind. Parrish actually liked him. Even this early in the development of a British nation, Parrish could still recognize that quintessential English trait, the charming eccentric!

He received his sickle, without he noticed, any protest at all from anyone. It seemed that he wasn't good enough to attend their ceremonies but they didn't mind having his strong back for their work. He shrugged off the unspoken insult and joined the other harvesters waiting at the edge of the nearest field.

While waiting he examined the implement in his hand. The two foot long handle was apparently a carefully selected piece of timber. He surmised that by dint of the fact that all the other sickles he could see had identical, slightly curving shafts of the same dimensions. Near the head of the shaft, just below where the cutting stone was embedded, was an engraved symbol, looking like a bloated hour-glass with a small bud at its top for a head. Even Parrish's artistically uneducated eye recognized it as a very crude carving of a legless woman with oversized and very rounded hips and breasts. The cutting stone itself was a very skilfully knapped eighteen inch length of dark, high quality flint, tapering to a blunt point but with an almost shave sharp edge along its inside face. The stone was wedged and securely lashed into the head of the shaft.

All the harvesters now had a sickle and waited in a long line at the edge of the first allotment. Parrish looked along the line, feeling like he was back on parade, the women waiting solemnly a few paces behind. A few bodies down the line from him stood Klud. He felt Parrish's gaze and gave him a curt nod of acknowledgment. Parrish returned it. What were they all waiting for?

As if in direct answer to his question, the flower and feather man suddenly started to chant and dance about, arms raised and waving in the air. He flitted in and out of the small allotments, all the time continuing his crazy singing and dancing. Parrish smiled. Not a patch on Fred Astaire he thought, then criticized himself for being so frivolous. This odd ritual was obviously a very serious matter to the people of Danebury.

Finally, the flower and feather man stepped aside, beads of sweat glistening on his forehead.

"She is ready." he said with heavy reverence.

"Thank you Earth Goddess!" cried the harvesters as one. All except Parrish. He was totally unprepared for the sudden outburst. The flower and feather mans words he fully understood, the chant he only grasped as far as 'Earth'. Goddess was not yet in his vocabulary.

Before he had a chance to ask anyone to explain it, the harvesters moved en mass towards the first field of wheat, Parrish with them, and started in. Parrish was not wrong. It was indeed hard and back breaking work. To cut the wheat stems as close to the ground as possible meant stooping low. Particularly in the case of the tall man, it was suddenly a long way down to the ground, compounded by the fact that for him, the handle of his sickle was far too short. Made for these Neanderthal midgets, he grunted in a private joke. And it was just a joke too because, despite the discomfort, Parrish could not deny the fact that he was enjoying himself. It was the first time he had witnessed the whole population of Danebury working as a single coherent unit and he took a secret pleasure in being a part of it.

The harvesters mowed their way systematically through the chequered field system and it became increasingly plain that the whole crop intended to be cut in the one day. Even though the sun was now only pleasantly warm on the bent backs of the workers, the labour made it feel hot.

Shortly after the sun had peaked in the clear sky, one man called a halt.

Parrish still did not know that this one man was the Chieftain. He would find out only when the Chieftain decided that he should know.

Everyone retired gratefully to whatever shade they could find among the outbuildings by the corrals or beneath the wall of the hill fort. There the women waited with food and refreshment. Parrish had not even noticed when the ladies had disappeared to get the food, a short while before.

He found Oona sitting among several small groups of people who were squatting or lounging in the shade of an outbuilding. Spread out for him on a piece of hide was a selection of cuts from the smoked meats that hung in the roof space of their hut, a skin bag of cool water and a handful of large green apples, freshly picked. He thought they looked like giant Cox's pippins.

Parrish smiled. A picnic.

She held up one of the apples as he stood motionless in the sunshine. He accepted it and examined the fruit.

"Sit?" she asked, offering the ground beside her.

"Good idea." Parish agreed, forgetting for a moment and replying in English. He stretched tall, which in itself attracted the attention of the people close by, and rubbed the small of his back with his free hand.

"Not so good to be tall, Parrish." came a voice from behind him, the words not a question, just a flat statement. The tall man was instantly aware of a sudden humbling of the people nearby, who were only moments before watching with interest. He turned and found himself looking down at the little man with the hat of flowers and feathers. It was the first time Parrish had actually been so close to him. He was a small man even by Neolithic standards, not even five feet tall but he looked up into Parrish's eyes with a quiet arrogance. There was a dash of Sergeant Carter in the look and for a second Parrish was ready to challenge the stare, but thought the better of it. He did the reverse in fact, nodded in acknowledgment to him and sat down, taking a bite from his apple. After he had chewed and swallowed the pleasantly sweet mouthful, he looked up at the flower and feather man.

"Who is 'she'?" he asked in his slowly improving Gaelic/Celtic. There were gasps from the people on either side as he blatantly dared to question their revered holy man.

The little man was unmoved. His gaze switched from Parrish to Oona who seemed immediately to whither under his hard stare. Parrish fought the urge to jump to her defence, letting things run their course.

"Have you not yet told him about the great Earth Goddess. How she cares for us, feeds us and gives us our lives?" the little man asked her in a stern voice.

"His words are not yet good enough," she said humbly, "but he learns quickly. With your permission, I would like to wait until he knows more."

The unspoken truth of her words was that Parrish only understood the barest snatches of the short exchange. Too many unknown words and spoken too quickly.

The little man considered Oona's request for a moment, seemed satisfied with her explanation and nodded in agreement. Parrish didn't like to be talked about in front of his face when he didn't understand. He looked up and, keeping his temper tightly under control, asked again.

"Who is 'she'?"

" 'She' is the one who gave you that apple." was the little mans reply. He spoke slowly, like one would to an ignorant child, keeping it simple.

"Oona?" asked Parrish, puzzled.

"No." said the little man. "The Earth." And with that he walked away, seemingly magnanimous in his explanation. Everyone else relaxed and returned to their food, the show over.

By the day's end the entire crop had been harvested. Where once had stood glorious fields of wheat and barley was now patches of coarse stubble, interspersed with dozens of neatly bundled stooks of varying heights and sizes. The people finally returned their sickles to the care of the flower and feather man then moved as a crowd back towards the welcoming confines of the hill fort, a small moving sea of smiling, tired faces. One of the smiles belonged to Parrish. He felt that he had really achieved something today and was bursting to tell someone all about it. But there was no one. Oona walked a few paces behind her master, as was proper, and his smile died on his face when he realized he was still alone in the crowd.

Suddenly, from among the throng, a hand clapped him on the arm and he turned to see Klud at his side.

"You did well Parrish." he said, speaking slowly. Parish knew it was to be helpful in allowing him to understand and not in the condescending way the little man had spoken, implying he was an idiot.

"Thank you. I am tired."

"That is how it should be. Sleep well." Klud slapped him on the bicep again then moved off among the crowd.

It was only a brief exchange of words, but there were similar exchanges going on all the time in the crowd around him and for the first time, just for a short while, Parrish really felt that he was a part of

Danebury.

The stooks dried quickly during the next few days to a crisp, sandy colour. When the process was complete the women gathered them up and threshed them with long switches, working in shifts. They beat the wheat, small batches at a time, in a purpose made chalk bowl in the ground. That operation alone took several days. The bare stalks were removed and the wheat grains sifted through woven mats held high in the air. The breeze took away any particles of dirt, dust and of course, the chaff. A final winnowing was done by hand, tossing the grains into the air to remove the last of the chaff.

Parrish was fascinated by it all. To him the system was extremely old and outdated, the work itself incredibly labour intensive. What totally astounded him though was how efficient it all was. The storage pits in the ground around the edge of the village quickly filled up with fresh, clean grain. The seeds to be used for next year's planting were carefully packed into large clay jars that in size and shape reminded him of big wicker linen baskets. The tight fitting lids were then sealed down with woollen caulking and tallow fat, before they were whisked off to some storage place he didn't know the location of. Nothing was wasted. The wheat stems themselves were flattened and woven into mats. They had a multitude of uses, as a bonding agent for large wall repairs on huts to help hold the mud in place, for bedding mats and floor coverings inside huts, soft and flexible baskets and a hundred and one other applications.

Parrish would have liked to try his hand at a few of these skills but Oona talked him into not asking by explaining that it was really woman's work. He should concentrate more on his hunting skills. Besides, he wouldn't have to make his own flour because when there had been a plentiful harvest like this one, there would be gifts. When all the storage pits were full and next year's seed safely stored away, the remaining grain was immediately ground into flour and all the women of the village got together for a great bake. Then the ladies, all carrying loaves, would visit every family hut, where the holy man who led the procession would hand out bread to everyone. It was not a tradition as such but just a ritual sharing out of the excess from the harvest. It was not that common an occurrence either because more often than not there was not even enough grain to fill all the storage pits. Oona offered the suggestion to Parrish that perhaps he was good luck and the Earth Goddess smiled on him.

Parrish just smiled to humour her but was intensely curious about this mysterious Earth Goddess and what the flower and feather man had to do with it all. It took a whole evening for Oona to give him a general understanding of their beliefs.

She explained that the Earth Goddess was not at all mysterious. She was the land and everything on it. She was nature.

Back in the mists of time, Dannu, for that was her real name, had placed man upon the land, shaping him from a single ray of the suns light, giving him form so he might cast his own shadow. She gave him all the fruits of the land to live on. All the other creatures of her Earth had a mate for the continuation of their lives and so she brought him a woman, plucking her from the night sky as a falling star. This woman was Dannu's gift from her to him to use.

The Earth Goddess could be bountiful in her gifts or she could be harsh. To offend the Earth Goddess could be mortally dangerous. She could punish a great wrong by stopping the crops from growing or not allowing the sheep to have lambs. In a rage, she could wipe an entire village from the face of her land. Bad people could die terrible deaths and, even worse, not be allowed to return to the arms of the Earth Goddess or take their stall in the great shrine house of the spirits.

Parrish pressed Oona on these last points. It seemed, as far as he could make out, that if someone died and was offered up to be returned to the arms of the Earth Goddess, she would not accept them if their bodies were incomplete. He pressed more but there the conversation broke down completely, a combination of Oona not knowing all the answers and Parrish not having a big enough command of the language. Yet.

And what about the flower and feather man?

Oona explained that he was the village's link between themselves and Dannu. Their guide to her will. He performed all the functions necessary for the village to do her bidding, serve her and pay homage. She spoke through him and vice-versa. It was a position of great importance and he had been chosen very carefully. She could not explain that when the village, or any village for that matter, had chosen their holy man, he left the encampment to be educated in his new vocation at a special village that was devoted solely to the Earth Goddess and her mediums. This village was away to the north-west, near the site of Dannu's greatest temple. Oona was grateful that Parrish was at that time content with the explanations she had given. She did not know much more and feared she might say the wrong thing and offend the Earth Goddess. Never had she known a man who asked so many questions. He wanted, almost needed it seemed to her, to know about everything.

And Oona knew why.

Sometimes, when Parrish watched a person or event from his vantage point at the top of the knoll, beside his little wicker shed, Oona spied on him. She was astounded by the way he could sit, sometimes for up to half a day, without moving or even, it seemed from a distance, without breathing. Her suggestion that the Earth Goddess smiled on him was not an idle comment.

Oona firmly believed that while he sat motionless and apparently rooted to the ground, he was in contact with Dannu through her earth, even if he would not admit it.

Oona did not, dare not, tell her beliefs to anyone else. She believed that the Earth Goddess had sent the tall stranger to her to be educated in the ways of mortal man. She felt that it was the greatest honour for her to be chosen for this task and that Dannu would not let her return to the arms of the Earth goddess until his education was complete.

Parrish, Oona believed, was a special man sent by Dannu for some special purpose. After all, had he not just appeared one day, walking out of the vast land, bringing the hot sun with him? He was plainly no normal man and had already given hints that he was capable of extraordinary feats. He could not even speak at first but could withstand the force of an entire wolf pack and, when challenged by one of Danebury's best warriors, laid the attacker flat before he could lay a hand on him. He was plainly much too big to have been born from a woman and he learned quicker than anyone she had ever known. Yes, his life was most definitely closely entwined with the Earth Goddess. Oona believed Parrish was Dannu's man and it was her honour to teach him.

Parrish in the meantime, had learned how the women ground the fresh grain in large, curved saddle stones with another stone called a quern. They rubbed the quern stone back and forth in the hollow of the saddle, feeding in handfuls of grain, pulverizing it into a grey powder. The women then formed this flour into flat, dinner plate sized patties, sometimes adding herbs or nuts. They baked the patties in the same clay ovens used to fire their pots and the result was a two inch thick, hard crusted, unleavened loaf. To Parrish it looked very wholesome and appetizing. Put a good topping on it, he thought, and it would be a serious pizza!

At the 'handing out of the bread' ceremony, the procession, headed by their holy man, made its way around the encampment. It visited all the huts including Parrish and Oona's, although their hut was not officially regarded as one of habitation, being actually a small storage facility. Parrish accepted the loaves offered him with a nod but the flower and feather man paid him no more or less attention than anyone else. The tall man handed the stack of loaves to Oona.

"It is good." she said. "I did not think he would visit us."

"It is good that he did visit us." replied Parrish flatly. "Or I would have taken some bread from him anyway."

"You dare not. It would offend him and so offend the Earth Goddess. To protect the village from her anger, the men would make you leave the village, or even kill you."

That remark surprised Parrish. Did the funny little guy really have that much clout around here?

He let the subject go. He could see that the old lady trembled at the mere thought of him forcing a showdown with the Earth Goddess' right hand man. In fact, the more he thought about it the more he knew it would be a stupid thing to do. He did hope however that the little man had at least a modicum of common sense, or he could have this village running around in circles. Parrish shook his head. No, he was sure the little guy was OK even if he did wear a silly hat. In the three or so months he had been at Danebury the place had been run in a well organized and productive manner. Besides, Parrish liked the flower and feather man and his gut instincts were hardly ever wrong.

Obviously the little man didn't run the village, even if he did have a big say in what went on. So the question then was, who did run the village? Someone had to be top dog, at least to sort out the day to day running of the place and settle any disputes, or the place would rapidly collapse into unmanageable anarchy.

He had not even considered the thought before but now it intrigued him. Every village usually had a chief. Who was Danebury's and was he deliberately avoiding him? There was no doubt a reason *for* this chief person keeping his anonymity and, after some consideration, Parrish decided to play along. After all, his absence had not affected Parrish so far, so why push it? He never even broached the subject of chiefs with Oona but thought on it as he tucked into the fresh bread, which was surprisingly light in texture and very, very tasty.

16

Parrish was taking a quiet moment for solemn observation. He stood beyond the corrals and outbuildings, at the edge of the recently decimated allotments. The vast, rolling forests that ended at the edge of the sheep dotted, well grazed open land before him were a magnificent, multi-coloured picture. Autumn was in full swing and the trees were a riot of colour, from dark, rusty reds to softly glowing yellows. Beautiful as it was, Parrish could not avoid the fact that it meant winter was on its way.

He did not know what type of winters these people found themselves on the receiving end of in three thousand five hundred BC but he was wholly intent on making sure that *he* would be prepared for the worst. It wasn't pessimism, just good sense.

With the autumn had come the rain. It didn't rain all the time of course, but the precipitation was quite regular and sometimes arrived in very heavy downpours.

Hence Parrish's pondering observations. He had only experienced half a summer and the transition into autumn, but he could already tell that the seasons seemed to be very distinct and individual, classics of their type. Assuming that as the case, it stood to reason that a hot, sunny summer and a wet then frosty autumn would inevitably lead to a cold and snowy winter.

Oona said that the summer had been a good one and Danebury had done well. Even so, Parrish saw that the people had not lifted all that far off what he saw as their poverty line and he feared for these people if the winter did indeed turn out to be bad. He did not fear too much for his own well being. He could look after himself and he was still his own man, not really beholding to the people of Danebury in any real sense. But still his thoughts kept returning to the hard conclusion that a severe winter would be a killer in the place where he now lived. And it worried him.

Parrish was still deep within his morose thoughts, motionless and staring out into the distance, thinking of the future, when he was jarred back to the present by a firm tap on the shoulder. He turned to look down at the man who had interrupted his train of thought. It was his friend the archer.

"I have found you Parrish" he said, then gazed off in the direction the tall man had been looking. "What did you see?"

"This coming winter."

"Can you see beyond today?" asked the archer, suddenly very interested. "Has the Earth Goddess shown you what is to come?"

"No" laughed Parrish, determined to immediately quash any rumours that might start about him being gifted with foresight. He now knew how these peoples simple minds worked. "I was trying to see it in here." He tapped the side of his head. "I wonder what it will be like."

"Cold." said the archer sounding slightly disappointed that Parrish was only a normal, if a bit forward thinking, man. "Your words are much better now. You are learning well."

Parrish nodded at the compliment. "What is it you want?" he asked.

"I have sought you out to tell you that your bow is ready."

"Great!" exploded Parrish with a grin. "Where is it?"

"Go and get your arrows. I will meet you here in a short while."

"Great!" repeated Parrish and clapped the man violently on the shoulder as he passed him on the way back to the hill fort. The force of the blow made the Neolithic man stagger but Parrish did not see, he was excitedly walking back towards the camps entrance. The archer, looking on after him, smiled at the tall mans sudden good humour.

Parrish was very proud of his arrows. It had taken him considerable time and effort to make them and he hoped to impress the archer with the results.

The shafts had been relatively easy to make after a bit of practice and a few early disasters. Oona had helpfully pointed out the correct type of trees to cut the best arrow making branches from. Apparently, so he had learned, it was also possible to use reed stems if a lightweight arrow was required but, with what was expected to be a powerful bow, that idea was ruled out. Parrish had warmed, straightened and scraped his shafts as he had been shown. His own arrows were much longer than all the other arrows in the camp because of his size and reach. They were thirty six inches long as opposed to the standard Neolithic twenty four inch arrow.

His arrowheads had been bartered for from the canny old flint knapper who had enjoyed a joke at Parrish's expense that day. For a large hock of smoked meat he had received a small basket of specially selected arrowheads, given with a broad smile. Oona thought it best not to point out that the flint knapper could make top quality arrowheads by the dozen while in his sleep and normally a single loaf would have secured him the heads. For her, it was enough that Parrish was pleased with his few dozen arrowheads.

They were duly fitted to the ends of the shafts which now began to resemble proper arrows. He made eight hunting arrows to start with and four barbed, broadheaded 'man stoppers' as he liked to call them.

The question of fletching feathers had initially caused Parrish some concern. He had still not yet managed to catch any wildfowl in his traps, having only recently put any thought or effort in that direction, content up to now to stick with the regular income of his more conventional traps. He decided to go looking for feathers. Just trawl through the woods in the hope that he might find a few to tide him over until his new hanging cage bird traps proved successful. Or so he hoped.

It was the first time he had decided to move out beyond the immediate vicinity of Danebury since he had arrived in the summer and so, to ensure that he would be able to find his way back, he pulled the little brass button emergency compass from his Survival Aids kit. It was the size and depth of a Rollo and inside it pivoted a four pointed star, the north point marked by two luminous dots, the south by one.

"I am going to look for feathers."

He felt decidedly stupid when he said it to Oona but the old woman was totally understanding. In a few minutes she had placed a loaf of bread, plenty of dried jerky and some fresh fruit into a soft leather sack with a long strap. Parrish looped it over his head and it hung comfortably at his hip. Across his other shoulder hung a water bag. He wore his woollen cape and carried his poncho in case it rained. That was it, he thought. Talk about travelling light. Oona watched him as he made his way through the camp and out of the main gate.

In the entrance way, as an initial bearing, Parrish checked his compass and suddenly noticed a strange thing. Looking up from the settling pointer, he gazed back into the camp, suddenly aware of the fact that in all the huts that he could see, the entrances faced him. Even the smaller storage huts, including the one he and Oona lived in. According to the compass, all the entrances faced south east, even the main entrance to Danebury itself! There was probably a very good reason for this, but it still struck him as very odd.

Parrish set off into the forest, heading due south, apparently unobserved by anyone in the hill fort. In fact several people watched him go, including the Chieftain and the flower and feather man.

He was to be gone more than four days before he returned with a nice supply of feathers for fletching. It was pure luck that he had initially set off in the right direction and stumbled across a good supply of feathers. At least *he* thought it was good luck. Oona was certain that the Earth Goddess had directed him.

Parrish was two days out from the fort and still heading southwards into the Hampshire Basin when he heard a sound that he would never forget, coming faintly to his ears on the slightly chill breeze. Heading in the direction of the sound, he emerged from a dense wood into a large natural clearing. Central in the clearing was the most enormous clump of tall pines. High up in the topmost boughs of the straight trunked trees was the biggest rookery he had ever seen.

At the sight of him, several big black birds lifted into the sky, cawing loudly. A humourless smile creased Parrish's face as he eyed the wheeling birds.

"I don't suppose you lot know anything about a helicopter?" he shouted up, making them cry all the more. He ignored the cacophony of sound and moved swiftly across the open ground and into the shadowed shelter of the pines. On the forest floor beneath the evergreens there was, as is usual with pines, no undergrowth, just lots and lots of bird droppings. What delighted Parrish though, was that scattered on the ground among the muck lay plenty of preened, moulted or otherwise discarded feathers. He moved at his leisure among the dark trunks and soon had a fine collection of good sized, jet black wing tip feathers, ideal for fletching. The sheer volume of bird droppings told him that the rookery had been there a very long time and was probably going to remain so. That suited him fine and it was his intention to return periodically, whenever he needed fresh feathers for more arrows.

After placing his new prizes carefully into his sack, he made his way back to the edge of the cluster of pines. Just as he was about to emerge into the open, a large helping of fresh droppings landed with a wet slap on the sleeve of his combat jacket. He just looked at the mess while the cawing from above seemed to turn into laughter.

Fair enough, he thought, I can take a joke. Besides, I've got what I came for and isn't it supposed to be lucky to be spotted by a bird? He laughed with the birds for a moment then crossed the open ground back to the main forest and wiped the mess from his sleeve with a handful of fallen leaves. Throwing the dirtied leaves to the ground, he saluted the rookery in a gesture of thanks, turned on his heel and headed back to base, on a north bearing, leaving the big black birds calling noisily after him.

It wasn't quite the reaction he had hoped for when he joyfully showed Oona his feathers. She was shocked and dismayed.

"They are from the sky spirits!" she cried. "You must take them back. Say that you did not kill a sky spirit to get the feathers. Say you did not!" She put her hands to her head in an agonized way.

"Jesus," said Parrish in English. "Keep your hair on, they're only bloody feathers." He tried to calm her, thinking quickly to try and put the distraught old lady at her ease.

"I did not kill any crows, er, sky spirits." he corrected. "I have found where the spirits live and these are feathers they had no more need of and had thrown away."

"Is this true?"

"It is true. The sky spirits are unharmed and did not mind me taking the feathers." OK, so he lied about the last bit.

Oona nodded, a bit calmer. "I must go and tell the holy man. He must know this." And with that she left the hut and went off into the camp as fast as her old legs could carry her.

Parrish was waiting outside in the weak autumn sunshine when Oona returned, following a few paces behind the flower and feather man. There was purpose in the little mans stride.

"Is it true what Oona says?" he asked bluntly. "That you have visited the home of the sky spirits and they have allowed you to take some of their feathers?"

"I took the feathers from the ground beneath their nests." Parrish explained for a second time. "They had been thrown away because the sky spirits had finished with them." He shrugged. The conversation would have seemed ludicrous if it wasn't for the fact that these people took the whole thing so seriously. After all, they were only bird feathers.

The flower and feather man considered the new information. He seemed momentarily to be out of his depth.

"It is very rare for men to visit the spirits where they live. Perhaps they allowed you the feathers as a reward for your tracking skills."

Parish thought the man's reasoning was totally off the wall but decided not to upset him unnecessarily by contradicting it. To help pacify the man, he laid out his thirty odd feathers on the ground, selected the best one and offered it to the holy man as a gift. A gift from the gods?

The little man thought for a long, long moment, then nodded as if in agreement with his own reasoning and accepted the feather. He looked Parrish sternly in the eye.

"It looks as if the Earth Goddess really does smile on you, Parrish. Take care that you do not offend her. Her punishment is swift." And with that parting remark he spun on his heel and strode briskly off into the camp, holding the feather out at arm's length in front of him.

Parrish looked accusingly at Oona. Oona the gossip. She cowered under his stare and retreated swiftly into the shelter of the hut. When she had disappeared from view he smiled. Primitives!

Returning to the edge of the bare allotments clutching his arrows, Parrish found the archer waiting. In his left hand he held his own bow and a clutch of arrows. In his right, still unstrung and ramrod straight, was the most beautiful bow Parrish had ever seen. Of course, the tall man was biased in his view. Before he had arrived at Danebury the only bow he had ever seen was in Errol Flynn's hands when he played Robin Hood in that famous film.

The bow in question was a single straight piece of yew, skilfully shaped, the grip at its centre whipped tightly with leather thongs to provide a non slip surface. Leaning it against his shoulder, apparently unconcerned with Parrish's mounting excitement, the archer held out his hand.

"Let me see your arrows." Parrish handed them over. The archer inspected them closely, paying particular attention to the fletching. "Very good, Parrish. Soon, if you keep in practice, you will be making the best arrows. I had heard of your black feathers. Not all in the camp think it is right to use them."

"What do you think of it?" asked Parrish, smarting from having his arrows called second rate after he had spent so much time and effort on them.

"I am a bowman. I think only that if your spirit arrows fly with the same ease as the spirits they came from, soon they will be much sought after."

Parrish just nodded. "Can I have my bow?"

"But what will you offer me for it?" asked the archer, hoping to catch the tall man on the hop and perhaps do as well from the exchange as the knapper had. Word had got about that Parrish was still inexperienced when it came to bartering. The archer was to be disappointed because this time Parrish was ready for the question. He pushed his hand deep into the pocket of his combat jacket and produced a small square of flat, folded grease proof paper.

"This will help you make good arrows." he said and gingerly unwrapped the paper while the archer looked on with curiosity.

It was a fresh, new and shiny Gillette razor blade. One of the ten blades that army regulations stipulate must be carried at all times in a soldiers personal wash kit. The archer was obviously mystified by the strange object.

"What is it?" he asked, baffled.

"It is a special cutting tool." Parrish went into his well rehearsed sales pitch. "It is made from a very special, secret stone and it will trim feathers and split quills much better than your finest flint."

"My flints are the sharpest in the camp." said the archer scornfully and plucked the double edged blade from Parrish's palm, unfortunately, by its top and bottom edges. Blood flowed as the blades cut into the pads of his finger and thumb. The small man didn't yell or even flinch but his face registered complete surprise. Parrish took back the razor blade and carefully wiped the small droplets of blood from it.

"If you fit a handle along its centre, following the slot, you will have a tool that will trim feathers with ease. As you see, it is very sharp."

The archer nodded, sucking his finger and thumb in turn. He took the blade a second time, this time holding it in the centre as Parrish did, and examined the two cutting edges more carefully. He still managed to cut himself again.

"I have never seen anything like it." he said finally and Parrish knew he had a sale. "What is it made of?"

"It is called 'metal' and you must guard it well. It is very rare here." If only he knew how true that was, thought Parrish.

"Agreed." said the archer and handed Parrish the bow while he carefully packed away his new prize in its paper wrapping.

The tall man inspected his bow more closely. It was as thick as his wrist at the whipped grip and the carefully shaped prods tapered gracefully to nocked tips. The overall length of the unstrung bow was actually a few inches taller than the man holding it. Parrish guessed it at six foot three.

"Thank you ..." Parrish suddenly realised that he didn't even know the man's name. "What are you called?"

"I am Mars." said the archer, secretly enjoying the compliment of having his work appreciated. The tall man's face said it all.

That's appropriate, thought Parrish, god of war and all that.

"Well, thank you Mars, it is a good bow."

The Neolithic man just nodded and handed him a small leather pouch. In it were three bowstrings of twisted and braided gut. Parrish selected one and uncoiled it. It was slightly greasy to the touch. Hooking one looped end in the bottom nock of his bow, he jammed the end along the edge of his boot and, with a firm pull, bent the bow and engaged the string in the opposite end nock. Now strung, his bow still dwarfed the one held by Mars. Parrish had apparently primed his bow in the correct manner because the small man nodded sagely. Putting his own arrows on the ground, the Neolithic archer selected one and nocked it to his string. He turned about and faced the hill fort, or more exactly, the mud and thatch outbuildings thirty yards away, directly in front of them. Their wattle and daub walls, which Parrish knew from his own inspection that very first day at Danebury, were about four inches thick.

"I will shoot an arrow into the wall." Mars said. "You do the same. Watch carefully how I draw and aim the bow."

Planting his feet roughly twenty inches apart, he stood side on to his intended target and drew his bow, pushing with the bow hand while at the same time pulling with the arrow hand. At full draw, the archer's chest was framed inside the bow, the bow string drawn back to the ear and the arrow elbow raised to the horizontal.

Mars released the missile in a smooth, almost fluid motion and it blurred its way across the gap between them and the mud wall, burying itself several inches into the hard, sun baked surface. Parrish nodded at the demonstration of skill.

Before he could nock his own arrow the archer took hold of his bow arm and tied a long, flat guard stone over his jacket sleeve, on the inside of his forearm. Only then did the tall man notice that Mars wore one too. Parrish nodded his thanks then nocked his own arrow to his string. The archer interrupted him again by adjusting the black fletched arrow on the string, turning it till the single feather was on the outside. Parrish made a mental note of it. Copying the small mans smooth action, he drew the big bow back to his ear, expanding his chest and keeping the arrow elbow raised. The effort required to complete the action made him grunt.

"Well done Parrish. I have tried but could not draw it fully."

Parrish barely heard him. His concentration was absolute and the effort required to keep the weapon at full draw was considerable. Taking careful aim along his arm at the target arrow, sticking starkly out from the mottled surface, he released. The bowstring smacked loudly against the stone guard on his forearm. Neither man saw the fired arrow clearly during its brief flight. There was a slight whooshing sound and, with a small burst of dust, the missile passed cleanly through the wall, leaving a small hole about a foot above the first archer's arrow.

"Shit!" said Parrish softly in English.

"Yes." agreed Mars, not understanding the word but grasping the sentiment.

They walked to the wall, inspected the hole then went inside the hut. The arrow was lodged firmly into the opposite wall, wrecked by its passage through the wattle and daub, the fletching stripped clean away.

The two men walked back out into the cool air and Parrish, a smile on his face, tugged a few times at his bowstring.

"I could shoot a few wolves with this." he said.

"Yes Parrish" agreed Mars and put his finger to the tall mans right cheek. Not understanding, Parrish did the same and could feel the mottled, lined surface he had first noticed when recovering from being attacked. Before he could raise the subject with his tutor, the archer strode off back to where their arrows lay and Parrish followed. Mars pointed out into the barren fields.

"I have placed a target, see?"

"That upright skin stretched on its frame?" asked Parrish, noticing the object for the first time. "About forty yards away?"

Mars didn't understand 'yards' but nodded. He nocked another arrow, drew, aimed and released in one flowing movement, almost it seemed, in slow motion. The arrow flew a graceful shallow arc and with an audible 'pop', punched through the taught skin.

Parrish copied the demonstration, only more slowly, and loosed his own arrow. The length was good but he missed to the right and the missile thudded into the earth a few yards further on.

"Not too bad Parrish. A little practice and soon you will be able to hit a deer every time that far away."

"Or a man." said Parrish.

"Or a man." agreed the archer, apparently unconcerned at the suggestion of a more controversial target. "Let us see what your reach is."

With that he nocked a third arrow and, aiming into the air at about a thirty degree angle, let fly. The speeding arrow was a thing of grace and beauty as it crossed the sky and fell to earth a good ninety plus yards from where they stood.

"Well shot." said Parrish and readied his own bow. He drew, the arrows fletching a jet black slash alongside his cheek, aimed up at thirty degrees and smoothly released. While the arrow was still in flight, Mars spoke.

"It is the furthest I have ever seen."

The two men watched in fascination as the arrow rifled through the air, finally falling to earth over two hundred yards away. Parrish turned slowly to his companion.

"It is truly a great bow. You should be proud to have made it and I am proud to own it. There is no other like it." The final statement Parrish felt sure was indisputable.

"You are the only man who could draw such a bow." nodded Mars, returning the compliment and together they unstrung their bows and walked forward to retrieve their arrows. No more words were spoken. The two totally different men were united in the common respect for skill at arms.

Parrish returned to his hut and proudly showed Oona his bow. The only comment she had to make was that it was very big. Parrish was a bit crestfallen at her apparent disinterest but, almost as if to cheer him back up, she produced from among her own belongings a leather quiver she had secretly made. It was long enough to accommodate his giant arrows and Parrish accepted the gift gracefully, enchanted with the gesture.

"Thank you." he said with feeling and, bless her, the old dear went all coy on him. He slotted the arrows home, slung the quiver on his back and tried a few draws from it, laying each arrow that he pulled experimentally across his bow in the process. Something the archer had done suddenly came back to him. He put a finger to his cheek.

"Oona, what is this?"

"It is your mark." she replied. "It tells what you have done."

More curious now, Parrish went to his webbing and rummaged through a pouch, looking for the small reflective surfaced heliograph plate that was in there somewhere. Peering at his reflection in it, he examined closely the marks on his face. He had a tattoo, bright blue in colour! A cross hatching pattern similar to a noughts and crosses grid and below it a row of five big round dots.

"What do you mean, it shows what I have done?"

"It is the sign of the wolf killer." she explained. "The dots say how many."

He was surprised that he had not noticed the marks earlier. Thinking on, he recalled that most of the men in the camp sported tattoos of one kind or another.

"Do all tattoos mean something?"

"Of course. Why have a mark that does not say anything?"

"What do the other tattoos say?"

"Each is different." The expression on her face said she was explaining to him something that even a five year old knew. "They speak of good hunting skills, great feats or victories in battle."

"Then there are many brave warriors in Dane-bre." He had seen several men who were absolutely plastered with tattoos. Klud was one of them.

He thought on it for a moment. He should have been annoyed but wasn't. In fact, he kind of liked it. It was a bold statement and a sort of trophy, something to be worn with pride. A medal of honour and achievement. He smiled. Eat your heart out Sergeant Carter.

Oona stood watching Parrish for a moment while these thoughts whizzed around inside his head then, realizing that he was paying her no more attention, went on about her business. Parrish fingered his tattoo for a moment more, then picked up his bow and began to examine it in minute detail.

17

Parrish could regularly be seen, away on the far edge of the grazing land, practicing his archery whenever time and weather permitted. The heavy rains had started to give way to frosts and cold winds. Most of the leaves were now gone from the trees.

Mars had warned the tall man against excessive use of his bow in very cold conditions and Parrish respected the archers advice, taking care to protect his weapon from damage by not over flexing the timber when the wood was cold.

The tall man paid closer attention now to any signs and actions within the hill fort. He was, on the one hand, enjoying the small victories that came his way such as the success of his new thatching at repelling the rainwater and frost. Also, his increasing accuracy with the longbow at ever longer distances. On the other hand, small defeats that he registered as an individual were also being inflicted on others throughout the camp. What affected one affected all. The rains and then the frost seemed to slow down the pace of the entire village. Buckskins were difficult to dry and woollen capes were only waterproof up to a point. The ground around the huts soon turned into thick mud and even a simple act like starting a fire could be a long and frustrating process.

More and more frequently, Parrish would find his traps empty. The animals had either migrated or simply stayed under cover, sheltering from the inclement weather. He knew that soon some of the beasts he relied on for food would start their winter hibernations and the number of animals that fell to his traps would dwindle even more. Throughout the camp he could see other people doing as he himself had already started to do, dipping occasionally into their winter supplies.

He watched a hunting party go out on a trip that unfortunately coincided with a long clear spell of dry weather that allowed an almost permanent, heavy frost to lay. Only four days later the party returned cold, hungry and dejected. It was the first time Parrish had seen a party return empty handed. The heavy disappointment could be felt throughout the entire camp.

Another sad first for Parrish was hearing from Oona that there had been a death in the camp. He didn't know the dead boy but that didn't make the news any more palatable. From the old ladies rudimentary description, Parrish surmised that the lad had caught a cold then died from the resulting pneumonia. Oona didn't seem to dwell to long on the subject. What did it matter how you died. When you were dead, you were dead.

It was with morbid curiosity that he watched from his lone vantage point how these ancient people treated death. There was a small, sombre ceremony inside the hut where the deceased had lived. Then a family procession, carrying the body and being lead by the flower and feather man, left the camp. The little man kept up a constant quiet, soft chanting. The words were unknown to Parrish but the feeling of the song was appropriate enough. It gave the tall man no pleasure to notice that the black feather he had given the holy man now had pride of place on the top of his hat.

The procession walked slowly across the frost whitened ground for about three quarters of a mile to a small knoll in the east. The sun rose directly over the knoll and Parrish felt sure there was some significance in that. In the distance, he could see the little silhouettes moving among the sparse trees atop the knoll.

"What happens there, Oona?"

"It is where we are offered up to the sky spirits." she answered in a revered tone of voice.

"And when the spirits come, what happens then?"

"When they have finished their work, the frame that carries the soul is put into the care of the earth. When the Earth Goddess decides the time is right, she will collect the frames and re-unite them with their souls. Then the dead will be re born and can again walk in the sun."

Parrish nodded solemnly as a mark of respect but he didn't have a clue what she meant.

The bereaved family finally returned from the eastern knoll and the camp once again dropped back into normal routine. The people seemed to just shrug off the death but Parrish couldn't help feeling sorry for the one woman who remained sad. She received no comforting from anyone. He wanted to go down and try to offer her some soothing words but he did not. There weren't any.

The weather grew colder.

Parrish noticed signs of bustle among the men of the camp and knew what it meant. He called Oona over.

"There is going to be another hunting party isn't there?"

She nodded.

"How do I go about joining it?"

"Why would you want to hunt for the people?" she asked, surprised."You owe them nothing."

Parrish just shrugged. It somehow seemed like the right thing to do.

"I will ask." she said and went off into the camp.

The flower and feather man arrived a short while later and together they walked back the way he had come. The journey ended outside the large living hut with the front porch that sported the carved pillars and painted skulls at its entrance. Under the shelter of the porch, warming his hands by the fire that burned just outside it, sat a man, several layers of woven matting insulating him from the cold ground. Parrish was aware of watching eyes peering timidly from behind the door blanket that hung across the huts doorway behind the man.

Oona waited outside the porch, head bowed. As the pair approached, the waiting man rose to his feet. The flower and feather man lead the way under the porch awning and sat. Parrish did likewise and finally, the third man sat down.

He was quite impressive, although not in stature, only being about five foot three and of a medium Neolithic build. He had a lot of tattoos which told Parrish something, but he had a certain air. The presence of a man who knew what he wanted, commanded respect and got it. A man who knew what went on about him. A man in charge.

There was a brief, tense moment of confrontation as the two men challenged each other with their eyes. Parrish held the other mans stare long enough to let him know that he was not frightened or intimidated by him. When he saw it register in his eyes, then and only then did he lower his gaze as a mark of respect. There was an audible sigh from the flower and feather man as the tension eased.

"I am Coran." said the man suddenly. "I am Chieftain of Dane-bre."

Parrish bowed as deeply as he could in his sitting position, a gesture that seemed to be appreciated by the man it was aimed at.

"Greetings Coran, Chieftain of Dane-bre. I had wondered when we would meet."

"You knew I was Chieftain?" asked Coran, surprised.

"No, but I knew there must be a leader. I wondered why he had not sought me out."

"I have watched you Parrish. There was no need for you to know me until it was necessary. You have so far done no harm to the village and so you have been permitted to stay."

"Then you are a good leader Coran. It is a wise man who watches first before deciding how and when to act."

Coran nodded, accepting the compliment simply as a statement of truth.

This opening exchange between the two men left both the holy man and Oona open mouthed. It was very rare for the Chieftain to ever explain his reasoning's to anyone and it was positively unheard of for another man to speak to the Chieftain as an equal. Neither of the two men involved in the exchange were in the least bit perturbed.

Coran had already gauged Parrish as a man of extraordinary power and a far reaching outlook. The tall man had posed questions already about what lay ahead for both him and Danebury. The Chieftain was well in formed at all times. There was also the strong rumour and distinct possibility that the tall man was in some way connected to the Earth Goddess. He had no intention of bringing the wrath of Dannu down upon the village by acting rashly with this man.

Parrish himself already had the Chieftain figured as a man of intelligence and at least limited forward thinking. This man knew what went on and controlled the camp with just the right balance of guidance and discipline. The simple fact that Danebury ran smoothly and its defences were in good order was testimony to this and it was because of it that the man had Parrish's respect.

"You speak well now Parrish. You learn quickly."

It was true enough for, although Parrish still had a little trouble with the pronunciation of some of the longer words, he had put in four months hard work to learn the language. He was just pleased it was a simple language.

"Oona is a good teacher."

"Your woman tells us that you wish to join our hunting party." Coran glanced at Oona who immediately lowered her gaze even more.

"It is true."

"Why would you want to do this?"

"Because it is plain to see that food is getting more difficult to hunt. Did not the last party return with empty hands?" Parrish waved in the general direction of the camp.

"This is true," replied Coran," But you did not answer my question."

"I would like to help the village. It, you, have allowed me to live here. I have a bow now and I would like to offer my skill. I have a debt to the village of Dane-bre." The reasoning was pretty thin, thought Parrish, but at least it's the sort of language they would understand. It wasn't reason enough and he was disappointed by Coran's reply.

"You cannot hunt with the village."

"Why not?!" It was half question, half indignation.

The flower and feather man, shocked that Parrish should question the Chieftains judgment, interrupted the tall man.

"You do not understand Parrish."

"Huh?"

"We know you respect our worship of the Earth Goddess but we think that you do not believe in her. Are we wrong in this?"

Parrish took a deep breath. The big question. No one likes to have their religion shot down and he wondered how they would react. He took the plunge.

"I cannot lie." he said slowly. "I do not believe in the Earth Goddess."

Oona put her hands over her ears. The holy man shook his head violently in disagreement. Coran gave him a hard stare.

"But," he continued," I do respect *your* belief in her and I would not knowingly do anything that would offend the people of Dane-bre or their Goddess."

There was a long silence. Parrish realized that he might just have shot himself in the foot by speaking the truth. One word from the Chieftain now and he would be out of Danebury on his ear. He didn't consider being put to death a possibility. The people didn't work like that.

Parrish was right, but for the wrong reason. He had no idea at all how much the Neolithic community connected him, however misguided that connection might be, with their Earth Goddess and would not even consider killing him.

"Your words and actions are of a true man, Parrish." said Coran finally. "I respect the truth and that is why I have allowed you to stay with us. It is also the reason why you cannot hunt with us. If you do not respect the Earth Goddess you cannot ask her to guide you with tracks and to steer your arrows. She would not join us on our hunt if you were with us."

Parrish understood the statement, correctly, to mean that if he couldn't attend the ceremony the night before because he didn't believe in it, he couldn't go on the hunt. Attempting to argue the point would just be a waste of breath and he knew it. It annoyed him to once again be cut off from real involvement in Danebury, remaining still an outsider. But, as he had just said, he respected their views.

Biting back his anger and disappointment, he nodded to both men and rose purposefully to his feet. Something else that would not normally be tolerated by the Chieftain. No one was permitted to stand over him.

"Then I shall hunt alone." said Parrish defiantly and strode away.

Oona looked pleadingly at the Chieftain and he waved her away. She hurried off after her master.

"What will you do now?" asked the holy man.

"Leave him. I have watched Parrish and learned much. He can trap food and he can shoot a bow but I do not think he can track and hunt. He will soon learn that I am right in my decision."

"And what about the Earth Goddess? He openly denied her existence."

Coran looked at the holy man.

"Do you think that he has any contact at all with Dannu?"

The holy man paused before answering. "Yes. Yes I do. He has done things that only the Earth Goddess would allow. I believe she smiles on him constantly."

"Yes." agreed Coran. "I too see that he must be from Dannu's arms. No normal man could do the things he has done. I have never seen a man that learned so quickly."

"Or survive a wolf attack, or catch so many fish, and what happened with Klud." added the holy man.

"Yes." repeated the Chieftain. "These things only the Earth Goddess would allow. And yet she has blinded his eyes to her for some reason. Could it be to test us? To see how we treat him? Perhaps she wishes to see if we are worthy of her good fortune?" He looked to the flower and feather man for answers to his questions.

"I do not know." said the small man, feeling the full power of the Chieftains stare. "But if it is a test, she would not allow us to know."

Coran considered for a long moment, then nodded and waved the holy man away. The small man left the cover of the porch feeling distinctly like he had somehow just had a narrow escape.

The hunting party departed from Danebury early the following morning. Parrish gave them a good head start before setting off himself, following their trail into the bare forest. He had independently come to the same conclusion as the Chieftain, admitting to himself that he could not track and hunt, but he was still determined to prove that he could bring home a kill of his own. The only way he envisaged accomplishing just that was to follow the hunting party at a discrete distance until they had led him unknowingly to their best hunting ground. Once there, he would head off on his own. There was no fear of him not finding his way back to camp whichever way they went, he had his co pass. Then would come the hard bit, actually achieving a kill. His best chance would be to move well away from the hunting party, settle in what he hoped would be a good spot, and do what he was good at. Wait. And hope that some unsuspecting beast would pass nearby.

His main enemy then would be the cold but he tried to look on the bright side. His hexi stove would guarantee him warmth and hot food when he needed it. He also had a fully waterproof poncho in the event of rain. The temperature was close enough to freezing for there to be a distinct possibility of some snow. The Neolithic hunters on the other hand, had to rely solely on their woollen capes for any added warmth and protection from the weather, while it was unlikely that they would enjoy a fire or hot food at all during their hunt.

The party was easy to follow. With no need for immediate stealth so early on, they just stomped their way through the frost covered leaves of the forest floor.

Apart from occasional dense thickets of holly or brambles and blinds of close growing bushes, the forest was open enough for Parrish to catch the occasional fleeting glimpse of movement from the party a couple of miles ahead of him if they happened to be on rising ground. This happened periodically because of the gently undulating terrain. The whole troop, with Parrish tagging along unseen, moved steadily north eastwards for the entire first day.

There were no fires as the travellers settled for the night. Parrish, still a couple of miles behind and south east of the hunting parties position, was sheltering under his poncho on land that would, in fifty five centuries time, be levelled as part of the construction of the Andover ring road.

It was not a very comfortable night and all concerned were more than ready to move off again at first light.

It was after noon when Parrish came to the site where the trail split into two. No doubt they had split up to increase their chances of success. After a moments consideration the tall man chose to follow the left trail. It got preference over the right simply because the parties original direction had been north east. When they had separated, the left hand group headed more directly north. That meant that when returning, Parrish could just head south on a back bearing and thus take a more direct route back to Danebury. A shorter return trip.

The trail was harder to see now and it was painfully obvious to Parrish that if he had trouble following the tracks of eight men, it would be nigh on impossible for him to track a single animal. He knew the trail was of eight men because he had counted sixteen persons in the hunting party as they had left Danebury. When they had split up into two groups, he had no doubt they would break into even parties.

The second night was colder than the first. After settling in a small hollow, Parrish dug a hole in the hard earth with his survival knife and put his little stove in it before lighting the waxy, white paraffin fuel blocks. He risked the small fire and the chance of being spotted, balancing it against the need for some hot food. The food itself was reviving, warming the inner man, while the heat from the flames boosted his morale. Parrish was grateful for it but extinguished the stove immediately the food was hot. It was not just to save on fuel blocks. His army training was coming to the fore and he had gone tactical to the point of smearing his face and the back of his hands with cam cream. After eating and packing away his kit, he settled down in the dark.

In the middle of a forest so big that a squirrel could probably travel for a hundred miles without ever leaving the high branches, Parrish remained quiet and still, just listening. A chill wind moaned softly in the tops of the bare trees but apart from that the world around him was silent. He had no difficulty in coming to the simple conclusion that it was going to get very cold and there wasn't a lot going on in the wilderness. It did not bode well for the hunt.

At first light he was glad to be up and moving, still following in the footsteps of the reduced hunting party. The day went slowly. There was no sun, the sky grey and overcast.

Up ahead of him the six men and two youngsters, who were there to hone their hunting skills, had slowed dramatically. One of the trackers had picked up a deer trail and the rest of the party followed his lead, from then on moving slowly and carefully. They tracked the cautious animal through the forest for the next few hours. It was slow work in the cold, the deer always moving roughly northwards but seeming to just keep ahead of them, a flitting shape among the trees, just out of bow range.

The deer stopped, quite suddenly, beside a particularly thick blind of dense undergrowth in front of a cluster of holly bushes. It froze, ears pricked, tail twitching and eyes peeled. Something had alerted the animal. Its nose sniffed the air urgently, hoping to pick up a warning scent. The hunters assumed it was trying for theirs but the cold breeze blew west to east across the forest, between the hunters and their prey. The men edged slowly forward into bow range, taking full advantage of the deer's indecision. It was still motionless, apparently not sure which way to move in order to avoid possible danger. Finally getting to within forty yards, the lead tracker let fly an arrow which went deep into the deer's flank. The animal cried out in pain and tried to get away but only managed to travel a few yards before several other arrows from different archers brought it down.

Parrish heard the deer's death cry. It was very close. Carefully, he readied his bow.

The hunters had gathered around their prize, smiles on their faces and quiet congratulations on their lips. Two men knelt beside the carcass and started removing the arrows.

With a furious, ear shattering roar, a brown bear barrelled its way through the blind behind the kill. He was as hungry as the men who were invading his territory, and looking for a final meal to help fortify him through his impending hibernation. The dead deer was his, easy meat.

Before the group of men could even register full surprise, the bear was upon them. A backhanded paw sent one man reeling to the ground as the bear pounced on the deer carcass. Of the two kneeling men, one was killed outright by slashing claws that opened his chest wide, exposing slippery wet, still pulsating internal organs to the sky. The second man had gained his feet before he was struck a glancing blow which was still powerful enough to send him sprawling, blood flowing from his slashed shoulder.

One of the youngsters, quicker to recover than the rest of his still retreating companions, managed to release a hastily fired arrow which did not improve the situation at all. It jabbed ineffectually into the bears shoulder, infuriating the beast even more. It wiped the arrow away and looked for someone to vent its fury on, choosing the injured man lying groaning on the ground before him. The unfortunate man shielded his face with his good arm in a futile gesture as the bear reared spectacularly up onto its hind quarters, claws ready to slash, teeth ready to tear.

There was a solid sounding thud. The bear froze in his upright position, suddenly surprised and puzzled. Not two seconds later there was a second thud. In reaction to it, the bear let out a mournful howl. Its head went up and the beast teetered for a moment then fell backwards to the ground. The animal's powerful limbs peddled frantically for a few seconds, raw coughing sounds coming from its throat. A final breath came out of the bear in a long, rasping sigh, and it went limp and still.

The hunting party was astounded. All their bows were now ready to fire but there was no need. After a few moments of stunned silence they all moved hesitantly closer, still not convinced that the bear was dead.

Needing attention, the injured man groaned and the two youngsters went to his aid. The man who had been cuffed to one side struggled to his feet, very fortunate not to be injured at all. Another hunter glanced briefly at the other man on the ground. There was no doubt as to his condition.

As if drawn by a magnet, the entire group, including the injured man who was being supported by the youngsters, gathered around the dead predator.

Sticking out of the bears chest, quite close together, were two arrows. They were deeply embedded, not more than a foot of each shaft was visible.

The fletching on the ends of the shafts was jet black.

As one, the men turned, peering into the forest in the direction the arrows had come from.

There was nothing to be seen.

18

"You did not get anything?"

"No!" replied Parrish bluntly.

He was not a happy man and the last thing he needed was guarded sarcasm from Oona. To the rest of the camp it seemed like he had set off on his hunt full of bravado and rich boasts, only to return a mere four days later empty handed. He had promised, not delivered and made a fool of himself.

Parrish didn't care about his loss of face. In his present mood he didn't care what the Neolithic nit-wits thought of him. He was only worried about what would happen when the hunting party returned and what had happened in the forest became known. Beating the hunters back to Danebury by a day or two just gave him more time to brood on the outcome of it all. They could well be his last days in the hill fort.

Parrish well remembered his conversation with the Chieftain. Coran had said he could not hunt with the village. Parrish said he would hunt alone. He had both lied and disobeyed the Chieftains decision.

It had seemed like such a good idea at the time, to follow the hunting party unseen to their hunting grounds. He'd been careful and as long as they didn't know, there would be no problem. That had all changed when he'd given himself away by putting two of his very distinctive arrows into that bear. Of course, he couldn't have just stood by and watched while the beast turned the hunting party into mincemeat. He had saved the men, but at what cost to himself? The Chieftains word was final. When Coran found out he had done specifically what he'd been told not to, that would be it. He'd be lucky if the whole camp didn't send him out into the wilderness with an arrow up his arse!

For the next two days, until the hunt returned, Parrish was on tenterhooks. He busied himself as best he could, readying his equipment so he could move out quickly when ordered away. Oona wasn't sure what was happening but she didn't like it. When she tentatively questioned his actions or offered to help, he flew off the handle. The old lady retreated into the background, offended and upset. Parrish immediately regretted his actions but was in no mood to apologize. He had his own worries.

He didn't attend the grisly heart eating ceremony when the party finally did return. The catch was not huge but at least they'd had some success, with several deer and an old wild pig that looked too tough to eat at all. Parrish was not there to join in the elation. He stayed inside the hut and no amount of coaxing by Oona would make him budge. A final check of his kit made him realize that he really needed a backpack of some sort. He'd be leaving Danebury with his arms full.

The rest of that day passed uneventfully. Parrish knew that Coran must have been told and was trying to make him sweat. He was succeeding!

The following morning, Parrish was still inside the hut, lacing up his boots while Oona went out into the frosty air to start a cooking fire. The temperature inside the hut was not a lot higher than outside and Parrish clapped his arms around himself to keep warm. He was just wondering how long it would be before Oona could rustle up some hot food when the old lady burst in through the door blanket. Little crystals of ice that had formed on the outside of the blanket flew in every direction as her sudden entrance dislodged them from the weave. She gestured to the outside, a look of awe and fear on her face.

"What?" asked Parrish. "WHAT?"

"It is the Chieftain!" she gasped. "He comes."

Even Parrish knew that the Chieftain never visited people at their huts. They always went to him. Oona was astounded. Parrish was just filled with impending doom. This is it, he thought.

"Parrish!"

The call did not sound angry, just firm and demanding. A silence hung in the air. Oona, more fearful of the Chieftains wrath than that of her master, tried to usher Parrish out to meet him. The tall man stopped her gestures with a raised palm, then stooped through the doorway and emerged into the cold, stinging air to face the music.

The Chieftain stood beside Oona's unfinished fire. He was well wrapped in furs, his features partially obscured by the small clouds of condensation that burst in front of his face every time he exhaled. In his hands were two instantly recognizable arrows. Parrish eyed them and the Chieftain held them out.

"Yours?" The question sounded mocking.

Without a word, Parrish took his arrows. They were clean and one had been fitted with a new flint head. Coran just looked at him. The tall man shrugged. Neither man seemed in a hurry to say anything. The Chieftains gaze was unwavering and Parrish could feel Oona's eyes too, peeping from behind the door blanket at his back. He dropped his eyes in submission.

"You travelled with the hunting party Parrish." It was a damning statement. To say 'not exactly, a couple of miles behind actually', would have been splitting hairs and insulting Coran's intelligence.

"I did not intend them to know. Once they had led me to where they hunted I would have gone on alone."

"But you travelled with them. Against my decision."

"Yes." Parrish bowed his head. He decided then to save Coran the trouble of actually ordering him out.

"I will leave Dane-bre. I disobeyed you and it was very wrong of me. I am sorry." He heard Oona gasp and found himself briefly wondering if it was because of the news of his impending departure or of him disobeying the word of the Chieftain.

Coran's expression never changed but he smiled inwardly. He had already gotten what he had come for. A humble apology from the tall man and the understanding that *he* was the Chieftain and what he said was not to be taken lightly.

"You will not leave, Parrish."

"Huh?"

"Only the Holy man and you know that I decided not to let you hunt with the village." He shot a hard stare in Oona's direction and she got the warning message. "Everyone else thinks that the Earth Goddess steered your tracks to the same place as the hunters to help them kill the bear with your powerful bow."

"Did they not wonder why I never showed myself?"

A brief smile crossed Coran's face. "I just told them you probably had your reasons for not doing so."

Parrish understood. He was still a man of mystery and who knew how his mind worked? The villagers still thought of him as stupid and ignorant of their ways. Coran seemed to be able to read his mind.

"They think you are stupid and so you have lost face." he said.

"That is of no real matter. I tell you, there are a few who think you are special Parrish, but there are many that think you are of no real use to the village and that I should cast you out." He waved his hand in a dismissive gesture. "That is of no matter either. I have my own thoughts." Coran was obviously referring to the men of the camp, the women not even being allowed to voice an opinion. "But, if I thought the truth might ever be known about you disobeying me and cause *me* loss of face, you would not be here now."

Parrish wasn't sure if that meant he'd have been immediately ejected from Danebury, or killed on the spot.

"But I still went against your decision and disobeyed you." He waited for Coran's retribution.

"You were fortunate. My decision was wrong." There was another gasp from Oona at the revelation. Parrish waved her silent as Coran continued. "The Earth Goddess smiles on you Parrish. She smiled on the hunt too, even though you were with them and so, I was wrong. The catch was not good but still better than the empty hunt before it. I would not upset Dannu by turning you out into her forest when she is about to send us hard weather. You must stay."

Parrish nodded, a weight lifted from his shoulders. It surprised him when he suddenly realised just how desperately he wanted to stay in Danebury.

"Thank you, Coran, Chieftain of Dane-bre."

"I warn you now to take care, Parrish. Do not disobey me again."

There was another silence as the rest of the threat went unsaid. Both men knew that it was no idle threat.

"There is bad weather on the way?" Parrish asked, seizing on a chance to change the subject. Coran nodded.

"But how do you know?"

"The Earth Goddess told me."

"But how?"

"She will speak to you too, when the time is right." Coran said it as a true statement and not in an attempt to baffle the tall man he liked so much, but who had no idea of things that every other person in Dane-bre knew to be simple facts.

"If there is bad weather coming, will there be another hunt before it arrives?"

"There is no time."

"Oh. I was going to ask if I might join them." Parrish knew he was pushing his luck and the Chieftain might become angry, but he desperately wanted to be involved in the life of the village. To his great surprise, Coran laughed out loud.

"I knew you would ask that." he said, smiling up at the tall man. "The answer is still no. Accept the truth, Parrish. You do not know how to track and hunt. Perhaps next summer, when the game is plentiful, we will teach you and then you can hunt with us."

Parrish nodded, both agreeing with the man's statement and accepting the offer of training, knowing that giving 'spare time' was a great gift when manpower at Danebury was always at such a premium.

"I look forward to it." The tall man smiled.

Coran nodded and started to walk away. He had gone only a few paces when he half turned, seeming to remember something as a last thought.

"He is grateful." he said over his shoulder.

"Who?" asked Parrish.

"The man you saved."

"Perhaps he will teach me to hunt?"

"If he lives." was the Chieftains parting remark and he strode briskly away.

Parrish watched him go and let out a long breath. It seemed he had somehow gotten away scot-free.

Not so! He soon had to suffer the immediate pain and a following few days more of discomfort when the holy man arrived to put another tattoo on him. The mark of the bear.

From elbow to wrist, on the upper part of Parrish's forearm, the flower and feather man cut a number of diagonal slashes into his skin with a sharp flint. Then he scored a ring around his wrist and cut three spreading lines on the back of his hand, like the ridges on the back of a leather dress glove. Parrish gritted his teeth but wouldn't give the little man the satisfaction of crying out. He had a good mind to ask for his black feather back. The holy man wiped away the blood and rubbed dark blue dye from a special, patterned clay cup that he had brought with him, into the fresh cuts with his fingers. When he had finished and left the hut, with an annoyingly satisfied smile on his face, Oona was ready with the soothing, heady, foresty smelling poultice.

"The arm marks are the layers of the bear's fur." the little man had explained before he left. "On the back of your hand is the sign of his claws and the ring shows that he is dead. You have learned our words quite well now. You can learn the words of our marks too."

It was true enough but Parrish wasn't really interested. He didn't even bother to reply.

Oona of course, was so proud that Parrish thought she might actually explode! She bustled about, tending his arm and unable it seemed to do enough for him. Apparently there weren't that many bear killers around. Her joy came to an abrupt end when they received another visitor a few days later. A man Parrish did not recognize called him out into the cold air.

He looked drawn, his face lacking colour, but apart from that, healthy enough. He stood back from Parrish, wary of the tall man. One hand was tucked into the belt cord of his tunic and he favoured the arm, taking great care not to jar it. Under his other arm was a fur bundle.

"Yes?" Parrish was curious as he looked down at the man who seemed intimidated by his closeness. It was not his intention to put fear into the man but he never the less enjoyed the sensation of power.

"I am Gant." said the man.

"Good." said Parrish, baffling the man with the unconventional answer. He smiled. "What can I do for you?"

"You have already done it." Now it was Parrish's turn to be baffled.

"Huh?"

"Your arrows saved me."

"Oh," Realization dawned and explained his injured shoulder. "That's OK." The okay was in English but the man understood the general gesture of the phrase. "I was glad to be of help."

"But this is rightfully yours." Gant held out the fur bundle which Parrish accepted and handed to Oona who had been watching and listening with gleeful intent from behind her master. She was revelling in all the reflected attention. There had been more visitors in the last few days that the whole of last summer. She unrolled the bundle and the untreated bear skin spilled onto the ground. It was quite a size, even by Parrish's standards.

"Thank you, Gant." Parrish nodded in gratitude and the small man turned to leave, careful of his wound. "Wait!" Parrish dived into the hut and returned with one of his arrows. He didn't know if it was one of the actual arrows but that didn't matter. "Here."

Gant looked at the arrow with its black, crow feather fletching, then gingerly touched his shoulder. He knew that by rights he should be dead now and the fletching on the big arrow had come from the sky spirits. There were strange forces at work around this tall man.

"Take it." Parrish offered out the arrow again. The smaller man was still undecided so Parrish applied a little Neolithic psychology. "Carry it when you hunt. It protected you once, who knows, it may protect you again."

Gant accepted the gift then. He bowed to Parrish and, without another word, walked slowly away, reverently cradling the arrow in his good arm.

Parrish looked down at Oona, still holding one edge of the rolled out skin.

"That needs stretching, scraping and drying. I will make you a frame for it."

Oona's shoulders sagged. Her master's triumph had suddenly turned into more hard work for her.

19

The bad weather arrived just as Coran had predicted. Parrish tried to convince himself that with all the cold and frosty days they had experienced, it was only a matter of time before the weather turned really nasty, but the Chieftains announcement was uncannily accurate. The wind veered around to the north and for the next few days the temperature never rose above freezing at all. The sky got greyer and heavier. Then it snowed.

Danebury tried to pre-empt the weather as much as it could. Parrish watched as the sheep were rounded up and herded into the corrals. He helped carry a good supply of animal feed into the barns and the sheep needed no second bidding to get out of the cutting wind and into where there was food.

A number of the animals were killed and carried off for butchering. They were very carefully selected, causing the least damage to the well being of the flock. A few of the older rams and about two dozen sheep that were not carrying unborn lambs. There was no heart eating ceremony for these beasts, they had not been hunted, and the skinned and quartered carcasses were taken off to the great centre hut. Parrish wondered once again what it was like inside. He did not know that he was soon to find out.

The next morning the encampment awoke to find itself shin deep in snow. It seemed to immediately motivate everyone. Every family gathered all the firewood they could and stored it inside their huts. Parrish and Oona worked together and stocked firewood inside their own hut but there was not a lot of room in their small hovel. They stocked more fuel along the outside wall beside the entrance. Parrish's ace in the hole as far as firewood was concerned was his old wicker shed, still stacked up to its low roof with well dried timber from the summer.

People moved whatever else they thought they might need that was usually kept outside, inside if they could. Parrish's bear hide was now as stiff as a board on its drying frame but it was still utilized as a more solid door against the cutting wind. At least it didn't have to cope with a direct assault, the north wind blowing from the opposite quarter, onto the back of the hut.

It continued to snow on and off during the day and visible movement dwindled away to nothing as the white carpet deepened and began to drift in the steadily increasing wind. Danebury became like a ghost town.

Parrish consulted the little Survival Aids zip-o-gauge thermometer attached to the toggle of the zip on his combat jacket. Even at midday, the inside temperature of their hut was a cool, zero degrees Celsius. Loading up the fire warmed it up some but, by their very design, the huts allowed masses of heat to escape through their thatching. And still the wind increased, the combined snow and wind chill factor making the outside temperature almost unbearable.

"Fuck me it's cold." said Parrish out loud in English. Oona nodded in agreement, not with his unknown words but with the heartfelt expletive.

"There is going to be a blizzard." she said, matter-of-factly.

"You don't say?" said Parrish sarcastically, listening to the wind beginning to howl outside. Oona was hunched over the fire in the middle of the floor, trying to heat up some smoked meat by suspending it above the flames on a stick spit. Parrish joined her beside the fire, picking up another log on his way. He tossed it into the greedy flames and squatted down next to the old lady.

"How often do you get blizzards?" he asked.

"We nearly always get snow. Bad blizzards come about one in four winters"

"How long do they last?"

"Some are short. Some are long." She shrugged. "If Dannu is kind it will not be longer that a day or two."

"And if she is angry?" Parrish screwed up his face in expectation of the bad news.

"I have known two blizzards that lasted more days than the fingers on one hand." She nodded as if the tall man might not believe her. "It is true!"

"I know." said Parrish. "I've been on exercise in Norway and was snowed in at the barracks for a week once."

Oona gave her master a quizzical stare and Parrish realized he was not concentrating and had mixed English words with Gaelic/Celtic ones. How could the old lady know what 'Norway', 'barracks' and 'week' meant. It must be the cold, he thought. He smiled down at her lovable old face and hugged her with his arm.

"I believe you. In fact, I have a nasty feeling that this blow is going to be a very bad one." Parrish warmed his hands at the fire and Oona went back to her cooking. She'd already had a bad feeling about the blizzard and now it had been confirmed by the Earth Goddess, spoken from her mans own lips. She shuddered.

That night the pair slept as close as they dared to the fire, having to wake at regular intervals to stoke it. The flames seemed to consume fuel as fast as it could be fed.

Dawn broke grey and featureless. Parrish reluctantly but necessarily had to leave the shelter of the hut to collect the rest of their firewood. He estimated the wind speed at around fifty miles per hour. The snow was waist deep and where it had drifted up against the only hut he could see, it had almost totally engulfed the building. Only the top third of the thatch, snow free from the rising heat inside, proved that there was actually a building there at all.

The driving snow stung his face and hands, chilling them in moments. The icy wind seemed to knife straight through his clothes without even slowing down. He worked fast in the strength sapping snow, handing logs to Oona who stood in the doorway, and between them they quickly transferred all the logs inside. The old lady finally replaced the frozen bear skin door and lowered the door blanket behind Parrish as he slumped, fatigued, in front of the fire. The pair looked at their new supply of fuel. There didn't seem to be a hell of a lot of it.

The rest of the day dragged by. The blizzard howled outside and the only thing keeping it at bay was the dancing flames of the fire and its rapidly dwindling supply of fuel.

The couple didn't get much sleep that night and it was no comfort at all to know that the rest of Danebury was suffering too. After dark the temperature dropped even more and when the last of the logs went onto the fire in the small hours of the morning, Parrish began to have serious doubts about any long term prospects for them both. The arriving dawn coincided with the fire finally dying away to glowing embers.

The blizzard didn't appear to have even reached its zenith yet and the temperature inside the hut dropped steadily. Parrish couldn't shake the feeling that neither he nor Oona would live to see the coming night. Suddenly he remembered his ace in the hole.

"Oona. I'm going to get some of the firewood from my old hut." He made to rise but she held on to him.

"No." It was bold of her but times were desperate.

"But we need the fuel or we will surely die!"

"In such weather you could only make one trip." Her statement was undeniably true. "And how long would the wood that you could carry back last?"

"Not long I know, but at least it would give us some time."

"We must use the trip to go to the great hut."

"What?" said Parrish, baffled.

"When the weather is very bad," she explained," the whole village goes to the great hut. The Earth Goddess watches over us and we live there until the storm is past. We must go to the shrine house or we will indeed die." It was one of Oona's knacks to state the obvious, even if Parrish did not always understand.

He waved the idea aside.

"Even if what you say is true, they would not let me enter their great hut."

She could hear the resentment in his voice.

"They would not turn you away, Parrish" said the old lady.

"Oh yes they would. I am not part of their village."

"I think you are, my son." she said. More than you know, she thought.

Her words were not spoken loudly but they seemed suddenly to carry immense power and conviction. Parrish just looked at her for a long time, weighing up the very limited options, then gave her a smile to gladden her heart.

"OK." he said, all at once at ease with what was truly a life or death decision. "Let's do it."

They gathered up what they could carry. Parrish stuffed his pockets with dried meat pieces and slung a pair of smoked hocks around his neck. Oona loaded up his skin sack with bread and looped it across her body. They were already wearing as many layers of clothing as possible but they draped the skins that made up their bedding around their shoulders. Parrish carried his bow and quiver of arrows across his back. He wrapped his scrim scarf around Oona's head, covering her ears, and secured it under her chin.

"Ready?" he asked.

"Ready."

Parrish pulled down the door blanket and wrapped it around the old lady. It hung on her like a great cape, reminding Parrish that he was glad of his own cape, snug against his back, outside his combat jacket. Finally he threw the rigid bear skin aside and stepped out into the howling wind and driving snow. The force of it made him stagger.

Vision was limited to a very few yards, almost a total white out. Parrish squinted down at the little compass held tightly in his hand.

"Keep close behind me!" he shouted to Oona, his voice barely audible above the wind. Her nodded reply was only just visible under all her wraps. He led off into the village, passing huts he knew were there but could not be seen. Oona followed him faithfully, unable to see how her master knew which way to go. He was being guided by Dannu, she decided.

It was slow going as Parrish kicked his way through waist high drifts, deliberately trying to clear an easier path for Oona. Every dozen steps he looked back to make sure she was still there, the snow swirling around her. It was at least one small blessing that they were heading in a southerly direction and the harsh wind was on their backs.

The distance from their little hut to the great 'shrine house' as the old lady had called it, was not more than one hundred and fifty meters. It took them an agonizing, bone chilling, fifteen minutes to cover the distance. As the building loomed up in front of Parrish, seeming to suddenly appear from out of the swirling whiteness, he turned to shout the good news to Oona.

She was nowhere to be seen.

"Shit!" Parrish turned into the teeth of the wind and followed his plough marks in the snow. Only twenty paces back, but out of sight, the old lady lay exhausted in the snow. Her tired limbs could no longer battle against the deep drifts. She was ready to give up when a pair of snow encrusted legs appeared before her eyes. Parrish scooped her easily up into his arms and hugged her tightly to his chest.

"C'mon mother." he shouted. "This is no time to be taking a rest, we are nearly there." She tried to bury herself into his broad chest as the tall man turned his back to the wind and followed his tracks once more until he reached the great hut. Working his way around the wall until he found the entrance, he shouldered his way through the snow and ice encrusted blanket. The still air beyond it was a blessed relief.

There was a wattle and daub wall in front of him, creating a passageway that led off to his left. He moved along it for about five paces, realizing that it was a windbreak and insulator between the way in and the world outside. At the end of the passage was another wall and he had to turn right. He stepped into the main area of the hut. It was warm and for a moment Parrish just stood, still holding Oona in his arms.

"So, Parrish!" It was Coran's voice, rising above the hubbub of other voices. They all fell silent. "We did not think that you still lived. Enter, you are the last one."

One of Coran's wives was sent across to meet them and silently guided the pair to where the Chieftain stood. Parrish set Oona down and stood there awkwardly, feeling out of place and aware that all eyes were on him. He took a long look around in defiance. On one level his military eye was noticing everything but on a more personal level, he was totally astounded by the sheer scale of the place.

The hut was huge. At least one hundred feet across, it was circular, open plan and high roofed, a gigantic version of the tiny hut Parrish had lived in for the last five months. Timber supporting pillars came down from the roof, plunging deep into the ground to form a ring around the inside of the building, about fifteen feet in from the outside wall. Running from these pillars straight back to the wall were heavy, wattle panels, separating each section into large stalls. As the tall man glanced about he could see that each stall held an entire family unit and some of their possessions.

The whole place was laid out like a huge clock face. It was the only way he could describe it. The entrance way and short passage was at the six o'clock position, or south east. From seven, around the western side of the hut, to ten o'clock, was taken up with stalls. Opposite them, from two o'clock, around the eastern side, to five were more of the same. Each one held a family unit, varying from eight to as many as fifteen people. A larger, double stall from ten o'clock to eleven, was the Chieftains. Opposite him at one o'clock was another larger stall, half full of firewood. It fed the enormous stone ringed fire that burned brightly in the centre of the floor, big enough for the women of a dozen families to cook at.

The whole thing impressed Parrish enormously but what really left him slack jawed was the shrine at the twelve o'clock or north-west position, facing the entrance. The base of it was an ornately carved, stone plinth. On it, rising majestically up into the roof space of the hut, brightly painted with swirling patterns and slashing lines was a great, bulbous sculpture of a rounded, squatting woman.

The Earth Goddess.

From the dim space behind the huge piece of stonework, the flower and feather man emerged and approached Parrish, who still stared up at the awe inspiring statue. The little Neolithic man stood beside Parrish, dwarfed by the height of the twentieth century man, and spread his arms wide as if to embrace the vaguely Buddha like statue.

"Is she not beautiful?"

It wasn't the word Parrish would have used to describe her but there was no denying the impact the sculpture had or the time and effort that must have gone into making it. Sir Henry Moore would have been green with envy.

"She staggers me!" he said finally.

The holy man nodded, satisfied with the answer, and returned to his place behind the statue. Parrish continued to stare.

A hand appeared on his shoulder and he turned to find the Chieftain at his side, smiling to see the tall man so impressed.

"This is your stall, Parrish." He indicated the empty stall next to his own.

It had a deep bed of fresh straw on the floor. Oona had by no means recovered from her ordeal in the blizzard but was determined to do her duties and busied herself spreading their bedding skins out on the soft, springy stems. She helped Parrish out of his extra garments, propped his bow and quiver in one corner and hung the hocks of meat on two of the pegs that lined both walls of the stall. Hung on the pegs along the opposite wall to the meat, were five bleached white wolf skulls and a bigger, bear skull. He moved closer and inspected them.

"They are your trophies, Parrish." said Coran as if that explained it all and, satisfied that his strange neighbour was happy with the arrangements, returned to his own stall.

The tall man took another look around the great hut. Apart from a few men who continued to look at him in a not too friendly manner, the other people had lost their interest and paid him no more attention as he scanned the interior. All the other stalls had trophies decorating their walls, to a greater or lesser degree. He saw, with a twinge of repulsion, that many of the trophies were human skulls.

Not wanting to invite trouble by offending anyone, no one likes to be stared at, he sat down on the straw in the middle of 'his' stall, let Oona bustle about as she saw fit and just watched. He tried to be discrete but could not help continually following individuals about with his eyes. It was totally fascinating to watch the entire village living in close harmony under one roof.

For a while the howling blizzard was forgotten. He sat motionless for several hours, engrossed in his observations.

The women of the various families clustered around the fire, cooking for their men and children. Oona joined them and the ladies chattered among themselves while the food was being prepared. The gossip seemed to go unnoticed by the men, the area immediately around the fire apparently female domain.

The men talked among themselves, visiting each other in their stalls and sometimes gathering in a particular stall where a group discussion was taking place. The kids ran and played about in the no-man's-land between the fireside and the stall entrances or in the firewood stall. Babies tumbled about in the straw, well wrapped up and never out of their mother's sight.

Hanging from the roof in the centre of the hut was a huge collection of different meats. Parrish now knew where the freshly butchered sheep had ended up.

The Chieftain seemed to preside over them all, resplendent in his double stall, being waited on by his wives, and beckoning with a wave of the hand when he wanted to talk to a certain man or find out what was being said by who.

Towering above everyone, visible from every stall, was the great statue of the Earth Goddess. Parrish estimated that she must be at least ten feet tall and weigh over five tons. The holy man bustled about behind the statue. Parrish's viewing angle allowed him to see quite well into the dimly lit back space. From the jumble of stuff he could see it was plain that the little man lived there. At the back of the space was a large stack of big clay storage jars. Another mystery solved. That was where the seed grain for next year's crop had gone. He smiled at the analogy. Taken into the protection of the Earth Goddess.

The day drew to a close. Oona served her master with hot food but Parrish noticed that she did not eat much herself. The old lady was not looking too well either, he could see the recent ordeals had taken it out of her. He wanted to tell her to take a rest and allow him to help her but he knew she would not have accepted his offer.

The Chieftain finally called lights out and all the tallow lamps were extinguished, the interior of the hut plunged into the dancing half light of the fire. The place was comfortably warm but Parrish had observed the women throwing logs onto the fire with scant regard for the shrinking supply in the store. It had already halved since his arrival only half a day earlier. Having experienced running out of fuel once already, he didn't relish the idea of going through it again. At the present rate, he estimated that the population of Danebury would run out of firewood late the next day. He was a tired man but fell into a restless, worried sleep.

20

Parrish was woken by the sounds of bustle. He opened his eyes and peered sleepily out from his stall into the centre of the great hut. Most of the women were moving urgently around the fire, many pots steaming away at the edge of the flames. Propping himself up on one elbow, he watched for a few minutes, allowing the last vestiges of sleep to leave him. All the other men of the camp were up and about and he wondered why he'd been allowed to sleep in. It didn't matter. The place was nice and warm, the irregular rising and falling howl of the blizzard outside just a muted background noise, and Parrish felt better for his long sleep.

Now fully awake, he had a good stretch and scratch and turned his thoughts towards food. All the women looked productively busy, all that was except Oona. Parrish turned to find her still asleep, her face turned to the wattle wall. He gave her a nudge.

"Come on sleepy head, wake up. Where is breakfast? This is no time to be sleeping on the job." He got no response and gave her a more forceful nudge. She stirred slowly and gave out a low groan. Parrish leaned across and turned her onto her back. She looked awful. The colour was gone from her face, leaving her skin grey and pasty. She was drawn, her eyes sunken and the wrinkles on her face seemed suddenly very deep. He felt her forehead. She was cold.

"Oona." He was immediately worried and upset. "What is the matter?"

She coughed feebly.

"I am sorry Parrish." she croaked. "I cannot seem to move." She made to rise but slumped back. "There is no strength in me."

Parrish experienced a dreadful sinking feeling in the pit of his stomach.

He patted her face, put a cheerful smile on his own and wrapped her gently in his cape.

"Don't worry. You will be all right." he lied. "Just lay still. I will get you some hot food."

"No." croaked Oona but the tall man was already moving away towards the fireside.

Leaning over the squatting women at the edge of the fire, Parrish asked one of them for a pot. She of course could not refuse but looked at him strangely. He returned to his stall, rashered off some meat from a hock, cut it into small pieces, added some water and put the pot into the hot embers. All the time Oona was shaking her head. Did he not understand? Men do not cook. He was making her look bad and himself lose face.

Parrish was unaware of everyone staring in silence as he squatted among the women, stirring the contents of his cooking pot. By doing women's work and, even worse, doing it in front of the whole village, Parrish showed himself to be inferior.

Coran shook his head. The tall man had still not learned enough about the ways of Dane-bre. He was sure one or other of the warriors who did not like Parrish's presence in the camp would seize upon this gross sign of weakness. The Chieftain knew his people well for he was not wrong.

A man stepped from a stall on the opposite side of the fire and pointed at Parrish, still engrossed in his urgent cooking.

"This is the man who has brought the blizzard upon us!" His voice commanded attention, his finger pointing accusingly at the stranger among them "He offends us all in the presence of the Earth Goddess." The pointing finger switched to the stone shrine. There were several murmurs of approval at the outburst.

"What?" The bewildered Parrish rose slowly to his feet.

"You have brought the blizzard upon us!" repeated the man angrily.

"Rubbish! There is always snow in winter and very often blizzards. I have nothing to do with it."

The man took offence at being told he spoke falsely and snatched up his flint headed axe, waving it threateningly in Parrish's direction. The entire hut was hushed, intently watching the battle of words. Feeling the attention of everyone on him, the man brandishing his axe rose to the occasion.

"You are nothing Parrish! You do nothing except woman's work." He pointed at the pot in the fire. "Your trophies are nothing and you do not respect the Earth Goddess. You should leave Dane-bre NOW!"

Parrish's face darkened. He had not been awake very long. He had eaten no breakfast and the only person he really cared about in Danebury was lying ill, very probably dying. And then, to cap it all, a man he didn't even know jumped up, called him names and ordered him out of the village. Parrish lost his temper.

"Listen asshole! What I do or do not, as long as it does not offend Dannu or the Chieftain, is nothing to do with you." He pointed an accusing finger of his own. "You laze about all day while the women work hard all the time." He could call people names too. "I say that *you* do nothing. I say your trophies are nothing." He waved at the row of human skulls on the pegs in the man's stall. "I say that you stole them!"

There was a shocked gasp from the watchers and Parrish knew he had gone too far. To call a warrior a thief was the ultimate insult. It had taken Klud many months to recover his loss of face after the incident with Parrish's webbing that first day and *that* attempted theft had been from a man who had absolutely no standing in the community.

He wished he could take back that last sentence but it was too late now and he had to stand by his words. He backed away from the edge of the fire, knowing that action was now inevitable.

His Neolithic accuser did not even hesitate. Letting out a furious cry and waving his axe above his head, he rushed around the fire towards Parrish, his path clear as people backed away to give the men room to fight. Parrish waited, relaxed and ready, arms held away from his sides and feet spread. Coran watched with keen intent, as did everyone else. In the background Klud was shaking his head in disagreement. He had experienced the tall man's hand to hand fighting to his own cost.

The Danebury man rushed at Parrish full tilt and swung his axe in a killer blow. The tall man swayed away to one side, skilfully avoiding the chopping blade and, with an outstretched foot, tripped his attacker as he ran by. The Neolithic warrior sprawled full length on the earth floor beside the fire but kept his grip on his axe. He scrambled quickly to his feet and turned to rush Parrish in a second attack but was shocked and surprised to find the tall man standing directly before him, practically toe to toe.

Parrish had closed with his opponent quickly, even as the man fell. When the smaller man regained his feet and turned, raising his axe to attempt a second attack, he was in close and ready. With his left hand Parrish grabbed the raised weapon by its shaft, virtually hanging the Neolithic man up by his arm. With his right he delivered a short jab to the solar plexus.

The breath whooshed out of the smaller mans lungs and he finally relinquished his grip on the axe and grasped his midriff, doubling over. Now holding the flint axe aloft in his left fist, with his right Parrish karate chopped the bowed man smartly on the back of the neck and his opponent crumpled to the ground. Turning the prostrate man onto his back with a kick, Parrish stood over him and raised the axe to strike. Their eyes met. The Neolithic man expected no mercy and waited for death.

He's brave all right, thought Parrish. If nothing else, these men know how to die. What a waste.

Holding the axe to one side, the tall man reached down with his free hand, grabbed the front of his opponent's buckskin tunic and hauled him roughly to his feet. Spinning him around by the shoulder, he pushed the man away, making him stagger. Every face in the hut registered bewilderment.

"Why do you not kill him?" Coran demanded, voicing everyone's thoughts. "He insulted you!"

"No. He is wrong about me not respecting the Earth Goddess but he is right about everything else." answered Parrish. "I deny bringing the blizzard but I cannot prove it. I *do* do women's work and my trophies are nothing to his. He is a great warrior with many man skulls. Real trophies. I wrongly called him a thief. It was I who insulted him." Parrish walked slowly back to his stall, furious at himself for his loss of control and rash actions. He had been determined not to do that. In his anger he swung the flint axe with all his might and struck the support pillar nearest him. The weapon bit deep into the timber with a loud thud. He left it wedged there, turned to face the people and shrugged.

"Besides, would it not be a great waste to lose such a brave warrior over a simple bowl of soup?"

There were more murmurs of approval, this time for him. A wise statement. The tall man dismissed the whole episode with a wave of the hand, checked to see that Oona was comfortable then went back to his broth, which was coming to the boil.

Coran returned to his stall, satisfied with the conclusion of the incident, a signal for everyone else to return to whatever they had been doing before.

The battered warrior staggered back to his stall and was met by Klud, who helped him to sit down. The man rubbed his stomach and massaged the back of his neck.

"What happened?" he groaned, "I was beaten before I could even touch him!"

"It is quite wondrous to watch. In battle he moves like no man I have ever seen." Klud fingered his misshapen nose, a testament to the words. The other man nodded, the two united by being on the receiving end of Parrish's assaults.

"Perhaps the spirits guide his hands?" suggested the seated man, searching for a reason to explain their utter ineffectiveness against the tall man. Klud shrugged.

"If that is so, do you think that the Earth Goddess would find his presence offending? Would he be given the power to beat Dane-bre's best warriors?"

"You speak wisely Klud. Perhaps we are both lucky to have learned this without being killed by Dannu's man?"

They both nodded sagely.

Parrish heard none of this. He was busy tending to Oona. She was gravely ill and it upset him. She managed only a few spoonfuls of the meaty broth that had started all the trouble. Worse still, she insisted that he eat the rest of it. While he did so it was difficult to hide his guilt and worry.

He nursed her on through the day but the old lady grew steadily weaker, it was distressing for him to stand by, powerless to help. He choked back a tear. All he could do was keep her warm and make her as comfortable as possible. The warmth she so desperately needed came from the fire and he watched with growing concern as the woodpile dwindled rapidly.

Around midday a cry went up that there was no more wood. Parrish knew the drill. The residual heat would keep the place bearably warm for a few hours more but by evening, fuel would be desperately needed for the coming night.

The only other combustible material he could see were the wattle panels between the stalls and they wouldn't last five minutes.

Mid afternoon, as the temperature began dropping noticeably, Parrish went to see the Chieftain.

"Yes?" Coran waved him in and as he approached, all the man's wives lowered their eyes, an act which Parrish found somehow degrading for him as well as them.

"I know where there is firewood." he explained. "But to bring it here I will need some men. To help carry it."

"Where?"

"In my old first hut."

"That stupid square one?" asked the Chieftain to which Parrish nodded. He was shocked to realize that these Neolithic builders considered his wicker shed, which he thought was such a good piece of work, totally non functional.

"That is no good Parrish. How will you find it out in the blizzard?"

"The same way I found my way here from there."

Coran never even paused to consider the options because there was nothing to consider. If the blizzard continued any longer than one more full day, it would be a choice of freezing slowly inside the great hut or quickly outside while trying to find fuel. Either way the end result was the same.

"If the men will help you, you have my permission to try."

Parrish nodded his thanks then strode out to the centre of the hut, next to the dying fire, to draw attention.

"I have been told I do nothing." he said loudly, the hut falling silent at the sound of his words. "Now, I can do something but I will need help. I know where there is wood for the fire but I need some brave men to help me carry it here. Who will come with me?"

"Where is this wood?" came the question from the crowd.

"At my old square hut."

"And how will you find your way there in the blizzard?" scoffed another voice.

Parrish had a sudden flash of inspiration. "With the help of Dannu." He looked sideways at the flower and feather man who watched from in front of the stone shrine. Time to chose a side, he thought.

There was a tense moment of silence before the holy man nodded, turned to face the huge statue, opened his arms wide and started to chant in low tones.

Everyone knew that to blunder blindly about in a blizzard was to invite a swift death. The people murmured to each other before eventually falling silent again. Parrish stood for a long moment, sensing defeat. His faith in the people of Danebury and in human nature drained away. He was on the point of turning his back on the entire village and giving up trying to become a part of what he had hoped would perhaps be one small step in the development of mankind. It was so sad. All these people were going to die, and they wouldn't even help themselves. His shoulders dropped and he started to turn away.

"I will go with you, Parrish!" came a firm voice across the still air of the hut. Klud stepped forward from the crowd. Parrish gave him a smile. There was another stony silence. Coran watched intently from his stall behind the tall man.

And then another man stepped forward. Parrish recognized him immediately as Mars the archer. He gave him an acknowledging nod, realizing that he had now reached his limit as far as friends in the village went. Then, to his surprise, a third man stepped out in his support. It was the warrior he had beaten in their fight only half a day earlier.

"I will go with you." he said and Klud stepped up beside the man, clapping him on the shoulder.

"Well said, Hass."

"And I." said a higher voice and a boy stepped hesitantly out from the crowd. It was Tomps. Parrish smiled again. A few months ago he would have dismissed the young volunteer out of hand, but not now. The lad was fourteen summers old. In only two more years he would already have his first wife and be a man. On his shoulders then would be all the responsibilities that went with being head of a family unit. Provider, warrior, hunter and protector. A lot for a young man to take on but, in these Neolithic times, he would already be halfway through his short life. If he was lucky he might live to see his thirtieth summer. Very lucky and he could possibly live to the ripe old age of thirty five. Parrish knew there was no one in the village older than that. How Oona had survived so long he didn't know.

He didn't particularly like the idea of the youngster going out into a blizzard but this was truly a man's world and he had made his first stand as an adult. To refuse his offer of help would embarrass him greatly and cause him to lose face. Besides, when it came right down to it, the fire needed all the fuel they could get it. On the other hand, Parrish didn't want dozens of people wandering around aimlessly all over the camp in a blizzard. A party of four was all the untrained personnel he felt he could control.

"Good. That is enough." he said in what he hoped was a positive sounding voice. "Wrap up well and meet me at the door shortly." A hubbub of discussion broke out as Parrish turned away and returned to his stall. His eyes met Coran's and the Chieftain nodded. It had been handled well.

Parrish knelt beside Oona. "I will be back soon. I am going to get some firewood to keep you warm."

She gave him a weak smile that never reached her eyes. He gently patted her cheek, then started to don his extra clothes.

At the entrance to the passageway Parrish checked his men. They were all well prepared. He pushed the fur hat tighter down on Tomps' head so that it covered his ears.

"You stay close." he said to the youngster. "Use the bigger men to shelter from the wind if you can and always walk in our steps. It will be easier for your smaller legs."

Tomps nodded vigorously.

"OK men." Parrish waved his hand in the best wagon train tradition in an attempt to raise their morale with joke. "Mooove OUT!" His Neolithic companions just stared at him. "Sorry." said Parrish sheepishly and gave an embarrassed cough. "Let's go."

Before they stepped out from the still air of the passageway into the blizzard, he took his bearing with the little brass compass. There were no degree markings on it but it was still accurate enough for their short trip of just over one hundred meters. Finally satisfied, he nodded and they all stepped out, staggering in the teeth of the wind. The other four followed the tall man in single file as he led confidently off into the featureless whiteness with Tomps bringing up the rear. They were all bowed forwards as the chill, cutting wind bit into their faces and hands.

Parrish checked his compass regularly every ten paces and counted off his steps. His confidence was rewarded when he felt himself climbing up a distinct slope and with a combination of outstanding compass work and blind luck, he hit the wicker hut dead on. As they topped the rise, the force of the howling wind was incredible. The group fell gratefully into the little pocket of calmer air on the lee side of the shed.

Oona's words came back to Parrish as he considered transferring the firewood to the great hut.

"How long could the wood you carry last?" she had said.

He signalled to the four to wait. "Stay here." he shouted. "I will be back soon." Before the group could argue he staggered off and vanished, immediately swallowed up by the swirling snow.

He didn't go far, only to Oona's hut. Inside he found the frozen bear skin, stiff on its wooden frame. He went to his webbing which still hung on the wall, dug out his bundle of paracord, and tied a length of it to the top corners of the frame. He had made himself a very crude sledge.

When he reappeared as if by magic out of the snow storm, wrestling with his bear skin and frame, the waiting group thought he had gone mad. Waving for assistance, he laid the skin on the snow and started loading logs onto it. The rest followed his example and they soon had the sledge fully loaded with firewood. Parrish looped the green cord under his armpits and over the back of his neck and set off back along their track, dragging the laden sledge behind him. The three other men pushed the load while Tomps kept any loose logs from falling by the wayside.

The cold was bone chilling, muscle paralyzing and strength sapping but the strenuous exercise made the blood pound in their veins. It was a welcome sight when the great hut appeared suddenly before them out of the snow covered, wind whipped landscape. Parrish felt like he and his squad had been out in the storm for ever although he knew it could not be more than half an hour.

When the load was finally push/dragged into the main area of the hut the group were greeted with welcoming cries and happy voices. Willing hands took the timber away and in a brief time the fire was once again blazing brightly.

Coran stood beside Parrish as he and his helpers grateful warmed themselves by the dancing flames.

"You did well. I have ordered more groups of men to follow your track and bring in the rest of the wood. I am told there is easily enough to see us through another night."

"Thank you Coran." Parrish bowed at the compliment. "But it could not have been done without my good friends and brave warriors." He turned to his companions who grinned at the recognition of their deed. The grins died on their faces when they saw the tall man frown. "Where is Tomps?" Everyone looked around but there was no sign of the youngster.

"He was still with us when we started to return." said Hass.

"Yes." agreed Mars. "That was when I last saw him too."

There was a shaking of heads.

"No one is to blame." said Coran. "He was brave, but not strong enough. It is sad. He would have made a good warrior."

Parrish couldn't believe his ears. Surely they were not just going to give up on the lad? The youngster had willingly put his life on the line for them. The tall man bit down on his rising anger. He had finally learned not to blow his top but he was not prepared to stand idly by while there was still a chance to save the boy.

"The blame is mine. I should have watched him more closely." He turned on his heel and ran towards the passageway.

"Parrish!" called Coran but the tall man was already out of sight. He had to work on the assumption that the boy had at least stayed with the sledge some of the way back and hoped that he had not strayed from the track, still visible in the snow. Parrish knew he would not be able to stay out in the blizzard for very much longer without putting himself in peril.

Keeping the track very close on his left side he waded through the deep snow just off the track, in the hope that Tomps had merely fallen to one side. Visibility was now so poor that could only just make out the returning second group with its loaded sledge as they passed him by. Bent to their own task, they never noticed him at all.

By the time Parrish had reached what he estimated to be the halfway point he knew he had to turn back or else he would need to be rescued himself and he couldn't see that happening. With a hollow feeling of defeat in his chest, he crossed the track and headed back, the task a little easier with the wind now on his back. As the hut came into view, when he was only a few paces from the entrance and had given up any hope of finding the boy, Parrish tripped over an irregular hump in the snow. Not even bothering to regain his feet, he rolled in the whiteness back to the hidden obstacle and swept back the drifting cover to find Tomps lying there unconscious.

Poor bugger, thought Parrish, he had been so close.

Shoving his hand down inside the boys clothing, he felt the front of his chest. It was still warm and he could feel a heartbeat. He picked the limp boy up, slung him unceremoniously over his shoulder and hurried as quickly as he could back into the great hut.

Emerging into the deliciously warm environment he was immediately met by Tomps worried and highly animated mother. She led the tall man to a stall on the right of the fire and, following her directions, set the lad gently down on the soft, furs covered straw. Tomps mother cooed over him as Parrish gently removed the boy's outer clothing. The unconscious lads cheeks, nose, the point of his chin and most worrying, his hands, were white, waxy looking and very cold. After feeling them, the woman started to rub the hands in an attempt to help warm them. Parrish quickly stopped her.

"No mother." he said. "I have seen this before. It is called 'frostbite'."

He used the English word. "You must not rub. Do not put him near to the fire either. Give him warm drinks when he wakes, keep him wrapped up and let him warm up slowly. Tell him that the frostbite will be very painful but that will pass. He must be brave for a while longer. If the Earth Goddess smiles on him he will not lose any fingers to the coldness. The feeling will slowly return to his hands but they will blister and give him more pain. This too will pass and then he will be well. Do as I say and tell him this so he knows what will happen and not be afraid. Do you understand?"

She nodded. "Thank you, Parrish." she said, her eyes cast respectably downwards. The tall man put a finger under her chin and gently lifted her head until he achieved eye contact.

"I am glad to do it. When he is awake and wants to know what has happened, come and tell me and I will talk to him." He smiled, winked at the woman and got a small, shy smile in return. Satisfied, he rose to his feet, left the stall and returned to his own one. Oona was even weaker and it was agony for him.

To do so much for the boy and yet be helpless to save her.

21

Parrish knew he badly needed rest and tried to get some sleep but could not settle. Oona's condition worried his so much that he could only doze fitfully. After a couple of hours of restless cat-napping he finally gave up on the idea. Outside, it was now night and the storm still raged, but the great hut was warm and quiet. Parrish checked Oona for the umpteenth time and held her hand.

She tried to offer him a brave smile but the corners of her mouth somehow would not turn upwards.

"Do not worry." he said, kneeling over the old woman. "I am here and I will not let any harm come to you."

"I am beyond harm." she croaked. "You must be ready to offer me up to the sky spirits."

"No way." he smiled. "There is plenty of life in you yet." It sounded so hollow when he said it. He knew it and so did she.

"If you say so, my son."

"You just rest. If you want anything, anything at all, just call for me. I will be here."

The old lady nodded slowly. Her eyes closed and she drifted back into sleep. Parrish sat beside her, still holding her hand.

A footfall at the entrance to his stall made him turn. Klud stood there, leaning against the supporting pillar that had the axe embedded in it. He pointed with his chin at Oona.

"Why do you bother with her? She is just an old woman and soon she will be dead."

Parrish knew it was the truth but it still hurt to hear.

"She once tended me when I was sick. I must do the same for her. It is my debt."

There didn't seem any point in adding that he really cared for the old lady. It would be wasted on the Neolithic warrior with his accompanying Stone Age attitudes.

Klud nodded in the acknowledgment that debts must be paid.

"I am here because I see that you do not eat. She cannot cook for you." He again pointed at Oona with his chin. "When you are hungry and feel you can leave the old woman, I invite you to eat with me at my stall. There is plenty of food and my family would welcome you."

Parrish was dumbfounded by the unexpected and very complimentary invitation. It was rare offer, he knew. He was honoured and said so.

"It would be my greatest pleasure and a true honour to accept your offer but first I must tend to Oona. With your permission, I will join you and your generous family when I can."

Klud gave an almost regal nod of agreement and turned away without another word. He was actually honoured that the tall man had accepted his offer at all and was more than satisfied with the 'maybe later' answer.

The night drew on. Coran called lights out and the hut once more sank into semi darkness. Parrish still could not find sleep and periodically dozed.

It was in the early hours of the morning, with the hut quiet and still, when he heard his name called softly. He snapped wide awake and moved quickly to Oona's side.

"I am here." he whispered.

"I am so cold." she said, her voice barely audible even in the night hush. Parrish put his back against the wall beside her and held the old lady in his arms. Her head rested against his chest while his arms wrapped around her frail body. Head bowed, his cheek was on her forehead and they stayed that way for a long time, Oona feeling Parrish's' physical and emotional warmth while he listened to the old woman's soft breathing and felt the slow rise and fall of her chest.

"She comes." said Oona suddenly. So quiet was her voice, like the merest rustling of breeze blown leaves in the high branches, that only a few inches from her mouth, Parrish still had to strain to hear the words.

"Who?" he whispered.

He got no answer. A final breath sighed easily out of the old lady and her chest stopped moving. No fuss, no struggle. She went limp in his arms. Parrish hugged her close, bowed his head deep into her hair and started to cry.

"Don't go Oona, please don't go."

"It is her time, Parrish." said a female voice from the entrance to his stall. He never even bothered to look up and acknowledge the mystery woman who so rudely intruded on his private grief.

"But I need her." he sniffed.

"No. You have learned. She taught you well. Now you must let her go."

The voice was soft and soothing, yet strong with honesty. The quiet, almost melodic tones had a strangely calming effect. Parrish hugged the body of the old lady for a moment longer as a powerful, comforting feeling washed over him. He believed the truth and wisdom of the soft words. The tears stopped.

"You are right, I ..." He looked up to see this wise woman. There was no one in his stall except Oona and himself. Laying the old woman's body gently down on the straw, he stepped out into the main area of the hut, totally bewildered. The place was quiet. Not a single person stirred and he saw no one.

Scanning the interior of the hut carefully for any sign of movement, his eyes eventually fell on the huge shrine of the Earth Goddess. In the dancing half light of the fire her rounded form took on a rich glow, an almost pulsating, skin like quality. Drawn to the statue, he walked quietly over and reached tentatively out before laying his palms firmly on the cool stone.

Parrish stood like that for some time, eyes closed as if in meditation.

A small noise close by jerked him back to his senses and his eyes darted, determined this time to see the mystery woman. He was again disappointed. By his side, looking solemnly up at him was the flower and feather man. Neither man moved as they looked deep into the others eyes, each searching for the others thoughts. When the holy man finally spoke, Parrish knew. His logical, twentieth century mind tried to deny it but he was sure it had not been just an imagining.

"When she speaks," said the little man," you should listen."

In an unexpected gesture of compassion, the Neolithic holy man patted Parrish tenderly on the arm, then turned and left him to his puzzlement, walking over to stand at the entrance to the tall mans stall.

Parrish just stood, as still as the statue that towered over him, wrestling with his conflicting thoughts. Reason against the unexplainable.

Eventually, with no idea how long he had stood, frozen before the Earth Goddess, he turned and joined the holy man. Together they looked in at the still, lifeless body of Oona. Her face was relaxed. There was no pain in her features. She looked at peace.

"Will you show me how to offer her up to the sky spirits?" asked Parrish quietly without taking his eyes from the body of the old woman.

"It will be my great honour to teach you this." replied the holy man in the same soft tones.

They again looked into each other's eyes. This time, the little man smiled at what he saw there. He nodded, a look of pride and satisfaction on his face. Again he laid his hand on the tall mans arm.

"When the storm is past we will go together." He looked down at the body. "All of us." He gave Parrish a reassuring smile them returned quietly to his place behind the shrine.

Parrish wrapped Oona carefully up in her bedding skins, kissing her on the forehead before covering her face. Then he lay down in the soft straw, calmly closed his eyes and fell into a deep, dreamless and relaxed sleep.

The following morning Parrish once more slept late. When he finally awoke he again watched the regular bustle and immediately noticed that there was something different in the air. An edge of light heartedness, almost relaxation. The formerly ever present underlying tension was gone. It took him a few moments to pinpoint the reason why. The howl of the storm was now barely audible and, like everyone else, he knew it was passing. As Oona had faded away, so was the blizzard. He looked across at the shrouded body and was surprised to find himself smiling. Not gone, he thought, just moving on to another place.

He stood, stretched, then left his stall to warm his hands at the fire. Rubbing the sleep from his eyes, he scanned the interior of the hut and caught Klud's eye from his stall on the opposite side of the building. Parrish accepted the unspoken call and approached the stall.

"Come." beckoned the warrior. "Come and sit." Parrish squatted beside the man and the warrior immediately conducted a brief introduction of the other people around him.

"These are my wives." That was all the attention and description the three women got. Parrish couldn't even see their faces, they cowered so low. "This is my eldest son, Bart." The sixteen year old nodded and Parrish returned the gesture. "He has one wife." The girl Klud pointed out was even younger than the boy although it was difficult to see much of her. She too was bowed but also hid behind her husband. "There are two younger sons and my middle wife is with child." He reached over and patted one woman's slightly bulging belly. The two small boys were playfully fighting in the back of the stall and paid him no attention. They looked very close to the same age and Parrish guessed they didn't have the same mother.

"You are fortunate, Klud." Parrish had no wish to offend the warrior after his most generous invitation, although he found himself becoming more offended the more he learned about how these Neolithic men treated their women. They were not considered or even allowed to be people with a free will. Just chattels to be owned by the men. He knew without having to ask that a man bartered for the woman of his choice. "You have many fine sons."

"Yes. I hope the unborn child will be a son too but the Earth Goddess has already been generous. If it is a girl baby, then so be it."

You can't argue with logic like that, thought Parrish sourly.

"How is the old woman?" Klud asked after what he thought of as Parrish's family.

"She is dead." he said flatly.

"Are you not sad?" asked the warrior, somewhat impressed with the blunt delivery of the statement, especially after the way he had been seen fussing, unnecessarily in his opinion, over her the night before.

"Sad that she is gone, but happy that she can now return to the arms of the Earth Goddess."

"Ah." nodded Klud. "And you know that this will happen?"

"Yes. She told me."

"Who, Oona?"

"No." Parrish paused. It was as if saying the word would mean admitting to himself that he now believed what, until last night, he had thought was just superstitious mumbo-jumbo. Perhaps too, Klud would be offended if he thought that Parrish was taking his god's name in vain. "Dannu."

Klud's eyes went wide.

"She spoke to you?"

Parrish nodded. Both the other men and the four women now stared openly at him. The two boys in the back sensed something of importance had just happened, fell silent and also looked at the tall man. He raised his hands in a gesture of surrender.

"I would like it if no one spoke about this."

"But why?" exploded Klud. "It is the greatest honour to be visited in person by ..."

"Until last night, I did not believe. But now I am not so sure. It would not be well taken by others if I suddenly say that something has happened to me. An unbeliever."

"I believe you." Klud rested his hand on Parrish's shoulder. "I think you are a man of honour. Strange in many ways and thoughts, but still a man of honour."

"You are wise and I thank you, but it is still my wish that no words be said about it."

"So be it." Klud looked darkly at all the other adults in his stall and they got the message loud and clear.

There was an awkward pause. The two men looked blankly at each other. Parrish rubbed his stomach.

"Any chance of some food? I am very hungry." he asked in a light tone, desperate to get away to some other subject. Klud laughed and clapped his hands smartly together. As one the women were galvanized into action.

Towards the middle of the day the people started preparations to return to their own dwellings. The wind had just about died away to nothing and only a light dusting of snow floated out of the grey sky. The fire inside the great hut was dying but there was no longer any panic to find it more fuel. Parrish knew that as soon as the villagers had made their way back to their normal homes there would be a sort of slow motion stampede, through the deep snow, to the forests edge. There would be many trees felled before the end of the day.

Parrish began to gather up his own belongings. There wasn't all that much to collect. He was to leave Oona's body in his stall, at the holy man's suggestion. He thought it would be a good idea to let it lay peacefully under the gaze of the Earth Goddess for a few days, until the village had found its feet.

The old woman could wait until the people were settled. Parrish thought it a wise move. Oona would certainly have agreed with it.

He visited Tomps before the lad's family left the hut. The youngster was well on the road to recovery. He was walking freely about although he didn't know exactly where to go. His actions as a man, while still in the last throws of boyhood, had put him somewhere between the two distinct camps. A sort of adolescent limbo. His face was red and veined, taking on an almost ruddy, wind burned complexion and he spoke very little. It still hurt to move his jaw excessively. Large purple, fluid filled blisters had come up on most of his fingers and it was obvious by the way he treated them that they were very painful. He bore his pain silently.

"Do not worry." Parrish told the lad. "The blisters will pass. Your hands will soon be good once more." He got a not too certain nod. "You did well, Tomps. Your father is proud that you showed such courage. He and I both think that when you are full grown you will be a great warrior. The people of Dane-bre will be glad to have you in their village."

Tomps father nodded, more to please the tall man by agreeing with his words than to allay any feelings of disgrace that the boy might have that he had let down the village by not completing the task he had set out to do.

Parrish knew this and for once used the fear that he put into the weaker minded men of Danebury deliberately, to protect the boy. He thought Tomps had guts and didn't want his fragile but growing confidence undermined by any harsh words once he was out of sight. He gave the youngster's father a discrete but hard eyed stare before returning to his own stall.

Coran met him there and offered him into his own stall next door. The two men squatted in the now vacant space. Coran's wives, his brothers and the children had cleared away all his effects and were now busy outside, in the process of making his personal hut habitable again. He felt in no way guilty or obliged to help them in any way. He was the Chieftain and they were simply doing his bidding.

"You have done well Parrish. The village is in your debt."

"No." denied Parrish. "I did not bring the firewood in for the village.

It was simply for myself. I needed the warmth. If it warmed the others too, then that was just their good fortune."

Coran smiled at the tall mans lie. He found himself liking the stranger even more for his modesty.

"Like it or not, you are now joined with the village by your deed and their debt. You do not understand our ways, I know, so I will tell you this so it will not offend you later. The village must work together in some things or it will surely die. It is my duty as Chieftain to see that this work is done. When I order work to be done by you, be it working on the guard ditch or simply tending the flock, it is for a reason and it *will* be done. I will not hear argument and I will not hear refusal. Do you understand me, Parrish?" He fixed the tall man with a piercing look.

"I will obey your orders Coran, Chieftain of Dane-bre." said Parrish formally. He didn't like the way he was being spoken to. It smacked of Sergeant 'mad dog' Carter, but he understood the need for discipline more than Coran would ever know, and accepted the ground rules that were being laid down.

The Chieftain sensed the tone of displeasure in the tall man's voice.

"I understand you better than you think Parrish, but you must show respect. You are a man who can see ahead and I know the village will do well from your presence here. You know many things that no one else except Dannu knows. I too would like to know these things and would like you to know that I am ready to listen if you were to offer me any advice."

Parrish knew exactly what he meant. He was hoping that he might be furnished with any suggestions, directions or even instructions, as long as it was just between the two of them. But of course he wouldn't come right out and say that. He was after all the Chieftain and was expected to know all things. His word was right.

"I would be honoured if you felt that my advice was even worth listening to and, if I am to live my life here in Dane-bre, it is my duty to try and help the village in any way that I can."

"That is good." Coran smiled at their agreement. "There will be hard times ahead but we will bear them out. With my guidance, your help and the good fortune of the Earth Goddess, the village will last for many more summers."

Parrish nodded in agreement. He felt it prudent not to say that he knew for a fact Danebury would last right through the Stone, Bronze and Iron Age, until the arrival of the Romans.

"You are a good and wise Chieftain." he bowed. "But now, I must return to my own hut and make ready for the coming night."

"Very well." The Chieftain dismissed him, treaty making over. Parrish went back to his stall and gathered his belongings into his arms. Coran stood idly beside him and looked in on Oona's covered body before eyeing the tall man.

"You are alone now. It is not good for a man to do women's work. You must take a wife. Soon."

Parrish almost dropped his kit! He hadn't even considered the idea of taking a wife, let alone two or three like the others.

Sex was very low down on the agenda of life in Neolithic Britain, he knew. It was one of the things he had observed while watching village life, especially in its condensed form during the storm, when the whole village lived in the one hut.

There were none of the elaborate fertility rites he had expected to see when he first understood exactly where he was. That was just a modern, idealistic fantasy. In the twentieth century, the archaeologists had put much emphasis on this supposed fact. Findings of big hipped female statues, sculptures, icons and carvings had seemed to re-enforce their views. Perhaps it was so easily believed because twentieth century man was obsessed with sex.

Where he was now, in the pre-history of time, his first hand knowledge of Earth Goddess symbolism and their worship of the mother earth had made him see the truth. For all its technology and science, modern man knew little or nothing of the true power of nature. What's more, they showed her no respect.

In many ways, modern man was more backward in his idea of understanding nature than the so called primitive notions of Neolithic man. He wondered what Dannu would think or do if she knew how men were going to treat her earth in five thousand years time.

As far as sex for himself personally went, he could generate no interest. The realization had been a shock at first. It was not that he didn't have a normal sex drive. It was just that he could see no outlet for it and so his libido had slowly faded over the months. He had obviously looked at the women of the time and quickly found that they held no sexual attraction for him whatsoever.

For a start, they were so small. He feared that he might break them if he actually tried anything. Another thing was that he could not abide the way they cowered and bowed submissively to all men. He knew that when a man decided to mate with one of his wives, for that's what it surely was, there were no feelings of love or any other emotion for that matter. It was sex on demand with no female response. Wham, bam, thank you ma'am, only without the thank you. As his friend 'Clive' had once described one totally emotionless woman he had encountered in a state run brothel in Denmark, just a de-luxe willy warmer.

That was how Parrish saw Neolithic women.

No, he had not considered taking a wife and he didn't intend to. He smiled half heartedly at Coran and said, very non committally.

"We will see."

"Yes." agreed Coran in a puzzled tone. The tall mans attitude to women astounded him more than anything else that he did or said. It was a painfully simple subject as far as the Chieftain was concerned. A man takes a wife, gives her his seed and hopes that Dannu smiles and gives him sons. Why must Parrish have such trouble with so simple a thing?

He watched the tall man make his way towards the exit of the great hut and shook his head.

Such a strange man.

22

Clearing the snow away from the immediate area in front of what was now truly his hut was made easy by the use of a shovel. He had borrowed it from one of the huts he had passed on his return. Each family hut had a positively massive collection of different wood, bone and stone earth working implements and it was of no real matter to loan out a single item. The shovel he used was made from the shoulder blade of a small elk or large deer, judging by its size. He soon had a working area cleared and set off with all the others to cut himself some timber. His former firewood store on top of the rise was no longer to be seen. After all the logs had been removed from it the storm had immediately flattened the then unsupported wicker shed.

He felled a good sized tree with his large chopping axe, trimmed off and sectioned the smaller branches, carried them back to the hut and started a fire inside. Then and only then did he return to the main trunk and start cutting it into portable sections. This was the pattern throughout the entire camp for the next several days. Everyone's main concern was gathering fuel. Even the small children dragged individual branches or small bundles of kindling wood to their houses. Every little helped.

Parrish was all the time amazed at the effectiveness and long lived keen edge of his lumber axe. Lashed and wedged firmly into a good sized shaft, the four pound, house brick sized stone head bit deep into the wood swing after swing after swing. Without pushing himself too hard, he felled, trimmed and logged six trees in three days and at the end of it his axe was as sharp as when he'd started.

He was also impressed with the way the hardy little sheep had weathered the storm. They had immediately been let out into the corrals, quickly turning the ground there to mud, so the barns could be cleaned out. Less than two dozen of the animals had perished, frozen where they stood, nearest to the open but barred doorways. The flock was still over two hundred strong and in pretty good shape although they dived hungrily in when the heaps of silage were tossed into the enclosures. When the potentially dangerous, deep drifts around the forests edge had gone and the snow had become shallower and more easily navigable, then the animals would be released back out into the pastures.

The dead animals had been conveniently kept at sub zero temperature by the blizzard once they had died, being still fully edible even though the carcasses were a week old. The meat was handed out fairly as usual and some of the women set too with the fleeces and bones to make tools and clothing.

After the storm, the air was clear and sweet but still very cold. The covering of snow did indeed thin out but stayed for several more weeks. Occasional dustings that fell, mostly during the nights, kept the land covered in a crisp white blanket several inches deep. Even so, on most days the low winter sun shone brightly, dazzling the people of Danebury with its bright reflection from the whiteness of the landscape. Parrish watched with amused interest at how these not-so-stupid people defended themselves against the brightness, obviously knowing how incapacitating full blown snow blindness was. They counteracted the glare by cutting narrow slits in an oblong piece of bark and tying it across the bridge of their noses, secured at the back of their heads with short lengths of leather thong. Parrish himself stopped the entire village in its tracks when he paraded through the camp on his way out to the forest wearing his 'blues brothers' sunglasses. They couldn't fathom out how he never bumped into anything. How could he see where he was going if his eyes were not visible? He lost count of the number of times he let people try on his shades to prove that, although you couldn't see in, you could still see out. The villagers found this truly astounding!

Four days after the storm had passed, the flower and feather man notified Parrish that it was nearly time to offer Oona up to the sky spirits.

Very early the next morning he returned to the great hut and stood at the entrance to his stall. He was as presentable as he could make himself. His boots were clean and polished. He wore the first pair of buckskins that Oona had made for him. His combat jacket was clean, neat and pulled in smartly at the waist by the webbing belt that he had painstakingly removed all the pouches from. On his head at the regulation angle was his beret. The bugle horn badge over his left eye, first introduced to the uniform by the foresters of Germany in 1744 and the emblem of the Light Infantry since its inception in 1968, was buffed to a golden, glowing sheen.

The holy man ignored the strange headdress, which was more than the rest of the village had done when he made his way to the shrine house, and softly sang his strange songs over the old woman's body. Parrish stood silently by, flat faced, waiting until the ceremony was finished. He no longer found amusing the little mans outrageous, feather festooned hat with its interlaced dried flowers, or his odd woollen cape that had more of the same decoration interwoven among the thick threads. He now understood their symbolic connection of the spirits and the earth.

Finally, the holy man nodded and Parrish stepped forward and scooped the small body up into his arms. He followed his lead out of the hut and the two man procession slowly made its way through the mud of the encampment and out of the main gate before heading off to the east, across the ankle deep virgin snow to that little knoll in the near distance.

They climbed its slope, threading their way through the small bare trees that dotted the rise. At its top Parrish saw the rough wooden trestles. Most were empty but two he could see held human remains. It was excarnation he realized, the bodies held up into the sky in the same way the North American Indians treated their dead. He now knew what it meant to be 'offered up to the sky spirits'. Easy pickings for the crows. It definitely wasn't the way he wanted to go but it was clearly how Oona had wanted it.

The flower and feather man selected a trestle and chanted while circling it. He gave a sign to Parrish who stepped forward and laid the body carefully down on top of the platform which was at chest height for the tall man. It didn't matter which way the body was laid upon the trestle platform, the whole assembly being built on a north/south axis. The holy man chanted some more, took a handful of earth from a leather pouch on his belt and threw it across the body, before he gently turned its head to face the rising sun. Then he bowed deeply and stepped back, bowed once more, turned and started off back down the slope of the knoll. He noticed that the tall man was not following and turned to call him. He looked on, surprised, intrigued but above all respectful, as he saw the tall man pay his own last respects.

Face expressionless, Parrish stepped back one long pace, then snapped to attention. After a moment's pause he brought his arm up in a crisp, sharp salute, holding it for five long seconds before whipping the arm smartly back down to his side. Then he 'fell out', turning to his left, stamping again to attention and marching off, past the silently watching holy man and away, back down the steep slope towards the camp.

The snow eventually melted away into the earth and the weather resorted to long periods of frost and cold, interspersed with mini thaws and bouts of rain. Parrish noticed that pairs of men had started to be sent out to watch the flock, and not just at night this time. He was about to ask if there had been wolf signs found in the forest or did they expect visits from the predators at this time of year, when the first lamb appeared.

Fair play, he thought, and smiled as he watched the little creature staggering about, almost permanently attached to its mothers teats.

Apart from the four, well defined seasons, Parrish had no real idea exactly where he was in the year but it was a known fact, explained to most kids while still in primary school, that lambs start to appear from the middle of February onwards. At least now he could assume that the worst of the winter was probably past.

Well, that's good news, he thought. Shame I missed Christmas though.

He gave a snorting laugh on remembering that *that* man wouldn't even be born for another three thousand five hundred years!

Danebury was even busier than usual now. The women were baking and sewing, grinding corn, making bone needles or spindle whorls with chalk or clay weights, ready to spin the wool that would be sheared from the sheep in two full moons time.

The men were just as occupied, repairing any storm damage to the living huts before concentrating on tool preparation for the tilling of their fields for the new planting. They were expected to start on the now weed strewn allotments as soon as the warmer, dryer weather appeared. Their antler picks, bone headed hoes and shoulder blade shovels were all being sharpened and readied for use. Great attention was also being lavished on all their hunting weapons.

Any damaged or blunted heads were replaced, whipping was closely inspected and sling ammunition and supplies of arrows increased.

Parrish noted with alarm that the men of Danebury were also readying their barbed, broadhead arrows that were definitely *not* hunting weapons. He asked Klud what was going on. The warrior's first reaction was surprise before he grasped the reason for the tall mans curiosity.

"Oh yes, I forget. You do not yet fully know our ways." He fixed Parrish with a look of patient reasoning. "The winter was very bad, yes?"

"Yes."

"Well, we here at Dane-bre saw our way through the season quite well, with the good fortune of the Earth Goddess and your help."

"We all did our bit." Parish returned the praise that Klud was bestowing. The warrior nodded briefly but did not dwell on it.

"Other villages may not have been so fortunate."

"There are other villages around?" asked Parrish, swooping on the choice snippet of information. Klud just nodded but did not expand on the subject. He would not be swayed from the explanation he was in the middle of pointing out to his ignorant friend. He repeated himself.

"They may not have been so lucky."

"So?"

Klud shook his head sadly. "Sometimes Parrish, I think that you have learned nothing from us." he sighed. "If some other village that has suffered the Earth Goddess's wrath is to survive, it will need food, supplies or whatever else it is short of. From a village that has the things it needs."

"I see." Parrish understood now. "A raiding party."

"Yes!" The Neolithic man nodded emphatically, reminding Parrish somehow of the patronizing Chinese caricature that Benny Hill used to do.

"Thank you!" he said, nodding just as emphatically. The two men smiled at each other, enjoying the light-hearted mickey taking.

"You had better check your own arrows, Parrish." advised the smaller man and Parrish did as was suggested, worried now about the prospect of imminent attack from some other distant, mysterious camp.

Shit, he thought, and just as things were looking up too.

It seemed strange to him how he appeared to be the only one who was at all worried by the unknown threat of possible attack. Everyone else seemed to take it in their stride, with a resigned attitude of, if it happened, it happened. Parrish managed to stay tense and alert for the next couple of days before even he succumbed to the general feeling of apathy that prevailed in the camp. It was inevitable. No man can remain in a constant state of instant readiness indefinitely, it would completely drain him.

In any event, the days continued to pass uneventfully and the bustling village of Danebury began to look forward to the advent of warmer weather.

Once it had arrived, the preparation of the fields could commence with gusto. The village had been so impressed with the more than ample yield from the last year's crop that they were quite keen to begin this year's. By the end of the winter season the grain supplies would normally be getting low but there was still a good reservoir of the precious seed in many, as yet unopened, storage pits. Bread was still freely available in the camp, a rare occurrence in early spring. The people were sure the Earth Goddess was still smiling on them and they had high hopes for a second good crop.

Parrish did his bit, along with all the other men, doing his stint as shepherd when requested. He took a perverse pleasure in shouting 'mint sauce!' whenever any of the woolly creatures strayed too close to him but couldn't help smiling to see the little lambs trotting obediently along beside their mothers. Their short bleats for more milk seemed as natural a sound in the air as the singing of the birds in the forest.

"What is 'mint sauce'?" asked his co shepherd, towards the end of the days watch. The little man, who had not spoken a word all day, had been hushed in the shadow of his towering partner. Awed by the man's presence and his natural, confidant air, he was almost afraid to speak for fear of saying the wrong thing. The rumour still circulating around the camp among the lower echelons was that Parrish was Dannu's man. Some even wondered if speaking to the tall man was to be heard directly by the Earth Goddess. Finally though, the little mans curiosity got the better of him.

"Huh?"

"What is 'mint sauce'?" The look on the Neolithic man's face told

Parrish that he was expecting some profound, deep meaning reply. He laughed.

"It is just a special preparation that is eaten with lamb where I come from. The sheep are supposed to know this, be frightened and run away. Of course they do not, but I still like to do it."

"Oh." said the smaller man in a disappointed voice. Parrish laughed again and shrugged his shoulders.

"Stupid I know, but it is just a bit of fun."

His partner obviously didn't understand the concept and Parrish walked away, leaving him to try and figure it out, a devilish smile on his face.

Dannu was obviously looking out for her man, well that's how the villagers saw it. The following day, when he had finished his final stag as shepherd and was safely in the shadow of the fort, working by the corrals repairing storm damage to some barn thatch, it happened.

A warning cry went up from across the pasture and everyone looked to see the source of the shout. One of the two shepherds for the day was running at high speed towards the hill fort. His partner was nowhere to be seen. The running man let out a second warning shout. Half way through, the yell turned into a cry of pain and he pitched forward onto his face. Even at the extreme distance, Parrish could still make out the slender shaft of the arrow that stuck stiffly out of his back. The unfortunate man squirmed on the ground in agony but Parrish no longer watched him. His eyes were on the tiny figures that swarmed out of the distant tree line and were charging towards the fort. As the mob passed the stricken, prostrate Danebury man, two men bludgeoned him quickly and mercilessly to death with their war clubs.

"Contact!" yelled Parrish. "Into the fort! Into the fort!" He herded the two women who had been bundling his thatch for him towards the gated entrance. It was fortunate that almost everyone else was already inside, still waiting out the unsettled weather prior to the imminent ploughing. The few that were not yet safe behind the defence ditch and palisade like wall were at least close by and sprinted towards the entrance. Parrish waved them all past him and was the last man in. The great gate banged safely and securely shut while the strangers that charged towards it were still several hundred meters away.

23

Every warrior in the camp was up on the parapet and peering over the wall at their unknown attackers. They had gathered in a large group about one hundred and fifty meters beyond the defence ditch, safely out of arrow range. Parrish moved up beside Coran and, not taking his eyes off the mystery men, asked the big question.

"What happens now?"

"I am not sure." was the man's quick answer. "Their attack was bad. It is likely that they intended to watch and wait until many of us were outside. They were probably spotted by one of the shepherds. Perhaps he who gave the alarm?"

Several men near them, who had been listening to their Chieftains words, nodded in agreement and Parrish nodded too.

"Yes. He did well and died bravely." No one felt obliged to mention the fact that the man was running away when he was killed, very probably leaving behind the body of the man who really did raise the alarm. "The main thing now, is what will they do next?"

All eyes were still firmly glued to the massed men beyond the fort wall, every man jack of them armed to the teeth. Parrish counted about thirty. The number compared quite closely to the total number of warriors in Danebury, making it plainly obvious that whatever village they had come from, it was almost certainly its full complement of men. Some raiding party!

"They may or may not know that we have no well inside Dane-bre, but can be sure that we will have enough water to last us many days." said Coran suddenly, apparently thinking out loud. "It is unlikely that they will wait until we run out. It would be a very long time before we would be forced to go outside the fort."

"Weeks." agreed Parrish.

Coran and the nearby warriors looked quizzically at the tall man, not understanding the English word.

"You are right Coran." Parrish corrected himself. The Chieftain opened his mouth to speak again but was cut off by a shout from beyond the wall.

"Coran!" The cry carried clearly across the gap between the two factions. "Coran!"

"I hear you!" shouted back the Chieftain.

"You will open your gate and give us what we ask, or we will kill all your sheep, take what we can carry and burn the rest. Do you understand me?"

There was a murmur of dismay from the men along the parapet and Coran shook his head. Parrish on the other hand couldn't help but admire the ultimatum. If anything was going to get these people what they wanted, that was it. He also wondered how the unknown caller knew Coran's name, and looked at the Chieftain, who was deep in thought.

As if to make sure that his threat was not a bluff, the mystery man in charge of the sieging warriors signalled, and a number of sheep were dragged bleating to the front of the group. In a violent display of their intent, the animals were killed in full view, their heads smashed in by eagerly swung war clubs. A wave of shock went through the men along the wall. Even as Parrish watched, he could see their morale plunging. They needed those animals he knew, they were the village's lifeline. The opposing force obviously knew this too and their clever leader was making full and effective use of the farmers Achilles heel.

Coran had quickly pared his thinking down to two options.

"We either go out and fight them, or surrender like women and let them strip the village bare." he said bluntly and another uneasy rumble travelled along the line of men.

Parrish knew what the Chieftain was thinking, trying to figure out the losses that might be sustained in an attack. He looked over the man's head, down the line of men with their slumped shoulders, weapons hanging dejectedly from their hands. His own mind raced.

He tapped Coran on the shoulder, gestured with his head and the two men moved away to confer in private. Parrish had an idea and he put it to the Chieftain, the whole plan hinging on the fact that these Neolithic warriors had no real concept of battlefield tactics. It was a simple plan, it would have to be for a number of reasons. Firstly, they are the only ones that seem to work. Secondly, it had to be understandable to these simple men. Thirdly, it had to be easy enough for Coran to explain to his men. The words would have to come from his mouth or he would lose face before his warriors and, as Chieftain, he would have to be seen to run the whole operation. He put his idea to Coran, explained in simple terms what to do, the orders to give and the expected outcome.

"Are you sure it will work?" asked Coran finally. He was concerned not only of losing the battle and loosing face, but the possibly very high number of casualties if it failed. What point is there in being Chieftain if there is no village left to be Chieftain of!

"It worked against the Zulu warriors and there were many more of them than the defending men." The explanation itself didn't mean all that much to Coran but the tall mans words were full of confidence. He deliberated for a few moments then nodded, grim faced.

The Chieftain gathered all his warriors around him and slowly and carefully told them what was going to happen and what they had to do. There were to be no mistakes and no releasing of arrows except on his order. Any man who disobeyed him would feel his wrath afterwards. It was plain by the expression on their faces that they were not sure of the plan, but Coran was Chieftain and his word was right.

When everything was fully clear and understood, they all gathered before the main gate. There were several nervous glances at Parrish. The men didn't know it was completely the tall mans idea but they were well aware that the Chieftain had conferred with him and had apparently come up with this completely untried plan during or immediately after the talk. Parrish ignored the glances but the pressure he suddenly felt was enormous. Had he just committed these men to a violent death?

At Coran's command the gate was swung open. The men ran swiftly out into the open, past the overlapping ends of the defence ditch and lined up along its front edge, removing their quivers from their backs and thrusting several arrows into the ground beside them. The opposing warriors watched the whole exercise in baffled silence. The unknown leader of the group was a bit surprised. It was usual for two opposed bands to rally themselves before the attack but he had never before seen men string out in a line to do it.

One hundred and twenty meters of open ground separated the two forces and they eyed each other in an uneasy silence. Time dragged slowly by.

Parrish stood to Coran's left. Like the others he had an arrow already nocked to his bowstring.

His plan would only work if they were attacked, not the other way around. And still no one was ready to make the first move. Tension was thick in the air.

"Which one is their leader?" Parrish asked the Chieftain. Coran pointed with the end of his bow to a striking individual at the head of the mob facing them.

"That man with the white fleece jerkin. It is the sign of their Chieftain. Why do you ask?" Parrish was half temped to ask how Coran would know such a thing about a band of people he had never seen before, but thought the better of it.

"We must make them attack us or the plan will not work."

He planted his feet firmly and steadied himself, speaking softly under his breath to boost his own morale, unaware that Coran and a couple of the men either side of him could also hear the words.

"Fuckers think they are safely out of range. Well, we'll see about that!"

He drew back the big bow, grunting with the effort, eyeing the distance between him and his target. It was not as difficult a shot as it looked. He had done it successfully many times during practice. The question was, could he now do it when it counted? He sucked in a deep breath, let out half the air in an audible sigh, and took careful aim. He released.

The arrow rifled through the air, crossing the open ground in under two seconds, watched intently by one and all. The fleece jerkined leader saw the missile heading towards him and laughed at the feeble attempt. He knew the shot would fall well short. When he realized his mistake it was too late. He had barely started to turn away when the speeding arrow struck, hitting him with a hard thud, loud enough to be heard even by the distant line of Danebury warriors. The barbed flint broadhead buried itself deep in the man's chest and he died where he fell.

A cheer went up from the line of men but Parrish was in no mood to accept any praise. He had just killed a man in cold blood.

For a brief time confusion reigned among the dead Chieftains warriors but the mood quickly turned to one of anger. The waiting men of Danebury could all see the rising fury in the way the others moved and acted. The level of tension increased rapidly, culminating in a sudden roar from the distant men. They rallied, raised their weapons and started to race across the gap between them and the Danebury line, yelling and screaming at the top of their lungs.

All along the line men shuffled and swayed uneasily. Parrish could almost feel the high tension and fear in the air, like a hot blast of air on his cheeks. It was at once both terrifying yet thrilling.

The combat instructors at basic training camp called it going into fight or flight mode, signalling the high rush of adrenalin. They would have been proud of the warriors of Danebury for every man stood his ground in the face of the threatening death that rushed towards them.

When the charging mass of men had closed to about eighty meters Coran gave a shout and almost as one his men drew their bows and released. A shower of arrows arced across the gap towards the running group. Only a couple of men fell to the first barrage, many of the arrows actually falling to earth behind the closing band. The line drew once more and, at the Chieftains order, launched again. The gap was lessening all the time and the second fusillade of shots was much more accurate, perhaps seven or eight men falling wounded or killed. The men drew for a third time and, to their credit, did not release until Coran gave the order. The temptation to do so was strong, even Parrish had to check himself. The Chieftains shout went up when the attacking men were only twenty meters away. The phrase 'wait till you see the whites of their eyes' sprung briefly to Parrish's mind, acknowledging the fact that Coran was undoubtedly a natural born leader. At such short range, every arrow flew straight and true into the advancing men and most of the missiles struck home. Men fell screaming right across the width of the attack and, with well over half the men down before they had even got within fighting distance of the Danebury men, the advance crumbled. The warriors that were still able, turned and fled back the way they had come.

The complete success of the tactic fired up the Danebury men to fever pitch almost instantly, Parrish included. Victory was theirs, the enemy routed.

As one a great cry went up from the line and they hurled down their bows, drew their battle axes and war clubs and charged off after the retreating men. The blood fuelled, white hot adrenalin thrill thundered in the men's veins as they ran screaming and shouting in pursuit.

"Remember Agincourt!" yelled Parrish, just as caught up in the melee and, drawing his survival knife, charged across the open ground. Because of his greater size and stride he rapidly outstripped the other Danebury men and closed with the tail enders of the retreating group. He rushed up behind the nearest man and thrust his knife violently into his back. The unfortunate warrior went down with the blade still embedded in him, Parrish losing his grip on the knife as the man fell, the weapon lodged firmly between the warrior's ribs.

Parrish was by now out of control, high on his aggressive fury and charging blindly on, unaware that all the other Danebury warriors had given up the chase and were dumbly watching him, astounded.

He quickly overhauled the next man and brought him down with a bruising rugby tackle. The two men rolled apart and Parrish came quickly to his knees, searching for a weapon. His eyes fell on a discarded battle axe and he snatched it up, turning swiftly to face his opponent.

They stood less than ten feet apart, each poised to strike, both armed with flint axes. There was no room to rush at each other and the men just stepped up, going for the kill. It was almost a fatal mistake on Parrish's part. He found himself attacking a man who was at one with his chosen weapon, whereas he was using one that was totally alien to him. His attempted blow was quick but clumsy, poorly timed and ineffective. His opponent, although smaller and with a correspondingly shorter reach, was more successful and it was only a swift and evasive body movement that saved Parrish from immediate death. The swinging axe struck him a glancing blow on the side of the head and he felt the blood flow freely down his cheek.

The little man's eyes glittered at the sight of the wound and he eagerly attacked again, bringing the lethal weapon over his head in a potentially skull splitting blow. Parrish defended himself by holding his own axe in front of his face, gripping it tightly at both ends, and blocked the downward strike across the shaft. Before the Neolithic warrior could draw back for a third attack Parrish punched him on the chin. The man rocked back with the force of the blow. Parrish hurled the useless axe aside and leapt on the man and they fell to the ground, grappling together. With a surprising display of strength the little man kicked himself free and once again they both leapt to their feet. This time it was the warrior who was faster and he lunged, going for the face, gouging for the eyes. Parrish defended himself as best he could and as his hands protected his face, brought his knee up hard into the little mans groin. The blow didn't connect fully but the effect was still enough to distract the little warrior from his attack. Parrish seized the opportunity, took his opponents head roughly in his hands, tilted the face up towards him and ruthlessly head butted him on the bridge of the nose.

Stunned, blinded by tears and with blood streaming down his face, the warrior cried out and sank to his knees. Parrish grabbed a handful of the man's hair, jerked back the head and raised his hand, ready to smash down its stiffened edge on the exposed windpipe.

It was the second time that he had held a man's life in his hands, but this time it was not controlled and contained, like an unarmed combat training exercise. It was wild and savage, a bloodthirsty fury that now controlled him and not the other way round. A feeling of revulsion at the discovery of how powerful his primeval side was, suddenly threatened to choke him. As quickly as it had come, the fighting rage evaporated away. Parrish found himself looking down at a blood spattered, defeated enemy. A feeling of disgust swept over him when he realised how close he had come to delivering a totally unnecessary 'coup de grace', just to satisfy his blood lust. He slowly lowered his hand. When he released his grip on the beaten warrior's hair the man slumped and just knelt before him, shaking his head to try and clear his vision.

"Kill him Parrish, kill him!" came a nearby cry from one of the Danebury men, a chant that was immediately taken up by the others. He looked around, shocked to see all the men, watching the fight intently, gathered only a few feet away, the blood lust bright in their eyes. Parrish felt sick to his stomach. He looked back down at the subjugated warrior, who still knelt, head bowed, now expecting ritual death.

He reached down and offered the man his hand. The warrior looked up in surprise and confusion at the tall man, who offered his hand again. The chanting and yelling spectators fell silent. Parrish offered his hand a third time and the kneeling warrior hesitantly reached up and grasped the tall mans forearm. Parrish gripped his opponents arm and pulled the man to his feet. The two stared at each other intently for a long moment, the confusion on the small warriors face quite apparent. Parrish nodded in a brief bow. The smaller man hesitantly did the same.

"You are a great warrior." said Parrish slowly. "You honour me greatly with a good fight. I honour you in return with your life. Go."

The Neolithic man gave him a disbelieving look.

"Go." he repeated.

To his credit, the man didn't just turn and dash off. He bowed deeply to Parrish, eyed the other Danebury warriors with distrust and then turned away. Obviously keen to get beyond arrow range but still defiant enough not to be seen to hurry, he jogged off after his compatriots who were now disappearing into the forest, carrying as many of their dead as they could, including their leader.

Parrish turned to face the men of Danebury, his eyes daring anyone to draw an arrow against the departing man. When he was sure the warrior was safely away, he strode over to the still silent men, shouldered roughly through them and walked slowly back to the fort, stopping on the way to retrieve his knife and pick up his bow and arrows.

The others just stared after him.

"He is truly the strangest man." said Coran. "I have never seen a man so born to fight, yet not ready to kill." The rest of the men nodded in agreement. Then the Chieftain signalled and the party broke up. The men wandered gleefully off among the carnage and started to collect their grisly trophies.

Parrish returned to his hut, cleaned up his face and tried to gather his thoughts. His actions on the battlefield had shocked him. Was he reverting to animal savagery? Is that the effect living in primitive conditions has on a man? He looked around his little Neolithic hovel, just about as basic a dwelling as it was possible to get, and decided there and then that he would build himself a better, less crude place to live. Somewhere with at least a few creature comforts. A place where he could afford to relax a little. He set off to find Coran.

The village was deserted and he wandered through it wondering what the blazes was going on. When he reached the main gate he could hear the distant babble of excited voices. Following the sound to its source, he found himself out beyond the animal pens, at the excrement pit. It was a huge hole in the ground, surrounded on three sides by mini forests of tall nettles, where the whole village dumped its waste. All the villagers were there. Parrish edged his way through the throng to see what the great attraction was. The smell from the pit was strong this close up but that didn't seem to deter anyone. He pushed through to the front of the crowd and witnessed another sort of Danebury ritual.

The bodies of the warriors that had been killed, all now headless, were being systematically quartered and the separate pieces thrown into the cesspool. The sight of limbs, brutally hacked off with flint axes and tossed into the mire, disappearing into the filth with a wet slap, made his stomach churn. What repulsed him even more were the looks of absolute glee on the faces of the people. Even the women and children.

Coran appeared beside him, smiling broadly. He saw the ghastly expression on the tall man's face and took it to be one of bewilderment.

"Do you see what we do Parrish?"

"Oh, I see it all right." He held his tongue, rather than say what he really thought about the awful spectacle.

"But you do not understand." He called the flower and feather man over and spoke into his ear. The little man nodded then led Parrish away to a quieter corner, near the animal barns.

"The Chieftain has told me to tell you about this." He pointed at the backs of the people crowding around the pit.

"I'm not so sure I want to know."

The holy man dismissed the notion with a wave of his hand.

"It is a warning to any others that would dare attack us. Their bodies will share the same fate."

"What, to be chopped up and tossed into a pool of shit?" asked Parrish incredulously. As if the men cared what happened to them once they were dead. But, of course, he knew they did.

"It is a warrior's greatest fear. To die a good death but not to be able to return to the Earth Goddess."

"Huh?"

"When you return to her arms, you must be complete." The little man once again had that look on his face as if he were explaining some simple truth to a child. "She will not take you unless you are.

How can you go and take your stall in the shrine house of the Goddess without being whole? Besides, if your body is not offered up to the sky spirits, how can they take you to her?"

"I see."

"Yes. And without your frame, your soul cannot be re born again and walk in the sun. You are lost forever."

Parrish nodded and, explanation over, the little man hurried away back to the join the crowd. Suddenly remembering, he returned and made a final speech.

"You no doubt will not know this either. Tonight there will be a big celebration of our victory in the great hut. You must be there for you too have trophies."

"I don't give a toss about trophies." The idea of having a human skull hanging in his stall he found quite repulsive.

"Pah!" dismissed the holy man and once again hurried back towards the pit, determined not to miss anymore of the fun.

By nightfall the whole village was once more inside the great hut. Blazing briars ringed the outside of the building while the inside was well illuminated by the roaring central fire and plenty of tallow lamps. The light threw into stark relief the new whiteness of freshly cleaned skulls, proudly displayed in many stalls.

It seemed the warriors had wasted no time as far as trophies were concerned. The heads of the slain men had been removed, emptied and boiled before being cleaned and proudly displayed for all to see.

Parrish himself had two skulls to his credit and somehow they didn't look quite so grisly when lined up alongside his other trophies. One had belonged to the man he'd knifed and the other to a warrior who had been found with a black fletched arrow embedded in his body. He even had his arrow returned to him, being told that the missile had almost passed completely through the chest. To top that, many congratulations and great emphasis was put on the fact that, although the skull was not his to show, he was acknowledged as the killer of the attacking villages Chieftain. He waved the praise modestly aside and secretly wished all the gloaters would piss off.

The Chieftain finally called the meeting to some sort of order and made a long speech, praising all his warriors for their great bravery, skill at arms and for fighting a good fight. There were roaring cheers when he pointed out individual feats of courage and skill. Someone called out that the Chieftains plan had been a great triumph, proving his worth as Chieftain. To this he received a great cheer, accepting the adulation without so much as a glance in Parrish's direction. The tall man grinned with the realization that, even this far back in time, some things remained the same. Leaders still took the credit for other men's efforts. To his surprise the smile on his face felt good and, for the first time since the battle, he started to relax.

When Coran had finished, the flower and feather man stepped up and turned to face the stone statue with his arms raised. This time in the language of the village, he started chanting and the people listened with great satisfaction as their victory was sung to the Earth Goddess.

Coran came over and stood beside Parrish and together they watched the ceremony.

"I did not mention you when I spoke of good deeds, Parrish."

"I noticed."

"Do not be offended. They all know how well you fought but you did not kill the man you bested in battle. To some that is a sign of weakness and I would not make glory of it." Parrish was not in the least bit offended and nodded in appreciation of a sound leadership decision. The smaller man continued. "You are a strange one but still both brave and clever. I am honoured that you shared your plan with me and allowed me to take charge of the battle."

Parrish was staggered by this frank admission and appreciation of his assistance and looked around to see if anyone else had witnessed their Chieftain paying homage to a supposedly lesser man. No one had, for Coran had chosen his moment well, the rest of the village engrossed in the holy mans chanting rhetoric. He nodded to the man.

"Without you to lead the warriors, the whole plan would have been nothing. You are a great leader, all the more so because you are not too proud to admit that you needed a little help and accepted it when offered. With you as Chieftain of Dane-bre the village will stay safe and strong."

Coran clapped the tall man on the shoulder and laughed.

"Yes, I did well did I not?"

"Every warrior was proud and honoured to fight with you today."

The two both nodded solemnly for a moment then laughed out

loud, sharing the moment of camaraderie. The holy man's chanting finished at that moment and a rumbling hub-bub of voices broke out.

Coran clapped his hands loudly and several men ran behind the shrine, re emerging with an assortment of drums. Some were slotted horizontal logs while others were upright, hollowed out barrels of wood with skins stretched tight across the tops. Setting them down in front of the statue, they started to beat on them with sticks and their palms. A throbbing, rhythmic beat began to pulsate through the air. Men started to dance around the fire while the women and children joined in with clapping hands.

The noise was almost deafening but not at all unpleasant. The deep beat crept inside Parrish's head, as it did to all the other people. He knew immediately how powerful it was and reckoned that a good rock band would have given a year's earnings to steal a recording of it.

The celebrating went on into the night and it was not long before Parrish found himself hauled up by friendly hands and dragged out into the dancing throng. Just about every man and boy was now on the floor, dancing, jumping and stamping around the fire to the throb of the drums. Parrish's whole body seemed to be pulsating along with the sound and he couldn't help himself as he started disco dancing to the overpowering rhythm. He swung his arms, gyrated his hips and nodded his head to the vigorous tempo. Others began to copy his actions and the people in the stalls watched with ever growing excitement, clapping and chanting, driving him along. The whole floor was now gyrating in the same manner as the tall man, revelling in the discovery of a new dance. Finally Parrish went completely over the top and stopped the whole show by emitting a high pitched shriek and moving backwards across the earth floor doing the Michael Jackson moonwalk. Every one stopped and stared. The drums died away and the great hut fell into silent amazement.

Parrish froze on the spot, feeling all eyes on him. He turned full circle looking for a way out but found none. In desperation he rushed over to the drums and began beating on one with his hands.

"Drums, drums!" he shouted and the drummers, seeing the discrete nod from Coran, started the beat up again and the dancing slowly resumed. Parrish did not return to the floor, making straight for the sanctuary of his stall. The Chieftain again walked over to join him.

"Sorry about that." Parrish apologized hastily. "I got a bit caught up in the beat."

"No matter Parrish. That is what it is for. That was quite a display. Perhaps one day you will teach it to me?" The tall man laughed nervously, not sure if the Chieftain was being serious or sarcastic. "Will you not dance again?"

"No. I have danced enough. While we speak though, I have a request. I would like to build myself a better house. Have I your permission?"

"Of course."

"I will need some help."

"That is all right, Parrish. As you know, the village is in your debt."

"Thank you."

The Chieftain nodded and walked away. Parrish sat down in his stall and immediately started to plan out the construction of the new house in his head.

He never got very far. The beat was strong and unavoidable. Soon he found himself clapping his hands and laughing along with the other people, relaxed and thoroughly enjoying himself for the first time since he could remember.

It was a great party and he wondered what time the buffet started.

24

For the next few days the flower and feather man was kept very busy tattooing warriors, Parrish included.

The mark for taking another man's head was apparently a single, continuous line around the neck. Above this line were then drawn circles, each one about the size of a man's thumb nail, each circle representing a taken head. Parrish was credited with three kills *and* had to suffer the added grief of having one of his circles completely coloured in with the blue dye, necessitating many small cuts within the circle to achieve the desired effect. When he complained about the process the holy man scoffed.

"Do you not know how rare this mark is?" he asked in an incredulous tone. "The sign of a Chieftain killer is nothing to be annoyed about. Be still."

Parrish was not impressed and was very glad of the pain relieving poultice that Klud's first wife applied to his neck immediately after the skin cutting torture was finished. He had to admit that he now found it more interesting to look at other men's marks. Klud had eight 'head circles' to his credit. Coran however had circles that went right around his neck above the line and several more below it. A most impressive tally by Neolithic standards. Parrish pushed from his mind the thought that technically the man was a mass murderer.

And so it was that many men with sore necks, but never the less proud of their new medals of courage, turned their attention to the less glamorous subject of cultivation. The weather was doing its best to stabilize, giving the first hints of early spring. In the space of a few consecutive days, the allotments were dug. Parrish had been allocated a section of one families plot. They were the relatives of Oona's original family and he was handed her piece of the small holding, the piece she had allowed to go completely to seed the past year. It was somehow reassuring to know that he hadn't risen above the level of still sometimes being handed the shit end of the stick.

The symbolic scythes were nowhere to be seen when it came to basic ground clearing but the work rate was very much the same. With the whole village working once again as a team, the job was done in less than two full days. When the plots had been finally cleared and the topsoil turned, muck from the excrement pit was spread over them, the filth transferred from the pit to the plots using birch bark buckets. They themselves were discarded afterwards. It was a foul job and was of course done by the women.

Either Parrish's resolve was slipping or he was becoming a bit more Neolithic in his outlook because even he stood back and let them get on with it. The muck was allowed to lay on the bared earth for a couple of days in the hope of some rain driving it into the ground, before it was finally turned in by hand. It was probably just a side effect but letting it lay for a while also starved any new weed shoots of the sunlight they craved and helped keep them at bay for a while longer. Parrish wondered how these Stone Age people had learned the concept of feeding the earth with nutrients, although he was in no doubt that the plots needed it. Using the same patch of ground year after year without any respite or replenishment would soon drain it of all its goodness.

It was during this time that the bodies of the two shepherd's who were killed during the first moments of the attack on Danebury, were offered up to the sky spirits. The sad procession towards the knoll only received the occasional glance from the people working the land. Parrish watched the faces of the dead men's families and understood how their sadness was worsened by the fact that the bodies were headless. Even so, they were still offered up to the sky spirits. He asked the flower and feather man about that fact after the ceremony was over and the little man nodded sadly.

"They cannot join the Earth Goddess in her great shrine house without their heads but the rest of their bodies are complete. Although the heads were taken away as trophies, it is still possible that at some later time they may perhaps be returned to the families. Then the two parts can be re united. It is most unlikely but, while the chance still remains, we must make sure that the rest of their bodies have been prepared."

Parrish understood the reasoning, and he was sure the holy man did too, that the whole thing was a gesture to give the families of the dead men something to hold on to in the hope of saving their close relatives souls from being forever lost. If you have to believe in something, he reasoned, that's as good a thing as any.

While all this was going on Parrish, capitalizing on the long periods of waiting between gardening operations, had started on his new house. Much to the dismay of the rest of the village, he had again settled on a building with corners. The people were also less than impressed with the site of his planned house, the patch of raised ground in the north-west quadrant of the hill fort, where his original wicker shed had once stood.

He planned to build, with the help of the other villagers, a log cabin. *And* it would have a thatched roof and a stone fireplace with chimney. That would mean he would have to have a separate smoking shed for his meats but he was prepared to waive that disadvantage against the mental comfort of living in a more modern styled, 'house like' house.

Even though the Neolithic people thought the tall man's idea of a house was ridiculous, it did not detract from their commitment to the building project. Together with the tall man they cleared and levelled a rectangular patch of ground before beginning to cut down the trees he had selected and marked. Parrish still respected some of the criteria laid down for house building in Neolithic times. He made sure that the plot was laid out so the entrance of his cabin would face south east, as per all the other buildings inside the encampment, but other concepts he introduced were totally alien to the locals.

Such as windows. Admittedly they were only two small square openings, one on each side of the cabin, fitted with wooden shutters that enabled them to be closed during the cold season or opened to allow a through draught in the summer. To the people of Danebury, at that moment in time, they appeared to be a total waste of time.

Although the overall shape of the cabin was rectangular, a wattle and daub partition wall was to be erected inside to give a storage room and also a second door between the squarer living quarters and the outside world. He planned to stagger the position of the doors using the same principle as the entrance passageway inside the great hut. Most of the storeroom would eventually be taken up with logs to fuel the fire in the living room. It made Parrish smile just to think of the words 'living room'.

He helped but mainly directed when it came to laying down the logs as they were cut and transported, by hand, up to the top of 'his' rise. The logs were all selected pines that after trimming were more or less telegraph poles with the bark still on. After notching them a couple of feet in from either end they were laid down in an interlocking pattern to build up the four walls. The logs for the two opposing long sides were very carefully chosen for their straight trunks.

They were heavy and awkward to carry and it was fortunate that Parrish deemed it necessary only to take the walls up to shoulder height. The two ends of the cabin were much easier, especially the door end. He could not deny that the Neolithic builders knew their onions when it came to the construction and angles of thatched roofs and bowed to their superior knowledge, intending to do the same. He built up the gable ends with ever shorter logs until he had two high apexes that were linked by a main roof support spar that spanned the gap between them. The building was by now beginning to take on a definite shape. Parrish stepped back to look at the overall design and was quite pleased with it. Apart from the fact that the roof would be a steeply angled straight line, the cabin closely resembled a Dutch barn in shape.

The work progressed smoothly. Kids were quite happy to mix up great mounds of daub and push it into the joints where the logs butted up against one another. They then started smoothing it out and eventually both the interior and exterior walls were virtually smooth. Parrish himself, with a small band of men, laid down and tied a criss-crossing frame of boughs from the main roof spar down to the walls in preparation for the application of the thatch.

It was at that point that Coran called a halt to the building work. Parrish was keen to carry on now that his place was taking shape but respected the man's decision. There were now more important jobs at hand. Besides, there weren't any stems of a suitable length yet grown that could be used as thatch.

All the other jobs to be done, including building the wattle and daub partition wall, building up the fireplace and chimney with stones and clay, plus any furniture he might decide to make, he could do himself.

The time had come to seed the land. This needed the whole village and involved another Earth Goddess ceremony, which started with the flower and feather man singing to the shrine. At a given signal, a troop of men solemnly carried out the precious clay jars full of seed. Everyone then filed out of the camp and crossed to the allotments, the procession led by the holy man and the Chieftain, followed by the grain carriers and then the rest of the village. At the site of the freshly prepared earth the holy man appeared to bless the ground, well that's what it looked like to Parrish, each plot visited individually. The grains were then handed out to each family which meant that from that point on they became their responsibility. Finally the plots were seeded, one after the other, watched by everyone.

Parrish thought it highly amusing that, on Coran's instruction, the children were to be used as living scarecrows to keep the birds at bay. It was quite a trial for the youngsters. They plainly wanted to run wild and play but were expected to stay close and protect the seeds. In Parrish's opinion it seemed a rather responsible job to be left in the hands of children, although he could see how it would impress on them at a young age the importance of bonding together as a single village unit. He didn't find it quite so amusing when he realized that the same kids that started their scarecrow jobs before dawn, were still there at dusk.

He asked Coran if he might be allowed to organize the little scarecrows into a fairer, more even system. It would be just as effective at protecting the precious grains but cause less wear and tear on the kids. The Chieftain thought that he was wasting his time, especially when he had a house to build, but told him to carry on if he so wished.

Early the next morning all the children were in front of the allotments, gathered around the tall man. To them this was an honour in itself considering what a great warrior he was *and* friend to the Chieftain. They listened intently to his instructions.

The youngsters were to work in groups of four. Parrish knew that they couldn't count, no one here could count, so he tagged each group with necklaces. These were leather thong loops with little clay doughnuts threaded on them, one bead for group one, two for two and so on. They didn't have to know how many beads were on their necklaces, just that they had the same number as the rest of their particular group. The little squads were to do shifts, or stags, of roughly three hours each. Parrish pushed a tall stick into a bare patch of ground and, along the arc that the shadow the stick would make, he placed four big round pebbles. It was a very rough and ready clock/marker to indicate the six, nine, noon and three o'clock positions. This early in the year the first and last shifts would overlap well into the night so four shifts would be enough. The plan was that when one stag was ending and the next about to start, one of the kids on the ending stag would run and find the four for the following one. A simple system, allowing everyone to do their fair share of the work but still have time to play. As long as the sun shone that is. If it did not, Parrish would come down to the allotments at regular intervals and change the shifts personally. It was no big deal to him.

He explained the stag system slowly and fully to the youngsters who were all very excited at being involved in some kind of 'plan'. Especially after the Chieftain had used a great plan to defeat the enemies of the village. It was a double bonus that they could do the Chieftains bidding and guard the important seeds yet still have time to play. But best of all, they were absolutely thrilled to be each given a unique bead necklace of their very own!

"If this 'plan' works, perhaps the Chieftain will use it again in the future." said Parrish to the excited youngsters gathered before him. "Do not let me down and the warriors of the village will look well upon you. If something does go wrong or you do not know what to do, come and ask me. Do NOT at any time leave the fields unattended. Do you all understand?" There was a chorus of cheers. "Then we are ready. Little warriors with one bead, start your work."

The four with single beads on their necklaces dashed off towards the allotments, the rest of the kids yelling after them. Parrish laughed and clapped his hands to see the spontaneous explosion of joy. He turned and looked down at the milling kids, once more getting their full attention.

"Do not forget. People with two beads," he held up two fingers, "must be ready when the stick shadow crosses the next stone. Away you all go." He waved his arms in the air and the rest of the children scattered and dashed happily away back towards the hill fort, chattering excitedly amongst themselves.

Coran never said he approved of the scheme but then he never said anything at all. Parrish took that to mean OK and to let the children carry on, running their stag system successfully and with virtually no adult supervision.

He smiled to see the kids working well and still being able to have some fun. They should make the most of it during their short childhoods.

The kids themselves thought that the tall man was the second greatest man in the entire village.

After the Chieftain of course.

25

The construction of the fireplace and chimney progressed slowly. It was very much like building a dry stone tower, trying to get the stones to interlock as closely as possible and sticking it all together with clay for mortar. Parrish made quite sure that he had a double thickness of stone at the back of the fireplace, plus an air gap, to insulate the log wall behind it from any latent heat. He had sited the whole thing in one corner of the room, using the two converging walls as added support for the chimney stack until it was fully dry. The total effect, when the construction was finished, reminded him of a huge, stone embedded clay teardrop that had run sluggishly down the inside corner of the cabin, setting solid when it had spread out upon touching the floor. The fireplace itself was a huge, bulbous thing with a gaping mouth, ready to consume anything combustible that was put in it.

He burned a fire in it constantly for a few days to ensure that the clay fully hardened in case it rained and washed away all his hard work. To him it looked odd to have a roaring fire inside a shell of a house with no roof. To the people of Danebury the whole thing looked utterly stupid and they shook their heads sadly, not in the least to see all the wasted smoke that was being deliberately funnelled away up into the sky.

The weather took on a more spring like quality. The ewes had finished their lambing and at a glance it seemed as if there were hundreds of the little things. The crops weren't the only things that had made good use of last year's fine seasons! Parrish had once tried to count them but gave up before he reached three figures, the little bleaters wouldn't keep still! Even so, there were enough of them to allow the villagers to enjoy an occasional meal of tender lamb.

Buds had sprouted everywhere on bush and tree and the whole encampment was as pleased as punch to see the allotments grow a close green carpet of little shoots. There appeared to be no bare patches and this reinforced the villages hope for another good harvest. From Parrish's vantage point the plots looked like a great jumbled collection of huge, misshapen snooker tables. The sun packed a bit more warmth and the days were lengthening. There were also now more dry days in a row than wet ones and the village, the ground and distant, green budded forests began to dry out.

Parrish tried to figure out exactly where he was in the new year. The lambing had finished and, in a conversation with Klud, had been told that in two moons time the sheep would be sheared. He wasn't overly excited at the prospect of giving haircuts to the increasingly shaggy beasts but the soldier in his platoon whose dad had run a sheep farm once told him that sheep were usually sheared around the end of April to early May. By his ready reckoning, Parrish estimated it was now about the arse end of March.

The ongoing building work of the log cabin came to a distinct halt for a second time when Coran called the whole village together and announced that everyone was to lend a hand in cleaning up and repairing the village defence system.

The palisade wall was sound enough and only required a few basic repairs, replacing the odd rotted timber support here and there, and so just about everyone was directed to tidying up the ditch. The bottom of it was now dry, which was what Coran had no doubt waited for, but it was cluttered with fallen branches, items of discarded rubbish, rubble from numerous small pockets of erosion along the top edges of the ditch and masses of dead leaves.

Armed with an assortment of hand tools, the people of Danebury bent willingly to the task, spurred on by the memory of the repelled assault on the village not one full moon before. The cleanup operation was time consuming but deemed completely necessary by everyone concerned.

The ditch was tackled in sections. The men laboured down in the bottom of the six meter deep artificial gully, clearing away the bigger branches and shovelling chalky rubble into wicker baskets. These baskets were lowered down the steep sides on ropes and, when full, hauled back up to the top by groups of women who then took them away. The children were assigned their own task, a mini-system of the male workers. They followed along behind the working warriors, clearing up the smaller, residual pockets of rubble and all the dead leaves. As the whole ensemble moved steadily along the curving length of the ditch they left behind them a clean and tidy, deep and very steep chalk white scar in the earth.

Parrish was of course among the men in the bottom of the ditch and, snatching a moment's break, stood up to wipe the sweat from his brow. He looked up to watch the women on the rim, hauling steadily on their ropes to raise the heavy baskets. A smile creased his face at the secret pleasure he got from being a part of the team when the entire village worked in a co-ordinated effort. He watched the intent and the determination on everyone's faces as they bent willingly to their work, admiring the great determination and sense of purpose that he could almost feel radiating from them all.

At the head of one of the tug-of-war like teams that pulled on the ropes, a girl of perhaps fifteen reached over the edge and grasped a basket as it reached the rim at her feet. Hands gripping the edges of it and with an intensive effort, she attempted to jerk the heavy load over the edge and onto level ground. With a sharp, tearing sound the bottom fell out of the basket and the load tumbled and rolled back down towards the bottom of the ditch and the toiling men. Someone shouted a warning and the warriors scrambled aside for safety, everyone looking up for the danger. They were all in time to see the unfortunate girl as she wheeled her arms desperately in an attempt to regain her lost balance but failed. With a terrified shriek she overbalanced, toppled and fell.

Like a rag doll she tumbled untidily down to the bottom of the ditch.

Parrish wanted desperately to shout to her to spread her arms and legs to stop the rolling and so lessen the chance of injury, but all he could do was watch dumbly along with the others as the girl bounced her way down the steep slope. Almost at the same moment as she hit the bottom there was the sound of cracking bones, clearly audible to one and all.

The girl screamed shrilly and finally rolled to a stop. She just lay there on her back among the pieces of rubble, making high pitched keening noises. The warriors slowly gathered around her and looked curiously down. At first it seemed that not a soul was ready to help her. Parrish pushed his way through the crowd to get to her but was beaten to it by another man he did not recognize. The stranger just stared down at the stricken girl, shaking his head disappointedly.

"Father!" she cried and reached up to him. The man looked at her very apparent injuries and shook his head again.

"You are beyond help." he said, turned his back and calmly walked away through the throng.

Parrish had heard the brief exchange with amazed horror and, if it wasn't for the fact that he intended to help the girl because no one else seemed either bothered or capable, he would have taken time to punch the callous bastard in the mouth. He would have been even angrier if he had understood the real reason for the man's disappointment.

His daughter was indeed fifteen summers old as Parrish had so rightly guessed, and ready to be bartered off as someone's wife. She had been, up to the moment of the accident, in prime condition and would have fetched a good price. Now she was worth nothing, beyond help.

Parrish knelt beside the girl and checked her injuries. He winced. They were pretty bad considering there wouldn't be even basic medical facilities for at least another five thousand years. Her knee length leather skirt had bunched high up over her thighs, revealing her broken legs for all to see.

Her right leg was broken at the midway point between hip and knee, easily diagnosed by the way her lower leg had rotated, with the knee and foot pointing out at right angles to the line of the leg. Around the point of the break swelling and discolouration was already becoming apparent. It looked quite horrific but was still not as bad as the girls left leg. That had broken very badly below the knee. The bottom half of her lower leg was bent at a completely unnatural angle and the tight skin of her shin had split open, punctured by the jagged end of the bone that stuck out of the flesh.

The poor girl's arms, legs and one side of her face were badly scraped but these were secondary considerations. Parrish bent down for a closer inspection of the wounds. The injured girl was already beginning to go into shock. He turned to look up at the gathered crowd and made to give out instructions to them. Before he could utter a single word the girls farther re-appeared carrying a war club. He moved around to stand beside the girls head and raised the weapon to deliver a killing blow.

"NO!" shouted Parrish and jumped between the attacker and his intended victim, giving the man a dark, threatening stare.

"She is beyond help, Parrish. It is best that she be killed swiftly." came Klud's voice from among the crowd.

"Rubbish!" said Parrish vehemently. "*I* can help her."
"She is not yours to help." said the man with the club. "I have lost a daughter who was ripe for barter. She cannot be helped. Let me kill her."
The sheer unfeeling, mercenary attitude of the man at first astounded Parrish then made him furious. He slapped the club violently from the man's hand, grabbed him by the front of his tunic and drew back his fist.
"PARRISH!" barked a warning shout from above them on the rim of the ditch. Everyone looked up to see the Chieftain standing there looking down, arms aggressively crossed and a threatening look on his face.
"He is going to kill this defenceless girl and I think I can help her." Pleaded Parrish. "Do not let him do this."
There was a long silence.
"Please!" Parrish reached up with his free arm, appealing to the Chieftain who just shook his head.
"She is not yours to help, Parrish. The girl belongs to her father and he can do with her as he pleases."
Parrish reluctantly released his grip on the man's tunic and looked him in the eye. The smaller man's mind was already working. Here was a chance for him to get at least something for the now worthless girl, no matter how small.
"What would you give me for her?" he asked, eyeing the tall man defiantly, chin tilted up. If it had not been such a desperate situation Parrish would have happily smashed his arrogant face in.
"I have nothing with me now but if you will trust me I will see that you receive something of mine for the girl." he paused, hoping for an immediate agreement. He got none. "On my honour."
The man considered only for a moment. He knew that whatever the tall man gave him, it was sure to be something extraordinary. The whole camp was well aware of Mar's strange shiny knife that cut cleaner than any flint. He nodded.
"On your honour, Parrish." he reminded the tall man.
Parrish gave the man a tight, angry bow then turned away and faced up towards Coran.
"With your permission, Chieftain?"
Coran nodded curtly, no sign at all of any emotion on his face,

turned away and was gone from sight.

Parrish knelt down beside the stricken girl and offered her a friendly smile.

"Do not worry, I will help you."

She was very frightened and in great pain. Her teeth chattered as the shock took hold and her skin was cold and clammy. At the sound of his words all she could do was look back at him, wild eyed like a cornered, wounded animal.

"This is going to hurt sweetheart." he said in English, his voice soft and tender. "I'm sorry but I've gotta get you out of this hole." He slipped one arm under her narrow shoulders and gently wormed the other under her knees. She cringed with the pain. He took a deep breath and lifted. She didn't weigh much at all. As she came up into his arms her legs swung for a moment before coming to rest against his side. She screamed with the pain and fainted. He was glad for her then. The onlookers just shook their heads and parted silently for him as he made his way through the group towards the cross pole ladder, the only route out of the ditch.

Ignoring the eyes on his back he climbed the ladder deftly without using his hands and hurried away to his hut, holding the girl tightly to his chest and leaning back in an effort to stop her legs swinging unnecessarily. The injuries were already bad enough without him having to move her while they were unsupported.

Parrish laid the girl gently down on his fur covered bed and set to work on her legs. The open fracture wasn't bleeding too badly and so he left it while he worked on the other break, letting the gentle flow of blood clean out the wound. He tried to remember what he'd been taught during the first aid lectures he'd attended periodically during his training. Going on the courses had just been a good skive at the time but now he wished he'd paid more attention. He pulled his personal first aid kit from his webbing and spread its contents out onto his jacket, laid on the earth beside the bed. It was hardly what he would have called extensive, the whole lot was packed inside a plastic thirty five millimetre film tub.

There were four fat Brufen tablets, six more of Paracetamol, half a dozen dumbbell sutures rolled tightly up, a single band-aid and a pair of sealed antiseptic medi-wipes stuffed in to stop the whole lot rattling.

"Shit! How am I'm supposed to treat major injuries with just a plaster and some aspirins?" For a moment he was at a loss as to where to start. He raised his eyes to the heavens. "Beam me up, Scotty." he said quietly, took a deep breath and forced himself to get started.

He covered the girl with his long woollen cape to keep her warm against the shock then left the hut to fetch an assortment of branches to use as splints and supports. It only took a few minutes and he returned with an armful of pieces, determined that he would have a ready selection immediately to hand.

He was grateful that she was still unconscious. Her breathing was regular, if a little shallow, which was another effect of the shock. Parrish tucked the makeshift blanket more tightly around her torso, rolling up the bottom to reveal her battered legs.

After feeling for the break under the swelling, he grasped her right knee firmly and attempted to gently rotate the leg back to its proper position. He could feel the ends of the bone grating together. The girl groaned. Taking another deep breath, he pulled on the knee with one hand, the other holding her pelvis firmly at the hip. Twisting the knee with a movement of the wrist, he felt the two ends of the bone pop into place and when he released his grip the leg stayed in the correct position. Parrish smiled at the initial success. He quickly selected and laid two splints either side of the limb. They stretched from the crotch to the ankle and he strapped them tightly to the leg, completely immobilizing it.

He turned his attention to the left leg. It posed him much more of a problem. The bone stuck jaggedly out of the skin. Parrish was also sure that the other, unseen bone was also broken because the leg had shortened by about two inches.

He again gripped the girl by the leg, this time at the ankle and knee. With a steady pull he stretched the limb back to its original length. The fortunately unconscious girl groaned again. With a soft sucking sound the visible piece of bone disappeared back inside the leg. When he released his grip on the ankle, the leg started to pull up from the point below the break and Parrish knew that at least one of the bones had not butted together. It had to be the jagged one.

"Shit!" he hissed and unwrapped one of the sealed medi-wipes. After carefully cleaning his index finger with it, he poked his finger into the warm, wet wound. He could feel the ends of the bone and, with a combination of pulling on the ankle and prodding about with his finger, he managed to roughly align them. His second and last medi-wipe went on cleaning up the wound before he butted the two edges together and held them in position with four of the dumbbell sutures. Finally satisfied, he strapped more splints to the girls left leg. Then he covered the closed wound with his last field dressing and used some of the long end of the bandage as part of the strapping to secure the splints. At last he sat back, suddenly realizing that he had been sweating profusely. He cast a critical eye over his makeshift body repairs. Both the girl's feet now pointed the right way and her legs looked the same length.

He tidied her up. Completely contrary to all the teachings of the medical instructors, he used the still antiseptic but now dirtied medi-wipes a second time and cleaned out the worst of the scrapes on the girl's arms, knees and face. One of the deeper cuts on her cheek received the lone plaster to cover it. He finally sat back on his haunches, felt her forehead once more and tucked her up in his cape, covering her legs as well.

"Sorry sweetheart, but that's the best I can do. The rest is up to you now."

Parrish sat with the unconscious girl all the rest of the day. The only thing left for him to do was to make sure she was as comfortable and warm as possible and be ready to offer words of support when she finally awoke. If she ever awoke. At dusk, as the light faded and the shadow of night darkened and began to spread across the land, Parrish heard a small, almost polite cough from outside his hut. He listened for a moment and the cough came again. Rising quietly to his feet, he left the girls side and stepped out into the twilight. Klud's first wife stood there. In her hands she held two clay bowls, steam rising invitingly from their contents. Her head was bowed and she spoke without looking up.

"I thought that you might be in need of some food." she said in a hushed, almost apologetic voice. Parrish knew that any woman who dared to think for herself risked severe punishment from her man for what was seen as by him as insubordination. The woman was taking a great risk in trusting him. She held out the bowls. Parrish peered in at their contents and smiled knowingly to see that while one bowl was obviously for him, the stew thick with chunks of meat and a huge crust of bread, the second contained the thin, strong smelling soup that Oona had fed him when he had been injured.

"Does Klud know that you are here?" he asked.

"No." There was a note of panic in her voice as she suddenly feared that she might have misjudged the tall man. He took the bowls from her.

"Then go quickly before he finds out." The woman turned to go. "And thank you, mother." he added gratefully.

The woman paused, nodded briefly then swiftly vanished into the shadows of the village huts.

Parrish returned to his bedside vigil, placing the girl's strength giving broth at the edge of the fire to keep it warm and tucked hungrily into his own stew. It tasted good. He looked at the girl for a second then threw a sideways glance at her bowl of broth beside the dancing flames.

"You're welcome to that soup girl." he whispered softly in English. "Take my word for it, it will do you a power of good but it tastes like shit!"

26

The girl awoke with a start, jarring her immobilized legs. She cried out in pain and Parrish, who was asleep on the hard cold ground beside her, jerked upright.

"What the fuck ...?!" he blurted before he remembered where he was.

He looked at the girl. She was now laying very still, teeth gritted against the almost solid, heavy throbs of pain that pulsed their way up from her legs.

Parrish knelt beside her and rested a hand on her forehead. She wasn't hot but was still sweating. He couldn't blame her for that.

"Hurts, eh?" he said.

The girl just stared at him. With the fire that now burned low, directly behind him, his face was in shadow. She did not know who he was.

"How do you feel?"

"I am not dead?" she blurted out before realizing that she had asked a question of a man without his permission.

"Not yet." said Parrish and turned to the fire. He threw a few logs onto it and lit a few tallow lamps. He tested the thin soup with a finger. Still warm. When he finally returned and faced the girl she recognized the profile of the tall man and turned away.

"Do not be afraid." he said. "I am trying to help you." The girl just lowered her eyes, no easy task when lying flat, but she still succeeded in looking totally subservient.

"Look at me!" snapped Parrish, instantly annoyed at her submissive posture, feeling somehow insulted by her need to bow to what she no doubt saw as his Goddess given superiority. Reacting to the order as he himself would have to a barked command from Sergeant Carter, her head snapped round to face Parrish. Finding himself suddenly comparing his actions with that of 'mad dog' did not sit well with him either and his voice softened.

"I did not mean to shout." he apologized. There was no reaction from the girl. He asked her again. "Are you in much pain?"

She just nodded an affirmative.

"Eat some of this. It will keep up your strength."

The girl drank the soup he offered without protest, Parrish totally missing the point that she took the food not because she was hungry or because she needed it, but because to her, a man had ordered her too. When she had emptied the bowl, and Parrish was surprised that she had managed to eat it all, she just looked at him, uncertain about what was going to happen to her next. He could only see the pain in her eyes.

"If the pain gets very bad, you must tell me." She just nodded and Parrish began to get annoyed at trying to hold a virtually one sided conversation.

He smiled down at her anyway and put a reassuring hand on her shoulder. "If you want to ask any questions of me, do so."

The girl's eyes widened. Surely he must know that it was not proper for a woman to ask anything of a man. She shook her head.

"No questions at all?" he asked, surprised.

"No. It is not allowed." she said in a hushed voice.

"Rubbish!" he scoffed. "In my house, I say what is or is not allowed. If you want to ask me something, I say that you can." It was then that he understood the reason for her apparent reluctance to accept his help. The idiotic Neolithic notion of complete and utter male dominance. He decided to turn this antiquated idea to his advantage.

"In fact, I order you to ask me any questions that you might have." She just stared at him like he had gone out of his mind. "Do not be afraid. I will not hurt you but if you do not tell me where it hurts I cannot help you either."

The concept of a lowly woman being helped by a warrior staggered her. She nodded slowly in acknowledgment and there was a long silence that dragged on for several minutes.

"Well?" he asked suddenly, making her jump. The muscular spasm jarred her legs and she cried out again. Parrish put a steadying hand on her shoulder.

"Easy girl, easy." Her eyes had an agonized stare and her breathing was sharp and ragged but she didn't cry or wail as she had when she fell. He marvelled at her control. Eventually she settled back to a slightly more relaxed condition as the waves of pain subsided. She looked down at her legs, covered by his cape.

"My legs do not move." she said very quietly, her voice full of cowering respect. "Are they still there?" As soon as she had launched the question her eyes screwed up as if in anticipation of a physical blow.

"Yes." he smiled, trying to put the girl at ease and pleased with the breakthrough. "Would you like to see them?" His hand moved towards the edge of the makeshift blanket. The girl shook her head, a frightened look on her face and he pulled back his hand. "They are both broken."

"Then why am I not dead?"

Parrish couldn't believe how calmly she said the words.

"Because I say so!" he snapped.

The girl cringed at the sudden anger in his voice and sank back into her cowering silence. She was totally baffled by the whole experience that was happening to her. By all that was right and proper, she should now be dead, beyond help as her father had said. But she was not, apparently because the tall man had said so. She was not stupid. She knew some of the things that the people of the village said about the tall man. He was a great warrior and rumoured to be Dannu's man, but did he also have the power of life in his hands as well as death?

Parrish inwardly cursed himself for snapping at the timid creature and loosing what little rapport there was between them that had managed to start up. Getting the girl just to say a few words was like pulling teeth! Silence again reigned in the hut. He leaned over her to regain eye contact and spoke softly.

"Try to get some sleep. If the pain becomes too great, do not be afraid to wake me and say so. Do you understand me?" She nodded. "Good." He tucked her in once more.

"Now sleep."

Her eyelids snapped instantly shut and he shook his head sadly. He settled back himself onto the floor beside her, glad of the extra warmth from the flames now they had taken hold on the fresh logs. Despite all the wrangling and irritating hassle, he fell quickly into an exhausted and restful sleep.

It was dawn. Although Parrish was just dozing and already on his way out of sleep towards consciousness, he was helped along by a prod in the shoulder. He turned over slowly.

"Huh ...Wha ..?" he mumbled in English.

The face before his was filled with pain. Even so, the eyes automatically lowered and her voice was soft, almost apologetic.

"The pain. It is very bad. My legs."

Parrish sat up, rubbed the sleep quickly from his eyes and rested a hand on her forehead. She was sweating again but thankfully still not hot. At least she didn't have a fever. He got his water bag down from its peg and gave her a long drink, straight from the spout. It was much appreciated by the girl. She was thirsty from fluid loss, induced by her sweating and the action of shock.

"Legs hurt a lot, eh?" he asked and she nodded. He uncovered her lower limbs and checked them over. They had swollen and the bandages and strapping was very tight but he had expected that.

"Wiggle your toes."

They wiggled. Parrish nodded his satisfaction. He looked up to give the girl a few words of encouragement but they remained unsaid, halted on his tongue by the look of horror on her face. She stared wide eyed down at her strapped and splinted legs. Parrish had to admit that his primitive work didn't look particularly confidence inspiring. He patted her reassuringly on the arm.

"Do not worry. It is just to keep them still so that they will mend." She seemed unconvinced and he couldn't blame her. He smiled. "I will undo the straps to ease their tightness. You will see that your legs are still complete."

He re did the bandaging one section at a time so he lost none of the rigid immobility. The girl never complained while he worked although he knew it must have been very painful. The wound was still closed and so far seemed free of infection.

"Better?" he asked when he finished. She nodded humbly. He smiled back then set about rustling up some cold food for breakfast. They ate in silence, watching each other, him staring openly, her stealing brief glances through lowered eyes. Her appetite was poor but she managed to eat some. All the while she tried to keep her body as still as possible but her arms were constantly mobile, hands twitching.

"It is very painful?" he asked, knowing it was a stupid question but feeling he had to say something.

"Yes."

“Do you think you can bear it until the sun is high?"

"Why?" She instantly became frightened again. It sounded to her like some kind of ultimatum. Perhaps the moment of her doom.

"Because that is when I will return. I must still help with the work on the ditch."

"Oh." She considered for a few moments, as if testing the water of her pain with a mental toe. "I do not know."

Parrish understood. He plucked out a Paracetamol tablet from his little black plastic tub and gave it to her. Then he poured some water into one of the plain, round bottomed clay cups that were fired in their tens in the village kilns. She looked down with puzzlement at the flat round pill in the palm of her hand.

"You swallow it." explained Parrish, smiling. "Here." He offered her the water.

"Will it... will it hurt me?" she said timidly.

"No." he laughed. "It will help to ease the pain. Trust me." He was sure that it would relieve her suffering. In fact he was a bit worried about the size of the dose. Her body mass was quite small and as no Neolithic bodies had ever felt the effects of a strong analgesic, he felt that it was a rather powerful drug to use on her. He was suddenly unsure about giving it to her at all but bowed to reason. Don't be stupid, no one had ever overdosed on a single Paracetamol tablet.

She looked down again at the white pill and was plainly unconvinced.

"How will this little white stone help my pain?"

"If I told you, you would not believe me, even if there were the words in your tongue for me to be able to tell you. Just swallow the 'little white stone' and try to get some rest. I will come back at noon."

She dutifully swallowed the pill and chased it down with a draught of water. Then she lay back and stared blankly up at the thatch above her. Parrish nodded.

"Good girl. I must go now. Rest and I will be back as soon as I can, OK?" She looked at him when he spoke the English word. He knew her legs were giving her grief and just wished he could do more for her.

"OK?" he repeated with more emphasis, eyebrows raised. She finally nodded. "Good." He moved to the doorway.

"See you soon then ... er... sorry, I do not know what you are called."

"Juli." she said flatly and Parrish suddenly felt he had somehow insulted her by apparently not being bothered or even needing to ask her name sooner.

"Well, at least that is a good English name." he said brightly. There was no reaction from her. He smiled thinly and was gone, leaving the poor girl alone with the pain and the uncertainty.

Parrish worked through the morning with the rest of the men as they continued their steady way around the circumference of the fort. No one said a word about the incident the previous day.

At one point he stopped for a drink of water and, after he had quenched his thirst, offered the bag to Klud. The warrior accepted it gratefully.

"Klud. With your permission, I would like to ask your wife if she could make for me some of that healing poultice." The Neolithic warrior never even bothered to ask which one of his wives the tall man was talking about. He just nodded approval.

"Do you need this for the girl?"

"Yes."

"She still lives then." he said in a surprised tone but shook his head. "She will not walk again. I still say that it would be best if she were killed swiftly."

"Well I do not!" said Parrish curtly.

"You have not traded anything for her yet." Klud bluntly reminded his friend. "She is still the property of her father and if he says she is to be killed, it will be done and you would not be allowed to stop it."

Only a few months earlier Parrish would have exploded, drawn his knife and made a threat. But he had learned.

"You are wise as always my friend. I do not know this man. Can you find him and send him to my hut at the end of the day. Tell him that if he comes, I will give the bastard his blood money."

Klud didn't understand the English phrase or its half hearted translation but never the less understood that the tall man was not pleased with the girl's father for some strange reason.

"I will." he said and without further ado the pair, mutually knowing that the conversation was over, once more bent to the task before them.

At midday Parrish checked on the girl as he had promised and was pleased to find her sleeping, no doubt a result of the painkiller. He didn't disturb her, left the hut quietly and strolled across to the Klud family hut. Respecting their privacy, as was proper, he did not enter but called the man's wife out into the daylight. His voice was obviously recognized because the right woman, the one who had brought them both the illicit food the evening before, emerged from the doorway. She stood bowed before him.

"I have spoken with your husband and he has agreed to allow me to ask you if you would make for me some of the pain easing poultice." Parrish knew that if Klud had said so, she had no choice but to do his bidding but he felt obliged to put it to her as a polite question. She just nodded.

"Thank you mother." There was a pause while the woman waited to see if there were any further instructions. When he said nothing more she turned away as if dismissed. Not once had she looked directly at him.

"Oh yes." he added and she froze in the door way. "The soup was *very* much welcomed." Without any further acknowledgment the woman disappeared into the darkness of the huts interior. Parrish shrugged and headed off back to work.

As the day drew to a close and the shadows again grew long, Parrish had a visitor. He still did not know the man's name and had no intention of asking. When he heard his own name called from outside, he let the man wait for a long moment before finally stepping out to talk with him.

"Yes?!"

"I have come to talk trade over the girl." he said. Parrish glared down at the Neolithic man but it was just empty posturing and the little warrior knew it. The bargaining right was his and, although it was unnecessary, he reminded the tall man of his oath.

"On your honour, Parrish."

Parrish found it difficult to restrain himself from giving the little shit a good slap. He instead gave the briefest of nods and ducked angrily back inside his hut. The girl was plainly frightened by the sound of her father's voice. The voice of doom.

Parrish went straight to his webbing. Until that moment he'd had no idea what he would give in exchange for Juli's life but, in a sudden brainwave, it had come to him during the last, aggressive words the man had spoken. He pulled one of his two remaining thunderflashes from the ammo pouch, winked knowingly at the girl and re-emerged into the evening air. Initially without a word of explanation, he simply handed the object to the man who took it hesitantly, eyeing it with caution. He was plainly baffled by the offering.

"What is it?"

Enjoying himself now that he had the upper hand, Parrish laid a tall tale on the man.

"It is a little something from the stores of the Earth Goddess." The man's eyes widened and he quickly thrust the thunderflash away from himself, holding it out at arm's length. "Clearly we have all seen the angry storms that Dannu sometimes throws across the sky, with loud roars of thunder and bright flashes of light." The man nodded, his eyes never leaving the cardboard tube in his hands. "Well. Held safely inside that thing that you now hold is one crash of thunder and one flash of light. To release them back into the air you must first undo that wrapping." he pointed to the binding of white tape with its loose end. "Beneath it you will find a small flat piece of wood and a long bud. Draw the wood across the top of the bud and it will release a fire which tells the thunder and lightning it is free to go."

It was all Parrish could do not to burst out laughing at the astounded expression on the stupid idiots face. If 'Clive' had been here he would be wetting himself to hear an eight second fuse called a 'bud'.

"How did you come by this?" the little man whispered.

"I cannot say, but believe me, my words are true." He sealed the deal with the magic words that meant all to a Neolithic warrior. "On my honour."

There was no more need for debate. The man nodded with satisfaction, safe in the knowledge that he believed the tall man had tricked himself. He had done well. Such a treasure to trade for an injured, useless young female.

"The worthless girl is yours." he said and hurried off with his prize before the tall man had a chance to change his mind. Parrish scowled after the man then ducked back into the hut.

The girl had listened to every word and now looked even more frightened that ever. To her it now seemed more true than ever that her new owner really did walk alongside the Earth Goddess. What would happen to her in the hands of such a man? Her 'new owner' grinned at her broadly and rubbed his hands together.

"Well that should sort out the little shit." he said and winked down at her. "You are in the clear now Juli and, with a bit of luck, the little bastard will pull the pin on his new toy and blow himself to fuck!" He laughed out loud and clapped his hands together loudly. "BOOM!"

The girl still looked at him, as frightened as ever. Grinning, Parrish sat down beside her. She clearly did not join in his pleasure.

Although it had seemed like a great idea at the time and a way to teach the nasty little man a lesson, the more he looked at Juli's worried face the quicker his euphoria faded. He suddenly wished he hadn't done what he just had. From deep in the recesses of his mind, an Army instructors words came floating to the surface.

"A mark eight thunderflash in no bonfire night banger. It is to all intents and purposes a grenade, only with all the shrapnel removed. It is still VERY dangerous."

Parrish knew he had done a very stupid thing and instantly wished he could take the pyrotechnic back. But of course he could not.

Still, he thought. It's in the hands of an ignorant cave man. The chances of him actually getting it to work are pretty slim. And besides, Parrish told himself, if something unpleasant did happen, him wanting to kill the poor girl meant he'd bloody well asked for it.

27

There were no big bangs heard in Danebury during the next few days and any gift or trade that been passed between the two men concerning the girl was never mentioned in a single conversation throughout the camp. The warrior concerned was keeping the whole thing quiet and Parrish took that to mean that he was keeping his new trophy to himself, to gloat over in private. Like an individual art collector, the little man was keeping his gift from Dannu for his own private delectation. Parrish guessed that it probably now had pride of place on the man's wall and he breathed a secret sigh of relief. In all probability it was now very unlikely that the thunderflash would ever be detonated. In the cold light of day Parrish realized that no matter how nasty the little swine was, he didn't really want to see the man hurt after all.

Juli went through a protracted period of suffering before the swelling and pain in her legs subsided to a more tolerable level. Parrish did what he could for her. The poultice was a blessing, doing sterling work on the wound on her left shin by easing the pain and keeping infection at bay. When her pain became too much to bear he would give her another Paracetamol but had to ration them, lest they run out before she was able to handle the hurt unaided. He used four during the first week after the accident, mostly at night. After that her body seemed to settle and the poor girl could sleep right through the night unassisted.

The inner man, and woman too, was being fortified not only by Parrish's basic field cuisine but with bowls of food from Klud's wife. Particularly in Juli's case. The pair even began to receive the odd bowl of morsels from other women in the camp too. Always under cover of darkness and also, Parrish was sure, without the knowledge or blessing of their men folk. These women risked serious reprisals to do this. It seemed he had uncovered, by his act of kindness to the girl, a close knit network of mutual assistance among the women. A sort of covert community within a community. A sub culture within a culture.

None of the women actually asked after Juli but Parrish knew they were all silently cheering for her. They were all aware that something unprecedented had happened concerning one of their number and were intent on doing everything in their limited powers, without upsetting the camp status quo, to ensure that it came to a successful conclusion. Juli knew it too, if not by the attitude of the women she never saw to the tall man and herself, then by the quiet visits outside during the dark evenings and the more than ample food he seemed to have on hand at any one time. She knew, as did everyone else in the entire village, that since his old lady had been offered up to the sky spirits, the tall man had fended for himself. He did all his own washing, cooking, mending and fetching of firewood and water. It was wrong for such a warrior to do this but no man in the village knew the answer to his problem and no women would even dare to offer their help. If only they were allowed, because they would have gladly helped. They had not forgotten his earlier generosity and his general courtesy and kindness towards them.

One evening as he sat beside her, the two of them steadily spooning their way through a bowl each of hot food that Juli knew he had not prepared himself, Parrish suddenly stopped with his spoon halfway to his lips. The girl was staring in fascination at the metal utensil, a part of his issue KFS. He tipped its contents back into the bowl and offered the spoon out to her to touch. She refused.

"KFS." he said, the English lost on her. "Knife, fork and spoon." He pointed to each in turn as he laid them on top of her blanket. She thought he was trying to teach her and dutifully repeated the words for him, not doing too badly for a first attempt at a foreign language.

"For eating this good food with." he unnecessarily explained and scooped up another spoonful into his mouth. When he finished chewing he swallowed and nodded. "And it is good too." He eyed her quizzically. "You *do* know that the women of the camp are looking after you, yes?"

Juli nodded and to her surprise Parrish's face dropped. He felt a sudden sharp pang of envy. "You are fortunate that you have people who care for you girl."

"Yes." she said, noticing the sadness in his usually so confident voice. She couldn't explain it but she suddenly felt the need to offer him some small gesture of support, as he had constantly done to her since he had pulled her out from under deaths dark shadow. She smiled at him.

It was the first glimpse of emotion Parrish had seen from her apart from the ever present fear and sullenness. He gazed at her intently and for an instant, Juli's constant, aching pain was forgotten and she gazed back at him on even terms. For the first time too, Parrish looked at her and saw an actual person. A young girl, rather than just a tight lipped patient and a constant, worrying burden.

He had to admit too that, for a young Neolithic woman, she wasn't exactly ugly. The swelling around her cheek, eye and chin had gone. Apart from the yellow bruising along her jaw line and the clusters of small scabs that were all that remained of her scraped face, her features were pretty well back to normal. She had an oval face, framed by long and wild, dark brown hair that straggled down her back and cascaded over her shoulders. Apart from the recent superficial damage her face was pretty well blemish free, courtesy of her young age. She still had all her teeth. They were framed by a good shaped mouth that wasn't too big. Her cheekbones were quite high and her nose was the right size. He somehow hadn't noticed before but her eyes were a light blue colour and had a twinkle that hinted at some hidden, secret knowledge. They also had the constantly darting, hunted look that every woman in the camp had. Parrish chose to ignore that and looked for the twinkle. At least it seemed like she had a capacity for some intelligence, he thought.

His eyes were all of a sudden boring deep into hers, almost it seemed right into her mind. She crumbled under his stare, feeling that she had offended him, made a bad mistake and been too familiar. Just as her smile began to fade his appeared. They were locked together by the moment before Juli finally lowered her gaze, as much from embarrassment as respect.

"No, do not turn away." said Parrish, trying futilely to snatch the moment back. "You looked almost human when you smiled then."

She wasn't sure if he was being sarcastic but looked back at him, once more flat faced.

"If you wish me to smile ..."

"Do not be stupid. No one smiles to order. I would just like you to feel free to smile when you felt like it." He knew that it was another female trait that was frowned upon in these Neolithic times. "At least when you are inside my house."

"If you so wish it."
"Do not start that again." he growled, the softness gone as quickly as it had come, his voice back to its normal, hard edged confidence. She lowered her eyes once more and concentrated her attention on her food. Parrish did likewise and they were back again to eating their food silently, two completely different people, culturally, physically and mentally. Sitting close together by the warm fire and yet miles apart.

The days passed steadily and village life rose once more to full bloom, reflecting the natural world. Spring was upon the land and the forest was a bright, fresh, living green, the new, young canopy stretching northwards as far as the eye could see.
Danebury's ditch repairs were successfully completed without further incident and the villagers reverted to caring for their individual family units. Hunting parties once more began their regular forays into the wilderness. It was during these times, when the women had virtual free range in the camp, that it seemed to Parrish there was almost a constant flow of ladies from every hut in the place, apparently casually passing by his little, out of the way hovel. They would nod politely and steal glances past him towards the entrance to his hut through veiled eyes. They were hoping for some small glimpse of Juli he knew, seeming almost desperately curious to know what he was doing to her.
Everyone had seen her terrible, broken beyond repair leg injuries and marvelled at how he had managed even to keep her alive.
During a lot of this time Parrish left Juli alone while he worked on the interior fittings of his cabin. The partition wall was soon up, daubed and had hardened off. He had already decided to build himself three items of furniture in an attempt to make the place more convivial for him when he eventually moved in.
First he made himself a sturdy table roughly six feet by three. It consisted of a lot of long poles lashed side by side over a framework made from more of the same. The actual top of the table was of course uneven and it didn't stand too solidly on the earth floor at first, but it was definitely recognizable as a table. He felt better just looking at it. Flushed with the success of his first creation, he immediately

followed it up and made himself a 'set' of four stools to go around the table. With circular cross sections of trunk for their seats and three legs each, they looked like tall milking stools. With only three legs they were stable whatever surface they were stood upon and, once the seat areas had been scraped flat, they were quite comfortable. He immensely enjoyed just sitting on them.

Next came what he thought of as his finest piece of work. His bed. It was built in the same fashion as the table only it was six foot square and sat solidly on half a dozen eighteen inch high log legs. He carefully pushed daub into all the grooves between the long poles and then smoothed the mud across the entire top until it was completely flat. Parrish had to admit to himself that all he had really done was raise up the earth floor he usually slept on to a more accessible height but it still looked like a bed and that was the effect he was after. A more modern familiarization. Once it was covered in woven mats and his bedding skins, he was sure it would look really inviting.

He felt quite satisfied. The place was coming along nicely and all he needed now was the thatch for the roof. That would have to wait for a while until the meadow grasses that grew near the river beyond the flint mine were taller. Their stems would serve as a suitable summer thatch until the harvest was in and the cabin roof could receive a secondary, more hard wearing cover. Until then Parrish had gone just about as far as possible.

The full moon had passed and the time for shearing began to draw near. All this time, poor Juli had been incarcerated in her splints. For well over a month now. Parrish spent every evening sitting with her to try and ease her boredom. He was most impressed with the stalwart way she seemed to take it all in her stride. He knew that if it had been him stuck inside a dark hut for several weeks, never seeing the sunlight or having any visitors, he'd have been climbing the walls long ago. Juli however rarely complained and, when she did, it was always with good reason.

Their conversations were still very limited but she had lost a little of her timidness towards him. His concern for her welfare was genuine enough and she no longer feared what the next day might bring. It was still very difficult for her to start a conversation or ask any questions even though the tall man openly tried to encourage her. It was something that had been drummed into her all her life not to do and it was very hard to go against that grain.

The evening when Parrish had put the finishing touches to his bed and returned smiling and mud spattered, she could feel something in the air. Something concerning her. He knelt beside her and patted her on the shoulder.

"It has been over a month, sorry one moon cycle." He corrected himself for slotting an English word into the sentence. "You still must not walk yet but I think you would benefit from some fresh air. Tomorrow I will carry you out and sit you in the sun. Would you like that?"

"Yes. Thank you." Her eyes dropped.

"What?" He knew that look by now.

"You will look bad if you are seen tending to me by the people of the village." she said and Parrish was suddenly charmed that she should be concerned for his image and standing in the community.

"I do not care what people think but I understand. Do not worry. I will not shame myself or you."

She smiled briefly at him and he grinned back. He liked her smile.

"Can I have some water to wash myself with?" she asked. It was easier for her to ask him questions if the questions themselves were menial.

"Of course." Parrish took the request to mean that she wanted to tidy herself up for the women who would visit her when she sat outside. He was sure that they would come. "I need to clean myself too." He looked down at his muddied hands and arms. She nodded in agreement.

He brought her in a couple of bark buckets of clear water and, leaving her to her ablutions, went back outside and wiped himself down. The job only took him a few minutes and he ducked back inside to dry himself by the fire. He stopped just inside the doorway. Across the fire from him Juli was sat upright on her bed skins, naked from the waist up. She was in the process of wringing excess water from her long hair.

Parrish couldn't help it. He stared. Juli just looked up and stared right back. She made absolutely no attempt to cover her body. Her skin was milky white like smooth porcelain and her pert, jutting breasts were tipped with small, tight nipples, very dark against the surrounding whiteness.

"Sorry." he blurted and backed quickly out again.

Juli stared after him, astounded. She could hardly believe it. He was actually embarrassed and she wasn't exactly sure why. But she liked it.

Parrish gave her a long while to finish the rest of her wash before he re-entered the hut. She was once more laying flat on her back, fully clothed, hair glistening wet and face scrubbed clean.

"Better?" he asked as if nothing had happened. She nodded and smiled at him with just a hint of a new found confidence. He coughed loudly and quickly busied himself preparing some food.

The next day, around mid morning when the sun had had time to warm the air, Parrish prepared a bed on the ground outside the hut with a roll of padding so Juli could sit up against the wall. When he scooped her up into his arms, her legs still stiff and rigid in the splints, her arm snaked around his neck, seemingly of its own accord. He never mentioned it so she never took her arm away.

Placing her down gently on the bed and positioning her legs to be as comfortable as possible, he crouched beside her and patted her small feet.

"One more moon and we should be able to throw these away."He touched the rough and ready supports. "I will cut you a pair of crutches." Her eyebrows raised in silent question. "Sticks to help you walk while your legs are still strapped." he explained. "In a few more days you can start to move about but only slowly and with great care. If you do too much too soon the legs will break again and that would be bad. Very bad." She bowed in understanding. If he said bad, then he meant it. "Good. Then I will leave you to rest."

"Thank you."

He nodded, threw her a smile and left, heading off into the village towards Klud's house. The warrior had promised to give him some hints and tips on sheep shearing and handling.

When he returned in the afternoon Juli was laid back on her makeshift lounger, eyes closed, apparently asleep. As he drew close her eyes flicked open and she smiled at him for no apparent reason. That secret twinkle was in her eye. He squatted beside her.

"You look happier." he said. "Does the sun feel good?"

"Yes. My legs do not hurt at all."

"That is good. Have you been alone all day?"

"Many women have been to see me." She looked away into the distance, thinking back on what they had discussed together.

"Well, do not be shy." he said curiously. "What did they have to say?"

She laughed at his interest in worthless, women's gossip. It was strange that a great warrior should care at all what women said.

Parrish found himself once again looking at her closely. It was the first time he had heard her laugh. He liked it.

"They were all very interested it these." She touched her splints. "And they wanted to know if they would be tied to me forever." She had no intention of mentioning how even more fascinated the women had been to be told of the tall man's strange ways and unexpected kind acts. When she had revealed how he had actually been embarrassed by her nakedness, all the women gasped, at once saddened and charmed. Sad that he did not have the apparent strength to impose his rightful will and be master in his own house and yet charmed by his seemingly young innocence.

He was a mystery to the people he lived among, an enigma. The more they discovered about him the less they understood him. He was all at once a great and feared, unbeatable warrior and at the same time an ignorant child, innocent in the ways of the world.

The women, with Juli central in the discussion, had talked this over at great length during the day and had finally come to the conclusion that he was indeed a true, mans warrior but also carried the womanly cares of his mistress, Dannu the Earth Goddess. They almost envied Juli for being so closely involved with such a rare man. The girl puffed out her chest, for the first time proud of her owner and his many great achievements.

As Parrish squatted beside her she found herself looking at him in a new light. No longer so much in fear, now much more in fascination. The tall stranger was a man apart. One day, she decided, when she could pluck up the courage, she would ask him where he really came from.

A footfall broke her chain of thought and she looked up as Parrish rose to meet the approaching man.

"Greetings Mars." he said. The warrior nodded to him but his eyes were on Juli's legs.

"That is very interesting." he said and squatted down to inspect the splints. At no time did he acknowledge or show any interest in the girl herself, just her legs. "I had heard about this and decided to come and see for myself."

Parrish smiled, both at the effectiveness of the village grapevine and also at Mars's technical outlook on things he did not understand. The unknown did not frighten him as it did some of the weaker minded men of the camp and Parrish had no doubt that if Mars had been born in the twentieth century, he would have been some kind of scientist.

The two discussed the splints and their purpose for a few minutes with Mars asking searching questions as Parrish explained in simple terms the principles of how bones repaired themselves if given the time and kept still. The Neolithic warrior was deeply interested by it all but remained sceptical.

"And you are sure that your wife will walk again?" he asked the tall man.

"Yes, I ... *Wife* ?!" Parrish blurted out, stunned.

"Yes, wife." repeated Mars. "Do not pretend you did not know. You traded for her and so she is now your woman." Parrish was just agog at the sudden realization and the smaller man laughed at his puzzlement. He clapped the tall man on the shoulder "If you can make her walk again you will have done well for your trade. She is young and ripe. She will be able to work hard for you for many years." Parrish was still speechless. "Sleep well tonight my friend for the shearing starts tomorrow and you will be glad of the rest." He laughed again at the look on his friends face and walked away, his chuckles still echoing in the air.

Parrish stared down at Juli and opened his arms in a 'how did this happen' gesture.

"Wife?" he asked again.

"Yes." said Juli, wondering what all the fuss was about. "Are you not satisfied with me?"

"No ... I mean yes. I am just so surprised. All of a sudden I am married."

"What is 'married'?"

"It just means to be with wife." he answered absently.

He knew now that Juli was his responsibility for the rest of her life. Still, looking on the positive side, what Mars had said was definitely true. Once she was well again she could indeed take care of him as Oona had done. He would be free of all the menial chores. He knew that was a Neolithic attitude but it was still undeniably true. It would be good too to share his cabin with someone. He would no longer be alone. The idea began to appear more favourable the more he considered it. Perhaps Coran had had a good point when he'd talked to him about wives.

He sat back down beside his new wife and stared out into space. Juli remained quiet alongside him, letting the man's thoughts run their course.

Finally, he turned and looked into her eyes.

"Nothing has changed between us." he said. "But it seems that you are mine now and so I will take care of you. Do you mind this?"

"I am honoured to be yours." she said, baffled as to why he felt the need to state the obvious.

"Yes, but do you mind?"

Juli just looked at him for a long moment. What a staggering question to ask a simple woman. No female had ever had a choice before, never even being consulted as to which man became her husband. She just went with which ever man made the best trade with her father. She tried to think the question through objectively but it was very difficult. She had never had to do that before. Unable to reach an answer that way, Juli closed her eyes and listened to her heart. Then it was easy. Decision made, she looked back into his powerful eyes and spoke to him boldly for the first time.

"Parrish, I would rather belong to you that any other man in Danebre."

He saw the truth in her eyes and smiled, leaned in close and gave her a brief kiss on the lips.

"What was that?" whispered the girl in a puzzled tone, putting her fingers to her mouth.

"It is a part of the 'married' ceremony where I come from." He smiled, then rose effortlessly to his feet and once more headed off into the village, to talk to some of the other 'married' men.

28

The shearing wasn't half as much trouble as Parrish thought it was going to be. In fact it all went rather smoothly. All the other men were quite willing to help him out and give him advice when they discovered that shearing was another everyday skill that the tall man knew nothing about. Even the animals themselves seemed almost to be co-operative for him.

There were perhaps two hundred and fifty sheep that needed to be shorn. That number did not of course include the dozens of lambs. With over thirty warriors cum shearers to tackle the job it was no surprise that, with a ratio of only eight to one, the whole flock had its woolly coats removed in a single day.

With flat, scallop shaped cutting flints the wool was removed by the technique of grasping a big handful of fleece with the free hand and cutting under it with the stone knife as close to the skin as possible. Parrish had naturally assumed that a freshly sheared sheep would look smooth and bare.

He had seen many like that from his car window as he had driven down country lanes near the barracks. They however, had been sheared by twentieth century machinery and the Neolithic reality was very different. He could not help laughing at the sight of the steadily growing mob of ragged, tufty looking animals that had had their fleeces more or less hacked off!

The freshly shorn wool was taken away by the women to be washed and then processed, manually of course. Once it was clean and dry, it was teased out into long strands and then spun into a single coarse thread, that gradually built up on the long, slender, bone whorls weighted with a stone or piece chalk, that the women deftly spun with their fingertips. It pleased Parrish to return to his hut a few days after the shearing to find Juli sat up on her lounger, a pile of fleece beside her, deep in concentration as she teased the wool out. He could see that she was glad to be back into the system of the camp and doing useful work, no matter how small her contribution might be.

He cut her a pair of crutches from two appropriately shaped

boughs, padded them with skin and wool wrapping then trimmed them to the correct length after offering them up to Juli's reclining body. It reminded him of how Oona used to size up the buckskins she made for him.

Parrish gave them to her to try, picked the girl up from her bed and supported her while she teetered about on the totally foreign devices. He had to regularly remind her not to slump onto the crutches and steadied her by the shoulders to help her remain straight. It was the first time he had been close to her now that she was upright. Even though she stood a diminutive four feet ten inches in her splints, Juli wasn't as short as he had first thought, but the crown of her head didn't reach much above his shoulder. She was still young though and there was the possibility of maybe another inch or two to come.

It took Juli a few minutes to master free standing and a little while longer to get to grips with actually moving about. She tottered unsteadily around the fire place outside the hut, waddling precariously from side to side in a lurching, rolling gait with Parrish close behind, arms ready to catch her if she started to fall. The joy on her face when she finally managed a whole lap around the fire blackened ring of stones unaided was obvious by her smiling face. Parrish lowered her back down onto her bed against the wall and she sat still for a moment, puffing from the exertion.

"I did it." she smiled. "I walked."

"Yes." Parrish laughed. "Well done. We will have you on a bike next."

"Bike?"

"It... never mind, but very well done with the crutches. They are yours to use when you need to get about until I decide that it is time to remove the splints." He raised a finger of warning. "Do not try to do too much though. Use them a little at a time and at no time go very far from the hut. OK?" He looked long into her eyes to make sure the point went home.

"I understand."

"Good. You must save your strength and not put too much of a strain on your legs yet but the exercise will do you good and get the blood flowing. That too will help you to get well." He patted her on the arm. "I know you do not understand all the reasoning of what I say but you must trust me."

"I do." she said truthfully.
"Good."
"Can I try it again?"
He lifted her back to her feet and handed her the crutches while she steadied herself by leaning on him. It didn't happen very often but if an innocent opportunity arose, she took full advantage of a touch. She liked to feel him. To her he seemed big, strong, solid and reassuring.
"Ready?" he asked.
"OK." she said with a smile and Parrish laughed. He stepped back out of her reach, snapped to attention and gave the tiny girl a crisp salute.
"Carry on, soldier." he barked in his best Sergeant Carter voice. Juli frowned at his suddenly strange behaviour. "Go on." he said in a softer tone, smiled and sat nonchalantly back down against the hut wall. Juli began to totter her way once more around the fire while Parrish watched, apparently all casual and relaxed but inwardly coiled like a spring, ready to leap to her immediate assistance if she started to get into difficulty.

It was a few days later that the flower and feather man called Parrish aside and told him that it was time. Time to put Oona into the earth to wait for the call of Dannu. The sky spirits had completed their work and carried off her soul and it was now the duty of her family to make sure that her frame was ready when the time came for them to be reunited. The holy man said that 'family' meant him, which made him smile.
The odd looking pair went to the great hut where Parrish stood by and watched the little man sing a song of announcement to the shrine. Then he was handed a carved wooden tray with odd, swirling scroll and circle markings on it and together the two walked once more to the lonely knoll away in the east.
Atop the offering up trestle that Parrish had laid the body of Oona on almost five months earlier, were the old ladies bones. Picked clean by the black winged birds and washed white by the spring rains. The holy man chanted around the trestle one more time then removed from it the skull, rib cage and the long thigh bones, placing them reverently on the ceremonial tray Parrish held.

"What happens to all the other bones?" he asked, not finding the idea of the rest of the old woman's remains being carried away by scavenging animals or just allowed to be lost, very palatable.

"They go into the excrement pit." answered the flower and feather man evenly. "In that way, even they eventually find their way back into the Earth."

Parrish considered it and, although putting the bones into the pit wasn't exactly a nice way of achieving the desired end, the idea of going back into the ground was satisfactory enough.

At a nod from the holy man, the pair once more set off, Parrish bringing up the rear with his bone laden tray held out in front of him.

Travelling north-west away from the knoll, they passed by the allotments and carried on into the wood that hid from view the stream that supplied Danebury's water. They crossed the stream via a shallow ford and walked some more, emerging from the woods perhaps a kilometre or so further on. After being led into a large natural clearing, Parrish found himself halted before a long, grassy mound of earth with deep ditches either side of it. A long barrow!

The site was most impressive. The mound was a good two meters high, over six meters wide and sixty meters long. The twin ditches that flanked the barrow paralleled it but did not enclose its ends. The earth that had been removed from them had obviously gone into the construction of the mound itself. The whole massive earthwork was, unknown to Parrish at the time, aligned along an east to west axis. At its eastern end, nearest them, was a stone lined entrance, guarded by a pair of stone sentinels, standing tall like grey sentries either side of it. The flower and feather man bowed deeply to the barrow and Parrish did likewise.

He then watched in silence while the little man spent a few minutes working with a flint, repeatedly striking it obliquely across a knobbled, well used piece of iron pyrites held over a tinder bundle. The thin, weak sparks needing a lot of cajoling to finally produce a glowing ember. Next he coaxed it into flame and used it to light a pre prepared torch that waited ready just inside the entrance. Without a rearward glance he led the way into the bowels of the long barrow. Parrish was surprised that he had no need to stoop when inside the mound. There was at least a foot of clearance between the top of his head and the roof above them, although they had to walk in single file. At the far end of a thirty foot passage lined with cold slabs of stone, the narrow tract billowed out into a wide, roomy chamber perhaps ten feet wide and twenty feet long. Parrish found it difficult to judge its actual size in the flickering, shadow throwing torchlight but he knew what he was in. A crypt.

Around the walls, from floor to ceiling were rows of stone shelves. They were not in themselves very remarkable, it was what was on them that staggered Parrish. On these shelves were skulls and bones, all neatly stacked. There seemed to be hundreds of them. Parrish just stood, open mouthed. Without a word the holy man took the skull from the tray and found a place for it among all the others. Watched in silence by his tall companion he did the same with the ribs and long bones. Then he bowed deeply to all the bones, facing each wall of the chamber in turn. Parrish bowed too and this time not just because he was copying the little mans lead. For all the staring, empty eye sockets, the place was in no way grisly or repulsive. He was genuinely affected by the serene, almost holy, church like feel of the place.

After a moment of silent contemplation, the flower and feather man led the way back up the passage and out into the daylight, extinguishing the torch and replacing it in its holder when they reached the entrance. Walking out beyond the two sentry stones the pair turned again and once more bowed to the long barrow. This time Parrish too bowed with real feeling.

They both stared at the burial mound for a few moments. The holy man waited, he knew that the tall man would have questions. He always had questions.

"Is everyone there? All the people who have ever lived at Danebre?"

"Yes." answered the holy man. "All that is except the Chieftains."

"Where are they?"

"They wait for Dannu, each in their own chamber, on the great plain between our village and her temple." He pointed away to the north-west.

Parrish knew instantly that he was referring to Salisbury Plain.

Whenever any soldiers went on exercise there they needed only to take a brief glance at the operations map to see that there were more burial mounds and tumuli than you could shake a stick at. And they were only the ones that hadn't disappeared by being ploughed in or built on.

"When a Chieftain dies," continued the holy man to save Parrish asking the question he knew would come next, " The whole village carries him in honour to the great plain where his own chamber stands ready to accept him. Unlike all the other villagers, he is buried complete, sometimes with his most treasured possessions, ready to be re born and once again lead his people in the sun."

"It is good." said Parrish, nodding solemnly in agreement with the sentiment. "I feel sure that the bones of the people rest easy here, protected by the Earth Goddess."

"Yes. And one day Parrish, your bones will lie here too."

Parrish frowned for a moment. It was a good feeling to at last be considered a Danebury man but the idea of his bones sitting on a shelf was a bit disconcerting. He knew that twentieth century archaeologists had a penchant for digging up ancient barrows and displaying any bones they might find there, under glass in some museum. He dismissed the thought. Once you were dead, you were dead. Unlike the rest of the people he now lived with, he didn't care that much what happened to his bones once he was gone. After all, they would be of no consequence to anyone anyway.

"I could not ask for more." He bowed respectfully to the flower and feather man and together they walked in silence back to the hill fort.

29

Juli soon became very proficient on her crutches and also the centre of attention for most of Danebury's inhabitants. The warriors were curious but feigned aloofness. How could they have any interest in the activities of a mere woman, no matter how strange those activities might be. The women were simply delighted to see the girl up and about, all be it in a cumbersome and restricted way. They knew that she really ought to be dead. The children were absolutely astounded. They clustered and milled around her like a pack of excited, yapping puppies and Parrish regularly had to shoo them away lest one or other of them accidentally got under the girls feet and cause her to fall.

She never went too far from the hut, as she had been instructed, but there was no shortage of people who wanted to see her and watch her do a few demonstration laps around the building. She soon had to stop when she got tired and hot.

The weather was comfortably warm now and the sun shone brightly, high up in the sky. Parrish had made a scouting trip to the riverside meadows to check on the growth of the grasses there. They were just about ready to be cropped and dried to thatch his cabin roof and he was eagerly looking forward to the job. It seemed like everything was growing like crazy now. The wheat fields were knee high and the forest was dense, the earth dark and shadowy beneath its shady leaves. Even the kids in the camp seemed to be shooting up.

Parrish sat down beside his little wife and shared a cooling drink with her. She handed the cup back to him with a smile. Parrish was happy to see her happy. He had worked hard on bringing the girl at least partway out of her shell and from under the oppression that she had been stifled by since birth. She in turn understood that she was to be more open and questioning only around her man or in the privacy of their hut, but she was quite beginning to enjoy her new found increased freedom of speech, even if it was still quite limited. Once she had finally conquered her fear of asking a question of a warrior and expecting a blow in return, she tried to tap into his mass of knowledge regularly. From Parrish's point of view, most of her questions were still menial and pointless but he understood that it was the actual asking and not the content of the question that was significant.

"In a few days it will be time to take away the splints." he said, watching for her reaction.

"Will that also mean that I will no longer need the crutches?"

Parrish laughed.

"You quite enjoy being a star, yes? A little bit of fame?" She frowned, not understanding the idea of fame as a measure of popularity. He carried on without bothering to explain. "I would like you to use the crutches for a little while longer, until the strength can build back up in your legs, but they too can shortly after be thrown away."

"And then I can walk once more without help?" she asked hopefully.

"I should think so."

"This is good." she said, suddenly deep in thought. Parrish had expected a bit more jubilation at the imminent release from her restrictive bonds but wasn't getting quite the response he had anticipated.

"Is there some problem?" he asked.

"No." she replied finally with a satisfied look on her face. "I was worried that I would have to make the long walk on my crutches. That would have been very hard."

"What long walk?"

"To the temple of Dannu."

"Huh?"

Juli shook her head. With all the things that her husband knew, so many things that she was sure even the Chieftain or the holy man did not understand, all that cleverness, and then he would suddenly admit to knowing nothing about a thing that everyone else has known since they were tiny babes.

"The long walk to the temple of the Earth Goddess." she explained. "Once a year, the whole village goes there and pays its respects to Dannu."

"Where? When? How far...?" Parrish pounced on the chance for a bit more information about the Neolithic religion.

Juli put up her hands to protect herself from the barrage of questions.

"I ... I do not know." she stammered. "The holy man would know these things but ... I... I am sorry ..."

He patted her tenderly on the shoulder. He had intimidated her with his unintentionally aggressive questioning. His keenness to know had gotten the better of him. He could see the hunted look coming back into her face again. It would be a long time before she was fully at ease around him, he knew.

"No, I am sorry. For frightening you. You rest for a while, I will be back soon." She looked at him as he rose to his feet, a puzzled look on her face. He smiled in reassurance. "I am going to take your advice and talk to the holy one." he winked down at her. "I've got a few questions for the little man."

Juli watched him walk off into the camp, knowing that there had never been anyone like him before. She could not believe how he could even dare to call the holy man a 'little man'. More so, she did not envy the holy man for what was going to happen to him. Her husband could be most determined when he wanted answers to his questions. She sometimes wondered if his hunger for knowledge might be a bad thing.

Parrish found the holy man sitting with Coran under the Chieftains porch. He approached slowly, following camp protocol, and called a greeting to the pair, who just nodded in reply.

"May I sit with you?" he asked.

Coran waved him down with a casual gesture of the arm and, even before the tall man had settled on the skins, said with a smile.

"What do you wish to know?"

Parrish smiled back.

"It is actually the holy man I have come to talk to but I am sure that you would know too."

"Know what?" asked the flower and feather man.

"I have just been told by my ... wife," Coran smiled smugly at the tall man's reference. "That the village seems to go on some long walk once a year. She says that the time for this walk grows near."

"It is true." Both Neolithic men nodded.

"Where do you all go?" Even now Parrish still had difficulty seeing himself as a villager.

"It is that way." The holy man pointed vaguely off to the north-west. "We go to pay our respects at the great temple of the Earth Goddess."

The answer didn't tell Parrish much more than he already knew from Juli. He pushed on, trying to get at least some idea of the distance and difficulty of this mysterious walk.

"How far?"

"Several days walking." explained Coran. "We pay homage to Dannu at our own shrine first, and then the whole village makes the journey to her great temple. There we worship her in a great ceremony, and then trade for several more days before returning home to the village."

"But, is there not the chance of Dane-bre being raided while the whole village is away?" He found it hard to believe that the Chieftain would leave the village totally unguarded but he had said 'the whole village' and he usually meant exactly what he said.

"Do not be stupid." interrupted the holy man. "No one will raid the village."

"Why not?" Parrish chose to ignore the stupidity insult.

"Because everyone will be at the temple." he answered curtly, as if stating an obvious and inescapable truth.

"Everyone?"

"Yes." It was Coran again. "*All* the people will be there, so every village will be empty. That is why we can trade with each other, and at the same time worship together without fear of attack on our homes. It is the one great gathering of the year."

"And there is no fighting between people who would normally be enemies?" Parrish well remembered the attack on Danebury earlier in the year.

"Fighting there is very rare and is heavily frowned upon by the holy men. To fight at the great temple of Dannu would be a very bad insult to her. It would be foolish to do this and risk her wrath."

"I see." Parrish thought it over for a while. The whole truce arrangement seemed pretty shaky to him. "When do we go?" There was no question that he would go too. Just to see what happened, if nothing else. He noticed that neither of the men corrected him at his inclusion of 'we' in the question.

"We must be at the temple before the morning of the day when the sun is high." said the holy man firmly.

"Huh? High? You mean like noon?"

"No." The little man shook his head. Sometimes it seemed that the tall man knew absolutely nothing. "The morning of the day when the sun will reach its highest point in the sky."

Parrish mulled this one over for a minute. It was like a clue in a crossword puzzle and, like the answer to all good clues, it came to him in a flash. The little man must mean the day when the sun reached its highest point above the horizon. The summer solstice! That meant June the twenty first and his eyes lit up at this gem of information.

"When is this day?" he asked eagerly.

"Some time shortly before the next full moon." answered the Chieftain.

The last full moon had only just passed so Parrish knew that this evidently big Neolithic event was a few weeks away yet but he knew that summer had now truly started and June was just around the corner. He got a great sense of security from just knowing where he was in the year and, by the same token, also found it hard to believe that he had really been at Danebury almost a whole year.

"We will all worship at our own shrine before we take the long walk, so make sure you have your gift ready." said the flower and feather man suddenly. Parrish shot him a puzzled look. "Each family gives gifts to the Earth Goddess in thanks for her bounties and to ensure her continuing good fortune." He explained to the tall man, his tone again showing his exasperation at having to spell out what was such a well known event.

The gifts were actually taken by the holy man for his own use but that was expected. After all, was he not the villagers go between to Dannu? The holy man chose this convenient moment to remind the tall man of the giving ceremony because it was well known that Parrish's gifts were most unusual and he secretly looked forward to whatever he might be given.

"I see." said Parrish again, not really sure that he did. He pondered some more. "How do you know when this high sun time is near?"

"It is to do with the stars." said the holy man, waving away any chance of an explanation. He arrogantly felt that it would be much too complex a subject to be understood by the tall man, even if he had intended to give away the secret knowledge that was handed down from holy man to holy man, which he most certainly did not.

Parrish in his own way did not feel the question worth pursuing either. He was no astronomer. He knew the big dipper and how to find the north star from following the alignment of stars at one end of the constellation. That and being able to identify Orion when it rose above the horizon during the winter nights was his absolute limit as far as reading the heavens went.

"Very well. I will be ready. Thank you for answering my questions." He got up, bowed deeply and left them.

"What do you think will happen when he arrives at the temple?" Coran asked the holy man, voicing both their thoughts.

"I cannot say." came the answer. "We both know that he is closely connected with the Earth Goddess but he himself does not. She may not wish all the other villages to know that her man is among us. Nothing may happen at all."

Coran just nodded and both men watched in silence as Parrish threaded his way easily through the village and its people, heading back to his own hut.

He gently questioned Juli some more when he had once again settled down beside her but she had nothing more to tell him, except on the giving of the gifts.

She explained that they were for the holy man's use so he could keep his closeness with the Earth Goddess, hearing her wishes and allowing the village to speak to her through him. It was understood that if the gifts were clothes then they were all to be made to fit him. Usually the gifts were a mixture of clothes, food and tools.

Parrish nodded. Now he knew how the little man managed to survive so well in Danebury without appearing to do any work. He was kept well supplied by the people, to be their medium to their Goddess. He scoffed. Nice work if you can get it.

"I see now why you would want to be rid of your crutches." he said. "A walk of several days would be most difficult with them."

"Will I still be able to walk that far once the crutches are gone?"

It was difficult to answer the question truthfully without knowing how far 'that far' was but he nodded.

"I think so but we must take care. If it becomes too difficult for you, I will carry you."

"But..."

"I know." He raised a hand to stop her from voicing her worries. "I will not show weakness if I can help it but, well, we shall just have to see."

A troubled look settled on his wife's face. He just smiled and patted her reassuringly on the arm.

For the next few days Parrish made regular trips to the meadows to cut the tall grasses and stack them in short stooks to dry in the sun and breeze. Coran gave his permission for two men to accompany him on the trips and help him in his work. There was no shortage of warriors willing to work with the tall man, something Parrish took as a great complement, but the Chieftains choice was final. The two men he selected pleased Parrish too.

Coran was wise in his selection and picked two men who were personally indebted to the man and also his friends. He knew that these people would work particularly well with the tall man. It so followed that the work itself would be completed sooner and thus return the three from their unprotected position to the safety of the hill fort that much quicker. Needless to say, this also returned the fighting force of Dane-bre to full force more quickly. The Chieftain knew how valuable Parrish and his knowledge was to the defence of the village.

One of the men chosen was Gant, he of the bear attack, who was grateful to the Chieftain for the chance to repay at least part of the personal debt he owed to the tall man. The other was Tomps. Parrish smiled when Coran had selected him and referred to the youngster as a man. If the boy's chest had puffed out any further when the announcement was made, it looked very likely that he would have exploded with a loud bang!

The Chieftain watched as the three set off along the path that led to the flint mine and beyond, armed with their bows, slings and reaping tools. Their jolly voices carried back to him in the clear air, and he nodded in satisfaction at his wise, well considered selection.

It was not usual for the meadow grasses to be cropped for roofing thatch but Coran understood that the tall mans odd shaped house needed a roof and was equally aware that, although Parrish had tried to keep his inner feelings to himself, it was important to the man that he move into his strange dwelling to settle himself down. Once again, the Chieftain was kept well informed. The uneasiness that swirled just beneath Parrish's surface confidence was as much a threat to the harmony and well being of the village as any attack from beyond the walls and Coran was not a man to stand idly by when threatened. No matter how insignificant that threat might seem.

After watching the slowly diminishing silhouettes of the men for a while, from his vantage point on the parapet of the defence wall, he dismissed them from his mind. The departing trio had looked vaguely comical as they travelled away, the small boy, the Dane-bre warrior and the tall stranger, but the Chieftain was not a humorous man. He had other things on his mind, and returned to his recent main pre-occupation, preparing the village for its trek to the great temple. It was now less than one moon away.

This was the time of year he hated most. Everyone began to get excited as the time for the long walk drew near but only the holy man knew the exact time and the people waited eagerly for his signal. Then there would be the offering of gifts followed by the trek, which finally led to the time of trading and that was what they all looked forward too. The once a year chance to exchange gifts and gossip, meet old friends, and perhaps make some new ones. But until the holy man gave that signal, Coran had the unenviable task of maintaining order in the village, a task that grew steadily more difficult.

Over enthusiasm could be a dangerous thing.

30

Juli awoke to find her husband crouched beside the fire, heating some water in the strange pots that he called mess tins. She had once asked him what they were made of and he had just said 'metal'. The word meant absolutely nothing to her.

She sat up and peered curiously into the steaming mess tins. Apparently cooking away in the hot water were two pieces of cloth. Parrish heard the girl's movement behind him and turned to face her.

"Good morning."

"Is it?" she asked, not sure why he should feel the need to tell her this. Parrish laughed. Juli frowned, unaware that she had said anything funny.

"Why are you cooking pieces of cloth?"

"Not cooking." he corrected, "Heating. How do you feel today?"

"I feel... um ... OK." She remained puzzled. That was the second strange thing he had said and she had only been awake a few moments.

"Good." he nodded. "Then today we shall have those splints off. In fact, right now is as good a time as any."

A mixture of gladness and trepidation filled Juli. It was indeed her great wish to be rid of the splints but she was frightened that when he undid the bindings, her legs, or at least a part of them, might drop off.

Parrish grasped the girl's ankles and swung her legs gently out of the bed and onto the floor. She obediently gathered up the woollen skirt she wore, holding it up near the tops of her thighs as he slowly undid the bindings one at a time, throwing the thongs aside. He would find some other use for them later. Finally, he undid the last one and lifted away the wooden support shafts. With a grin he held them up to Juli then turned and tossed them into the fire. She just nodded before staring down at her legs, afraid to move them. Parrish bent again to his work, attending to each leg in turn. He massaged and gently kneaded the calf and thigh muscles. The right leg looked as if nothing had ever happened to it. The left sported a pink, two inch scar on the shin but apart from that, seemed normal enough.

As he tenderly rubbed her bare legs, Juli watched, fascinated and at the same time, enjoying the feeling. She didn't know what it was supposed to do but it was very nice. As if reading her mind, Parrish looked up and smiled.

"This will help to get the blood flowing and reduce the risk of any cramps."

She didn't know what 'cramps' meant but believed him anyway. She had absolute faith in her husband now.

"OK. Now, try to bend your legs, slowly."

She started to pull her legs up towards her chest, managing to raise them a foot or so before stopping, wincing at the ache in her joints.

"They are very stiff." she said. "My knees."

"I expected as much." He turned to his mess tins and pulled out a hot cloth from one of them. It was hot all right but still bearable and, without ceremony, he slapped it onto the girls knee and wrapped it around the joint. Juli flinched at the initial contact but did not pull away. He repeated the exercise with the second piece of cloth and patted the hot wet compresses around her knees, massaging her muscles some more while he waited for the heat to work its way into the joints.

"The warmth will help free them up. It is expected that they would be stiff after being kept still for so long."

Juli just nodded, still enjoying the new sensations.

Finally he removed the pieces of cloth and got her to flex her knees again. This time they had much more movement but were still a bit on the stiff side. Satisfied, Parrish scooped Juli up into his arms and, with a supporting arm under her shoulders, lowered her feet to the floor. She stood for a moment, just getting used to the feeling of once again free standing. He moved around to face her and held onto her arms.

"Come on then." He took a pace backwards. Juli took a short, tentative step towards him. Then another, and then another. Parrish, still walking backwards, led her in a slow, halting lap around the fire.

"Good." he said. "Very good. Do they hurt?"

"No." she shook her head. "They are just very stiff and slow."

"That will pass. For now though you must still use your crutches. Only take very short walks without them for the moment. Perhaps in a few more days you can forget them too." He would give her a week, maximum, he decided. Then if she had not already discarded them, he would take them away himself. Things looked good. The girl smiled and, after he had stood aside, she slowly walked unaided around the fire, arms outstretched for balance. Parrish could see a slight limp but wasn't too disappointed. The results were much better than he had even dared hope for. He silently acknowledged the fact that the human body was a truly amazing piece of kit.

Juli returned to her husband and stood before him, a look of total joy on her small face. He smiled down at her, as happy with her success as she was.

"I have my legs back!" she exclaimed. "I have my legs back. Thank you Parrish." She laughed out loud and, in a moment of elation, hugged him around the middle, her head buried in his chest. He put his arms around her and patted her gently on the back.

The moment of joy evaporated and Juli recoiled from her uncharacteristic display of free expression. She pulled away, arms dropping limply to her sides, head bowed.

"Please ... forgive me ... I ..."

"Nothing to forgive, sweetheart." he said and she tilted her face up towards his, surprised at the sudden tenderness in his voice. He leaned forward and kissed her gently on the forehead. "Well done, girl. Now, I do not want you to start dashing around without your crutches, understand? You must take it easy. Be careful and build up your strength first. Yes?" She nodded. "Good. Now sit back down and I will see about some food."

He turned to leave. Juli put a gently restraining hand on his arm and he stopped in mid turn, sideways on to the small girl. She signalled for him to come closer and he stooped, as if to have some special secret whispered into his ear. The girl leaned forward and, copying what she had seen him do, kissed him lightly on the cheek. It was another strange and not unpleasant sensation for her.

"Thank you." she said gratefully. "Did I do that right?"

Parrish put his finger to his cheek and smiled warmly.

"Perfect."

She bowed her head at the praise.

He left without another word and Juli sat back down in the warmth of the fires glow, as the discarded splints burned brightly, listening to her husband's sudden burst of cheery whistling from outside the hut.

For the next week, while Juli exercised her legs and regained her strength, Parrish and his little band of followers carried all the dried stooks of meadow grass labouriously back to Danebury. They made several trips every day to complete the task. He was most grateful to his friends for their assistance and said so on many occasions. They would have none of it. It was their honour to help him.

Parrish worked very well with Gant. The warrior was an honest grafter and, although sometimes a man of few words, spoke wisely and learned quickly. He grasped the basic concepts of productive organization quite well.

The boy Tomps was changing into a man even as the other two watched. Parrish and Gant had discussed the subject together when they had stopped for a breather and the youngster worked on, that in itself a sign of his increasing maturity. His self confidence was growing in leaps and bounds and he now looked upon himself as a warrior rather than a boy. His continued association with the tall man increased his standing in the community and it was a measure of his new found confidence that other, older warriors started to show him some measure of respect.

"He is a man now." said Gant as they watched him carrying a pair of stooks on his back, up towards the cabin where the two men stood. All the women, and some of the men, parted to allow him passage. "You have done well."

"Me?"

"It is you and being around you that has changed him. You have given Dane-bre one more fine warrior."

Parrish felt a sudden flush of pride. Gant was right.

As Tomps approached the two men he was puzzled as to why they should both be grinning at him. Juli chose that exact moment to appear from around the corner of the cabin.

"I have brought food and water for you all." she said and held up her goodies. The three men nodded in thanks and helped themselves to the food. Juli looked up at the partially thatched roof. She had not yet been inside the odd shaped building and had no intention of doing so until her husband invited her to.

"You are doing well?" she asked.

Gant frowned at the woman for daring to ask a question. Tomps knew it was a very strange thing too but was not quite so surprised. He had learned to be ready to expect something out of the ordinary to happen whenever he was around the tall man.

Parrish shot her a reproachful look and Juli immediately bowed her head in apology, realizing that she had made a mistake. Gant nodded in satisfaction. He expected that the insolent woman would be severely punished later, when she was alone with her husband. To his surprise though, Parrish answered her question anyway.

"The roof is coming on very well. It will not be much longer before it is finished and we can move in." Juli's head was still bowed and he could not gauge her reaction.

"This is true." said Tomps through a mouthful of food. "The 'cabin' will be ready even before we take the long walk." He was pleased at his first chance to use the new, strange language word that the tall man had taught him.

"Yes," agreed Gant. "If we talk less and work more. Finish your food."

Tomps nodded agreement and gulped down his mouthful. Parrish smiled, winked at Gant and looked down at his small wife. She bowed to her husband and the other warriors, excusing herself, and walked away. The three watched her leave, following closely with their eyes her relaxed strides, only the merest hint of a limp still visible.

"I do not know how you did it Parrish, but she is fully healed. How is it that you can do such feats?" Gant looked expectantly at his tall companion, hoping for some sort of insight. Tomps was as well. He even stopped chewing.

"It took me many, many years to learn these things." Parrish stared on after his wife, proud of the achievement and suddenly recalling Carter telling him that his contribution to life would be fuck all. He smiled to himself in private satisfaction. "What I can do is nothing compared to the feats of the men who taught me."

At basic training all the raw recruits had thought that their instructors were nothing short of super human too.

"Where are these men?" asked Tomps. The question stumped Parrish for several moments. He could think of no feasible explanation to tell his Neolithic friends.

"I cannot say."

"Why?" asked Gant as if someone had snatched the very food from his mouth. Here was a chance to find out something about the tall stranger in their midst. "Would your answer offend the Earth

Goddess?"

Parrish laughed.

"No. It is just that you would not believe me if I told you."

"We would." said Tomps eagerly. Gant shot him a hard look. The boy still had much to learn about talking to his betters.

"OK." Parrish shrugged. Try this one on for size boys, he thought. "The men that taught me have not been born yet, and will not be born for a very long time."

The two Neolithic men just stood, stunned. They knew that what he had said was not possible, but also knew that the tall man was a man of honour and spoke true. Parrish noted their reactions and shrugged again.

"I told you, you would not believe me. Come on, let us get back to work."

Gant and Tomps looked at each other in silent awe then, bewildered, followed the tall mans lead and went dumbly back to their tasks.

It was a little later that same day and Parrish and Gant were perched high up on the apex of the roof, standing at the tops of cross pole ladders. They were busy tying down the bundles of thatch that Tomps had prepared on the ground below them, which were then hauled up by rope. From their high vantage point the pair had panoramic views of the entire hill fort and the surrounding countryside.

Juli had completely discarded her crutches now and the two men watched her long approach as she crossed the fields and entered the fort after filling some water bags from the distant stream. She walked easily and with confidence, her strength returned, and stopped on her journey to exchange words with other women that she passed by. They were delighted to see her fully recovered and were full of words of her praise for her husband.

The two warriors watched in silence until Juli passed almost right beneath them and had disappeared into the little hut.

"She is well now, and ripe." said Gant. "You will no doubt be hoping for a son." The words held no hint of expectation, the man just stating what he thought to be the obvious. Even so, they caught Parrish completely on the hop.

"Huh?"

"A son." repeated Gant. "You hope that the Earth Goddess will be generous and grant you a boy baby."

Parrish didn't know what to say. Gant stared hard into the tall man's face, a sudden look of suspicion on his own.

"You *do* want a boy baby?" he asked slowly.

"I have not really thought about it. I mean ... well..."

"You *have* given the woman your seed?" he asked, once again in the slow, suspicious tone.

"It... I..." he shrugged, unable anymore to look the man in the eye.

"You have not!!" he exclaimed incredulously. "I do not believe it! Parrish, what kind of a man are you?"

"She has been ill." blurted Parrish in his defence.

"That is of no matter! This is terrible news." He shook his head. "She must think that you are nothing!"

"Why?" Parrish was astounded at the man's sudden dismay.

"Why? Because you deny her her right. It is also your duty to give her your seed."

"Her right?"

"Yes! She is honoured by the Earth Goddess with the gift of being able to bear children. It is the one thing that warriors cannot do and is Dannu's great gift to every woman for faithful service to the warriors upon her land. You deny the woman her gift and insult her by not giving your seed."

Parrish's head swam. It was all coming at him a bit fast and he shook his head, bewildered at the sudden revelations. He looked pleadingly at his Neolithic companion.

"But, I did not know. She did not tell me this."

"It is not her place to tell you this." said Gant in exasperation. "And it does not even matter if you want to or not. It is her right to expect your seed and your duty to give it, for the honour of Dannu and the continuing of men upon her land." He shook his head. "You must put right this terrible wrong Parrish, or the Earth Goddess will be very angry."

Parrish nodded and waved for the warrior to calm himself.

"It will be done. It is not my intention to insult the Earth Goddess. Do not worry."

Gant looked into the tall mans eyes, then nodded. He knew that Parrish was a man of honour and spoke true.

"It is good that Tomps was not up here to hear this." he said, looking over his shoulder at the boy on the ground below them. "Your weakness shall be known just between us. Give her your seed Parrish, or the whole village will feel the wrath of Dannu."

Parrish nodded, astounded to suddenly discover how much importance these people put on something that he knew they did not personally care much about. The rights of women of all things. There was hope for these barbarians yet.

"Good." said Gant. "Now, we shall speak no more of it." He shook his head once more and the pair went back to the thatching of the roof, working in a subdued silence for the rest of the afternoon.

Tomps laboured on regardless, unaware of the heated discussion that had gone on high above his head.

31

It was the following evening when Parrish entered the hut armed with some very good news. Well at least he thought so anyway. The thatching was finished and he and Juli could now move into the cabin. Their cabin. There was already a good stockpile of firewood in the storeroom and at this very moment a fire burned in the hearth. He grinned at Juli, who was bustling about around the fire. Before he could open his mouth to speak, the girl offered him a large bowl of hot stew and a smile.

"Here, I know that you have worked very hard and so I wanted the food to be ready as soon as you returned. Please eat."

"Oh, right. Thank you." Parrish accepted the offering and without another word squatted almost obediently down beside the fire. Juli immediately joined him and they ate together in silence. The stew was very welcome and very tasty. As he devoured it he looked his wife over once more. He noticed that he had been doing that on a regular basis now that she was back on her feet. He didn't mind, he liked it. He cocked his head to one side. All things considered, he hadn't done too badly as far as wives go.

Juli was conscious of his examinations, but no longer self conscious of them. Parrish had told her many times not to fear him and to ask questions if she wanted to know or understand something. It was very strange for her at first, but now that she felt more secure in his presence it began to please her. The discoveries of things that she did not know, just by asking her strange and clever husband, excited her. Perhaps the tall mans constant hunger for knowledge was catching. She had discovered that she liked to learn.

She glanced up at her husband as he continued to stare, recognizing the look in his eye. It didn't happen often but when it did it meant that he was about to ask her a question. The thought bothered her. He was so clever and she was so stupid, that it did not seem right that he should ask a question of her. She feared that she might not know the answer and so disappoint him and it was her main aim in life to please her tall husband.

"You would ask me something?" She took the plunge.

"Well, yes. I have recently discovered that you have a right."

Juli gulped. She knew that this moment would surely come and did not know what would happen when it did. What kind of strange mating rituals did the mysterious tall man's people follow? It now seemed that she was about to find out.

"You ... you mean my right of seed?"

"Yes." There was a long pause before he continued. "You did not tell me of this right. Have I not said that you can talk freely to me?"

She thought that he was about to get angry and immediately bowed her head in submission. He carried on.

"Gant said that I am offending the Earth Goddess by denying you your right of seed."

"Gant should honour our privacy." she said quietly. To her complete surprise Parrish roared with laughter and slapped his thigh.

"Too right girl." he laughed. "Tell him to keep his nose out."

Juli looked back up at her husband. He really was such a strange man.

"Look." he said, suddenly serious. "It was not my intention to deny you your right. It is just that I did not know and, well, I do not know how you people do it." He tried to say it in an objective manner but could not stop his cheeks reddening. Juli saw the embarrassment and smiled as he suddenly took on that occasionally innocent, childlike quality that appealed to her so much. He was actually asking *her* about the giving of his seed. Had he never given it before? She asked him boldly.

"Is it your first time then, my husband?"

Parrish was at first shocked, then laughed again.

"No." If only she knew, he thought. "But it is with one of you people."

Juli often wondered what he meant whenever he referred to the people of Dane-bre as 'you people'. Were his own so very different?

"Do you want me to tell you how it is done?" she asked.

"Do you know?"

"Oh, yes." she said with some authority. "I have seen it done many times."

"But never done it yourself?" he asked, almost too casually. She shook her head. A virgin, he thought with a surprising amount of pleasure. They looked at each other for a while in silence.

"Well?" he said eventually.

"The woman is laid on her back." Juli said, very matter-of-factly. "The man gets hard and puts his hardness inside the woman." She uncrossed her legs, opened them wide and pointed at her groin in a totally unnecessary gesture which Parrish found quite distasteful. "Then he pushes in and out very fast for a short time and the woman has his seed. Then, if Dannu smiles, she will have a baby and, if Dannu is very generous, it will be a boy baby."

"And that is it?" asked Parrish in dismay. "Does the woman not get any pleasure from it?" Does the man even, he thought sadly.

"There is no pleasure." said Juli, puzzled at such a strange question. "It is duty."

Parrish shook his head sadly. The poor bastards don't even know what they are missing. It was almost criminal to throw away such a joy, not to mention the gross mistreatment of the poor woman who then had the added burden of carrying a child for nine months, no doubt still working hard during all that time. He hung his head in sorrow.

"Is something wrong?" asked Juli.

"Yes." said Parrish emphatically. "I am sorry but I cannot do it your way." It was the honest truth.

"Oh." Juli was surprised to find herself more than a little disappointed and it was not totally because of the prospect of offending the Earth Goddess. She had secretly begun to look forward to mating with the tall man. She couldn't explain her feelings fully, but she knew she liked to touch him and mating seemed a natural extension of that touching.

"Ah ... How do your people ... do it then?" she asked, not quite sure that she wanted to know the answer. For all she knew, it might be very painful!

He looked at her, reading the reluctance in her eyes.

"Do you really want to know?"

She paused for a second, then nodded.

"We do it slowly." he said, watching her reactions closely. "If it is done properly, there is great pleasure to be enjoyed by both the man and the woman. I am sure that the Earth Goddess would not deny her women some enjoyment when honouring her." Juli nodded, not understanding what he really meant but agreeing that the idea seemed reasonable enough to her.

"If the man is good, the giving of his seed, and the pleasure of it, is a gift from him to her." The girls eyes widened at the very idea of any gift being given from a warrior to a mere woman. "And sometimes, the pleasure can even be a gift from the woman to her man. It is true." he added, judging from the look in her eyes that she did not believe him. "And another thing. It is done best when the man and the woman are both willing."

"But it is the man's right!" said Juli incredulously.

"Where I come from, it is also the woman's right to say no." said Parrish, his tone hard. Juli shook her head in amazement.

"I have never heard of such a thing." There was a hint of disbelief in her voice.

"It is true." he said again.

After that there was a very long silence. Parrish knew that he had to 'give his seed' as they so quaintly put it in these parts, or lie to Gant and the rest of Danebury about it. He didn't like either idea much at that moment. It very much looked like he would have to lay back and think of England. His mouth began to set in a firm line. Juli watched him for a moment and came to her own decision.

"Parrish." she said softly. "I am willing."

"What?!"

"I will take your seed your way, just please do not hurt me."

Parrish was astounded. What a girl! His heart went out to her. He reached across, gently stroked her cheek with his fingertips and smiled into her troubled eyes.

"Sweetheart, the last thing I would ever do is hurt you. I am honoured that you are my wife and I also think that, in your own way, you are as brave as any warrior."

She smiled then.

Without a word the couple stood up. Parrish removed his combat jacket while Juli shucked out of her woollen summer clothes. It took her a few brief seconds. She stood naked before her husband while he was still struggling out of his shirt. He stopped and took a long lingering look at her pale young body. Too young, was his first impression. He was about to have sex with an underage girl. He dismissed the notion. She was his wife, already halfway to her grave as far as Neolithic longevity went, and willing.

Juli warmed to her man as his eyes wandered with obvious pleasure over her. She let him enjoy the sight for a few moments longer, then crossed to the bedding on the floor beyond the fire, and lay down upon it. Parrish could hardly take his eyes off her as he fumbled with his boot laces before being able to remove the rest of his clothes. When he was finally naked, he crossed to the bed. She suddenly recoiled from him, a look of fear on her face.

"What? What is wrong?"

"It is so big. It will tear me." she whined, her eyes locked on his groin.

Parrish looked down at his hardness. He didn't think it was *that* big.

"It will not tear you." he said, smiling softly at the back handed complement. "If a baby can pass through you, then I do not think I will cause any damage."

He lay down beside her and gently stoked her long, dark hair. She seemed so tiny next to him.

"Look." he said softly, trying to dispel her silly fear. "If you are frightened or I am at any time hurting you, just tell me to stop and I will."

Juli shook her head, tingling with the sudden closeness of him.

"I am still willing, my husband." The smile that he gave her warmed her heart. She suddenly knew what they were doing was right, as if she had received the blessing of the Earth Goddess. It was her task to take care of Dannu's man and, if what he said was really true, perhaps her pleasure as well.

This close up, Parrish found his Neolithic wife suddenly very appealing. It was the heady mixture of her small, almost frail looking body, her deep desire to please him and the restrained look of apprehension yet expectation on her sweet face. A big surprise when, up till recently, he had always thought all the Stone Age women to be sexually almost repulsive to him.

He leaned over and kissed her tentatively on the lips. She did not respond and he did not expect her to, but she did not turn away either.

Juli still thought it was a strange thing to do but liked it never the less. The surprise that it was so enjoyable increased even more, making her smile, when his soft kisses travelled slowly over her chin, down the line of her throat and onto her bare chest. Her eyes closed and she let the simple niceness of the sensations wash over her as he kissed, sucked and teased her hard nipples with his tongue.

Parrish wasn't sure if what he was doing was having any effect on Juli. He knew he couldn't judge much by her physical reaction or even lack of it. The effect he hoped he was having would be totally alien to her and so she would not know how to react. He just hoped that she might manage to throw off the repressions that Neolithic culture had burdened the sweet young thing with, at least for the moment that they were joined, and let her inner feelings show. He manoeuvred himself on top of her, raising his body clear of hers on his arms. As he looked down at her a sudden feeling of self doubt washed over him. Should he do this? Had he the right to take her, even if, in the eyes of everyone else, she was lawfully his wife? She was so young and by all that was right he shouldn't even be here. A man from another time and another place. A stranger in a strange land. At that moment Juli's eyes flicked open and he was drawn deep into the small pools of blueness. Her smile warmed as she gazed back at him and what he saw there surprised him. If it wasn't for the simple fact that he knew that in these hard Neolithic times there was no idea of, or even place for, romance, he would have sworn that she loved him.

Parrish had his simple fact wrong, although he did not know it and she could not tell him so. But the look was enough. Confidence restored, he lowered himself gently onto her, still taking a lot of his body weight on his elbows, and gently started to ease himself into her.

Small and delicate as Juli might appear to be, she was still a Neolithic woman and no stranger to discomfort. She took the stab of pain as he entered her with just the merest of flinches but the smile died on her face. Parrish saw.

"Is something wrong?" he asked softly, stopping.

She shook her head briefly and so, with a long movement of his powerful hips, he pushed himself in till he was fully enveloped. To Parrish the sensation felt so good. Almost too good and he had to fight the nearly overwhelming urge to immediately explode inside her. He had to hold on tightly to his control.

It was indeed a very tight fit for the young virgin and Juli felt that he completely filled her, almost as if she were impaled on him. It was terrifying and at the same time the most incredible thing she had ever experienced. She still lay completely motionless beneath him but where his body touched hers, both inside and out, she tingled with pleasure. If it was right or wrong to feel like this she did not know, but she trusted her man and knew that he was always guided by the Earth Goddess. This must be the great pleasure that Parrish had talked so determinedly about.

Just when she thought it could get no better, Parrish started long, slow strokes, kissing her as he did so. It was nothing at all like any other of the matings she had witnessed and she too suffered her own moment of self doubt. Was what her husband doing right? Should she submit herself to this apparently unnatural act? Parrish had said that if she said no, then he would stop. As she considered the thought the first shudder of sexual feeling flooded outward from her groin and made her gasp. It shocked her.

Parrish heard the gasp and felt a sudden rush of gratification. He let his full weight settle gently on her, feeling her fiery warmth, and for the first time since he had known her, really held her in his arms. He nuzzled her neck, at the same time increasing the rhythm of his thrusts. Not so fast that he might immediately excite himself to bursting point, but quick enough to keep the waves of pleasure washing over Juli.

She was suddenly adrift, lost on a sea of strange sensations. Her body seemed to light up inside. To Parrish's utter delight she slowly reached around him and pulled him to her, hands pushing hard on his back to keep him close. He kissed her hard on the lips and she couldn't help it, she kissed him back. It just seemed the right thing to do.

Parrish groaned softly then and Juli feared that he might be in pain. She looked into his eyes once more and saw something that both frightened her and thrilled her to the core. The raw need, plus something else. She had no word for it but knew that she felt the same.

The look was enough. A sudden, bursting sensation of white hot, flaming heat flared up at the place where they were joined together. With gathering speed it rushed outward to the very ends of her being, roaring inside her.

"Parrish," she gasped. "Something is happening. I do not know ... I am frightened, ... Stop!" Then her body thundered in its climax. Her power of speech was lost. It was all she could do to gasp. She clutched her lover to her as tightly as she could, holding on with all her might.

Parrish was with her as she peaked. At that same moment he let out a strangled cry of pleasure and his seed thundered into her. He hugged her so close that she had trouble drawing breath. He had never felt the like of it before. He knew it was as much a new experience for him as it must be for her.

They held on to each other so tightly for that brief yet timeless moment of physical euphoria, before collapsing as the moment ebbed away.

Parrish eventually lifted himself off Juli's trembling form and looked down at the young woman beneath him. Her eyes were full of wonder and admiration for him. He kissed her and she responded. They held each other, locked in the embrace for some time before he rolled slowly onto his back, welcoming her to his side as she snuggled up, resting her arm across his broad chest. At that moment he felt he never wanted to be apart from her.

They lay like that, not needing to speak, for a long time. Parrish felt Juli's, his woman's, breathing slowly regulate until he knew that she had fallen asleep, still holding on to him. He felt happily sleepy himself.

With his free hand he pulled the skin blankets carefully over their naked bodies. He closed his eyes, feeling the body heat of his wife and silently revelled in the sensation. Just before he fell asleep he remembered that he had some important news to tell Juli. About the cabin.

No matter, he thought with a smile, it wasn't *that* important.

32

The sun was shining and Parrish was being unbearably cheerful. When he and his wife had woken that morning, they had greeted each other by making love again. Eventually, it was all he could do to drag himself away from her and get to work on the days chores. Juli was just as reluctant to let him go. She also met the new day feeling too happy for words. The almost unearthly sensations that her husband had released inside her were undoubtedly a gift from Dannu, given to her through him. To start the day by worshipping the Earth Goddess was a great joy. Good morning he had said and she now knew what he meant.

Juli was somewhat limited to the extent that she could allow her joy to show, once she had left the sanctuary of their hut, but that did not bother her unduly. She was however most impatient to tell the other women of Dane-bre about the extraordinary Earth Goddess contact that her husband had allowed her to feel. And just how wonderful it did feel! They would be so envious of her closeness to Dannu's man.

"Greetings Parrish."

Parrish turned at the sound of Klud's voice. He approached from his family hut as the tall man passed by on his way towards the main gate. The warrior stood before him and nodded his head in the direction of the rise behind him.

"I see that your strange house is finished."

"What? Oh, yes." He had all but forgotten.

"It is indeed an odd looking hut but I think that it is right for you."

"Thank you Klud. You are indeed wise." It was the best compliment the warrior could have paid him. Parrish had long since gotten used to being called odd or strange. The two men gazed up at the cabin for a moment, its roofing thatch a light, sandy colour in its freshness, clearly visible from anywhere in the camp.

"I must move my things into it. Juli does not yet know that we shall live in there as from today."

"It is of no matter if she knows or not." said Klud, still finding it hard to understand the strange need his tall friend had to fuss over his women. The Neolithic warrior considered the idea utter nonsense but, as long as Parrish was happy and he did not offend anyone, then he saw no point in correcting his mistake.

"You will not sleep many nights there before this moon is gone." he said.

"Why is that?" Parrish pulled his eyes from the cabin he thought so attractive looking and stared quizzically down at the warrior.

"Because the long walk is near. Last night the holy man signalled the day. Tomorrow night we give Dannu her gifts at our shrine. The next morning we set off on the long walk." He patted Parrish on the shoulder and gave him a toothy grin. "You always need to know things, my friend. Well believe me when I say the great gathering at her temple will interest you much." He nodded then walked away, still nodding, apparently in agreement with his last statement.

Parrish watched him depart and shook his head. A great guy, even if he was sometimes too sure of himself. Then he laughed and walked back through the camp towards his cabin, nodding a cheerful acknowledgment to anyone that he passed.

He entered the cabin and gave it the once over for the umpteenth time. The fire had long gone out and he re kindled it. His rugged pieces of furniture were all in place and he was satisfied that there were no chinks of light in the thatch above his head. He opened the two window ports and beams of sunlight shafted in, giving a glowing warmth to the interior. It added to his overall feeling of joy. He nodded to himself in appreciation and satisfaction, then laughed as he realized that he was inadvertently emulating Klud.

Stepping back out into the daylight, he stood for a proud moment on his new threshold. His eyes scanned the village below him, a habit he had developed since his first, eventful days in Danebury.

Tomps suddenly appeared from between the buildings, running hard towards him. Parrish watched impassively as the young warrior charged up the slope. He arrived gasping and Parrish held up his hand to stop the lad from attempting to speak until he had regained his breath.

"Have you heard?" he finally asked, panting. "The signal has been given!" The excitement on his face was undeniable.

"Yes." answered Parrish casually, taking a secret delight in letting the wind out of the youngster's sails. "All troops are now on standby, operation long walk is go. Be ready to move out in forty eight hours."

"Huh?" said Tomps, copying the ignorant sounding grunt that his strange, tall mentor used when he didn't understand something.

"I know. Klud spoke of it to me not long ago."

"Oh." Tomps was crestfallen. He had hoped to be the one to break the good news to Parrish.

"Never mind." The tall man patted him sympathetically on the shoulder. "I am as excited as you. Klud tells me that it is a great event." The boys eyes lit up again and he nodded vigorously.

"Have you eaten?" Parrish changed the subject abruptly. Tomps shook his head. "Would you honour me by eating with my family?" It was the least he could do after shooting the lad down.

The young warrior was almost beside himself at even being asked such a thing. To eat with the tall man when they worked together was one thing, but to eat at his house was a real honour.

The pair walked down to the little hut with Tomps all the time trying to tell Parish everything that happened at the great temple of Dannu. His descriptions did not come across very well. Although he was now a warrior, the previous times he had visited the temple he had been but a boy and only remembered what he had wanted to. Parrish kept interrupting him with questions that he could not answer. It was of no matter. The tall man was for some reason in good humour and did not get annoyed on not receiving satisfactory answers to his queries.

They arrived at the entrance to his hut and sat down outside beside the as yet un-lit fire.

"Woman of the house!" shouted Parrish in a strangely happy tone of voice. "I have a warrior with me who is in need of food!"

Tomps nodded in approval. That was how he thought a warrior should instruct his women. He looked forward to getting his own wife soon. A few moments later Juli emerged from behind the entrance curtain carrying two bowls holding cuts of meat and some early summer fruits, mostly berries. She set the bowls down between the men and retrieved a water bag from a peg beside the doorway.

Tomps watched the girl closely. She seemed somehow different, almost too happy in her work. He had seen her but one day earlier and then she had just been a girl, not much older than himself. But today she was different. She seemed almost worldly wise, carried herself differently, proudly, and the look in her eye held some new, exciting secret. The girl was now a woman. As Parrish had changed him, so had he somehow changed her too. The young warrior noticed how the tall mans eyes followed her almost constantly. Anyone would think he had never seen her before. When she handed him the water bag their hands touched and held for a second and he definitely saw her insult him with a long moment of eye contact. But, instead of punishing her, he smiled. Worse, she actually smiled back!

Tomps found it all quite unnerving and could not contain his curiosity.

"Has something happened here?" he asked.

"That's the understatement of the year, matey." smiled Parrish, speaking in English. Ignoring her husband's unintelligible words, Juli nodded to the young warrior and touched herself low down on the abdomen.

"I have my husband's seed." she said proudly.

"Is that all?" Tomps found the answer most disappointing. He had expected to hear of some exciting new revelation from his strange companion. "I thought something important had happened, like the sign being given."

"It has?" asked Juli, suddenly excited.

Tomps frowned at the brazenness of the woman, daring to ask a direct question. The woman instantly knew she had overstepped the mark and made a mistake. She was still overwhelmed by the events of the previous night. She bowed deeply to the warrior.

"Please, forgive me, but it is indeed great news."

The lad accepted the apology with the merest nod of his head. Parrish smiled. It was a gesture that the boy had obviously copied from watching the actions of the Chieftain. It was good to know the youngster didn't consider him the only hero in the camp.

"Yes. The holy man has signalled. Tomorrow night we give at the shrine. And then the long walk!" He could not contain his excitement.

"That is all very well." said Parrish casually. "But that only gives me a short time to move everything into the cabin. Eat up your food so that I may get on with my work."

Tomps nodded and tucked into the free food. Parrish winked at Juli, who gave him a secret smile in return then shot a sideways glance up at the cabin on the higher ground behind their hut. It was an odd looking place but she was not too concerned. Where her husband went, so did she.

The briars blazed once more around the outside of the great hut, calling the people of Danebury to the shrine of the Earth Goddess. Inside, the great central fire burned brightly and every stall was well illuminated by tallow lamps.

It did not take long for the whole village to assemble there. The eager throng waited for the last few, knowing the ceremony could not begin until all were present.

Parrish and Juli arrived in good time but were not too early. He always hated to be the first arrival at a party. Eventually the hut was full, the village outside deserted. There was a wonderful, expectant atmosphere in the place. It buzzed with excitement.

The Chieftain left his stall, attracting all eyes to him, and in his slow, measured strides completed a full lap of the interior, passing the entrance to each stall with his hand raised as if taking a head count. When he had gone full circle and arrived at the foot of the shrine, he raised his arms high in the air and called to the Earth Goddess.

"Dannu! All my people are here. They have gathered in your presence and it is their great wish to honour you with gifts!"

There was a suitably long silence to allow a dramatic effect to build before the flower and feather man appeared from his place behind the shrine. Parrish had to admit that he looked quite spectacular, now he was dressed in full regalia. His hat was an absolute riot of colour with woodland flowers and different pieces of bright plumage, including the jet black feather from the sky spirit that Parrish had given him. His cape matched it for outrageousness. There were brightly patterned leather bands around his knees and ankles that had more feathers and tassels of coloured cloth dangling from them. They were a riot of animation whenever he moved. He turned and faced the shrine as Coran retreated to his stall. After a moment of silent expectation, the holy man raised his arms too and sang one of his unintelligible songs to the statue. Unlike the other songs of his that Parrish had heard before, this one sounded almost jolly. A song of celebration.

When the little man had finished the song he grasped the edges of his cape, held his arms out wide, spreading the bright garment like eagles wings, and started to dance. He followed in the Chieftains footsteps around the interior of the great hut, twirling and chanting, skipping and jumping all the way. It was a splendid display and Parrish was impressed and enthralled. He raised his hands to clap along. Juli noticed and stopped him with a hand on his arm. This was a solemn occasion, the celebrations came later. Parrish did not mind her timely intervention. He appreciated the discrete guidance.

Dance finally finished, the holy man stopped again before the shrine, bowed so deeply that he almost touched the floor with his amazing hat and turned to face the people of Danebury. Droplets of sweat beaded brightly on his forehead, face flushed with exertion.

"The Earth Goddess is ready and willing to accept any gifts you may wish to offer her." he announced very magnanimously.

Parrish smiled at the choice of phrase. He knew it was just about compulsory to give a gift, or risk the wrath of Dannu, not to mention everyone else in the village.

Every person in the great hut, including Parrish and the Chieftain, bowed reverently to the statue. The holy man took the bows graciously enough then stepped to one side, standing beside the plinth and looking on as people began to file up with their offerings. Parrish and his wife joined the queue and he watched with amusement the expressions on the little man's face as it lit up or frowned when he approved of or was not impressed by the objects offered. At no time though did he utter a single word.

As Juli had so rightly pointed out, all the articles of clothing were made to fit the small man. Obviously, the women who made the clothes could not offer up to their holy man the semi completed garments to ensure the fit was good. That explained to Parrish why the holy man always looked like a scruffy new age traveller, apart from his immaculate religious regalia.

He let Juli step forward before him to offer her gift first. It was not proper protocol but he didn't care. It was right as far as he was concerned. The holy man let the discrepancy pass. His eyes were fixed on the object in Juli's tiny hands. It was the little square heliograph from Parrish's kit. Juli had been assured by her husband that the flower and feather man would be most impressed with the strange object. He was not wrong. The signalling device was of no use to Parrish. There was no one for him to signal too, even if they could understand Morse code, and the sighting hole in its centre made it less than ideal as a normal mirror. He had another mirror anyway, on the inside of the lid of his Survival Aids tin.

Juli had threaded a length of leather thong through the sighting hole, turning the mirror into an eye catching, if useless, necklace. The holy man looked for an instant past the girl to her tall husband. He knew where the gift had really come from. He bowed briefly as he accepted the necklace, the only time Parrish ever saw an adult male bowing to a woman, and hung it proudly around his neck. He fingered the mirror, unable to identify the material it was made of. Juli then stepped aside, pleased that her gift was approved of, and stood beside her husband as he made his own presentation.

She was suddenly uncomfortably aware of the intense interest of everyone in the great hut. As Parrish offered his gift the people craned their necks to see. The unusual nature of the tall mans gifts were now almost legendary in Danebury.

Parrish held out his hand to the flower and feather man, palm up. On it was a short length of green paracord. Tied to one end of it was a neatly cut oblong of dark flint. On the other end was a two inch length of hacksaw blade. It was another survival implement that most infantry soldiers carried among their personal kit. A flint and steel.

"What is it?" asked the holy man, clearly unable to identify the object.

"I watched you when we were at the burial chamber." said Parrish, all the people hanging on his every word. Juli glanced at him. If he was feeling the pressure of all the attention, as she surely was, he was not showing it. He seemed supremely indifferent. The tall mans words carried clearly to the farthest corners of the round hut.

"This gift will make it much easier for you to light fires or torches." He took the item in both hands, holding up one end and then the other. "This block is a piece of good flint which I know is common place here, but this other thing is called 'steel', which is very rare here. When you strike one against the other it makes a spark, good and strong, which can quickly light tinder. Thus." He struck the steel a firm, glancing blow against the flint and strong, bright, hot orange sparks leapt into the air. There were gasps from some of the enthralled audience.

The holy man, trying to suppress his excitement, accepted the gift graciously enough and struck it himself a few times, creating his own instant sparks. His face was a picture.

"Thank you Parrish. It is a great gift."

Parrish bowed.

"I hope that you ... I mean, the Earth Goddess, will get much good use out of it."

The little man nodded and bowed in return. Parrish threw him a brief but crisp salute and turned away, leading Juli back to their stall.

They settled down to watch the rest of the gift ceremony. Parrish was pretty sure that no one would be able to upstage his gift. Juli looked proudly at her husband.

"How will you light our fires now that you have given Dannu your spark maker?" He turned to her and gave her a smug smile.

"I have more 'steel'." He patted the MOD survival knife on his belt. "And flint is always plentiful here." It was true enough. There was no need even to pick a loose piece off the ground. All the warriors carried at least some flint with them at all times, be it either arrow heads, dagger points or the small scraper flints in the leather pouches tied to their belts.

"Look. My father offers his gift now." said Juli, peering over Parrish's shoulder towards the shrine and the growing pile of goods in front of it. "What is that?"

Parrish turned to see as the man's words floated to his ears across the twenty meter gap between the shrine and his stall.

"Take this gift, Dannu!" The proud tone was easily discernible. It drew everyone's attention. The man plainly thought that his gift was something exceptional. "I give you back your trapped flash of lightening and your roar of thunder."

Parrish was horrified! He instantly recognized the object the man held in his hand. Tape already unwrapped, fuse exposed. Before he could utter a sound the man drew the striker smartly across the end of the fuse and it immediately began to fizz furiously. The entire hut was silent with astonishment.

"Juli!" Parrish barked. "Hands over ears, mouth open!"

Leaping up he left the stall like a sprinter out of the starting blocks. Although not understanding why, the urgency of his tone was not lost on her and she immediately did as ordered, clapping her hands to the sides of her head and watching in amazement as her husband dashed across the floor towards her father, who still held the fizzing thunderflash.

It took Parrish several desperate seconds to cover the distance and close with the blissfully ignorant man who just stared at his rapid approach in astonishment, the bomb in his fist momentarily forgotten. When he finally reached him, Parrish chopped the man smartly on the wrist, causing him to drop the thunderflash, grabbed him by the shoulders and dragged him roughly away. The holy man just stared down at the noisy, smoking cardboard tube that landed at his feet, as did everyone else.

"Do not touch it!" shouted Parrish at the top of his voice and threw himself face down on the ground, covering his ears. "GRENADE!"

The people who knew the tall man, Klud, Mars, Gant, Hass, Tomps, the Chieftain and, thankfully, the holy man who stood closest to the bomb, paid immediate heed to the urgent warning and took his lead. They too covered their ears and started to move hurriedly away. The flower and feather man had barely managed to protect himself from the imminent explosion behind the plinth of the shrine when the thunderflash detonated.

In the confines of the great hut the blast was just tremendous. Apart from Parrish and the holy man who did not or could not see the blinding flash, everyone else who was watching was momentarily dazzled by the intense burst of white light. They only had a split second to register the blindness. The blast from the detonation threw anyone who was standing to the ground. Others were bowled to the backs of their stalls although that was as much from their flinching reactions as by the explosion itself.

After the deafening roar of the mark eight had faded to nothing, there came an almost as impressive silence. Parrish rolled onto his back and sat up. He knew that not many could register the eerie quietness, their heads no doubt filled with ringing from the violent assault on their ear drums. The air was thick with dust, dislodged by the pressure wave, most of it from the thatch above them rather than blasted from the ground at the site if the explosion.

The people who had been wise enough and quick enough to cover their ears slowly lowered their hands, peering in wide eyed amazement at the thickly billowing dust cloud that filled the great hut and obscured their view.

The only sound was Parrish's almost hysterical laughter floating eerily from somewhere inside the all enveloping fog. He walked slowly through the choking cloud towards his stall, appearing like a phantom from the mist in front of the Chieftain and Juli. Tears of mirth ran unchecked down his cheeks and it was all he could do to keep his feet, he was laughing so much. The looks on their faces made him laugh all the more. His sides hurt it was so funny.

This was one party he could honestly say really did go with a bang!

33

To see the entire population of the village leaving the hill fort en mass, with the morning sun still low on the eastern horizon, was quite a spectacle. All the necessary preparations for a long absence from Danebury had been completed even earlier. No lit fires remained and fuel to re kindle them upon return, lay ready beside the blackened hearths in neat stacks. All the huts entrance blankets had been tied in place and the flock had been herded into the pens and supplied with ample food. The last man out swung the gate too to keep out any scavengers.

Knowing that the hill fort would be totally undefended and at the complete mercy of any would be plunderers who might just happen along, made Parrish feel uneasy. All his fellow voyagers however seemed completely unconcerned. There was no doubt in their minds that when they returned in seven or eight day's time, the camp would be just as they had left it.

The mini exodus set off with a murmur of excitement and the picture in Parrish's mind, of a tribe of North American Indians moving camp, was not that far from the mark. The throng moved steadily and with positive intent, not quite a Sunday school outing but still with a definite air of enjoyment.

Babes were carried in their mother's arms and the very young but able to walk trotted along, sticking like glue to their mothers sides. The older children ran almost manically about as usual. Parrish knew that the little tearaways would cover at least twice the distance as everyone else before reaching their final destination, charged as they were with the boundless energy that all kids have.

The women carried the bare necessities to make a basic yet serviceable camp while on the trek. A cooking pot or two, utensils and such, plus any personal items of their own. On their backs were crude packs, similar to knapsacks or bergens, that carried their items for trade.

Even the men, except for the Chieftain and the holy man, were not free from burden. They carried the precious water bags and small amounts of foodstuffs. Parrish could see that it was enough to get by with, but only just. He had correctly guessed that there would be a constant 'hunt of opportunity' during the journey, although that was not the main reason why all the warriors were armed to the teeth. Klud had patiently explained to him that although there was a truce and self imposed goodwill at the great temple, it did not mean that they were free from attack before they got there!

Parrish carried his longbow, the leather quiver full of arrows across his back, outside his cape which bulged unevenly over his fully loaded webbing. He noticed without surprise that everyone either carried or wore their own capes, their bed and blanket for the duration of the trip. Juli had her own knapsack too but Parrish insisted that he carry just about everything else. He was still concerned about the condition of her legs and the fact that she was not yet fully fit. After watching the women adjusting their packs before setting off, he quizzed his wife about their contents. They all looked similarly soft and not overly heavy, yet still quite bulky.

"That is because they all carry the same. Things made of wool. Capes, skirts, jerkins, bundles of yarn or even plain, unprepared wool. It is what we trade."

Parrish simply nodded, mulling over her answer. He had not seen it before but now began to get the first inkling of what was really going on.

"And these other villages?" he asked. "The ones we shall meet up with at the great temple. They will trade something different? Not wool?"

"Yes. We will trade our goods for theirs."

Again Parrish nodded, this time deep in thought. It suddenly seemed that these primitive 'cave men' were not quite so primitive after all. It looked like they operated, at least once a year, some kind of rough system of organized exchange. Inter village at least by the sound of it, perhaps even inter county.

His reference to counties was purely for his own benefit. It was the only scale of area he could think of that fell between local and nationwide. Anyway, he now knew he was not on his way just to see a religious gathering, but also to witness an annual fair or market! Klud was right. The gathering would indeed interest him much.

"Is everything all right, my husband?" Juli asked as he stood motionless, swirling the enlightening thoughts around in his head.

"Yes. I am fine. But if you are not, then you must say so. It is still very soon after the removing of the splints. If your legs start to hurt, you must tell me, and we will rest. I will not allow you to be injured again." He looked deep into her eyes to drive the point home. "Understand now, you must tell me."

She nodded, accepting his order without question.

And so the entire compliment of Danebury set off towards the great temple of the Earth Goddess, somewhere away to the north-west. A backward glance offered the observer the eerie, unnatural sight of the hill fort without a single column of smoke rising from it or any sign of movement. The place was a ghost village, deserted and dead, its lifeblood of people gone.

The sun started to climb steadily into the clear sky, rapidly warming the land. In nineteen eighty eight the weather would have been referred to as unseasonably warm for the time of year. Parrish thought it was anyway and soon removed his combat jacket, slinging it at the rear of his webbing, under his poncho roll.

With warriors well placed on the flanks and a couple more ahead on point, the mass of villagers moved at a slow but steady pace across the rolling landscape of prehistoric southern England, skirting along the edge of the sweeping forest of the north land.

The pace was not at all fast.

By Parrish's rough estimation they would travel not more than sixteen or twenty kilometres a day, about twelve miles. He had broached the subject to the holy man earlier and the little man nodded, saying he had allowed for that and that the village would arrive at the gathering point before three more nights had passed. They must be there by then, he had added in a more curt tone of voice, because the following morning was the day of the high sun. Parrish thanked him for the additional information, now knowing that their destination lay no more than fifty five to sixty kilometres away. Still a very long walk for the women and children but not more a very good stretch of the legs for the warriors who regularly hunted for Danebury's meat.

The general heading was always north westerly and, although the holy man did not always lead a straight path, Parrish had faith in the little man's directions. He did not doubt that he knew the way, so did not concern himself unduly with the route, concentrating more on observing the surrounding countryside while trying to memorize at least some of the natural markers along the way.

The roving villagers had, very early on, passed close to their own long barrow and would pass a few others on the route, more noticeably as they neared the great temple. They all bowed respectfully to any that they passed. Threading their way through the more open woodland that marked the edge of the great forests, they crossed what would one day be the open space of Thruxton aerodrome. In their own time, many people would gather there also, but for a vastly different reason. Parrish kept his eye on the position of the sun and stole the occasional glance at his compass. The general heading was always the same and he knew it was only a matter of time before they came upon Salisbury Plain.

Sure enough, the trees thinned rapidly out till there were none at all and the ground rose up to become the Plain proper. Here there was no cover and the warriors were always on their guard, eyes peeled and constantly scanning the distant, undulating line of the horizon. The holy man led the people steadily on, remaining on the Plain for the rest of the afternoon. Along with all the others, Parrish passed unknowingly through the small, slightly more hilly area on the eastern edge of Salisbury Plain which would at long length be transformed into a place that he knew like the back of his hand. The small town of Tidworth, home of the British Army on Salisbury Plain. Even so, the peoples little religious guide seemed more to be leading them around the north eastern edge of the open grasslands rather than cutting straight across it. As the sun began to set at the end of the first days travel, the villagers left the higher, open ground and returned to the safety and cover of the woodland. The Chieftain selected a suitable spot and the one hundred and thirty plus souls under his care and protection settled for the night. There were to be no fires though.

Coran posted his guards far out in the surrounding forest for an early warning in the event of a sneak attack. He had quietly and appreciatively observed how effective was the rota system that the tall man had employed when organizing the children who had watched over the fields. Now he copied it and used it to the same advantage, keeping his guards fresh and alert throughout the night. He also knew that by far the best watcher in Danebury was the tall man himself and so sent him back up onto the great Plain. There Coran knew he could rely on Parrish to see far and watch over a lot of open ground, saving the Chieftain from using too much of his limited manpower on that front.

Parrish did not mind the detail in the least, it was an honour to be given sole responsibility to stand watch on such a large tract of land, and he smiled at the Chieftains use of 'his' stag system.

He remained at his observation post, following his orders, until relieved by his replacement in the early hours, when the risk of attack was considered to be at its lowest. So still and quiet was he that his relief could not find him and Parrish had a bit of fun sneaking up behind the warrior and scaring the crap out of him! After regaining his composure the white faced, unnamed warrior enjoyed the joke with the tall man before taking up his own lonely vigil. The little man was proud of his keen eyes and could not understand how it was possible that he had not seen the tall man. After some consideration he came to the obvious conclusion that when Dannu's man was alone on her land she protected him by making him invisible to the human eye!

When Parrish returned to the camp site he also managed to slip undetected past the perimeter guard, which got the unfortunate man a tongue lashing from the Chieftain, and found Juli sleeping soundly, fatigued by the days march. He had kept a worried eye on her throughout the day. She did not admit it but found the continued walking hard going on her still unfit legs. When she awoke the next morning and found her husband sleeping soundly beside her, having gone to bed the night before without her preparing any food for him, she waited till he eventually awoke then went as close as she dared to actually scolding him for allowing her to be lax in her duties as a wife. He just smiled that charming smile of his and said that it was of no matter and he would eat now.

She shook her head in exasperation, checked to see that no one was looking and then kissed him before getting down to the business of preparing some hot food for her man.

Cooking fires were allowed during daylight as long as they produced no smoke, and the whole camp was well fortified with hot food before setting off on the second day.

The whole entourage finally left the open Plain before the middle of the day, descending into the lush lowland of the Vale of Pewsey and once more in the comforting protection of the woodland landscape. It was again hot and Parrish and all the other warriors were soon down to a single layer of clothing above the waist. The poor women had to struggle on with their individual loads and their trade packs. All the while, animal sounds could be heard from deep in the forests and the warriors kept their eyes peeled, as much for meat as for attackers.

During the mid afternoon, when the day was at its hottest, Juli moved close to Parrish and said quietly,

"I am very sorry, my husband, but my legs are painful. I must stop or I will fall."

Parrish nodded and immediately went forward to find the Chieftain. He explained to him that he feared for his wives still weakened legs and wished to stop for a while and check her over. There would be no need for the whole village to wait for them as they could catch up later. Coran was as baffled as Klud over the tall mans concern for a lowly woman, but nodded agreement to the request.

"Catch us up then, Parrish." he said. "Even you can follow a track made by this many people." Parrish nodded and smiled. The two men understood each other and it was their private joke, not an insult. "Do not fear if you have not caught up by night fall. We are drawing nearer now and tonight I will allow camp fires. You will be able to see us from a great distance."

"Thank you." Parrish bowed, and returned to his wife. They slowed their pace until everyone else had passed them by, then moved away from the glaringly obvious tracks of the recently passed mass of villagers and settled down a little way off in a sunny glade among some huge oak trees. He helped Juli off with her pack then shrugged out of his webbing, finally taking off his shirt and boots in an effort to cool down. Juli assumed this was what he wanted her to do too and followed suit, ending up sitting on the lush green grass naked from the waist up while her husband's fingers skilfully massaged her stiff, aching leg muscles. Parrish enjoyed the unexpected view as he worked, a constant grin on his face. When he finally finished teasing the poor girls knotted muscles into a state of relaxation he lay on his back beside her and she copied him again.

They both stared up into the blueness of the sky, which reminded him of her eyes, and soaked up the hot rays of the sun.

"Ah, this is the life." he said suddenly. "No problems, no need to rush and no hassles. You people do not do too badly here. In fact, in some ways it is a lot better than where I come from."

"Parrish." said Juli slowly without turning to look at him. She plucked up her courage. They were completely alone and now seemed the right time to ask him the question she most wanted to know the answer to. "Where *do* you come from?"

"It is a bit difficult to explain." he said, propping himself up on one elbow and looking down at her. "I come from a place not far from here. It is, or rather will be, a truly huge village called 'Southampton', but still it is a long time away yet."

"I am sorry. I do not understand."

He nodded and tried to explain it more simply, approaching it from a different angle.

"It is to do with time." he said. "Years, er ... sorry, summers. Look, how many summers are you?"

It was a question Juli could not answer fully but she did her best. She held up both hands in front of her face with all the fingers extended.

"At least this many."

"OK. Now, try to think of each finger as a summer and picture what you would see if you could go back to your very first summer but still be as old as you are now."

She frowned, thinking hard. It was the most difficult thing her husband had ever asked her to do.

"I would be older even than my mother and my younger brothers would not yet be born." she said eventually.

"Yes. It is hard to think of, is it not?"

"Is that what had happened to you? You have somehow travelled back down the summers to be with us here?"

"Well done!" said Parrish pleasantly surprised. "I did not think you would be able to reason that one out." She smiled at his sudden praise. "Yes. I have 'travelled back down the summers'." He quite liked the sound of her new phrase.

"How many summers?" she asked, thrusting her hands up in the air again. "This many?"

"No." Parrish shook his head, suddenly sad. He waved his arm at the trees before them. "More summers than there are trees in this great forest."

His face dropped as he remembered the twentieth century and all the things he missed from that time. Simple things that meant so much to him. His parents and friends, both in the Army and out. Basic soldiering. Music, motorbikes, beer. TV. The list seemed suddenly endless.

Juli frowned again, deep in her own thoughts. This time the concept of time travel escaped her. She looked at her husband and saw the pained sadness on his face. It greatly upset her to see him so. He seemed suddenly smaller, withdrawn to somewhere deep inside himself, not seeing or hearing. Her heart went out to him and she felt an overwhelming need to help him. She quietly slipped out of her woollen skirt and lay back in the sun, its warm rays washing over her nakedness. Reaching out, she touched his arm.

"Parrish." Her voice was soft and clear.

"Huh?" he said without looking up.

"I want your seed."

Parrish looked up at that and saw her laying there, bared in all her young glory. He smiled, kissed her tenderly then slowly removed his buckskins. Lifting himself onto her, he held her tightly in his arms, as if hanging on for his very life, and they made love on the lush forest floor, the pleasant, distant sounds of the forest all around them. This time the pure joy of it was her gift to him.

The sun continued to smile down, the warmth of it on his back adding to the overall feeling of goodness. He was suddenly alive again and as they both rose urgently to their crescendos their cries of natural pleasure added and merged with the sounds of Mother nature around them.

Finally they both lay back, hot but happy, under the constant gaze of the sun. Parrish was returned to his usual good humour and Juli was pleased to have given him her gift and restored his spirit. It was a power that she was only now just beginning to fully understand.

"Do you know?" he said suddenly. "That where I come from there are other ways of mating?"

"Other ways?"

"Well, what I mean is that it can be done in different positions. One of them is where the man lays on his back and the woman sits astride him. Then she has complete control. It is the woman that is in charge and she only allows the man go at the speed she wants."

"A woman in charge of a warrior?" said Juli, shaking her head. "Only allowing him to do as she says? No! Even during the giving of his seed, that is not right. It is not natural!" He voice was quite firm. It was the most definite statement Parrish had ever heard her utter. He sat up, a small smile on his face.

"OK. If you say so." He looked up at the position of the sun above the tree tops. "It is time we should be moving or we will not find the rest of the village until very late. How are your legs now?"

"They are much better."

"Good. Then we shall leave and I will carry your pack. Do not worry." He said quickly before she could protest. "You can have it back before we get within sight of the rest of the village."

She nodded in acceptance of his wise words and the pair started to get dressed.

Indeed, they did not catch up to the rest of the people of Danebury until late in the evening. It was almost fully dark when they finally approached the camp and Parrish noticed that there were no guards posted at all. Coran was right too about the camp fires being visible from a long way out.

Apparently, sometime during the afternoon a number of the outlaying guard warriors had stumbled across a small heard of wild pigs. When the lone pair walked into camp, several of the animals were being roasted on spits above roaring fires. It was a very welcoming sight and no sooner had Parrish and Juli settled down in a comfortable spot when generous helpings of hot meat were being pushed into their hands. It was gratefully eaten and washed down with fresh spring water.

Fed and watered, Parrish lay back on his cape and looked up at the bright stars he could see winking down at him through the gaps in the leafy canopy above his head.

"This is the life." he said for the second time that day.

Coran walked among his people to make sure that everyone had eaten and was comfortable for the night. He stopped beside Parrish and looked down at the tall man, with a glint in his eye.

"Rest well tonight." he said. "For tomorrow we arrive at the gathering point. You will see things there to interest you, my friend."

The tall man smiled and nodded and as the Chieftain strolled purposefully away, settled down to sleep, Juli, as ever, close beside him.

34

Everyone was eager and ready to get back on the trail, shortly after first light. Quiet voices buzzed with excitement. The Chieftain kept his people waiting only long enough to be sure that everyone was ready and there would be no early stragglers, then cast his eye towards the holy man who immediately took up the lead position and headed out across the valley floor. Still off towards the north-west but gradually swinging round to a more northerly direction as the morning went on.

The ground underfoot was rich and fertile. It sloped gently downward, flattening out beneath the denser congregations of trees, and the throng passed with innocent ignorance over the ground that one day countless navvies would labour on to create the Avon and Kennet canal. Across the valley floor and up over the long low ridge on its far side went the massed members of Danebury. The outlaying scout warriors closed up now and the whole village was in a much tighter group. Parrish could tell by the looks on all the people's faces that they were nearing their destination.

They came to a sparkling river that flowed past them in a west to east direction and eagerly forded their way across it. Parrish did not know the area above Salisbury Plain much at all and could not identify the river as the Kennet. He left Juli and went forward, standing with the holy man as the people who were first across waited for the rest.

"Are we very near?" he asked.

"Along the river that way." The little man pointed away to the west. "Only a short way now and we shall be there. We have travelled well and shall arrive even earlier than I thought. It is good."

The people of Danebury walked on again, following the more or less straight line of the river. Very soon they found themselves on a wide track that had recently been trodden by many feet. Then, those with keen ears could detect a faint, low droning noise, somewhere off beyond the dense trees. As they drew closer to the sound it became gradually more coherent and recognizable as the constant hub-bub of human voices. The track finally emerged from the woods into the bright sunshine. Before the people of the village was an extraordinary and welcoming sight.

"The gathering point." breathed someone happily.

Parrish just stood and soaked up the, for him, amazing spectacle. He was, as his old friend 'Clive' would say, totally gobsmacked!

It wasn't the fact that he faced a man made clearing over five hundred meters across. Or that it was bordered on the north side by a long row of high posts and on the other by the semi circular sweep of a large bend in the river which formed a natural boundary to the southern aspect of the clearing. It wasn't even the large circular hut that nestled up against the row of posts, almost exactly in the middle of the line, and that it very closely resembled the great hut at Danebury apart from the fact that it had many entrances instead of the one. It was the people!

There were literally hundreds of them. Just from a quick, estimating first scan of the crowd, Parrish reckoned there to be easily seven or eight hundred. He dumbly went with the flow of the Danebury people as they all made their way towards the centre of the clearing, looking all about and trying to make some kind of sense of the huge gathering.

It was immediately obvious that there were people here from many different villages. Although some people were wandering apparently at will through the crowds, he could see that the bulk of those there remained in concentrated groups. At least eight separate ones that he could identify. It was possible to define these groups by the way they dressed. Each one had at least one single piece of clothing or equipment that appeared particular or peculiar to that group. It was then that Parrish became suddenly aware that all the people of Danebury could be quickly identified by their woollen, calf length capes, unique to them alone.

The caped villagers found a suitable space in the ample clearing and settled there, watching everyone else, and similarly being watched by everyone. As they squatted down, taking control of their own 'piece' of ground, the Chieftain and the flower and feather man detached themselves from the group. They crossed the clearing, all the while threading their way through the wary throng, and entered the mysterious hut in front of the posts. Parrish craned his neck to see inside it but without success, he was too far away and the bright sunshine made the interior seem impenetrably dark.

Known to everyone present there that day as simply 'the gathering point', it was a place that the eighteenth century archaeologist William Stukeley, who uncovered the post holes that marked its position, called the Sanctuary. Sited beside the only real curving sweep in the entire length of the river Kennet and almost due east of the famous West Kennet Long Barrow, it was at the south eastern end of the one and a half mile long, stone lined avenue that led to greatest Neolithic monument in all of England. He of course had no way to determine the true purpose of his discovery.

Parrish now knew.

He watched for a while, sitting quietly among all the others of his village, while unknown people moved between the tight clusters of the other village camps. They talked among themselves, seeking out and renewing old acquaintances and he even saw the first, shy instances of trading going on, before the individuals moved back to the reassuring company of their own kind. As he watched, another band of some unknown village arrived along the same path as the people of Danebury, and found themselves their own place to settle in the clearing. The first of many small cooking fires were already burning, fuelled by wood taken from a huge stack of felled timber beside the Sanctuary area that had obviously been provided for that purpose. By whom he had no idea. Women were bustling about, already mixing more freely among their own sex as they made trips to the river's edge for water.

"Is it not most exciting?" asked Juli. She could not grin in public as she really wanted to but it did not stop her eyes shining.

"I should cocoa!" replied Parrish, forgetting himself for a moment and answering in English. Juli took the foreign words to mean yes.

"It will take a while for the different peoples to lower their guard but soon the talking and trading will start to grow. It is the one time of the year when the people of the different villages meet, free of fear. It is a time for friendship."

She had already removed her pack and started to prepare her own cooking fire, as was right and proper for the wife of a warrior. Parrish shucked out of his webbing but kept a good grip on his longbow and quiver. He was just as cautious as the next man, whoever he may be!

As the afternoon wore on yet another village group arrived, while the people who had already been there some time began to lose their edginess and started to walk more freely among the other gathered villages that squatted near their own.

Finally Parrish decided to take the plunge himself.

"I am going for a little walk around." he said to Juli. He didn't sound overly sure of his decision. "Just to see what is what and who is who. Is that permitted?"

"Yes." she said and smiled behind her hand. He had a strange way of saying things sometimes but she understood. She felt like she was instructing a young child on good camp manners. "Do not go too far though. Some of the other villages are more warlike than us and will take longer to settle before they start trading. After the great ceremony tomorrow, everyone will be much more at ease, trading freely and without fear."

Parrish nodded, once again grateful for the information, put his bow and quiver carefully down beside Juli and stood up. Taking a deep breath, he stepped clear of the ring of squatting Danebury villagers and started to walk slowly off towards the nearest, unknown cluster of village people. Juli watched him, clearly nervous and edgy, no different to any of the other people who were walking about. He would have been indistinguishable from all the other warriors there but for his black boots and towering height.

"Do not be too long." she called. "I will have some food ready soon." He waved back and tried to look casual as he ambled away.

He started to wend his way slowly between the assembled villages of people, all in their own little invisibly staked out areas of ground, being careful not to encroach on anyone else's territory. As much as he looked at them, so they stared back at him, intense curiosity written across all their weather beaten faces. Eventually he could stand the constant scrutiny no longer and made his way back towards the relative security of his own village. It was as he approached the massed collection of caped people that a loud call stopped him in his tracks.

"You!" The voice was undeniably aggressive. "Tall man!"

Parrish turned and looked at his unknown challenger, feeling the hush that fell over all around him who had also heard the call. A warrior approached with a confident, almost arrogant stride. He was backed up by four other men who followed a short step behind him. They were plainly not men of Danebury. Parrish touched his finger to his chest, a questioning look on his face. The unknown man stepped right up until they were only a single pace apart, and looked unflinchingly up into Parrish's face, a defiant look in his eye.

"Yes, you!" he barked. "You with your cursed spirit arrows. It is you who killed the Chieftain!" There was a pause for effect. "*And* when he was safe beyond the reach of normal arrows!" The last sentence was spat out as if distasteful.

Parrish now knew who they were, even if he didn't know the name of the village that they came from. He matched the man's hard stare. Now was no time to lose face.

"He was within the reach of *my* arrow." he replied levelly. "So I killed him."

The man spat on Parrish's boots.

"When he could not strike back!" He thrust out his right arm and jabbed his index finger into Parrish's neck, bulls-eyeing the shaded blue circle that was the sign of a Chieftain killer. "That is no mark of honour!"

Parrish raised his hands in mock surrender and half pivoted as if to walk away, for a moment standing side on to his opponent. Before the smaller man could utter another word, Parrish leaned in towards him and struck the Neolithic warrior a blurringly fast, well aimed blow to the temple. The man's head snapped back with the hard, jarring impact and he fell straight back into the arms of the man directly behind him, unconscious. Both men dropped to the ground, the second man dragged down by the dead weight of the first. Parrish pointed dramatically down at his still form and said to his companions in a forceful voice.

"Tell him when he wakes up, that if he insults me again, I will kill him too!"

The sound of fast approaching feet from behind made him whirl, dropping into a fighting crouch, arms raised in readiness. The approaching men were his own flower and feather man and two others that he did not know but recognized as the same by their similar garb. Seeing him coiled to strike startled them and they pulled up short, staying out of the tall mans reach.

"What is this?" said one of the strange holy men sternly. "There is to be no fighting or killing here. Not in the presence of the Earth Goddess!"

"There has been no fighting here." said Parrish as he relaxed and stood up, holding his arms away from his body in a peaceful gesture. "I did not lay a hand on the man."

All three holy men looked at the unknown warriors, two of them now kneeling to tend to their fallen comrade. The power of the stares made the previously brave warriors cower.

"It is true." said one, switching his own gaze to the tall man, a sudden look of awe on his face.

The group of holy men eyed the tall man for a long, long moment before accepting the explanation, finally nodding acceptance of his words and walking away. They had gone but a few paces when another call filled the air, stopping them and everyone else in their tracks.

"Parrish!" The voice was filled with authority. "Parrish of Dane-bre!"

All eyes turned to see another man striding confidently towards the tall man. This man had many tattoos and wore a white jerkin. He stopped before Parrish as the first challenger had done and held his eyes in a cool stare.

Parrish thought he recognized the man but wasn't quite sure. Suddenly, the man thrust out his hand. With a grin Parrish gripped the warriors forearm and the smaller man did the same.

"You remember me." the man said with a wry smile.

"How could I forget. You have been my best challenge in battle."

The man nodded at the compliment then looked down at the still unconscious warrior on the ground beside him. He released his grip on Parrish's arm, pointing.

"You have lost none of your skill I see." He gave the men who had supported their companion, a scathing stare. "This man is my friend and you will not challenge him again. It is fortunate that, unlike you, he has respect for the place of Dannu. Give thanks to her that he has allowed you all to live! Now go!"

They all bowed low and scurried hurriedly off, carrying the fallen man away with them. Parrish was a bit shocked by their sudden display of subservience. There could only be one reason for that.

"You must be their Chieftain." he said, simply stating the fact. The man nodded and Parrish bowed respectfully.

"Do not bow to me Parrish. You are proven to be my equal and so I would consider it an insult."

"As you wish." said Parrish cordially.

"I do wish." he said. "Because it was your deeds that made it so that I might be chosen as Chieftain."

"Not my deeds. My honour." Parrish had to fight the urge to bow.

"Well, it would be my honour if you would eat with my family after the ceremony is over. We can talk, perhaps trade and I can then return to you your black arrow."

Parrish's eyebrows went up.

"You are not angry that I beat you in battle?"

"No." The Chieftain shook his head. "To defend your village is right. You fought well that day. If I had been in your place, I would have done as you did. Only, when we fought our own battle, I would not have allowed you to live."

Parrish was not in the least shocked. He would have expected no less. He nodded, again having to stop himself from bowing.

"You speak true and wise words. I thank you for that... er ..."

"Danel." he said proudly.

"Thank you, Chieftain Danel. It would be my honour to eat with you."

Danel bowed deeply to the tall man, a rare occurrence for a Chieftain, then turned and walked swiftly away, leaving Parrish staring after him. Satisfied that there were no more surprising events about to happen involving the tall man, the holy men walked off too.

Parrish returned to Juli, glad to be back among the reassuringly familiar faces of his own village. She had a pot steaming away over a small but hot fire. He squatted down beside her and sat for a while in silence, thinking over the recent events. Juli busied herself with the food, knowing to let her husband think his thoughts in peace.

A sudden shadow fell across their little camp and Parrish looked up to see the Chieftain, *his* Chieftain, looking down at him. As he gazed up, so Juli lowered her eyes.

"I hear you have been making yourself known." Coran said flatly. Before Parrish could answer he was silenced by more stern words. "Do not start trouble here, Parrish. For if you do, I cannot save you. Here my power is nothing. The people now bow to the holy men of the great temple of Dannu. The life of every person at this gathering is in their hands."

Parrish nodded slowly, not taking the warning lightly. With him the Chieftains words always carried a lot of weight. Coran patted him reassuringly on the shoulder, satisfied that the tall man understood, and walked away, his back hiding the smile on his usually passive face. His words were not strictly true. He just hoped to avoid the chance of any more unnecessary trouble. The Chieftain no more feared for the life of his tall friend than he feared the wrath of Dannu for bringing the so called stranger to her temple. He was her man after all, even if he himself did not know it.

Alone again, Juli immediately quizzed her husband on what had happened when he had gone for his 'little walk around'. When he told her she gasped, almost spilling the contents of the cooking pot she was stirring.

35

Parrish's eyes flicked open as Juli crouched down beside him, just about to shake him gently awake. She pulled her hand back from his shoulder and a moment later he sat up.

"I thought you were asleep." she said.

"I was." Parrish quickly and vigorously rubbed his face with his hands to wipe away the sleepiness. "But something is going on. I can feel it."

He looked around. The whole clearing was bustling with people in the process of preparing to leave, the scene illuminated by hundreds of hand held, flickering, orange flamed torches. It was still dark, the stars twinkling down from their lofty perches in the vastness of the heavens above them.

"What is it?" he asked.

"We are all about to start the final part of the great walk to the temple. Everyone must be there before the coming of the sun." As she held out his combat jacket he looked again see all the others already dressed and starting to move, leaving their possessions behind beside their campfires. He shrugged the garment on, leaving his webbing where it lay. No one would steal it he knew, every person present in the Sanctuary abhorred theft above all other misdeeds.

A lot of the gathered throng had already moved off and the people of Danebury began to follow suit, heading through the night towards the great hut beside the line of posts. Juli kept close to her husband's side as they moved steadily towards the thatched building. She knew he would be constantly watching and trying to find out about everything he would soon witness and she wanted to make sure that he did not unintentionally offend anyone, particularly the holy servants of the Earth Goddess.

Gant and his family passed close by the pair as the people began to close up and the warrior thrust a lighted torch into the tall man's hand. Parrish nodded his thanks and held the beacon of light high above his head in an effort to see more. He soon had to lower it again when he entered the great hut, by now just shuffling along in the close crowd. The entrance to the hut was much larger than the usual

Neolithic doorway dimensions and he hardly needed to stoop at all.

Inside, the people thinned out into two lines that flowed past a familiar stone statue on a plinth in the centre of the hut. The graceful curves of the Earth Goddess appeared to be pulsating in the flickering light of the passing torches although the huge effigy, bigger even than the one at Danebury, was already well illuminated by tallow lamps suspended from the high, steeply pitched roof poles. As each person passed, they bowed deeply, some putting out tentative hands to fleetingly caress the smooth stonework with their fingertips. Parrish respectfully bowed when his turn came and then he was carried on through the back of the hut by the steady human flow and found himself back out in the open air, on the other side of the line of posts. Before him the people had both fanned out and moved forward until they had formed a long, oblong shaped block, stretching away into the darkness. The separate villages somehow managed to retain their integrity as individual groups but all the people were totally together in their solid, unwavering reverence and respect for their great Goddess.

Parrish looked out into the night. The leading edge of the crowd was only visible as points of dancing torch light far off in the dark but the two sides were more easily definable. They could spread no farther apart than thirty meters, hemmed in by two parallel rows of stones that tracked off in a north westerly direction until they too were lost in the darkness. Parrish, Juli and the rest of the population of Danebury were very close to the rear of the great congregation and he could not see the tight, tidy group of all the villages' holy men that waited in patient silence at the head of the crowd. When a runner from the hut reached them to say that everyone had passed through the hut and was ready, they raised their torches high and set off along the stone avenue at a steady pace. The people followed gladly. As he walked, Parrish watched in fascination the stones that lined the pathway. The impenetrable darkness beyond the light of the torches helped to give the false impression that it was the people who were stationary and the stones that passed them by, moving steadily off to the rear. Great, evenly spaced marching slabs of clean, sarsen stone, alternately pillar then lozenge shaped, varying from three to four meters in height and some he guessed as much as five or six tons in weight.

This astounding avenue of stones funnelled and guided the great torch lit procession across the gently rolling landscape of ancient north Wiltshire in an almost straight line for a distance of two and a half kilometres. As the last of the stones were swallowed up in the darkness behind him, Parrish was briefly aware that he passed between two high banks. It was still dark but he could make out their vague shapes at the edge of the light thrown by the torches, the orange glow reflected back by the white chalk of their steep faces. Then the ground became so flat and level that he knew it had to be manmade. The throng ahead of him had spread out and the people of Danebury did the same, merging with the mass of bodies forming a long line that curved away through the night before the ends rejoined to form a great ring of lighted torches, roughly two hundred and fifty meters across. Parrish and Juli now found themselves in the middle of their part of the ring of people, no nearer the front than the back. Everyone was silent, plainly waiting for something to happen, though Parrish had no idea what and somehow felt reluctant to ask anyone and risk breaking the reverent, church like atmosphere.

They stood that way for a while, no sound bar the soft fluttering of the flames. Waiting. Then, almost imperceptibly at first, the false dawn started to lighten the sky away to the east. It changed the colour of the sky from black to midnight blue, through the many shades of an ever lightening mauve to a glowing, ember red. It promised to be another fine and sunny day. As the sky lightened people began to extinguish their torches, dropping them to the ground and rolling them with a foot in the wet, dew covered grass. They reluctantly died in their hundreds with protesting hisses.

Parrish used his extra height to its full advantage, scanning the area around him as strange shapes began to reveal themselves in the strengthening half light. Great slabs of rough hewn stone seemed almost to creep stealthily up out of the receding night until they had surrounded the gathered multitude. Further back, behind the hulking megaliths, was a shadowy, high wall of clean chalk, sweeping right round to fully encompass everything and everyone, the gap to the south east where they had entered the only break in the barrier.

As the last vestiges of night were banished beyond the horizon and the early glow of daybreak fell upon the white chalk face, the light was instantly reflected back into the man made arena and everything became clearly visible, as if some mysterious, unseen hand had switched on invisible flood lights. The effect made many people gasp, including Parrish, who benefited from his totally unrestricted view of the whole event, for it was enough to take anyone's breath away.

Surrounding the hushed ring of over a thousand Neolithic people, where warriors unabashedly rubbed shoulders with women and children, was a circle of massive stones, most at least four meters high and some half as much again. Beyond the dark, perpendicular slabs was a wide ditch that was deep enough to render its bottom invisible from where the people stood. Banked up behind the ditch was a steep wall of pure white, immaculately clean chalk, at least seven meters high, towering over even the tallest of the great stones.

Parrish looked slowly about, jaw slack and eyes wide. His platoon had been shown photographs of this place when the light infantry were briefed on the importance of not damaging or destroying ancient earthworks or other archaeological sites during their exercises in the Salisbury Plain area. They were nothing like this though! Those twentieth century pictures in no way did justice to the place where he now stood, being just drab, faded and feeble images that completely failed to capture the majesty and grandeur of how it had once been.

As it was now. A mind staggering and unequalled monument to human endeavour, commitment and religious belief. Greater even than the more famous Stonehenge circle. Even so, from those pitiful prints he could still recognize the place and knew without a shadow of a doubt where he was. Avebury!

The magnificent stone circles of Avebury were first 'discovered' by the man many consider to be the founding father of archaeology, John Aubrey, when he was out fox hunting. It was January in the year sixteen hundred and forty nine. He wrote of it in his journal that Avebury:

'does much exceed in greatness the so renowned Stonehenge as a cathedral doeth a parish church.'

The sheer volume of manpower and effort required to build such a monument in those ancient times supports his sentiment.

The chalk bottomed ditch, dug labouriously from the hard ground, measures three hundred and forty seven meters across its inner diameter and is between seven and ten meters deep, enclosing a level area of twenty eight and a half acres. The seven meter high outer bank has a median circumference of one thousand three hundred and fifty three meters, in itself an incredible feat of Neolithic engineering. The volume of the ditch equates to an unbelievable three million nine hundred thousand cubic feet. The material from it had undoubtedly been used in the construction of the bank beyond it and so, using just antler picks and shoulder blade shovels, the people who laboured in its construction had removed from the earth two hundred thousand *tons* of chalk!

Independent of the many smaller stones lining the avenue that linked the ring to the Sanctuary beside the river Kennet, the great megalithic outer ring of Avebury has a circumference of three hundred and thirty one meters and contains one hundred and thirty roughly shaped sarsen slabs. These huge stones, weighing as much as sixty tons each, fall into two basic types, tall and straight sided or diamond shaped. The largest pair flanked the entrance to the temple, everyone passing between them as they finally complete their long walk. The skill, care and expertise of positioning and erecting these stones parallels the remarkable feat of the construction of the ditch.

In the centre of the great ring are two smaller stone circles. Both lying on a north-north west to south-south east alignment and one hundred and three meters across, they each consist of thirty high, broad slabs of sarsen stone. Inside each circle lay a single large, sculpted oblong stone resembling a sacrificial altar.

It was the north-north west circle of stones that was at the hub of the ring of people, who now looked towards its centre as the brightening of the sky signalled the imminent arrival of the sun. The altar stone at its centre was perfectly aligned with the impending midsummer sun rise. Around this stone stood a ring of flower and feather men that Parrish had never seen before, even among the previously unknown holy men he had seen since his arrival at the Sanctuary gathering point.

These men were older than most of the people who now watched them with baited breath. Their clothes were impressive if not too functional, plainly made for ceremonial use. They wore hats of fur that were crowned with fans of display feathers from the tails of some unidentifiable but colourful wild fowl. Their tunics were similarly adorned and the men wore the tasselled leg straps that Parrish had seen for the first time on his own village's holy man only a few days before. Around the men's necks hung strings of drilled stones of varying shapes, tiny miniatures of the great stones that now encircled everyone. Across their shoulders like mini capes were tied wraps of woven grasses, decorated around the edges with bright spring and early summer flowers. Their entire outfits were unmistakably symbolic to every aspect of the Earth and its life giving properties.

As one, this ring of undoubtedly highly revered men raised their arms into the air above the altar stone. As the very top of the suns orb became visible above the rim of the eastern edge of the earthen bank they started to chant. The chant was at first softly melodic and low in tone. As the men began to increase their volume it turned in to a song. The words were lost on Parrish, the language unrecognizable, but it was undeniably a good song. After only a short time he had to make a conscious effort to prevent himself from swaying to the steady rhythm. The holy men from the visiting villages, positioned at roughly equal spaces around the inner edge of the ring of villagers, started to join in.

The swooping and rising pulse of the song filled the bowl, it giving the sound a throbbing resonance as the musical strains rebounded from the walls of the earthen amphitheatre. The glorious chant had a spell binding, mesmeric effect on the hushed crowd and Parrish could see many people near him starting to sway ever so slightly, like corn ears in a gentle breeze.

During all this time the sun was rising steadily over the rim of the circular temple. Its bright rays illuminated the western side of the bowl. The line of shadow that marked the leading edge of unobstructed sunlight crept slowly back across the upturned faces of the crowd, towards the inner ring of stones and the central altar stone. Parrish watched, agog. The people's faces seemed to light up with joy as the warm rays illuminated them, many apparently unable to stop themselves from smiling, no matter what their sex, age or standing in their own community. No one objected. Even the giant stones beyond the crowd seemed to drink in the light. They seemed to swell in it, their surfaces changing dramatically from a dull charcoal black to a lighter, warmer, greyish white.

The sun's rays crept closer and ever closer to the inner circle of stones, the singing, chanting holy men and the almost magnetic altar stone at their centre. As the golden light at last reached the old men they brought their joyous song to a rousing crescendo and then, with perfect timing, every single chanting holy man inside the giant ringed temple of the Earth Goddess stopped. There was total silence. All eyes were focused on the altar stone. The sun's rays finally fell upon it.

The light caused an astounding transformation. It changed the stone from being a flat, black hulking table top of rock into a bright, almost living beacon! It took on a sudden, golden hue and gave the appearance of reflecting back the rays of the sun. Parrish knew it was impossible but he was witnessing it with his own eyes. The stone just seemed to glow with a soft, warm light, as if the whole solid block of rock had become a hollow model of frosted glass, lit from within by bright candles. From all around the crowd came gasps of wonder, amazement and blissful satisfaction. Parrish's mouth just sagged open in utter astonishment.

The two holy men who stood at each end of the long stone, seeming almost supremely indifferent to the spectacle before them, lowered their hands onto the bright rock. The rest took a few measured paces back, keeping their own hands raised high in the air. Without a single word of command from anyone, the massed people of Neolithic southern England began to walk in single file into the inner stone ring from each end, past the retreated holy men.

As they came alongside the softly glowing stone each person reached out and trailed or rubbed one hand along its top surface, glad and grateful for this once a year opportunity to touch the life giving warmth of the all powerful Earth Goddess.

There was no pushing or shoving at all from the crowd around Parrish, or anywhere else that he could see. They were all eager but no one was in a rush, everyone certain that they would be able to feel the warmth of Dannu long before the rock faded back to its former state of lifelessness.

"Is she not beautiful?" whispered Juli, her hushed voice full of feeling.

"She leaves me completely breathless." replied Parrish slowly. It was the honest truth.

The old holy men watched solemnly as the multitude passed slowly and simultaneously along each side of the stone. As Parrish and Juli approached the softly shimmering rock, he let her lead, partly because it was the gentlemanly thing to do but partly because of his own uncertainty. He was not totally sure he had the right to be there. Finally alongside, Juli touched the surface of the stone tenderly with her hand then trailed her fingertips along its top as she walked beside it. The smile on his wife's face was one that, up until that moment, only Parrish had been privileged to see. The action and the look of peaceful joy on Juli's face somehow reminded him of a picture he'd once seen. It was soft, romantic painting of a relaxed Victorian lady, serenely trailing her fingers in the water that flowed past the sides of the punt she was reclining in.

Parrish took a deep breath and stepped smartly up to the almost frightening, unnatural looking stone. He boldly reached out and placed his hand on the glowing surface. And immediately snatched it back. The damned thing was red hot! He moved along the side of the stone and tried once more. Again he snatched his hand back, burning his fingers on the surface that was too hot to touch. He blew on his scorched fingers, then inspected them to see how badly they were burned. They were perfectly normal. No scorching, singeing, reddening of the skin or marks of any kind. He wasn't sure quite what had happened and apprehensively eyed the holy men surrounding the stone. They all seemed suddenly to be looking at him with keen interest. He noticed then that the two old men at each end of the glowing stone were not actually touching it with their hands, their palms held an inch or so above its surface.

Trying hard to act as if nothing had happened, he caught up with Juli and followed the procession out of the other side of the inner stone circle and rejoined the rest of his village. Like all the others that had already passed the stone, they were watching the rest enjoy their brief moment of closeness with the Earth Goddess.

Finally the long procession past the altar stone was done. All the people had gathered once more beyond the smaller ring of stones and after a respectful silence the old holy men once more burst into song. It was a different chant but still one of rejoicing. Just about everyone was cheerful and smiling, for that brief moment all taboo's, restrictions and restraints forgotten. Once the second song had been sung and the last words died away, the holy men clapped their hands loudly and bowed deeply to the altar stone. Every single person in the great stone and earth circle of Avebury did the same. There was another long moment of silence, and then the people nearest the entrance to the temple turned and quietly made their way out of the earthen ring. Gradually everyone else followed suit, reluctantly leaving the still glowing altar stone to the private delectation of the old holy men of the temple.

The great Neolithic throng ambled in a now much more disorganized manner back down the stone lined avenue towards the Sanctuary. The quiet hub-bub of different voices had a hallowed edge to it as the people talked in low tones of their brush with Dannu. No matter how many times it was experienced, touching the Earth Goddess was always a moment to savour, not to mention being a great honour.

Juli walked as close to one side and behind her husband as she could without actually touching him. Obviously it was not permissible for her to show any outward affection towards him in public. In fact it was virtually unheard of in Neolithic times for a woman to show much emotion at all towards the man that owned her but Juli found it difficult to curb her wish to hold him. She felt euphoric after touching the Goddess, one part of the feeling due to the knowledge that her husband was Dannu's man and she had the individual privilege of honouring Dannu through him. She felt sure she was closer to the Earth Goddess than almost any other ordinary person would ever get. Except perhaps for Parrish himself.

The tall man turned as the village holy man appeared by his side. The little man never said a word as they walked along together, apparently waiting. Finally, Parrish smiled and obliged him.

"What is the other smaller stone circle for, the one opposite?" he asked.

"It is for the holy men alone." the smaller man answered. "Their own private ceremony happens when the sun is at its lowest."

"Huh?"

"In the cold season."

Parrish nodded. He knew the little man meant the winter solstice on December the twenty first.

"How is it that the centre stone is the only one that glows?"

"It just does." The holy man spoke as if he believed it to be the ultimate truth, which he did.

"And where do all those old holy men come from?" Parrish

struggled on against the empty answers. He was by now quite used to the little mans cryptic replies.

"You will soon find out." The holy man gave a knowing smile. "You will soon find out."

And with that he turned on his heel and vanished into the milling crowd.

36

Once back at the Sanctuary, the people mingled much more freely. There was very little if any of the inter village rivalry and mistrust that had been so evident the day before. Paying homage to the Earth Goddess had clearly settled the gathered throng and they were much more at ease with each other. For a short while at least there was peace throughout the villages of the south and the gathering point was a haven of good will.

It was a sight to gladden anyone's heart. People talked freely to each other, exchanging stories as well as goods. Unruly groups of children ran about with total abandonment and the women cooked, washed or just gossiped among themselves with no fear of recriminations from their men folk. As long as they still respected the normal hierarchy of village life they were left to themselves. In fact the whole scene resembled the normal life of one huge village, a thousand people strong.

Parrish himself had nothing much to trade. He felt that he needed nothing and so was in no way disappointed that he could not join in with all the busy bartering. He was quite content to simply stroll about, just watching the hundreds of little scenes and dramas going on all around the great clearing beside the river. A huge bazaar or market place was his nearest comparison and he drank in the whole experience with great interest, watching, listening and learning.

Incidents and events were happening all across the clearing, some Parrish saw, many he missed. Good natured arguments over the value of trade goods, friendly tales of daring do, recounts of great hunts by the men and family talk by the women. Talk too of great Chieftains, holy men and warriors, past and present. Parrish even heard his own name mentioned once before the talk went silent as he passed close by. Occasionally, an extraordinary little drama would spark off among the others and these he found most enlightening. One such event involved Tomps.

The youngster was simply going about his business, whatever that might be, when he inadvertently bumped into a passing warrior from some unknown village. The collision just staggered the unknown warrior but knocked Tomps onto his backside. He looked up to see who he had collided with and the mystery man made the mistake of laughing down at him. It was an innocent enough gesture, no doubt induced by the relaxed, mellow feeling that prevailed in the camp, but it was still an insult. Tomps jumped swiftly to his feet and stood up to the warrior, eye to eye, hand on the haft of his knife. Both were suddenly serious in intent and expression.

"Stand aside boy." said the warrior, a hint of annoyance in his tone. "I wish to pass."

"You will not travel very far or live very long if you cannot see a warrior when he stands before you." said Tomps with real gravel in his voice. "It is only because we are at the temple of Dannu that I have not already killed you for your insult."

The unknown warrior would have laughed again if it were not for the fact that he could see the boy was deadly serious. In all truth, it was the elder warrior who was showing restraint, but he would only allow himself to be pushed so far. He gave the youngster one last chance.

"You know that if you insist on fighting me, I will kill you." It was not an idle boast, just a statement of truth, the boy obviously no match for the older, battle hardened man.

Tomps took that as another insult and stepped back, drawing his dagger. The warrior started to reach for his own weapon but stilled his hand as another man stepped up behind Tomps and laid a restraining hand on the lads shoulder.

It was Klud.

The unknown man froze, eyeing the second Danebury man. He knew of Klud's reputation. Even if he had not, the man's marks would have told him that he would be a most formidable opponent.

"If you fight the boy, you must then fight me." said Klud levelly. There was no aggression in his voice. He too was just stating a fact. The stranger showed remarkable composure and looked slowly from Tomps to Klud and back again. The words had been phrased so that if he wished, he could still withdraw with his own honour intact.

"Boy's become warriors young at Dane-bre." he said finally, speaking directly to Klud and ignoring the youngster completely.

"It is true that he is barely a man, but he has earned the name."

Tomps chest swelled at that. The man made his decision, smiled thinly at the youngster then looked again at Klud.

"He still has much to learn, but I respect the words of Klud of Danebre, for he is known as a great warrior who speaks true."

With that he stepped aside and signalled for the youngster to pass. Klud patted the boy on the shoulder and the lad shot him a brief look of gratitude, then walked slowly past the stranger, ignoring him completely. When he was gone, leaving the two men quietly facing each other, Klud bowed deeply to the unknown warrior, who in turn bowed just as deeply back. Each knew that the other had, by using discretion and mutual respect, avoided unnecessary bloodshed in such a holy place over the rashness of a younger, inexperienced warrior. Finally, the two men went their separate ways and the Sanctuary remained a peaceful and pleasant place.

Parrish had watched intently from the sidelines. What surprised him most about the confrontation was that, as Klud had backed up Tomps, so he himself had been instantly ready to back up Klud. Not simply because he was a friend but because the honour of Danebury was challenged. Unlike the battle outside Danebury earlier in the year, he had not this time been directly involved, but would still have jumped in if needed. He knew that, if necessary, he would have put his life on the line for the honour of his village. It was a profound self discovery for him.

The evening was drawing in, the sun low in the western sky. Parrish sat with the others of his own village, quietly contemplating the events of this strangest of days. Juli handed him some food and he ate in silence, paying little attention to what he was putting in his mouth.

"Would you like to see what I bartered for today?" she asked, breaking his chain of thought.

"Mmm, yes. I would." he replied absently, but then smiled at his diminutive wife when he saw the look of hopeful expectancy on her face. "What did you get?"

He wasn't quite sure what she would produce from the tangled pile of articles on the ground beside her but was mildly disappointed when she eagerly showed him several large, darkly tanned, heavy and thick pieces of leather hide.

"Is it not the best quality skin?" she asked proudly.

He just nodded.

"The best leather for making strong foot coverings, belts and straps for carrying." she said with great authority and gave the pieces of hide a loud slap with the palm of her hand. "I had to bargain very hard for skins this good."

Parrish's eyebrows shot up.

"Does not sheep hide serve the same purpose then?"

"No." Juli knew what she was talking about. "Sheep skins are too soft and it does not grow thick enough. This skin is from a cow and is the finest heavy leather."

He nodded again, this time with much more enthusiasm and interest. It had never occurred to him that there might be some things that the people of Danebury could not produce for themselves. He was no longer disappointed in the results of her trade and reached across to feel the quality of the hide.

"You are right, it is very good skin. You have done well. So, this has come then from a village that grows cows instead of sheep?"

"Of course." Juli smiled at her husband's apparently almost regular need to state the obvious. Once again he showed himself to be innocently unaware of everyday things, and she loved him for it.

"What else can be traded here?" Parrish could see that even in this all encompassing Neolithic barter system, there were still things women did that went unnoticed by their men folk. If a warrior wanted new footwear, his wife simply provided them. How, did not interest the man, although the woman still had to be prepared for it. He detected mysterious female undercurrents of trade at work here.

"There are many, many things to be traded here." Juli knew well her husband's constant desire to know all things but there were some women's secrets that she was not prepared to divulge, even to him. She just gave him a knowing smile, that secret twinkle in her eye. "If you have enough goods and can barter well, you can exchange anything for anything."

"Anything?"

Juli nodded with the assurance of an experienced and knowledgeable trader.

Parrish had undeniable confirmation of her assuredness the very next morning and again it involved Tomps, although this time in a peaceful incident.

Bartering was still going on throughout the camp on the third and last day of the great gathering. The sun still shone, although it was only a matter of time before the weather broke. Parrish was standing in the centre of the clearing, having various different village groups pointed out to him by Juli. There was a sudden cough from behind him and the couple turned to see the youngster looking up at Parrish, a proud smile on his face.

"Tomps?"

"I have something I wish to show you." he said. "I would greatly value your judgment on it."

Parrish nodded, quizzically eyeing his wife, who just shrugged back. The lad stepped aside and ushered forwards a small girl who had been standing, almost completely hidden, behind him. She was wrapped in his woollen cape. It reached practically to the floor and, with her head bowed, all Parrish could see of the girl was the top of her head.

"Who is this?"

"Her name is Karin. I chose her and my father bartered much for her. She is now my wife!"

Parrish was speechless at the sudden revelation. He just stared down at the young couple. The very young couple. After a moments silence Tomps repeated that he would value the tall mans opinion of his chosen woman.

"Would you like to see her?"

"Er... yes." was all Parrish could say.

Tomps grasped his cape where it was wrapped around the girl's shoulders and pulled the garment away. She stood pale and naked, unveiled before them all. Parrish's slightly baffled look turned rapidly to one of disapproval. The poor girl had not even flinched and made no attempt to cover herself but he knew that she did not like it. Parrish felt embarrassed and offended for the girl, who was not permitted to speak up for herself, and turned angrily on Tomps, about to lash the boy with some harsh words. Juli tugged urgently on his arm. She immediately saw the change in her husband's face and realized that his innocence of their ways prevented him from understanding them.

"It is not wrong, Parrish." she said hurriedly, committing the usually unpardonable female sin of interrupting a warrior who was about to speak. "If someone takes a wife from another village, the woman leaves that village with nothing, not even the clothes she would wear.

A wise village Chieftain gives away nothing, no matter how small."

Parrish's anger died as quickly as it had lived. It all made Neolithic sense, even if it was embarrassing and uncomfortable for the individual concerned. Any village with a will to survive and a Chieftain worth his salt wasted nothing and clearly the welfare of the departing wife immediately became the responsibility of her new husband. Parrish tried to put aside his own embarrassment and did his best to give an objective opinion of the girl Tomps had chosen to be his wife.

She was even younger than the lad himself. He guessed her to be only fourteen years old and, head up, she would stand only four feet eight or nine. Her build was very much on the slim side, with a light bone structure. She had small hands and feet, was dark haired and pale skinned. Her small breasts were still pointed and underdeveloped and there was just the merest wisp of maiden hair at her groin. She certainly appeared to be fit and healthy enough. Parrish looked for as long as he thought Tomps expected him to look, then signalled for the lad to cover her back up. Once she was again wrapped in the long cape, he stepped closer and tilted her head up, his hand under her chin. She was plain looking but not unattractive, if underage and utterly obedient girls were what one preferred. He noticed with more interest a small scar high on one cheekbone and briefly wondered how it got there. The small face was evenly set but her dark eyes betrayed her fear and uncertainty. Parrish smiled down in an attempt to ease her worry. It was a wasted effort but he couldn't blame her. He knew that once all the villages finally left the Sanctuary, the poor girl would not see the people of her own village again until next year and would not know a single soul in the new community where she would spend the rest of her life.

"Do you know who I am?" he asked softly.

Silence.

"Speak!" said Tomps. "This man is my friend and you are free to talk with him."

The youngster's voice was doubled edged with the pride at declaring Parrish as his friend and also having power and command over another person for the first time. Someone who was duty bound to obey his commands. It was a heady, intoxicating feeling.

The small girl finally nodded in answer to the question and spoke. Her voice was high pitched, with a frightened quiver in it.

"I know who you are. Everyone knows. You are Parrish of Dane-bre. The tall stranger from the wilderness of the Earth Goddess. He who watches and waits. Asker of many questions. Carrier of the long reaching spirit arrows and unbeatable battle warrior."

Both Tomps and Juli nodded with proud agreement at the description of the man they stood with. Parrish himself was somewhat taken aback by it. He thought the description was all out of proportion and suddenly realized what had been said about him behind his back among the gathered masses at the Sanctuary. Even so, he could not deny he felt flattered by it and smiled down at the girl. She waited in trepidation for his reply. From her own lips, the tall man before her had a fearful reputation.

"Karin." he said with as much friendliness as he could muster, "If you are the wife of my friend Tomps, then you are my friend too. Do not be afraid of me." He nodded as if to emphasize the point. "And you will not be alone when we return to Dane-bre. You are welcome at my house and my wife Juli will be glad to give you any help should you need it. I give you the freedom to ask." Juli nodded agreement, a friendly smile on her face. Parrish pointed to Tomps. "Your husband is still young, but know now that he is a brave warrior. He will treat you well, I know. Treat him well in return and you will have a happy life at Dane-bre. OK?" He finished with a smile.

It was quite a speech and the girl hung on every single word. She never understood the tall mans last phrase but its tone was good. She didn't understand either how the woman Juli was permitted to smile freely in the presence of warriors, and had no intention at all of doing so herself, but she respected the tall mans words. It was known that he spoke true, if sometimes strangely, and was a great warrior who it was not wise to make angry. She nodded to him, still holding her head high even after he had removed his huge hand from under her chin. Parrish immediately warmed to the girl when she showed the small hint of spirit, which he thought a rare quality in a Neolithic woman.

"I have done well?" asked Tomps expectantly.

"You have chosen very well." said Parrish in all honesty, and clapped the lad on the shoulder. He thought for a second. "Do you want some advice on how to live well together, from someone who has no right to tell you?"

Tomps stood closer to his wife, as he saw the tall man doing with his own wife. "I will always listen to your words, Parrish. Speak."

He nodded and said his piece, talking to Tomps but all the time looking at young Karin.

"Do not expect too much of your wife too soon. Remember that at first her new village will be very strange to her. Also, do not be in a great rush to give her your seed, even if it is her right. And when you finally do, do it slowly!"

Tomps gave him a baffled look, as did Karin.

"Trust me." said Parrish in a serious tone. All the while Juli was nodding emphatically, a knowing look on her face.

That was good enough for Tomps, who nodded, bowed respectfully to the pair then turned and walked proudly away, his new wife only two paces behind.

Parrish looked down at Juli and exhaled noisily, still a bit stunned. In total disregard to anyone nearby who might be watching, she smiled broadly up at her wise husband. Before he could utter a word, she suddenly hugged him tight in a brief but heartfelt gesture of adoration before once more stepping back and behind him, as was considered right and proper for the lowly wife of a village warrior.

At noon, Parrish responded to his earlier invitation and ate food with the Chieftain Danel. It would have been a great insult to refuse him even though Parrish would just as soon not have gone. Danel and his family were honourable hosts and he was treated well enough, but all the rest of the village could barely conceal their dislike at having the killer of their former Chieftain among them. Parrish feigned indifference to it all but was on his guard the whole time. It was a strain.

As they ate, Danel spoke in brief, clipped tones about the village he now lead, and its unenviable position. They were still struggling along after the loss of most of their seed grain during the winter blizzard. The storm had caused their great shrine hut to collapse. Many of the villagers, mostly women and children, had been killed. Most crushed in the collapse of the building, then more by the continuing severity of the weather afterwards. Parrish briefly scanned the crowd, taking a quick head count of the villagers bunched in close around him. He estimated a total population of only about forty five souls. It didn't take a genius to figure out that being soundly beaten during their attack on Danebury had not helped matters either. Still, the Chieftain had high hopes for the continuation of his village if Dannu was generous and the coming winter remained mild.

He was not just relying on the good nature of the Earth Goddess to save his village though. In an almost unprecedented move by a Neolithic village, Danel had bartered most of his people's goods for some of another village's grain, as yet still not grown and reaped. It was a very great risk on his part. If the village who's grain they had already paid for suffered a poor crop and refused to hand over the agreed amount, it would be very unlikely that Danel's village could even mount an attack and take by force what was rightfully theirs.

It all meant that the life of everyone in his village hinged on his ability to judge the character and honesty of the Chieftain he had struck the bargain with.

Parrish could only nod in agreement, knowing that Danel could really do little else in the situation, without condemning his decimated village to imminent and unavoidable extinction. He felt somehow responsible for placing the great burden on Danel's shoulders but knew better than to offer any help. All he could do was hope that the man had made the right choice.

The Chieftain offered Parrish back his black fletched arrow, the object that had caused him to inherit all the problems he now faced. He accepted it gracefully, not wanting to run the risk of insulting the man by telling him he didn't need it. It was with some gladness when he finally said that he must return to his own village, and rose to his feet.

"Good bye, Parrish." Danel again grasped his guests forearm in the unfamiliar gesture that the tall man seemed to appreciate. "It is no secret that my people do not like you but, if you come alone, you would be welcomed at my village."

Parrish nodded graciously at the invitation, fully aware that at no time during their talk had he been told where the village was, and that if he did somehow manage to turn up, he would more likely be welcomed because of his reputation as a warrior rather than as a friend.

"Thank you, I am honoured. Good bye, Chieftain Danel. I truly hope that I will see you and your village here again next summer, once more restored to full strength."

Danel nodded back and finally released his grip. Parrish simply turned and walked steadily away, feeling the hard eyes of the Chieftains people on his exposed back. It made his skin crawl but he did not hurry. He was very glad indeed to get back to his own village, now much more appreciative of the good fortune that they enjoyed.

37

It wasn't long after he had returned from his visit when he himself was paid one by a delegation of four flower and feather men. One was his own holy man but the others were total strangers. They approached him with a distinct sense of purpose and waited patiently until he had risen to his feet before they addressed him.

"Parrish of Dane-bre?" asked one, totally unnecessarily. Parrish didn't even bother to reply. The man carried on after realizing that he was not about to receive an answer. "The wise ones of the great temple wish to speak with you."

"My pleasure. What is it you want?"

"We are not the wise ones." said the spokesman, surprised that he should not know this. "You are to visit them."

"I am?" Parrish feigned surprise.

"Yes." They all nodded as one.

"What if I do not want to?" He managed to suppress his smile at the looks of surprise and confusion on the four Neolithic faces. That was obviously not the expected response.

His own holy man stepped forwards, the little man getting as close as he ever would to asking the tall man to please do as he was asked without his constant questioning.

"Parrish, it is a great honour to be asked. Not many ordinary villagers visit the wise men in their shrine house. You cannot refuse."

Parrish resented being referred to as ordinary so let them all squirm for a few seconds before eventually nodding his agreement. There was obvious relief from the small men. They immediately stepped aside and gestured for him to pass. Now it was Parrish's turn to be surprised.

"What, now?"

Again they all nodded. Parrish shrugged, waved goodbye to a wide eyed Juli and set off in the direction indicated, towards the Sanctuary shrine hut. Once through it and among the stones of the long avenue, the holy men positioned themselves in pairs on either side of him. Together they walked on between the rows of stones in silence. At the far end, instead of entering the huge temple site, the holy men steered him away to the left and they skirted the outside of the chalk bank, following a narrow but well worn pathway into a thick line of trees beyond the temple area. On the far side of the trees was a field system. Very much like the one at Danebury but a lot bigger. They threaded their way between the various plots, moving steadily up the gentle slope of a long, low hill. A few individuals were working among the growing crops but they paid the tall man and his escort no attention. The disinterest was returned by Parrish. His eyes were fixed firmly on the large hillfort atop the brow of the hill.

In fact it was not a normal hillfort as he understood it. It was actually a causewayed camp. To the modern archaeologists who excavated the site quite extensively in the first half of the twentieth century, notably one Alexander Keller, the place was known as Windmill Hill. In general shape the whole place resembled a fat dumbbell, practically two separate villages linked by a wide, raised path. The surrounding defence ditch was not nearly as deep as the one at Danebury, nor was the palisade wall as high, though it still made a formidable deterrent. Parrish finally pulled his eyes from the sight on the skyline and turned to ask his holy man about the place. The little man gave him a 'not now' gesture and, in silence, the five men approached the entrance way at the south easterly end of the eastern of the two camps.

They entered via the unguarded portal and made their way through the camp without ceremony. Windmill Hill was just as any other Neolithic village apart from the conspicuous absence of a central shrine hut. This time many people looked up to see who was passing. Parrish nodded respectfully at a few of the individuals, who nodded hesitantly back before ducking quickly out of sight. He just sniffed, ignored the rest of the wary people and continued to look over the camp. The people who now regarded him with such interest were clearly the owners and tillers of the fields on the lower slopes of the hill. Judging by what he saw, the village was doing quite nicely thank you and densely populated, perhaps as many as one hundred and fifty strong, although even for that great a number the field system seemed excessively large.

The little entourage passed through the camp and up onto the raised causeway. It was just possible for Parrish to see over the top of the wall and down into the valley where he had just come from. To his surprise he could not see Avebury ring at all. The temple was well hidden behind the bank of trees beyond the patchwork quilt of fields. He turned his attention to the smaller camp ahead of him at the far end of the raised road. It appeared at first glance to be another circular camp, slightly smaller than the one he had just left, still with many smaller huts, but it had a single, extraordinarily large one, right in the centre of it. That was where the little group was headed. Strangely, this second camp seemed totally devoid of people and Parrish briefly wondered where everyone was. He soon found out. They were all inside the huge hut, and apparently waiting for him.

Passing through an ornately carved wooden archway, he entered a long, downward sloping wattle and daub tunnel that emerged into the centre of the hut. Stepping out of the far end, he found himself in the pit of what looked like a poor version of a Roman amphitheatre. Earthen rings ran around the inside of the hut, rising up and back in even steps towards the distant wattle wall. On each level sat motionless but watchful holy men of varying ages, all dressed in full religious regalia. Parrish started to spin in a slow circle, scanning the interior of the well lit if slightly smoky interior. He only completed a half turn. Above and behind him, the entrance tunnel exiting at its feet, sat a massive statue of the Earth Goddess, at least eight meters high! It totally dominated the interior of the hut. He stared at the huge effigy, momentarily forgetting the eyes of all the sitting holy men, who were watching his every move with keen interest.

"Parrish!" The voice was firm, yet still mild, with the rasp of age in it. Like the sound of rustling parchment. Even before he identified its owner, Parrish knew that the man would be old and weathered, with a face wrinkled by the ravages of time. He turned again till his back was once more to the statue, and faced the small, slightly hunched, cloaked and shrouded man who walked slowly but steadily towards him from the first row of seating. Parrish's escorts respectfully stepped aside and bowed very deeply to small man as he approached. He appeared not to notice them. Only when he had finally stopped before Parrish did he look up into the tall mans eyes. He was indeed old.

Shocks of unruly grey hair flowed untidily out from under his splendidly decorated hat. His eyes were dark, intense and piercing. His body may have been slow but his gaze proved beyond doubt that his mind was still quick. To Parrish he looked old even by twentieth century standards so he must have seemed positively ancient by Neolithic ones.

"Do you know who I am, young man?" he asked slowly in his dry, rustling voice. Parrish just shook his head, for that moment reluctant to speak, so was the reverence and respect that was demanded by his presence.

"That is of no matter." he said and offered the tall man a smile. It stilled the looks of disbelief from the men either side of Parrish who could not see how the holiest man of all could be unknown to anyone. "Do not be afraid, Parrish. We only wish to speak with you." He swept the great hut with his arm, indicating all the seated men around them.

"I am not afraid." Parrish pulled up his suddenly flagging confidence by its socks and spoke loudly. In fact his voice sounded unnaturally loud as it reverberated boldly around the building's interior. Wondering briefly if the place had been designed especially for its acoustics, he eyed the old man squarely.

"What is it you want of me, old man?"

The wrinkled smile broadened.

"I was told that you were bold and filled with many questions. Come, come and sit with me." He took his tall visitor by the sleeve, gently guided him to the first level of seating and sat down on the hard packed surface, patting the space next to him, bidding Parrish to sit too. He obediently sat. They were both now facing the enormous statue that towered above them.

"Is she not beautiful?" the old man asked proudly.

Parrish just nodded, no words necessary.

"I am told that you do not believe?" The old man's eyes never left the statue of the Earth Goddess. Parrish was suddenly acutely aware of the unflinching attention of everyone in the hut, waiting for his reply.

"Not so." he said carefully. "I am just not sure."

"And yet, she has visited you in person."

At that Parrish's eyes darted accusingly towards his own holy man but the little man did not so much as flinch under the hard stare. What else had the old bastard been told he wondered, but it was too late now and shrugged his shoulders in a 'so what' gesture.

"I could not say. I think it was just some woman that I never saw."

"With a voice so powerful, yet so soft, you could not help but heed her words and worship her." Still the old man's eyes never left the statue. Parrish could not deny his statement. "Believe me Parrish when I say that it was indeed her."

He shrugged again, hiding his confusion by pretending to be unconvinced. He doubted that he fooled the old man for a second. Time to change the subject.

"Why have I been sent for?"

"We asked you here simply so that we might speak with you. Since we learned of your presence, we have waited patiently until you came with all the others to the temple. We have watched you closely. The stone was the final test."

"Test, what test?" Parrish looked hard at the old man, who finally turned from his contemplation of the statue and eyed him with deliberate and close scrutiny.

"When you found the stone hot to the touch, we knew for sure."

"Knew what?!" Parrish began to get annoyed. The old sod was worse that his own holy man. Was it part of their Stone Age religion to answer every question with cryptic lines?

"That you were indeed sent here by Dannu. For what reason we do not know, but we are sure that all will be revealed in the fullness of time."

"Bollocks!" said Parrish emphatically in English.

The wrinkled old face furrowed in puzzlement.

"Rubbish." he translated for the little mans benefit. The holy man responded by waving away his word as if it were a pestering fly in the air before him.

"We know much about you, tall man." he said. "Dannu speaks to us too." Parrish thought he detected a slight hint of sarcasm then but wasn't sure. "She has much to say about you."

"Oh, really?"

Up until then Parrish had shown great respect to the old bugger but now he just scoffed. He knew bullshit when he heard it and also knew when a whole shovel load of the stuff was about to be thrown in his direction.

"Yes. We know that you are special, Parrish. Do you deny that you have fought wolves, fought men and fought the weather and still remain undefeated? We know that you are very brave but do not kill just for the sake of killing. And you can be as one with the Earth, still and silent and strong as the stones themselves."

Parrish scoffed again. All these past events were being twisted to fit in with whatever they wanted to believe. Everything the old man referred to had probably been told to him by the Danebury holy man or even the Chieftain. He decided to play them along a bit.

"So, you all think I am here because of the Earth Goddess?" he said sarcastically. "Nature in the shape of a man, sent to you by Dannu?"

"Yes."

Parrish laughed out loud, the sound bouncing eerily around the curved wall of the hut. All the watching holy men shifted uncomfortably in their seats. The laugh sounded somehow unnatural. Almost supernatural.

Not reacting at all to the heavy sarcasm, the old man let the laughter die away and then said softly.

"We know that you have travelled back down the summers to be with us now, my young friend."

The smile died on Parrish's face, his features momentarily going flat. He had only ever used that phrase with one other person. He was filled with bitter disappointment.

"Juli told you that, I know." he said, almost aggressive in his sadness at his wife's betrayal of him.

"I know of no Juli." said the old man, his eyes locked with those of his tall companion. "The words came from Dannu."

"Bollocks!" said Parrish again.

"It is true." The priest rested one gnarled hand on the tall unbelievers arm. "Dannu told us too how she called on her helpers to begin the task of sending you on your journey back down the summers."

"Huh?"

"The sky spirits." The old man did not feel in the least bit perturbed at having to explain to Parrish what, deep down he was sure he really already knew. "She told us how some of her sky spirits sacrificed themselves to bring to earth the man bird and start your journey back."

The words stunned Parrish. Was he now the one who was twisting words to make them fit what *he* knew? He closed his eyes and for a moment saw again the helicopter skimming up the valley at high speed. Then the black crows as they lifted suddenly up into the sky, smashing into the aircraft as it ploughed through the flock, causing it to crash. Seeing the event then as the first link in a long chain of events that would finally lead to him sitting here now in the great shrine hut with the high priests of the Earth Goddess. Nobody else knew about that crash. No one. How could they know. It was just impossible, too fantastic.

"No." he shook his head. "It cannot be. I mean ... I never... How? When did she? What else ...? "

The wizened old man patted Parrish reassuringly on the arm, seeing the tall mans bold confidence crumbling away.

"I cannot answer your questions, my son." His voice almost had that same calming effect of the mystery woman's the night Oona had died. Parrish felt drawn to the sound, rather than the words themselves.

"I did not understand the strange words that she spoke. What is a man bird?" He shrugged the question off. "That knowledge must be yours and yours alone. But that too is of no matter. All we wish to do is tell you that we are ready to listen if you have any special words to say to us." There was a hint of expectancy in his crusty voice.

Parrish looked down at the old man, totally baffled. An expectant silence filled the great hut. He looked slowly around at the banked wall of faces, all staring intently down at him. He had never felt so intimidated in his whole life.

"I... I... have no special words." he said slowly. Apologetically. "I am just an ordinary man, here because of an accident."

Once again the grey haired old man patted him reassuringly on the arm and felt the slight tremble there. He knew that the tall mans words were true. He gave a soft, resigned sigh and smiled at the tall stranger among them.

"It is of no matter, my son. When the time finally comes, we will all still be here. Do not be afraid, for the Earth Goddess is good and she is wise. She watches over us and knows all. We all have a place in her plans, a path to walk and a destiny to follow. You must do what you must do."

"But what is that?"

The old man just shrugged, thought for a long moment then rose with great effort to his feet. Parrish stood too, out of respect, towering over the Neolithic high priest. He looked down, a frown on his face, head full of conflicting thoughts. He received a warm smile in return.

"Parrish." the old priest said sagely. "You must follow the path before you. She guides you on your journey. We here will watch your progress with interest, pride and honour. It is my great wish that you will come and talk with us again next summer when we all honour the Goddess at her temple. As you say, I am old but I too will still be here to welcome you, if it is the will of Dannu." He nodded at Parrish, who suddenly felt dismissed. "Farewell, my son."

Parrish, even though he was still stunned, bowed deeply to the old man. In reply, every holy man in the hut stood and bowed to him. It almost unnerved him completely, the colour draining from his face.

The old man smiled at him once more. Odd as the tall stranger was, he couldn't help liking this most unusual and yet brave and honest of warriors.

Parrish's little four man escort stepped forwards again, as if in response to some hidden signal, and led him meekly back towards the tunnel entrance at the foot of the statue. At the tunnel mouth Parrish stopped and looked back across the floor at the wise old man. The two men's eyes met for a long second before the priest nodded, to him or the great statue, it was hard to tell. Finally, Parrish turned his back on the whole assembly and, with back straight and chest out, strode briskly back up the dark tunnel, to emerge gratefully into the warm, prehistoric sunlight.

38

When he returned to the Sanctuary, Parrish found the people of Danebury preparing to leave, as were the other remaining village groups. Several had already left.

The escorting holy men from Windmill Hill left him at the end of the stone avenue. Once among the massed villagers, the Danebury holy man went to sort out his own affairs before departure.

Juli had waited patiently, tense with trepidation, for her husband's return and was not cheered by the dour expression on his face. She could see that his thoughts were troubled and was too frightened to ask what had happened in the shrine house of the wise ones. She knew that Parrish was Dannu's man and here was Dannu's place. Was here his place too? He stopped before her, deep in thought and just stood, staring off into space. She picked his combat jacket and webbing from the ground, holding them loosely at her sides.

"We are leaving, Parrish."

"Yes." he said absently.

"Will," she hesitated. "Will you be coming with us?"

The question jarred Parrish out of his deep thoughts.

"What?! Of course. Why would I stay?"

"But what of the wise ones? The temple of Dannu? Did they not..."

"Their place is here at the temple." he interrupted. "Mine is with my village and my wife."

A great weight lifted from Juli's shoulders and she gladly held out his things to him. He accepted them with a small grin, shrugged into his jacket and slung on his webbing.

"Back to Dane-bre then!" he said cheerily.

She nodded happily and quickly gathered up her own items and bartered goods.

The village moved out of the Sanctuary shortly after, with a few farewell waves to some new found friends, and set off along the well worn riverside path. It was late afternoon and Coran wanted to get well away from the temple site before his people settled for the night. Even so, there were still a few hours of daylight left and the Chieftain had his people several kilometres south of the river Kennet by the time the sun was low in the sky. They camped among the trees of the forest, the many cooking fires doing their best to push back the steadily encroaching darkness. Around the dancing flames floated cheerful talk of the events, worship and trades of the last few days.

This night there was no familiar chill in the air. The twinkling stars were masked by complete cloud cover. Parrish knew the signs and, when he and Juli were settled, spent a short time tying off the corners of his poncho with paracord to nearby trees to make a low, slightly sloping shelter. Juli watched from the sidelines with a puzzled expression. She was not alone. Others watched curiously from a discrete distance. Finally, Parrish straightened from his task and beckoned his wife to come forward and slide beneath the taught, rubberized canvas.

"It is called a 'basha'." he informed her.

"It looks silly." she said.

"Perhaps, but it will make the night easier."

Juli couldn't see how, but kept the rest of her thoughts on the strange item to herself and wormed underneath it, as ordered. Parrish joined her and snuggled up close.

"This is nice, eh?" he asked cheerily.

Juli nodded and wriggled with pleasure against the warm bulk of her husband. The basha was clearly for the purpose of keeping them both from the prying eyes of the others. She hoped excitedly that this meant he might give her his seed tonight.

As Parrish had guessed, in the early hours the heavens opened and the whole of Danebury, with the exception of Juli and himself, had an uncomfortable remainder of the night at the mercy of the elements. Juli awoke in the morning to see the rain falling steadily, the whole forest dripping and the people nearby hunched miserably down in their sodden capes. Parrish prodded the underside of the poncho with his finger and smiled smugly at his wife.

"Do you still think it is silly?" he asked. Her answer was a smile and an emphatic shake of the head.

There were no breakfast fires. Everyone made do with simple jerky or fruit and were quickly on their way again. Coran had already put out his scouts and led the village onwards through the steady, drenching rain.

Parrish let Juli wear his poncho. She had to hitch up the ends to prevent them dragging along the ground but at least she remained dry. Parrish was no stranger to wetness and was pleasantly surprised at how, even sodden with water, his woollen cape managed to retain its warmth.

The pace was slow. As the day wore on and the rain refused to relent, it seemed to sap the previous day's enthusiasm from the walkers. Any early conversations eventually died away to silence and the walk became a subdued trudge to the constant patter of the falling rain. It was after midday, although it was impossible to tell without the benefit of the sun, when Coran called Parrish to one side.

"I have received word from the scouts at the rear." he said, very matter-of-factly. "We are being followed. Come."

The pair moved swiftly back through the group of travellers and off into the forest. Not more than a kilometre behind the slow moving villagers they met up with a single warrior who pointed off back into the area of forest that the village had recently passed through.

"It is only one man." said Coran, acknowledging the scout with a curt nod but addressing Parrish. "A man that you know."

"Oh?"

"Yes." The Chieftains eyes had a chilling glint to them as they bored into those of his tall warrior friend. "Speak with him."

Parrish fully understood the message, nodded, then moved stealthily off between the wet, dripping trees to intercept the lone stalker.

The forest was quiet, as if it knew something unpleasant was going to happen. The only sound was the deadening patter of the rain, slapping against the sagging leaves and bending the grasses and wild flowers wherever it could reach them unobstructed. Moving quietly through it all was the unknown, uncloaked man, following the glaringly obvious tracks of the village. He was soaked through but didn't appear to notice. In his right hand, down at his side but at a moment's readiness he carried his bow, an arrow nocked to the string but not under tension.

In contrast, Parrish's own bow was unstrung and leaning up against the tree that hid him from the strangers view. He stood patiently watching the man as he approached. When he had closed, unsuspecting, to within about fifteen paces, Parrish stepped suddenly out into full view. His empty hands hung loosely at his sides. The Neolithic man froze, grasped his bowstring with his free hand and half drew his bow, although still keeping the weapon pointing at the ground. He could see that the tall man was unarmed and he knew he was safely out of reach of his feared, unbeatable hands. The strange man's eyes darted swiftly around but he could see no one else. A satisfied grin creased his face.

Parrish knew the man all right. Even though he was still perhaps twelve meters away he could plainly see that the warrior sported a tremendous black eye and a cauliflower ear, the result of a hard blow to the temple. The two men eyed each other silently for some moments. The smile on the smaller man’s face broadened more as he realized that he had full control of the situation.

"What do you want?" Parrish’s harsh voice carried clearly through the background noise of the rain.

"Your head!" was the aggressive answer.

"Why?" asked Parrish unnecessarily.

"Because of this." The man cocked his head briefly to one side to indicate his facial injuries. "You attacked me in the gathering place of the Earth Goddess, insulting her. Then you did not kill me when I was defeated. You dishonoured me, made me lose face. Not just before all the other warriors but also before my own Chieftain. Now I am nothing in my village and so I have come to regain my honour."

"Hah!" Parrish scoffed. "You dishonour yourself. You insulted me and I was right to attack you. Then I showed you mercy, and respect to Dannu, by not killing you when I should have." The Neolithic man’s only reply was to draw back his bowstring a few inches more. Parrish continued.

"Tell me coward, how would you regain your honour? By following my village like a scavenger, then creeping up in the night and killing me while I slept, with no chance to defend myself? I see that your bow is ready. Would you kill me now when I am unarmed?" He shook his head. "You have no honour left to regain."

He expected the warrior to be enraged by the cutting insults but, to his surprise, the man simply laughed.

"Your words are wasted tall man. There is no one to hear them. Soon you will be dead and I will have your head for a trophy. The people of my village will believe that I beat you in an honourable fight and I will become a great warrior among them."

"I would waste no more words on you." Parrish said in disgust. "You shame me just with your presence. Kill me now." He held his arms away from his body in a gesture of resigned acceptance.

The smaller man grinned and slowly drew back his bow fully, raising it to bear on his intended target. Suddenly, as if by some grisly magic trick, several arrows seemed to sprout spontaneously out from different parts of his torso. His eyes went wide with pained surprise and his numbed hands released the arrow, unaimed. It went well wide of Parrish, vanishing among the waiting trees to his right. He stared at the tall man, the look of surprise frozen on his face, while Parrish gazed right back at him with cold eyes. Almost in slow motion, the would be assassin crumpled to the ground, twitched and was still.

From among the trees on either side of the body emerged Coran and several other Danebury warriors, still holding their bows, fresh arrows at the ready. They crossed the wet ground and stood around the corpse, waiting for Parrish to join them. He still stood motionless in the rain. They watched silently as he then collected his own longbow and then walked slowly over to join them. He looked almost distastefully down at the dead man.

"You were right Parrish. He was truly a man without honour." Coran's comment brought nods of agreement from the other warriors.

Parrish didn't even acknowledge the words. Lying on the ground before him was the one thing he had not seen, and had hoped he would never see, since he had arrived back in the Neolithic age.

The dead man indeed had no honour. Or respect. Or even plain and honest decency. He was a liar, a cheat and a coward. He would have committed cold blooded murder, purely for his own personal gain, and done it gladly. Until now Parrish had not seen the slightest indication, or even heard any second hand rumours, of the dark, sinister side of human nature. True, the people here could be cruel and brutal, but that was because of the cruel and brutal circumstances they lived under. Even so, there was no malice, jealousy or suspicion. The people were fair, straightforward and honest. As much as they were violent, they could be kind and trusting without any thought of redress. Here, a man's word was his bond. And yet here he had just witnessed man's evil nature first hand. He felt sick to his stomach.

Parrish recognized it immediately for what it truly was. It was the creeping disease that he knew, deep within his heart, would one day be the final death of mankind. In the time of his birth, the so called 'civilized' twentieth century, the disease was rife. There men tricked, cheated, swindled and even killed for personal gain. Or wealth or power. Or, worst of all, just out of perverse, malicious pleasure. There goodness, honesty, respect and reason were in the minority.

Parrish looked down at the man's body, with the rain falling unnoticed on the open, unblinking eyes, and hated him for showing that even here, in the early years of man’s ascent, the rot had already started to set in. He spat vehemently on the corpses face and without a single word turned and walked off back among the trees, his back hiding from the warriors of Danebury the look of utter sadness on his face.

39

Danebury was waiting, just as they had left it. Quiet, peaceful and, as anticipated, undisturbed. With the return of its people it immediately returned to life. Parrish couldn't believe how pleased he was to be back. Back home. It was now so much more than just a collection of mud huts, green fields and sheep. No one said a word but he was sure everyone else felt the same way.

Without the need for any transition time, the populous of the hill fort dropped straight back into the normal status quo that ensured the smooth running of a close knit village community. No one took any liberties after tasting the more relaxed, unrestricted regime allowed at Avebury.

Parrish watched it all with amazement and pride. Juli however could not understand his awe. To her it was simply what happened every summer. The women went straight back to their everyday tasks of collecting firewood and water, readying the huts, the children and setting to work on any items they had bartered that needed further attention. The men also knew their duties. Setting the guard, putting the flock out to pasture, checking the crops and quickly organizing the next hunting party. Parrish was not invited to be part of the hunt but was not at all offended. Best to let the experts get on with it and do what they were good at.

Many people had returned from the temple of the Earth Goddess somehow changed. Parrish knew that he was. For others too, life would never be quite the same. It seemed the holy man now treated Parrish with a bit more respect than before, although not much, and though he lacked some of the more aggressive qualities of a Neolithic warrior, the other men of Danebury knew that Parrish showed true greatness in other areas. They were more than proud to include him as one of their own.

The women of the camp too were quietly appreciative of the tall man. They were all aware of his offer of assistance to Tomps new wife. It was an unprecedented thing for a warrior to do but then they knew he generally treated women differently to other warriors. They also knew that he was aware of the women's usually unseen system of mutual assistance, or just simply looking out for one another, and kept the information to himself. He had their respect and gratitude.

The girl Karin was unsure of her position in her new village and deliberately kept a low profile in the camp. As if in direct response to Parrish's instruction to his own wife to help the young girl, all the women of Danebury took Karin under their collective wing, helping her wherever possible. On being told the camp rumour that Parrish was suspected of being very close to Dannu, she trembled with fear when Juli invited her, with her husband's blessing, to visit his house.

It was of course an honour to be asked to visit anyone's house. All Neolithic people valued the privacy of their own homes highly but the tall man seemed quite eager to have people visit him. The prospect frightened her.

Even the shape and construction of his house frightened her. Everything about the tall man was strange, different and out of the ordinary. Never the less, she went when asked, not wanting to offend and not daring to refuse.

She left his house feeling even more confused than when she had entered, but no longer quite so frightened. Such a strange man, if that was what he really was. Apparently, his fighting skills were legendary and yet he seemed so gentle, sometimes almost childlike. How could he command such respect from so many great warriors, from the other villages as well as his own? She could not believe either the amazing liberties that his wife took with her husband when they were in their own house. Bare faced smiling, sometimes laughing out loud and even asking questions! And the strange way she acted around him, touching him often and unnecessarily. It was almost as if she worshiped him and Karin was sure that the Earth Goddess would not allow any worshipping to be done except to her alone. Still, it was not her place to say and, when all said and done, at the end of her visit she did somehow feel happier and more relaxed. Looking down at the village spread out below her, as she left the odd shaped log cabin, she suddenly saw it in a different light and began to realize that Danebre was a special place and it was her good fortune to be a part of it.

Tomps himself was a changed man too. A wife was a responsibility. Something he had not really experienced before. He now had more considerations to make. Also, his acquisition of a wife, his growing friendship with Klud and the general increase in respect shown to him by other warriors, was putting a strain on his family. He was beginning to overshadow his own father and his wives. It was clear that he needed a family hut of his own and a separate stall in the shrine house. In due course he had approached the Chieftain to request permission to build his own house. A nerve wracking experience for the young man, having never spoken to the Chieftain before, man to man. It was in itself one of the first acts of a fully grown warrior and Coran formally gave him permission, suppressing his smile until the nervous young warrior had departed. When the other warriors of Danebury got to hear about the visit they all nodded in satisfaction. They too well remembered their own first visit to see a Chieftain.

Parrish was honoured to be asked by Tomps for his assistance in building the hut and gladly lent a hand. In fact, Tomps was amazed at just how many other warriors pitched in to help ensure that his house was sturdy, strong, warm and well built. He was much gratified by the display of comradeship.

By the time his hut was finished, bar the heavy thatch that Parrish's own house was also lacking, the summer had almost run its course. The weather had been very hot although there had also been several bursts of heavy rain during the season. The ground, plants and trees of the forest soaked the moisture up and everything grew rich, tall and green. Danebury's crop fields were a magnificent sight. It made Parrish smile, a smile enjoyed all the more for knowing that his friend Chieftain Danel and his village now had a much better chance of seeing the coming winter through without so much hardship. His purchase of grain was practically guaranteed by the excellent growing season.

The wheat and barley was now high, golden brown and ready to be reaped. The summer had been so good that the holy man decided to hold an extra ceremony and celebration of thanks inside the great hut. Everyone was of course there and it was a good time. A time for relaxation and the pleasure of good company, all under the auspices of the Earth Goddess. The central fire burned brightly and the people sat attentively at the entrances to their stalls.

The women and children listened with excitement and pride as the warriors took turns telling of great deeds, glorious battles, the winning of trophies, both theirs and others, or just wild, imaginative and entertaining stories of false gods, spirits, heroes and the supernatural.

Parrish listened to the tall stories with as much enjoyment as everyone else. It seemed that every village had its own star story teller and Danebury was no exception. Surprisingly, it was the old flint knapper that Parrish spoke to on occasion. It became suddenly apparent that while the man sat, chipping away at his lumps of stone, he watched everything and everyone. He also had a truly astounding capacity to remember. There was a murmur of anticipation when he took centre stage and it was well deserved for he recited at least one deed for each warrior present. Parrish blushed and modestly waved away the praise heaped on him when the old knapper told the tale of his battle with the wolf pack and his singular fighting skills. His red face made the whole crowd laugh. Parrish did not mind in the least and laughed along with them.

Eventually, no matter how much he protested, Parrish himself was pulled up to take centre stage and tell a story of his own. For a moment he was lost for words, looking around in panic at all the expectant faces, then suddenly remembered a tale he had always loved as a child. Once started there was no stopping him and, with much gusto, waving of arms and exaggerated gestures, he told the stirring story of King Arthur and the Knights of the Round Table. It had its difficult moments. For example, no one knew what a table was, but that was a minor detail and besides, did it really matter to these simple people? To Parrish the story was a mixture of ancient history and folklore. To the people of Danebury it was pure fantasy and they loved every moment of it. He received roars of approval when he had finished and the old knapper smiled broadly, adding one more story to his collection of tall tales.

Harvest time. The second one since his arrival in the Neolithic age but this time Parrish was invited, expected even, to attend the pre-reaping ceremony inside the great centre hut. Once again the drums beat loudly and the people sang in good voice their thanks to the Earth Goddess, before the flower and feather man asked her cordially for enough days of continuous dry weather to allow the village to reap, dry, thresh and winnow its crop. Parrish then joined in happily with the rest of the village in their appreciation of the graciousness of the Earth Goddess in giving them their crop in the first place. He didn't feel at all hypocritical. It didn't really matter that he knew it was more down to the sunshine, sound land management, light winds and heavy rain rather than a simple belief in a mysterious goddess that he still couldn't bring himself to fully believe in. For him personally, the real emphasis of the ceremony leant more towards the basic unification of every single person in Danebury towards one common aim. An aim that he was more than proud to be a part of.

The next morning, every warrior was duly given his ceremonial sickle and took his place in the line up before the fields that would ensure the perpetuation of the village through the following year. Once again the little holy man danced and chanted his way around the plots of wheat and barley until finally ending up at the head of the waiting line of warriors. After a moment's contemplation he stepped to one side.

"She is ready." he said with heavy reverence.

"Thank you, Earth Goddess!" cried the harvesters emphatically, Parrish included, and moved forwards en mass then bent to the task before them. As was their rightful place, the women were just a few paces behind, ready to tie the felled stalks into stooks then stack them to dry in the sun. Parrish remembered just how much he had enjoyed the work last year. This year was no different. With the warmth of the sun on his back and the warmth that comes with a sense of purpose, in his heart, Parrish worked hard, as did everyone else, until a halt was called sometime after midday for food and drink. Quite a bit of the crop had been cut already and there seemed no rush to return to the fields. The overriding feeling among the people was one of relaxed satisfaction and, when Coran finally did call the villagers back to work, they all went gladly.

With all the men bent to their reaping and all the women bent to their stook gathering, it came as a bit of a surprise when suddenly a single, guttural cry went up. It was quickly followed by a great chorus of blood curdling screams and yells. Like everyone else, Parrish looked up with a curiosity that quickly turned to horror at the sight of strange people, dressed in animal skins and brandishing war clubs and axes above their heads, charging with murderous intent towards them through the remainder of the uncut crops!

40

The unknown assailants had crept unobserved to the edge of the wheat, then moved stealthily closer through it until they were near enough to execute their surprise charge. There were no arrows loosed, the attackers were that close, and some of the Danebury men barely had time to straighten before the yelling aggressors were upon them.

Parrish could not identify the strangers but everyone else knew who they were. They were the hunter/gatherers. Mesolithic people.

These Mesolithic people were the last remnants of how people had once existed before finally turning to the farming system, introduced by the first migrating travellers from the continent, for their living. Of the once numerous bands of wandering nomads, there were only a few scattered tribes left. They roamed constantly across the forests and hills of Neolithic Britain, forever searching for fresh food, clothing and shelter, only staying in one place for a short while before moving on. Ever the opportunists, they would attack other small groups or even villages if they thought it a reasonable risk for a good return. Always on the lookout for easy pickings if they could strike hard and fast when their victims were unprepared.

This was how they saw the people of Danebury. With their guard down and preoccupied with other things. If the nomads could vanquish the virtually unarmed warriors and take the village, the pickings would be excellent and plentiful. Good food, lots of tools, clothes, women and plenty of trophies.

The Mesoliths charged aggressively in and at first it was all the warriors of Danebury could do to defend themselves, armed only with the sickles they held and the daggers in their belts. A savage, deadly chaos ensued, with every man for himself.

A wild eyed Mesolith leaped towards Parrish, swinging his stone axe in an assertive attempt to smash in the tall mans skull. The blow was stopped cold by a full powered parrying swing of Parrish's sickle which severed the wild man's arm midway between wrist and elbow. The man let out an agonized, high pitched scream, grasping his bloody stump with his free hand. Parrish brutally cut the man's cries short by dispatching him with a second slashing cut across the throat. Blood jetted into the air, splashing bright red across Parrish's face.

All across the fields came the cries, yells, screams and other awful, murderous sounds of ensuing mortal combat. Looking to his right, Parrish saw Klud vigorously pulling his own glistening red sickle from the chest of a fallen Mesolith. The Danebury warrior felt his tall friends eyes on him and met his gaze, waving his weapon triumphantly aloft, with a terrible smile on his face. Parrish nodded in appreciation of his fighting skills, just in time to see a stone ball, hurled from some unseen slingshot, smash into the back of the Neolithic man's head. Blood splashed. Klud's eyes rolled up in their sockets and he crashed to the ground. Parrish felt sure his friend must be dead. As if to make sure, a fur clad Mesolith stepped up with the intention of giving Klud the coup-de-grace, and taking his head as a trophy. Before Parrish himself could act, a smaller warrior leaped forward to defend Klud's fallen body. It was Tomps.

Whose head he took as a trophy made no difference to the Mesolith and he turned his attention to the Danebury youngster, swinging his axe with vicious intent. Tomps skilfully avoided the blow with a swaying body movement that Parrish immediately recognized. The lad had clearly been watching the twentieth century man when he had fought and now copied his moves. The Mesolith could not but help follow through when his heavy axe failed to connect and he exposed his side to attack. Tomps took full advantage and, with a wide swing that started from somewhere down near his ankles, buried his sickle into the man's ribs, right up to the hilt. The curved stone blade passed right through the man's body, which seemed to poise in motion for a moment, as if hung up on the weapon. Tomps had to pull hard to withdraw the sickle and the man dropped limply to the ground. Even though he witnessed with shock the full, brutal episode, Parrish's first thought was that now the boy really was a full blooded warrior.

A second attacker charged towards Parrish, yelling at the top of his lungs, snatching the tall man's attention from the youngster. Changing the sickle to his weak hand and drawing his flint dagger, Parrish made good use of his far superior reach and lunged forwards in a fencer's riposte, the astounded Mesolith running onto its sharp point, killed before he could even get within reach.

A sudden scream, much higher pitched and unmistakably female, next caught his attention and he looked left over his shoulder. The first of the Mesoliths to breach the Danebury line had crossed the cleared fields in an effort to reach the grouped women who cowered at their edge. Easy pickings for trophies.

Parrish began to sprint across the carpet of crop stubble towards them as the women backed away from their assailant until they could back no further, huddled together up against one wall of the holding barns.

Why didn't they just run away? The thought screamed silently in his head.

Another Mesolith abruptly blocked Parrish's path but he never even slowed down. With all his might he hurled his sickle into the man's face. What the resulting injury from the impact was he had no idea but the man fell as if pole axed. Parrish ran straight on by without wasting any more attention on the poor unfortunate. It made no difference. He knew that he would be too late to stop the killing. Running hard, he watched helplessly as the Mesolithic man raised his war club slowly into the air in a calculated action designed to cause the maximum terror to his helpless victims. He was about to deliver his first killing blow when the diminutive but unmistakable figure of the holy man seemed to appear from nowhere and leapt between him and the terrified group of cowering women.

"Stop!" he cried loudly, doing his utmost to look and sound menacing in a valiant attempt to instil fear into the man. His eyes turned up towards the sky. "I call upon Dannu to protect her daughters!" he shouted at the top of his voice.

The armed man simply laughed out loud and back handed the little man viciously across the face, sending him sprawling to one side. Again he drew his war club back fully in readiness to strike, but the holy man's brave stance had bought Parrish enough time. At that instant he thundered up behind the Mesolith, a terrible apparition of fury, eyes hard, teeth gritted and face glistening with fresh blood. He seemed to rear up over the unsuspecting man like some nightmarish spectre of doom. At that moment, he appeared so terrifying that the women feared him as much as the Mesolith. Before the unsuspecting nomad could even move, Parrish savagely grasped the man's head with both hands and twisted it so violently to one side that when the nomad's neck snapped it could be heard by everyone. The women looked on, speechless with horror at the swiftness and power of the killing. As the body gave one last nervous twitch Parrish coldly tossed it aside and almost as violently grasped the fallen holy man by his buckskin tunic, hauling him roughly to his feet. Blood was flowing freely but unnoticed from a cut on the small man's cheek.

"You did well little man." Parrish said. "That was a brave thing."

The holy man could only nod dumbly. In all his days he had never seen such a thing. He felt not one iota of remorse or pity for the dead Mesolith but accepted the fact that *he* was responsible for the man's death by calling up the terrible wrath of the Earth Goddess, which had swiftly arrived in the shape of the tall man.

Parrish shook the flower and feather man in an attempt to rid him of his dazed look and get his attention.

"Take the women back to the hill fort, quickly now. Do you hear me?" He shook the little man again.

"Yes. I hear you."

"Then go!" Parrish thrust him urgently away. Without another word the holy man immediately began to herd the women away towards the fort. For a brief moment Parrish was aware of Juli waving frantically from the crowd but he could spare no time to wave back. He snatched up the dead man's club and ran back into the fight, scanning the bloody melee as he approached, looking for the weakest area. Many bodies lay on the ground, some so mutilated that it was impossible to tell if they were Danebury men or their Mesolithic attackers. Tomps was clearly visible, still standing in defence of the fallen Klud, only now with three slain Mesoliths at his feet. The others seemed to be giving him a wide berth.

Nearby, two Danebury warriors were being cautiously circled by a band of five Mesoliths, each one looking for an opening in the defensive posture of the surrounded men. The two stood back to back, their bloodstained sickles drawing slow circles in the air before them. The Mesoliths were right to be wary. Each of the two warriors had a dead body lying at their feet. Parrish charged straight in.

"Bastards!" he shouted and smashed his stone club into the nearest man's back, squarely between the shoulder blades. The man crumpled to the ground, his spine shattered. The momentarily distraction it caused the other attackers was enough for the Danebury men and they leapt into their own attacks. Sickles slashed and blood spurted. The remaining pair of Mesoliths turned and fled, with Parrish and his two compatriots screaming in pursuit. The three gave up the chase after a dozen or so strides, once they were sure the men had been put to flight, and turned their attention to other targets.

The Mesolithic rush had finally faltered then been stopped by the spirited stance of the Danebury warriors. The concerted charge had quickly degenerated into individual duels or small group attacks. Although the nomads had attacked with vicious and vigorous intent, the men of Danebury were fighting for more than just food and goods. They were defending their homes and their families. Aggression had been matched with aggression and blow for murderous blow. It was simply kill or be killed.

On one side, two Mesoliths had leapt on a single, isolated warrior and simultaneously battered the man to death with their clubs. In yet another area of the same field, a warrior helped another of his village by side swiping a Mesolith who was closing in for the kill after inflicting a debilitating arm wound on his Danebury opponent. With a sweeping slash of his sickle the warrior tore the lower jaw right off of the Mesolith's face, then left him to choke on his own blood and moved on to seek out another victim.

The Mesolithic casualties increased. An ascending spiral of death as the decreasing number of nomads suffered under the onslaught of the greater force of Danebury men. After Parrish and his fellow warriors had put the first attackers to flight, the rest soon followed suit. It became a rout and, as quickly as it had started, the battle was over. The remaining Mesolithic men ran swiftly away towards the distant tree line where their own shocked women and children watched and waited. A few warriors chased them for a short distance but gave up when they were certain of the retreat. Battered and bruised, their numbers decimated, the Mesoliths quickly vanished among the great trees, undeniably wiser in the knowledge that it had been an expensive folly to attack the well motivated, well defended village of Dane-bre.

In the suddenly quiet aftermath, Parrish stood in the centre of the fields and looked slowly about. Never had he seen such carnage. Bodies, and the dismembered pieces of bodies, lay scattered upon the ground. The normally golden brown wheat stems were splashed with red, with patches of earth soaked dark with men's blood. He looked down at his own blood spattered hands and arms, finding it difficult to believe that not only had he taken part in the deadly combat, but that he was also personably responsible for several violent deaths. He'd had no real time to think in the heat of the fight, running purely on the concentrated intention of protecting his village, wife and friends. It was not a pleasant surprise either to suddenly realize just how good he was at inflicting injury and death. Almost in a daze, he began to wander about the battlefield, not quite sure where to go or what to do next. Other warriors were doing the same, only their intentions were obvious. Searching out injured Monoliths and brutally finishing them off.

A sudden, almost wailing cry went up that caught everyone's attention. A warrior who also wore the running, red badge of battle was waving frantically from the far side of the fields. The other men moved across and began to gather around the body at his feet.

It wasn't until he drew closer that Parrish recognized the caller as Gant and smiled at him, pleased to see his friend still among the living. Gant did not return the gesture, noticing Parrish only briefly before returning his distraught gaze to the body on the ground. The other warriors gathered slowly around until there was a crowd of men, all looking down in stony silence.

"What is going on here?" Came a gruff voice, and the crowd parted to let the speaker through. It was Klud, his face awash with his own blood, the great eyebrows matted with it. He was being supported under one shoulder by Tomps. Parrish was very glad to see his good friend still alive but this time could generate no smile. The two men reached the front of the gathered crowd and they too looked down at the body.

Coran lay on his back, sightless eyes glazed, his buckskin tunic saturated with blood. A Mesolithic stone axe was still buried deep in his chest.

41

Two days later, a much subdued Danebury village finished its harvesting. It was the final task in the clearing up of the fields that lay before the hillfort. Parrish had always thought that the annual wheat and barley crop was one of the foremost jobs of the people, but even that took second place now. First considerations were rightfully directed to the multitude of bodies, both attackers and defenders, that had littered the ground. For both groups there were proper rites and rituals to be observed.

Including the Chieftain, the Danebury dead totalled eleven, in comparison to the twenty three Mesolithic bodies. Only Parrish, who could count, knew the actual body count. To the people of the village it was enough that there were many dead warriors but many more dead hunter/gatherers.

Each of the fallen Danebury warriors was individually honoured in a sombre ceremony inside the great hut before the entire population carried its dead in a proud but grief filled procession to the lonely knoll in the east. Even the warmth of the rising sun could not lift the chill that seemed to hang over that sad place. Only the sky spirit birds would find pleasure there.

The relatives of the dead were grateful to Dannu that all the bodies were complete, even if some were in several pieces, guaranteeing at least that all the brave warriors could take their rightful places in the great shrine house of the Earth Goddess, one day to be re born and walk again in the sun. The only warrior not to lay with his face towards the rising sun in his wait for the sky spirits to carry him off was the Chieftain.

Coran's tightly wrapped corpse lay in state in his stall, watched over by the statue of Dannu. After the last of the harvest had been gathered, his people would carry him up onto the great Plain and lay him to rest in his own burial mound. As befitted a great Chieftain, his wishes would be honoured and he had always made it clear that his first concern was that the village should be safe and secure at all times. And so, the harvest would be gathered before any other duties would be performed. His body could wait to be entombed.

His burial crypt was ready and waiting. Work had started on it as soon as he had been elected new Chieftain. Often, a Chieftain's barrow would lay empty and waiting for many years before it was finally used. There was no fear of destruction or desecration to it. Everyone, no matter how great or humble, be they farmer or hunter, had the utmost respect for the dead. Except for dead attackers!

The Mesoliths were disposed of in the same way all other attackers were dealt with. The bodies were stripped of useful items then dismembered and the pieces consigned to the excrement pit. On such a large scale it was a truly terrible sight to behold but this time Parrish felt no repulsion as he witnessed it. This time the watching crowd did not cheer. This time there was merely an overriding feeling of grim satisfaction as the quartered bodies vanished beneath the surface of the foul looking and evil smelling brown slurry.

The many trophies, emptied, cleaned and polished, now adorned the walls of warrior's stalls. Parrish never knew who prepared his own, as he had always flatly refused to entertain even the idea of scooping the innards out of someone's head, but four more skulls now hung from the wall pegs of his stall. In fact his count should really have been five. The man he had hurled his sickle at died from the resulting skull fracture but Parrish had no intention of making a claim on the trophy taken by the warrior who had administered the unnecessary final blow. Unlike the rest of the Danebury warriors, he found no joy in boasting of kills.

Most of the warriors had at least one trophy to their credit. Those who did not were still acknowledged with the same respect. Every single man had fought well and upheld their own honour and that of their village.

Klud's single trophy seemed enough for him and he was the first to sing the praises of Tomps, his protector and now holder of three gleaming skulls.

"Is he not truly a great warrior?" Klud asked Parrish, his arm wrapped proudly around the lad's shoulders. Tomps was too embarrassed to speak, still feeling woefully inadequate in the presence of such skilful and battle hardened warriors, unable as yet to come to terms with the fact that these men looked upon him now as an equal.

"Yes. A real life taker." said Parrish in reply, hiding his inner sadness as he looked down at the young killer.

In fact, Parrish's own body count was the highest of all the warriors and he had praise heaped on him from all sides. He waved the accolades modestly aside, not enjoying the people's worshipful blood lust. His own heart was heavy with sadness for the losses the village had sustained. Many families had suffered not just the loss of husbands but of sons too. The grief was evident on the faces of many women who had been more attached to their men folk than they were ready to admit. Juli and the other women were already rallying round to support those who would find the following months difficult.

It was not unusual to find that, if a family suddenly became completely bereft of men, an unattached warrior would make an offer to the Chieftain and, if it were accepted, buy himself an instant family. Thus he made life easier for himself and also helped to hold the fabric of the village together. The Chieftain of course kept the warriors offering for himself, as was his right.

Juli was so happy that her husband had survived the battle. She could not believe just how distraught she had felt when suddenly faced with the terrible fact that she might never see him again. During the women's hasty withdrawal to the fort, the holy man had loudly declared that Dannu, acting through Parrish and protecting her man, would wreak deadly havoc on her enemies. It gave Juli no comfort, the first time she had ever doubted the words of a holy man, and she spent the most dreadful moments of her life waiting to see if her husband lived or died.

Seemingly just as the holy man had prophesied, the tall man did indeed survive, coming through the ordeal completely unscathed. Others were not so lucky.

Army trained, battle hardened warrior that he was, Parrish still had to choke back the tears to hear that not only was his friend Hass among the dead, but that Mars had been wounded. On receiving the bad news, Parrish had immediately visited Mars' house and respectfully asked to see the man and his wounds. Of course the archer was pleased to see his tall friend even though he was weak from his wounds and loss of blood. With the warrior's permission, Parrish inspected the man's injuries with grim efficiency. Apparently,

Mars had been beaten to the ground by an axe wielding Mesolith, protecting himself as best he could with a raised arm. Another nearby Danebury warrior had saved him from the final killing blow by despatching his attacker from behind. Parrish almost wished that he hadn't. Mars was badly injured.

He had suffered several deep axe slashes to his right shoulder and neck as well as having a large section of the muscles between his elbow and shoulder sliced clean off. When Parrish asked Mars to gently move his arm, the Neolithic man tried, grimacing with pain in the effort. Parrish immediately stopped him and told him to rest. He had seen enough. The bowman had some movement of his hand and lower arm but virtually none above the elbow. Parrish knew that as well as the severe muscle injuries, there was some nerve damage as well. If infection could be kept at bay, Parrish felt pretty sure that Mars would live. But he was also sure that if he did live, his friend the archer would never draw a bow again.

And so the harvesting was finally finished but not before the sickles, that had earlier been used to such devastating effect, had been washed clean, both physically and spiritually. The flower and feather man blessed every single sickle in a private ceremony that the warriors saw as necessary but Parrish just saw as a waste of a good days harvesting weather. He wisely kept his thoughts to himself. When the rest of the crop had been cut, tied and stood drying in the sun, the holy man next turned his attention to the tattooing of warriors. To the men this was another important task, confirming their battle skills for all to see.

As the little man skilfully cut more small circles into the neck of a wincing Parrish, the tall man asked when Coran would be laid to rest, in wait for the Earth Goddess.

"Very soon, Parrish." the holy man nodded. He knew he would have to explain how it would be done. It was a ritual that every villager knew well, so it was a fair assumption that Parrish probably did not know it! But this time the little man would not insult his tall friend with sarcasm. He had glimpsed the man's true greatness. Dannu had shown him and he knew now to treat her man with more respect.

"The whole village will carry the Chieftain on his last earthly journey to his resting chamber up on the great Plain. There we shall all honour him again before sealing him into the Earth. But there is one more task to be completed before we can carry the Chieftain to the Earth Goddess."

"Oh?"

"When the village carries out its old Chieftain, the people must be lead by their new Chieftain. Tomorrow, when the sun is at its highest, all the warriors will sit in judgment inside the great hut and, with the guidance of Dannu, choose a new Chieftain."

"That will be very interesting." Parrish nodded to himself, interrupting the holy man's cutting and making him hiss in annoyance. "I will watch the choosing very carefully."

"I do not think so." The little man wiped the blood from Parrish's neck and stood back to admire his finished handiwork.

"Why is that?" asked Parrish, suddenly forgetting his discomfort.

"Because you will not be there." He spoke the words flatly. His voice did not betray the fact that he had not looked forward to telling Parrish this. "You are not born of this village Parrish and so you can have no say in the choosing of its Chieftain. That has always been the Dane-bre way."

The utter disappointment on Parrish's face was plain to see. The holy man had nothing more to say. There was an awkward silence. He bowed to the tall man, a gesture that went unnoticed, and left him to his misery. Juli tenderly applied some of the pain easing poultice to her husband's neck but he hardly noticed.

He was rocked by the sudden rebuke. For over a year now he had lived among these people, eating with them, sleeping with them, learning their language and befriending them. Taking a wife, working with them, watching them live and even seeing some of them die. He had never felt as much a part of anything as he had a part of this village. And now, after all that had passed, to be told he was still not considered a villager at all. It cut him to the very heart.

All the rest of the day he sat glumly in his cabin, not speaking. Juli could not coax him out of his sour mood. She had never seen him look so defeated before and began to fear that, if he did not accept the decision and snap out of his sad disillusionment, he might choose to wash his hands totally of Dane-bre and just walk away. Take his long walk back and vanish into the wilderness of the Earth Goddess from whence he had come. Her fears were unfounded for Parrish had nowhere else to go but she could not know this. To her the fear was real enough. A grim silence hung heavy over the house of Parrish in the village of Danebury.

The following day, at the allotted time, every warrior in the village except Parrish went to the great hut to start the process of selecting the new Chieftain. He watched them all enter the building, from his vantage point at the top of his slope, then went inside his own cabin and sat on the edge of the bed, staring blankly down at the earthen floor. He had more or less come to terms with the men's decision and recovered from being rebuked by village tradition, but could not hide his disappointment at still not being considered a part of the village itself. Juli sat down beside him, hoping to give him some comfort with her closeness. He appeared not to notice her.

"How long does it take for them to choose the new Chieftain?" he asked suddenly without looking up.

Juli smiled. Even when full of sadness, he husband still had questions to ask.

“Sometimes it is very quick but it has been known to take a whole day."

"My money is on Klud."

"Money?" Juli tried the strange word on her tongue.

"I would choose Klud." Parrish corrected his sentence for her. "He is the best man for the job."

Juli shrugged. It did not really matter to her. Women never had any direct dealings with the Chieftain anyway. It was enough that, whoever was chosen, his word would be final. She would simply do as she was told.

"They choose who they choose." she said philosophically.

"Yes." Parrish nodded. "But I still would have liked to be there." Once more he stared glumly down at the floor. Juli desperately wanted to cheer her husband, to somehow draw him away from his sadness. Words he had once spoken the last time she had cheered him suddenly came into her mind. Taking a deep breath, she rose, faced the man she loved and began to tug at his clothing.

"What are you doing?" he asked, rising to his feet.

"You will see." Her voice was firm with a sudden authority she could hardly believe. She started to undress him. He smiled in realization of what she wanted and helped her, finally standing naked before her. She pushed him gently down onto the bed and he lay there, silently watching as she undressed herself. The feeling that she got simply from his eyes on her body sent shivers up her spine.

As she climbed onto the bed beside him he instinctively reached for her but she placed her tiny hands on his broad chest and pushed him back down against the soft bed skins. He frowned for a second, laying flat on his back, until he understood her intentions as she swung her leg across his body and straddled his hips. With a gentle hand she guided his swollen manhood to the entrance of her body and, in a slow, sensuous movement, lowered herself onto him until he filled her completely and she sat squarely on his pelvis.

A soft, loving smile settled on his face and Juli's heart soared. For a while they remained motionless, Parrish feeling the warmth of his wife's body and Juli in wonder at her husband's meek submission beneath her. Then she placed her palms squarely on his chest and began with slow, deliberate movements, to coax their bodies towards the shuddering, shattering crescendo that, until she had first taken the seed of this tall man, she would not have believed was possible. The sensations were wonderful and she found that, by regulating the pace of her movements against him, she could sustain their heightened pleasure for a long time.

She sensed when the time was near. Parrish began to lose himself in the feelings and started to thrust his hips with hard urgency into his wife's groin, but she pushed down with her hands on his chest and with her buttocks against his thighs, slowing him down to the speed of her choosing. She could not believe the power she was suddenly exercising over her husband. To have such control over a man. Especially this man. A great warrior. He who could dispense sudden and terrible death, a man of strength, yet still a gentle man and friend of the earth. Dannu's man. It seemed so wrong and yet it felt so right. To control such power, and with such ease. She knew he was under her power yet also knew that she was nothing without him. His strength was her strength. His earth power flowed through her.

The pure, unrestrained excitement of it all boiled up inside her and she could contain them both no longer. Her love for him and her worship of the Earth Goddess rushed out from the place where their bodies were joined and filled her entire being. She cried out in pure pleasure as she was filled almost to bursting with a totally shattering climax. Parrish was right with her and his fingers dug with cruel pleasure into the flesh of her hips as he held her tight to him in his own moment of sexual glory and fulfilment. Juli took his seed with pride, with gratitude and, above all, with love.

They lay beside each other for a while in a blissful silence, the sheen on their hot bodies reflecting the warm sunlight that angled steeply in through the window ports. Then Juli propped herself up onto one elbow and quietly watched her husband, who was staring up at into the rafters above them, deep in thought. Her eyes wandered over the contours of his body, taking in every curve from solidness of his muscles to the gentle rise and fall of his chest. It was a body that she took great pleasure in simply touching. A body belonging to a man like no other she had ever known. So tall and muscular, with strong, capable hands that could be so soft, or as hard as death itself. She took his hand in hers and gently stroked the back of it. It made him smile and that made her smile too.

"I can see that you have been thinking." she said. "Are you happy again now that you are not angry at the village?" At that Parrish smiled again.

"I was never angry with them. It was that I was not happy with me. For a while I thought that my days at Dane-bre had been a waste. That I had done nothing here."

"But that is not true!" blurted Juli in astonishment.

"I know, I know." He patted his wife's naked thigh to calm her. She too lay back then and looked up into the thatching as if that might help her understand her strange husband's thoughts more. "I have looked back at the past summers and seen what I have done since I came to this place."

"Why?" she asked, her brow furrowing in puzzlement. "What has happened is past. It is of no importance."

"It is to me." he said softly. "I know now that not being allowed to take part in the choosing of the Chieftain is not too big a loss of face for me. I have still done many things to be proud of."

Juli just nodded. She could not see the point of his words and just listened obediently.

"A long time ago, I knew a man." Parrish's voice took on a softer tone, as if he were suddenly talking to himself, or at least to no one in particular. Juli suddenly felt that she was about to learn something about her husband's mysterious past and hung eagerly on every word." His name was Carter. He once told me that I was no good. That I would do no good in this land and that I would always be nothing."

"He spoke these words to your face?" she asked incredulously.

"Yes."

"You killed him of course." she said very matter-of-factly.

At that Parrish laughed out loud. Juli frowned. She saw nothing funny when a warrior as great as her husband was so falsely yet boldly insulted.

"Now that I think about his words, they make me look back at what I have done here."

"You have done much." she said reverently.

Parrish nodded in agreement. Yes, he had done much. Against the odds he had become a part of a late Stone Age village, visited the temple of the Earth Goddess, made many new friends and even killed many enemies. He had helped a Neolithic village through trying and turbulent times. Perhaps his contributions might in some small way help carry the village and its people towards a more certain future. Who knows how far the people of Danebury might go? Perhaps he might even have a son by his tiny Neolithic wife and teach him to carry on the good work after he himself was dead? Who knew what the future held? Only Dannu, and she was not telling.

But now there were things that Parrish did see more clearly. As the wise old man at the great temple had said, he had a path to follow and it was his destiny. *Here* was his destiny. He now realized that when he had lived before, in the future, his life *had* been meaningless, just as Carter had said. But he had never been more certain that his new life here at Danebury was his true place and was already much more than the nothing that Carter had predicted. With a brief nod of self satisfaction he acknowledged that, just as he had always suspected, old 'mad dog' was full of crap.

When the man's hard, harsh words had cut Parrish, there was no way for him to see then that his life had not yet begun. His true time was now. He smiled. Perhaps he should have killed the hateful, bullying Sergeant as Juli had assumed. He shrugged. Who knows, maybe someone still would, far off in the future. On that very agreeable thought, Parrish sat upright on the bed and turned to look down at his diminutive wife. She looked quite demure as she gazed back at him, laying there in complete abandonment, wild hair tousled, eyes bright and breasts pale.

"You speak true words, my wife." he said with a broad smile and placed his hand on her flat belly. When he splayed his fingers they almost completely spanned the front of her stomach. "I have indeed done much and there is still much to do. I am honoured to help my village and I will give my support to the new Chieftain, whoever he might be and whatever he might want of me."

Juli could not see why he should speak such words. She did not doubt her husband's loyalty for a single moment. In fact, she secretly thought that if the new Chieftain was at all wise, he would do well to listen to what Parrish said. It was not so much what the new Chieftain might want, but more what he should learn from her tall husband. After all, was he not close to the Earth Goddess? She grasped his hand with both of hers and pressed it to her body.

"The Chieftain will always get what he wants." she said softly. "It is his right. But now I ask you my husband, what is it *you* want?"

Parrish's eyebrows shot up in surprise at the sudden, searching question. Indeed, it was a very good question and for a moment he was stumped for an answer.

"What I want," he said at length, "Is ... a son." With that he rolled on top of Juli, holding himself above her on straight arms. With a joyful smile on her face, she reached up to accept him.

At that moment someone outside the cabin called his name.

"Fuck off!" he hissed sharply under his breath. The call came again.

With an exasperated sigh he gave his wife a brief, tender kiss, rolled off the bed and pulled on his buckskin trousers. Juli hastily started pulling on her own clothes as Parrish tied off his waist thongs then strode easily across the room to vanish from her sight into the store room. She heard him sweep back the outside entrance blanket. Then silence. Swiftly tying up her bodice she ran after her husband, following him out into the sunshine. There she pulled sharply up a few feet behind him. He was standing motionless just outside the cabin, and she was as astounded as him at the sight before them.

The entire village was gathered on the sloping ground in front of the log cabin. Juli was lost for words, her eyes sweeping the amazing spectacle. The women and children were respectfully silent at the rear of the gathering and in front of them stood all the warriors. At the head of the crowd was the flower and feather man with Klud at his side. Below and behind the multitude, Danebury lay spread out in the warm sunshine. It was eerie, almost unnerving to see all its people and yet still see the village itself completely devoid of any movement or life. Like everyone else, Juli's eyes became drawn to then locked onto Parrish.

He too was stunned by the unprecedented event. For a brief moment he was worried, almost frightened that the people had some grim intention toward him but then dismissed the notion as stupid. As far as he was aware he had done no wrong. He crossed his arms over his bare chest, a subconscious gesture of imitation of how Coran had often stood, and finally spoke. The single word carried clearly in the stillness.

"Yes?"

The flower and feather man and Klud both took a pace forward.

"Parrish." said the holy man rather formally. "The warriors have come to a decision."

"I... understand." was the non committal and not completely truthful reply.

"Yes." The little man nodded before continuing. He knew he would have to explain the village's final decision to the tall man. In fact, it was such an unusual decision that he felt the need to review it again himself. Not that he was at all disapproving of it, but it was such an unheard of event.

"The choice for Chieftain was such an unusual one that the warriors all felt the need to ask the rest of the village for their view on it. All are agreed on the choice."

The whole village nodded vigorously. Parrish could not hide his surprise. He knew that warriors alone made all the important decisions in these Neolithic times. There was no democracy here.

"All? Unusual choice?" asked Parrish, suddenly not totally sure that he wanted to hear the reply. He could clearly see that something completely untoward had happened and knew that some big change was underway in Danebury. The holy man nodded.

"It has never happened before but, with the agreement of the whole village and the blessing of the Earth Goddess, I can say now that we have *all* chosen our new Chieftain." He paused. The hush that settled over the people was complete.

"Who?"

Parrish's word was barely more than a whisper but it sounded loud to the village people.

"You!" said the little man bluntly.

"What?!" Parrish was staggered. Juli gasped. Again the people of Danebury nodded vigorously and there were a few murmurs of agreement.

"The warriors and the people of Dane-bre have chosen you to be their new Chieftain." the holy man announced, more formally this time. "But!" The word silenced everyone. "But, you are not born of this village and so you are not bound by its decision. As far as is known, this has never happened before and so, we are all gathered here to ask you." He spread his arms wide to indicate the entire population who stood behind him. "Parrish. Will you take on the duties, honours and burdens of Chieftain for this village?" Expectancy and hope was bright in everyone's eyes.

"But... but I am not the right man for this honour." Parrish almost blurted out the words as he addressed the people. "I am ignorant of so many things when it comes to guiding a village and its people." He pointed to his friend Klud, who still stood silently beside the holy man. "Klud would be a better choice than me. He is brave, strong and true. I would gladly be led by this man."

The Neolithic warrior stepped up to him and bowed deeply at the great compliment. He rested his hand on Parrish's bare forearm and said quietly.

"Your words honour me but they are not all true. You are wrong when you say you would be no good as leader. We have talked of this already. You are wise with knowledge that no one else has. And I would be honoured to help guide you in any of your decisions my friend, should you need or want my help. With you as Chieftain we are sure that the village will live through many more summers. With you as leader and with the help of Dannu, the village will be strong."

Parrish had nothing to say. What could he say? He just stared out at all the people. Facing him were over one hundred souls who were all prepared to put their trust, their futures, their very lives into his hands.

Juli stepped up close and stood just behind her husband on his left, as was her rightful place. Klud then took his place on Parrish's right, where he believed Dannu had always meant him to be.

The holy man raised his eyes to the sky, thrust his arms upwards and cried out.

"Oh mighty Dannu. Great Earth Goddess. Seer of all things. Bringer of the seasons, provider of our food and giver of our lives. Guide this tall man and allow him to see the way and the truth." His eyes turned then to Parrish and he said in clear, loud words that could be heard by one and all.

"Parrish. Will you take charge of these people before you? Will you take up the task that the great Chieftain Coran has left for you? Will you be Chieftain?"

There was an expectant, almost strained silence.

A myriad of thoughts whirled through Parrish's mind, everything from gratitude and pleasure to doubt and worry. But the one thought that stood out clearly above all the rest was that of Carters voice saying, 'You are a waste of space, Parrish. Your contribution to life on this planet will be precisely fuck all!' He remembered it word for damning word. Parrish knew then. He knew his path, his destiny. All uncertain thoughts were instantly banished from his mind and he snapped to attention, bowed deeply to the people then looked the flower and feather man squarely in the eye. His voice was crisp, clear and certain.

"I would be honoured."

1996

42

The foot patrol was making its way northwards towards the pickup point on the brow of Upavon hill. The rendezvous with the helicopter was at virtually the most northern point of the area of Salisbury plain that was encompassed by the boundary line designating the domain of the Ministry of Defence. The little band of soldiers were on the last leg of a jinking, zig-zag route that the men of the patrol were sure someone back at command HQ had drawn up while under the influence of alcohol. Corporal Harrod, leading the infantry section, consulted his map and compass once more. It was really an unnecessary gesture but one that he hoped the men under his command would appreciate, thinking that they might acknowledge his apparent dedication to his duties if they were questioned about it later. In all honesty he knew where they were going, for he knew the Plain like the back of his hand. The real point was that he suspected, although nothing definite had been said, that this small exercise was to be included as part of the assessment that went towards his impending cadre to gain his third stripe.

The patrol was just half a kilometre east of Chisenbury and had only three more kilometres to travel before they reached their pick up point. Harrod allowed himself a small smile. Practically due north for another hour and then a cosy chopper ride back to the start point and Endex. After that it was just a short, if bumpy, ride in a four tonner back to Tidworth barracks for a hot shower and a cold beer. Even with the dreadful, tortuous route he had been given, everything had gone pretty much to plan. He felt very confident.

"How much further, Corp?" asked a private who came up alongside just as the corporal folded away his map.

"Three more clicks north." He picked up his rifle and pointed in the general direction with the barrel, then checked his wrist watch. "But we'll have to push it to be there by the time the chopper arrives." He led off without waiting for or expecting any reply. The other soldiers followed his lead and fell in behind, automatically stringing out in a well spaced line.

Only a kilometre and a half ahead of the men a dark green smudge of woodland lay across their intended path, labelled on the corporals map as Rowden's Cleeve. As one of the few remaining pieces of ancient woodland still standing on Salisbury Plain, it was quite unremarkable.

A single slash of green standing out on the rolling slopes of barren, treeless gorse, Rowden's Cleeve lay on a west to east axis. Although only a few hundred meters deep at its widest point, it was over a kilometre long. Paralleling the A342 road, its eastern end stopped at the border fence of Upavon Airfield and its western end tapered to a point a little way short of the river Avon. It was a tightly wooded strip, mostly of old oaks and ashes some of them several centuries old, interspersed with younger pines that had been planted about fifty years ago to give as diverse a habitat as possible to the local wildlife.

All of this was totally lost on Corporal Harrod. The only thing that mattered to him was the fact that Rowden's Cleeve cut directly across his intended path and was, according to MOD standing orders and the mauve hash marks printed across it on his map, strictly out of bounds to all military personnel and vehicles.

The patrol reached the southern edge of the offending copse and went to ground in a standard circular defence formation while the Corporal again checked his map. The annoying, persistent soldier who had expressed an interest earlier knelt beside the corporal and peered over his shoulder at the wrinkled paper.

"What do you reckon then, Corp?" He was trying to second guess the man, in his own way trying to impress because he had promotion hopes of his own. "Left or right?"

Harrod checked his watch again. Whichever way they went to circumvent the long thin copse, it would add another kilometre to their journey and that meant cutting it fine if the patrol was to arrive at the rendezvous before the helicopter. Even from his kneeling position he could see the daylight from the other side of the copse filtering through between the tree trunks. He considered. No one would know and he could rely on his men to keep their mouths shut. It was not much more than a hundred meters across and it would save twenty minutes travel time to the RV. He made a command decision.

"We're going straight through." The words raised a few eyebrows. All the men knew the standing orders and, even if they didn't, the 'out of bounds' sign hanging on the fence in front of them was plain enough. Corporal Harrod scanned the camouflage cream smeared faces with a hard stare.

"Single file. No wandering. Step in the man in fronts footprints. I want no traces left to say that we were ever here. Understood?"

"Yes, Corporal." they all chanted. There were a few sly, knowing smiles.

"Move out!" he said gruffly.

Again following Harrod's lead, they all climbed easily over the sagging wire fence despite their heavy bergens and followed him off into the trees. The terrain was pretty flat apart from an innocuous looking, gently lifting hump in the ground directly ahead. The Corporal's path led over the raised ground and he used it to his advantage, stopping at the top to look back and check that his men were moving cautiously through the green undergrowth, as instructed.

With a sudden, soft, rending sound, the loamy ground opened up under the combined weight of the man and his equipment and just swallowed him up. The other soldiers stared in amazement as he dropped out of sight. It took a moment for them to gather their wits before they all rushed up and clustered around the dark, gaping hole in the mound, taking care to stay back from its crumbling edge.

"Well don't just stand there!" Harrod's pained voice floated up from out of the blackness. "Call for some help. I think I've broken my fuckin' legs!"

The next day Rowden's Cleeve was a hive of activity, busy with military men and equipment. Several four tonners and Landrovers waited patiently beside the copse. To extract Corporal Harrod from his predicament and get him off to hospital the army rescue services had found it necessary to expand and excavate around the hole in the ground. Only then was it discovered that the Corporal lay in the bottom of a stone walled tunnel of ancient origin. After the injured man had been airlifted away, the officer in charge of the rescue had, with a somewhat cavalier attitude to the possibility of further collapses, explored the tunnel by torchlight. He had to negotiate several other small cave-ins and obstructive tree roots before he finally came up against a single perpendicular stone slab that blocked any further advance. There was scroll and line work carved into the face of the stone. Faint but definitely there and definitely man made. And that was the reason for all the activity.

The officer had a rough idea what the stone passage was and called the Tidworth liaison officer in to confirm it. The liaison man had, in the course of his work, formed a close association with the Royal Commission on the Historical Monuments of England. The RCHME oversaw the management and protection of all the ancient monuments, tumuli and prehistoric ground workings that were so numerous on Salisbury Plain. No archaeologist himself, the man still knew a burial mound when he saw it and, on seeing the tunnels end, realized that this one was still undisturbed, its occupant or occupants still entombed behind the sealed stone slab.

Informed of the discovery and intent on being part of any new historical find on its land, for good PR reasons if nothing else, the MOD was more than willing to assist in the exploration of the burial mound, gladly lending its men and equipment to the project. In preparation for the arrival of the specialists who were to open the tomb, the soldiers had been kept busy. They had shored up the unstable sections of the passageway roof, cleared away the debris from within the tunnel itself and, with the aid of a generator, set up a string of electric lights that now dully illuminated its interior. It was as much as they could do until the experts arrived.

The man chosen by the RCHME for the initial opening of the tomb was head of archaeology at the Iron Age Museum at Andover. Most of the museums experience at uncovering and decoding the mysteries of artefacts from the past had been gained from their extensive excavations of the nearby site of Danebury hillfort. It was felt that he was the most appropriate and readily available choice.

Professor Goodman was of course delighted by the opportunity. Not only was it an archaeologists dream to be in at the start of such a unique find but it was also very likely that, after the recovered artefacts had been studied and catalogued, many of the choicest items would become exhibits at his museum.

He arrived with a young female assistant who clutched an expensive camera, flash gun and several spare rolls of film excitedly to her chest. It was a thrill for her too, being just a lowly assistant and yet picked to help the professor. She realized it was rare to have the chance when so young to experience archaeology at the sharp end!

The grey haired archaeologist and his wide eyed assistant, led by the army officer, made their way gingerly along the passageway to the stone slab. After much excited examining of the dried but intact seal and the taking of many photographs of the carvings using the eye dazzling flash, Professor Goodman finally asked the officer for the stone to be prised carefully back. Two squaddies were called down into the tunnel and the others stood back while they went to work with a couple of crowbars, breaking the seal away from the edges of the stone then levering the slab aside. It wasn't as heavy as the two men had anticipated, being surprisingly regular in the thickness of its cross section. Between them they lifted it clear without too great an effort and propped it up to one side. Already prepared and waiting was a standing light which they carried in and set down on the smooth stone floor just inside the entrance of the tomb. When the switch was thrown, a harsh halogen light flooded the chamber.

Everyone peered in through the stone portal, craning their necks for a first glimpse of whatever treasures might be inside. The silence was complete as the small groups eyes fell on the remains of a body, lying on the cold stone in the centre of the chamber floor. It looked all at once grisly, grim, lonely and somehow defenceless. From young girl to hardened soldier, each and every one of them felt a sudden pang of guilt strike through their hearts. Although their intentions were strictly honourable towards the dead body, the tomb being opened purely in the name of science, they still could not avoid the nagging shame they felt. Like they were unscrupulous, skulking grave robbers.

The tomb itself was almost ten feet square, practically the same in height as it was in length and breadth. The stone lined walls and ceiling were cracked and fractured in places where tree roots had applied their constant and unstoppable pressure. Swirling, painted markings that had once brightly decorated the walls were now all but gone, faded and distorted by cracking and the many runs of moisture that had painted their own perpendicular lines down the stonework, erasing large portions of the originals. The people gathered at the entrance to the tomb saw none of this. Their attention was wholly concentrated on the remains upon the floor. The brown, parched skeleton lay in a bed of grey dust, only a few wispy threads still there to indicate that it was all that remained of the bodies burial robes. They had all crumbled away to nothing. Next to the bones, a streak of orange rust marked the spot where what looked like the corroded blade of a knife lay, virtually hidden under the dust.

The first person to snap out of the groups trance like staring was the young assistant, who jerked the others back to reality with the dazzling electronic flash of her camera as she took her first picture. Professor Goodman blinked rapidly a few times then entered the chamber and, being careful not to step on anything except empty floor space, moved to the remains and knelt beside them. Pulling a small hand held dictation recorder from his pocket, he started to speak slowly and clearly into it, those less enlightened than himself paying close heed to his words as they echoed around, breaking the almost unnatural quiet of the tomb. As he spoke, the girl began firing off flash after flash, taking dozens of pictures of the entire interior before turning her attention to the remains.

"The find is a single complete skeleton." he said, the words crisply separated to offset the echo effect of the chamber and tunnel beyond. "Male. Of undetermined age but definitely between twenty and sixty. Unusually tall. I would guess at least six feet. Also unusual is that he is laid flat and straight and not in the almost universal foetal burial position. Judging from my brief preliminary examination, it would appear that the man did not die by violent means. I can see no marks, abrasions or cuts on the visible bones to indicate any kind of severe wounding that might have caused death."

"What's that?" interrupted one of the soldiers suddenly, pointing down at a brown line across the throat area of the skeleton. It looked like a piece of leather thong or some other tough, fibrous material. Some kind of necklace. On one end of the thong, half hidden in the dust, was a small black disc no bigger than a coin. The officer instantly knew what it reminded him of and, before the professor could caution him against touching and disturbing the remains, reached down and lifted the mystery item clear. The thong slipped easily between the separated bones and everyone straightened to examine the object. The two archaeologists frowned down in puzzlement but the two squaddies and the officer recognized it immediately. One of the two privates scoffed.

"Hah. This whole thing is some kind of wind up!" he said in a disappointed, angry tone as if suddenly discovering that he had been tricked.

"I don't understand. What is it?" It was the first time the young girl had spoken. The officer cocked his head to one side and gave her a brief glance. She got the distinct impression that he wasn't very pleased either but was keeping his emotions under tight control.

"This." he said and held the black disc up between his finger and thumb for all to see, "Is an army dog tag!"

"But... but I thought they were made of metal?" she asked, suddenly very confused by the whole strange turn of events.

"You've been watching too many Yank war films, young lady." He didn't smile. "Modern British dog tags are made of a plastic fibre compound. They don't decay in adverse conditions. Don't rot, don't rust and are fire proof. And this is one of them!"

Professor Goodman had listened to the exchange in silence. He had been scanning the tomb with a critical eye. He shook his head, trying to fathom out the puzzle. He could not.

"I agree something is not right here." he said slowly. "But believe me when I say that this is no 'wind up', to coin your own phrase." He pointed at the gaping skull. "If you look closely at the jaw you will see that this man has a few fillings in his teeth. Metal fillings."

"So?" asked the disappointed soldier, shrugging his shoulders. He knew as well as anyone that most people who still had their own teeth had fillings in them. Some more than others.

"I don't know how new the fillings or the dog tags are, but believe me when I say that I *do* know that these bones and this burial chamber are both ancient. Old. Very old. Possibly even Stone Age."

The three soldiers had no cause to doubt the man's judgment, he plainly knew his stuff. Besides, if the top brass said he was the best, then that was good enough for them. Even so, they gave the grey haired man a puzzled look, not quite sure what his point was. He spelt it out for them.

"In the Stone Age there was no metal. At all. That is why we call it the Stone Age." He spoke softly, but with a finality that left the other men suddenly speechless.

The officer aggressively clenched his fist tightly around the offending black disc. He had sudden visions of the British Army being held up to ridicule as gullible fools on the receiving end of some elaborate hoax. The press would have a field day. He knew he would have to move fast to prevent a media nightmare. Shaking the fist that held the tag, as if threatening the other members of the little group, he said curtly.

"Well, there's a number stamped on this. That will identify its owner once it's checked against the army records. We'll soon get to the bottom of this!" He gave the bones a final, angry glance. The grinning, eyeless skull seemed suddenly to be laughing at him.

He quickly left the chamber and walked with urgent, purposeful strides back down the tunnel, leaving the rest of the party to their confusion.

43

The cloud filled sky was low and brooding, a dull battleship grey that was growing steadily darker. It hung almost oppressively over the little Gothic parish church that sat in the centre of its surrounding cemetery, the solid, fifteenth century stonework grimly matching the clouds in colour. There was a big storm coming.

Sergeant Carter, resplendent in his dress uniform, stood a discrete distance back from the open grave and the people around it. He wasn't quite sure exactly why he had decided to attend the funeral. Telling himself that he just liked to see things through was honest enough but that wasn't the whole truth. True, he had been involved when the whole sad episode had started, and the funeral was undoubtedly the end, but there was something else. Some unexplainable, deep inner compulsion that insisted he be there. He had found through experience that his gut feelings were nearly always right and so, even though he couldn't explain why, he was at the funeral. It wasn't as if he had even liked the dead man. In fact, because of the man's disappearance while he was still technically Carters responsibility, the sergeant was still a sergeant eight years after the unfortunate event. The serious blot on Carters record had killed his career stone dead. Even so, he was still an army man through and through. It was his whole life and he intended to stick it out to the bitter end.

His eyes scanned the other people who he shared the sad occasion with. Apart from the vicar and himself, there were only four other mourners present. The parents of the deceased were sullen and quiet, but there were no tears. They stood beside the polished wooden coffin that contained what was left of their son's body.

They were just an ordinary, nothing special couple, Carter thought rather callously. In their middle years but prematurely old aged. Grey haired and wrinkled. Beaten and bowed by the long years of worry and uncertainty. He didn't know their Christian names and had no wish to know, but he understood the mental anguish they had gone through. It seemed to him that they felt some sad relief now they were finally sure of their son's whereabouts and certain of his tragic demise. Perhaps now they could get on with their lives.

The other two people, who stood on the opposite side of the open grave, he remembered well enough. Dunn and Rabbett. Neither were in uniform and he knew why.

When he saw them at the inquest it was the first time he had laid eyes on them for many years. He remembered bitterly the events that took place after Operation Backfire had gone horribly wrong. After the incident on Salisbury Plain there had obviously been an inquiry but many, many questions were left unanswered. Both Dunn and Rabbett had pressed hard for more details at the time and been sternly rebuked for insubordination. Still they were not satisfied and, after coming up against an impenetrable wall of silence within the military, went beyond Army jurisdiction to try and find out what had really happened.

They foolishly attempted to put pressure on their military superiors and bring out into the open what had happened to their lost friend and how the Army, who they were sure knew, were covering it up. At one point the press had become involved.

Then their campaign for the truth suddenly stopped. Stopped dead. The two men retracted all their previous statements and refused to give any more interviews or even talk about their experiences at all. Carter knew that they had somehow been silenced by the Ministry of Defence. There had even been a whisper that the hard word had come down from Whitehall. Whether it was army intelligence, direct orders from on high, veiled threats or even simple, ruthless blackmail that had been used to stop them he didn't know. But when the two men were suddenly posted to the far side of the globe at short notice, seconded to battalions that they had absolutely nothing to do with, he knew for sure that they had been silenced. The two men finally bought themselves out of the service and left the Army under a cloud, embittered and disillusioned.

But they were there at their friend's inquest and still they got no satisfaction, for even that was a farce. It was so short that it barely qualified as an inquest at all. The only two testimonies that were called for came from a high ranking liaison officer who gave a short, guarded statement, and some archaeology professor who had plainly been cautioned against saying too much. The inquest established that the body that had been found was definitely that of Shaun

Parrish. Proved irrefutably by his dental records, by the matching general physical characteristics of the remains and by his family doctors medical records of bones that he had broken when he was young. And of course, his dog tag.

The grey haired professor had simply confirmed that, as unaccountable and mysterious as it was, the remains were very old. At that point the inquest was abruptly closed. Both Parrish's parents and his two crusading friends were outraged at the totally unsatisfactory outcome but they were denied even the chance to dispute it. They were politely but firmly ushered out, escorted away by military guards who were plainly there for that specific purpose. Carter slipped quietly out during the ensuing mêlée and made his way back to the car park. It was just as he was unlocking his car that the Professor passed by on the way to his own vehicle.

Carter quickly fell in alongside the grey haired man.

"Excuse me." he said, almost too politely. "You were the man that found the body weren't you?"

"And you are?" asked the Professor suspiciously, coming to an abrupt halt.

"Carter. Sergeant Carter. Parrish was under my command."

That seemed to be enough for the other man. He was glad to drop the guarded attitude that he had, in no uncertain terms, been told to adopt and was clearly uncomfortable with.

"Goodman. Professor Goodman." he said, copying the soldier's introduction. The two men briefly shook hands. "Yes. I discovered the remains."

Carter wasn't quite sure how to put the next question so he just plunged straight in. That was his style.

"So the body was definitely Parrish, but you said that the bones you found were old. Just how old?"

"Oh, at least five thousand years." said the Professor in a soft, almost casual, but final sounding voice.

"Jesus Christ!" Carter gasped.

"Oh no." said the archaeologist, shaking his head. "Much older than him!"

Carter could only stand and stare as Professor Goodman, glad to finally get the secret off his chest, walked to his car, climbed in and drove slowly away.

The soldier remembered all this as he watched the coffin being slowly lowered into the grave. Far off in the distance a single bolt of lightning flashed for a white instant, lighting up the underside of the low, dark clouds.

"Ashes to ashes, dust to dust." The vicar's voice was clear enough but dry and devoid of any real feeling. Just as the coffin reached the bottom of the grave a sudden, deafening clap of thunder rent the air, making everyone jump. They cast their eyes grimly up at the menacing, anguished looking sky.

The undertakers pulled up their lowering strops and moved discretely away. There was a long, drawn out silence. Carter, duty done, snapped to attention and gave the grave a crisp salute before marching stiffly away.

Totally ignoring their former Sergeant, Dunn and Rabbett moved around the gaping hole in the earth and spoke briefly to their dead friend's parents.

Their condolences and good wishes were heartfelt but seemed so futile. Parrish's mother knew well enough how their own military careers had been destroyed by their search for the truth concerning her son and she was grateful for all their efforts. She kissed both men on the cheek. Then the pair solemnly shook her husband's hand and, with a final nod, they too departed, sadness heavy in their steps. Neither man looked back. The vicar left the couple alone with their grief, glad to slip away before the threatening rain arrived.

The aging couple looked for a long time down into the grave, staring at the coffin that held their son. Then the woman started to cry. Painful, bitter tears that had been bottled up for eight long years. Her husband smiled sadly and, putting one arm tenderly around her shoulders, led her gently away.

The lone grave digger worked quickly for he too wished to be finished before the rain came.

Finally the graveyard was empty. For a few moments a single black crow circled lazily in the sky above the cemetery before it too moved off ahead of the impending storm. All that remained to show that anyone had even been there at all was the raised, fresh mound of earth and the new gravestone at its head that carried the bugle horn emblem of the Light Infantry.

The rain fell then. Big, heavy drops that slapped noisily against the ground, quickly filling the drains and running in long rivulets along the edges of the paths. Smaller runs trickled haphazardly down over the inscription on the newest headstone.

The words on it were brief, but they were enough.

Private Shaun Parrish
2nd Btn Light Infantry
Born 1960 - departed this life 1988
Sadly missed

DIED IN THE SERVICE OF HIS COUNTRY